THE KILLERS AMONG US
AN EXAMINATION
OF SERIAL MURDER
AND ITS INVESTIGATION

STEVEN A. EGGER, PH.D.

University of Illinois at Springfield

PRENTICE HALL, Upper Saddle River, New Jersey 07458

Library of Congress Cataloging-in-Publication Data

EGGER, STEVEN A.
    The killers among us: An examination of serial murder and its investigation / by Steven A. Egger.
      p. cm.
    Includes bibliographical references and index.
    ISBN 0-13-472424-0
    1. Serial murders. 2. Serial murders. 3. Serial murder investigation. I. Title.
HV6515.E34 1998
364.15'23—dc21

                        96-48016
                    CIP

Acquisitions editor: *Neil Marquardt*
Editorial production supervision
  and interior design: *Barbara Marttine Cappuccio*
Director of manufacturing and production: *Bruce Johnson*
Managing editor: *Mary Carnis*
Manufacturing buyer: *Ed O'Dougherty*
Marketing manager: *Frank Mortimer, Jr.*
Cover design: *Miguel Ortiz*
Creative director: *Marianne Frasco*
Formatter: *Stephen Hartner*
Editorial assistant: *Rose Mary Florio*

©1998 by Prentice-Hall, Inc.
Simon & Schuster / A Viacom Company
Upper Saddle River, New Jersey 07458

Printed in the United States of America

10 9 8 7 6 5 4 3 2 1

ISBN   0-13-472424-0
ISBN   0-13-894734-1

Prentice-Hall International (UK) Limited, *London*
Prentice-Hall of Australia Pty. Limited, *Sydney*
Prentice-Hall Canada Inc., *Toronto*
Prentice-Hall Hispanoamericana, S.A., *Mexico*
Prentice-Hall of India Private Limited, *New Delhi*
Prentice-Hall of Japan, Inc., *Tokyo*
Simon & Schuster Asia Pte. Ltd., *Singapore*
Editora Prentice-Hall do Brasil, Ltda., *Rio de Janeiro*

To my Father, Hartman D. Egger,
March 13, 1916 to April 14, 1997,
who is now tying flies somewhere
up there.

Contents

Preface   xiii

Acknowledgments   xvii

PART I
THE SERIAL MURDER PHENOMENON

1 Serial Murder   3

Introduction   3

Defining Serial Murder, 4   Why Do They Kill and Kill Again?, 6
Who Are the Serial Killers?, 8

Solo Predators   9

Ted Bundy, 9   John Wayne Gacy, 9

Team Killers   10

Henry Lee Lucas and Ottis Toole, 10   The Hillside Stranglers, 11

They Are All Around Us   11

Serial Murder Victims   12

Investigation of Serial Murder   12
Myths of Serial Murder   13

2   **Why Do They Kill and Kill and Kill?**   **15**

Serial Killers on the Couch: Explanations   15
Sources of Serial Murder Theories and Explanations   16
Common Characteristics of Serial Killers   19
Empirical Works   20
Case Studies   23
Psychopaths or Sociopaths?   25
Inadequate Socialization   28
Sex as a Motive   30
Variations on Power and Control   30
Similarities to Rape   31
Biological Predisposition   33
Anthropological Viewpoint   35
Problems with Explanations   36

3   **They Are All Around Us**   **38**

Introduction: We Are Strangers to One Another   38
Who Are They?   39
What Do They Look Like?   43
Some Are Very Quiet and Hard to Spot   44
Some Take Years to Catch   44
A Number of Serial Killers Have Not Been Caught   45
*California, 45   Texas, 46   New York, 46   Louisiana, 48
Indiana, Kansas, Missouri, and Texas, 48   Washington and
Oregon, 49   Washington, 50   Florida, 50   Massachusetts, 50
Connecticut, 50   Pennsylvania, Kentucky, Tennessee, Mississippi,
and Arkansas, 50   Michigan, 51   California and New York, 51
Kansas, 51   Maryland, 51*
Female Serial Killers   52
Categories and Types of Serial Killers   56
How Many Are There in the United States?   59
*FBI and CNN Disagree on the Numbers, 64   A New
Phenomenon?, 64   An Increase in Serial Killers?, 65*

International: A Global Phenomenon 66

*Russia, 66   India, Turkey, Thailand, and Nepal, 67   South
Africa, 67   Australia, 68   United Kingdom, 68*

Serial Killers Outside the United States Who Have Not Been Caught 71

United Kingdom, 71   Canada, 72   Poland, 73   Sweden, 73

4 Victims. The "Less-Dead"   74

Serial Killing of the Lambs in Our Dreams: Concept of the "Less-Dead" 74
Serial Murder Victims 77
Society's Throw-Aways: A Low Priority for Law Enforcement 79
The Killing Fields: Where Do They Hunt? 80
Investigative Value of Victim Information Quickly Dismissed 80

5 Serial Murder: A Growth Industry   85

Introduction 85
"Mutants from Hell" 87
The Profile That Isn't 87
Sound-Bite Answers 88
The FBI and Serial Murder Mythology 88
A Violent Culture 89

PART II
CASE STUDIES OF SERIAL KILLERS

6 John Wayne Gacy: Case Study   95

Social Environment 95
Family Background 98
Peer-Group Association and Personal Relationships 99
Contact with Defining Agencies 100
Offense Behavior 107
Self Concept 110
Attitudes 111
Recall of Events 112
The Demise of John Wayne Gacy 113

7 Henry Lee Lucas: Case Study   115

Social Environment 115

Family Background   116
Peer-Group Associations and Personal Relationships   118
Contact with Defining Agencies   119
Offense Behavior   123
Self Concept   125
Attitudes   126
Recall of Events   127

8   Kenneth Bianchi: Case Study   **128**

Social Environment   128
Family Background   129
Peer-Group Association and Personal Relationships   132
Contact with Defining Agencies   133
Offense Behavior   138
Self Concept   141
Attitudes   141
Recall of Events   142

9   Theodore Robert Bundy: Case Study   **143**

Social Environment   143
Family Background   146
Peer-Group Association and Personal Relationships   148
Contact with Defining Agencies   150
Offense Behavior   156
Self Concept   162
Attitudes   164
Recall of Events   166
Bundy's Last Con   166

10   Cross-Case Analysis: Similarities of Four Serial Killers   **167**

Introduction   167
Social Environment   168
Family Background   169
Peer-Group Association and Personal Relationships   169
Contact with Defining Agencies   170

Offense Behavior   170

Self Concept   171

Attitudes   172

Recall Of Events   173

Missing Persons Problem   173

Summary   173

PART III
THE INVESTIGATION OF SERIAL MURDER

11   Problems in Investigating Serial Murder   177

Defining the Problem   177

Seven Major Problems of a Serial Murder Investigation   179

Linkage Blindness   180

Commitment to a Serial Murder Investigation   183

Coordination of Investigative Functions and Actions   184

Managing Large Amounts of Investigative Information   184

Public Pressure and Mass-Media Pressure for Information   185

The "Less-Dead": Low Priority Leads to Low Clearance Rate   185

Law Enforcement's Lack of Knowledge of Other Agencies' Experiences with an Investigation: Documenting the Problem   186

Ted Bundy Case, 186   John Wayne Gacy Case, 186   Hillside Strangler Case, 187   Henry Lee Lucas Case, 188

Summary of Investigative Problems   188

Linkage Blindness: An Analysis   189

12   Different Police Strategies to Serial Murder   199

Introduction   199

Conferences   202

Information Clearinghouse   206

Task Force   207

Central Coordination Without Forming a Task Force   210

Psychological Profiling (Investigative Profiling)   211

FBI Model, 213   Canter Model, 220   Geographic Profiling, 222

Investigative Consultants   223

Forensic Consultants   224

Major Incident Room Procedures   225

Solicitation from the Public   226

Computerized Analysis System   227

Centralized Investigative Network   228

*Interpol, 228   FBI's Violent Criminal Apprehension Program,
229   New York State's Homicide Assessment and Lead Tracking
System, 233   Examples of Other Computerized Analysis
Systems, 235*

Psychics   235

Offender Rewards   237

Specialized Response Team   238

All Investigative Response Strategies Share a Common Focus   239

PART IV
THE FUTURE

13   Future of the Phenomenon   243

Introduction   243

Research Agenda for Serial Murder   244

Criminal Justice Failure: An Example   245

14   Future Investigation of Serial Murder: Recommendations   247

15   Jeffrey Dahmer and Beyond   250

Dahmer's History   250

*A Silent Psychopath, 251   Milwaukee's Horror, 252   Killing
Close to Home: A Megastat Serial Killer, 252   A Curious Evil:
Self-Taught Anatomy, 253   Killing for Company and Sex, 253
Addicted to the Slaughter, 254   Easy Prey: The Powerless and
Vulnerable, 254   A Drunk, a Loner, and a Weirdo, 254   Trauma
of His Parents' Divorce, 255   Beating the System, 256   Escape
From Apartment 213: The Arrest, 257   The Trial: Was He
Insane?, 258   His Father Writes a Book, 260   Alone With His
Thoughts, 260*

The Victims: The Forgotten Ones   260

From Jeffrey Dahmer's 179-page Confession   263

Beyond the Dahmer's of the 1990s   263

Final Comments   264

References   266

Appendix A   Case Study Source Material   276

Appendix B   Sources for Jeffrey Dahmer Case Study   281

Index   285

Author Index   293

PREFACE

This book presents the up-to-date research efforts of numerous fields of study applied to the problem of serial murder. It was written to provide the reader with a clear understanding of what is known about this horrific violence, what we think is known, and what we simply do not know. It is not the final word. Rather, it is a carefully crafted description and analysis of this phenomenon, which continues to frustrate as it fascinates. The book will answer some of your questions about serial murder. It will also pose a number of questions that are as yet unanswered.

In this book I will take you on a journey of the fantastic, the macabre, the gore, the fear, the horror, the unheard cries of the victims, and the nightmares of reality. I cover the killings and mutilations of "Jack the Ripper" to the carnage of Jeffrey Dahmer and then beyond into the unknown. While some of my writing is in the terms of academic research and empirical realism, you will be frequently reminded that these terrible acts of violence result in death, the termination of people's lives. The elimination of human beings caused by the actions of a killer who kills and kills until he or she is caught. I do not write about the husbands who kill their wives in a jealous rage. I write about killers who kill and kill and kill again.

I have written this book to create a better understanding of serial murder and its investigation. To reach this goal I have attempted to keep my readers in mind. They are university students of criminology, psychology, sociology, true crime buffs, mystery writers and readers, journalists, skeptics, the curious, and the professionals working in the field of criminal justice. Aside from my desire to contribute to the limited body of knowledge that is slowly emerging in this area, my more immediate concern is the black hole of misinformation that police officers and homicide investigators are bombarded with from the mass media's efforts to secure the "thirty second sound bite." Such brief explanations for the serial killer's behavior produce gross misperceptions and a number of myths surrounding the phenomenon of the serial murder.

The book is divided into four parts. Part I provides an overview and describes the six myths of serial murder, which I attack throughout the remainder of the book. The various theoretical explanations for the serial killer's horrific and bizarre behavior are presented. Unfortunately, these theories are either too simplistic or too limiting to provide us with answers to "Why they kill?" A number of examples of these predators and their trail of victims from across the globe are presented. I have labeled the victims of these killers as the "less dead" because they were less alive, considered for the most part, the throwaways of our society. Someone loved each of these victims, yet because they were prostitutes, homeless, vagrants, runaway children, or homosexuals, their deaths are ignored by most of our society and given a low priority on the coroner's list. This is followed by an explanation of how the mass media and the violence of these serial predators feed off of one another resulting in a growth industry. This feeding frenzy both attracts and repels us. We are fascinated with such violence, yet perceive it to be far from our everyday lives.

Part II presents detailed case studies of four infamous serial killers followed by an in depth comparative analysis of these cases identifying their similarities. The names of Henry Lee Lucas, John Wayne Gacy, Kenneth Bianchi, and Ted Bundy are well known to most of you. However, much of what is included in their case studies has never been documented or published before. I spent over forty hours with Henry, discussing his victims, his childhood, his love-hate relationship with his killing mate, Ottis Toole, and his hatred of women, whom he viewed as prostitutes. I met with John only once before his execution and had a brief conversation with him as he screamed at me from his cell on death row. In order to present the most accurate and reliable case studies of these killers I have networked and had long interviews with a number of homicide investigators who worked on these cases. In addition I interviewed journalists who have studied and written about them, victim advocates who tried to force the police to work harder to solve these cases, and a few true crime writers with a sincere interest in the truth.

Part III focuses upon the investigation of serial murder. Seven major problems faced by law enforcement agencies in investigating a serial murder are explained. The most important of these problems is "linkage blindness," the unwillingness of police agencies to share information on unsolved murders. Wherever I have lectured on serial murder and explained this major problem, investigators and police officers in the audience nod their heads and agree. This has been the case from New York to Florida or Kankakee, Illinois to Liverpool, England. Analysts with Interpol as well as homicide investigators in Edmonton, Canada and Amsterdam, Holland agree that "linkage blindness" exists and must be overcome for the police to more effectively respond to the serial murderer. Without the sharing of information on unsolved homicides occurring across police jurisdictions, state lines and national borders, the serial killer becomes immune from detection due to his mobility. I provide evidence of "linkage blindness" by describing the investigative problems in the Lucas, Gacy, Bianchi, and Bundy cases presented earlier.

I provide an extensive discussion of the various law enforcement responses to a serial murder investigation with a table comparing each of them. The fourteen different responses to a serial murder investigation that I identify are the result of my analysis of hundreds of serial murder cases across the United States, Canada, and Europe. An earlier and preliminary analysis of this effort was presented in my first book on serial murder. This current analysis was first presented at the University of Surrey in England for an investigative psychology conference and most recently presented to the National Crime Faculty by invitation at the Bramshill Staff Police College in England.

Part IV presents the future of serial murder and its investigation. An agenda for future research of serial murder is my challenge and plea for the continued research into this phenomenon. the questions I pose demand answers if law enforcement is to become more effective in identifying and apprehending these killers. For the sooner they are identified and caught the more lives can be saved. Finally, a detailed look at the gruesome Jeffrey Dahmer case is presented , followed by my look beyond these serial killers of today and how they may evolve in the twenty-first century.

When I was a homicide investigator on the Arbor Murders in Michigan in the late 1960s the term "serial murder" had not yet been coined. Today, almost anyone who reads the newspaper, watches television news, or goes to the movies knows what the term means. Although most people, when asked, will have a variety of different definitions that explains little about the crime. A number of years after my experience in Ann Arbor as a doctoral student at Sam Houston State University I had the opportunity to work on the development of the Violent Criminal Apprehension program (VICAP). This program was to be operated by the FBI in assisting local police agencies in solving multiple homicides. As a result of this experience I wrote the first doctoral dissertation on serial murder in which I developed a definition of serial murder and presented evidence of "linkage blindness." It is now almost thirteen years later and I still have more questions than answers regarding serial murder. Serial murder is indeed an elusive phenomenon!

Steve Egger

ACKNOWLEDGMENTS

The author wishes to acknowledge the assistance of the following people, without whom this book would not have been possible:

- Center for Legal Studies at the University of Illinois at Springfield, which provided support for portions of my research, and my valued colleagues of the Criminal Justice Program, for their continued support and encouragement.
- Richard Griffiths of *CNN Special Reports*, producer of "Murder by Number," a two-hour TV program on serial murder and Cable News Network, Inc., for providing me with the original transcripts and research material used in producing "Murder by Number," first broadcast in January 1993.
- Professor David Canter, University of Liverpool, for inviting me to England to the second International Conference on Investigative Psychology in April 1993, the third Conference in September 1994, and a special conference in May 1995 to share my ideas and concepts with police officials from around the world.

- Leo Meyer, deputy director of the Illinois Department of Corrections (retired), for his interest in my research and for taking me on tours of both death row facilities in Illinois, where in front of one cell I had a brief conversation with the late John Wayne Gacy.
- Captain Bobbie Prince of the Texas Rangers (retired) and the late Sheriff Jim Boutwell of Williamson County, Texas, for their patience and support of my interviews with serial killer Henry Lee Lucas.
- Jim Sewell, director of the Florida Law Enforcement Executive Institute, Florida Department of Law Enforcement, for valuing my research, inviting me to speak at the Institute in Tallahassee, and for introducing me to Paul Decker.
- Paul Decker, deputy warden of Starke Prison in Florida, for providing my with the opportunity to interview serial killer Ottis Toole.
- Michael Reynolds, author of *Dead Ends* (1992), the true account of serial killer Aileen Wuornos, for his continued support and willingness to discuss some tough issues with me at any time.
- My colleagues who have researched the difficult phenomenon of serial murder: Jack Apsche, Eric Hickey, Candice Skrapec, Ron Holmes, Peter Jenkins, Hannah Scott, Richard Krause, James Sparks, Jack Olsen, Roy Hazelwood, D. Kim Rossmo, Jack Levin, James Fox, Stephen Giannangelo, and others who continue to observe and study this phenomenon.
- Canadian anthropologist and author Elliott Leyton, who is considered by many of us who have studied this horrific crime to be the "Father" of serial murder research, for his willingness to share his analysis of the serial murder phenomenon and his encouragement of my research.
- All homicide investigators everywhere, but especially to Sergeant Frank Salerno of the Los Angeles County Sheriff's Office, who has investigated many serial murder cases, including the "Night Stalker" and the "Hillside Strangler" cases, to Lieutenant Ray Biondi, who investigated the Sacramento "Vampire Killer" and the Gerald Gallego serial murder cases, and to Robert Keppell of the Washington State Attorney General's Office, who worked on the Ted Bundy case, the Green River Task Force, and who recently developed the Homicide Investigative Tracking System for his state.
- The researchers, law enforcement officers, and students who attended the First International Conference on Serial and Mass Murder at the University of Windsor, Canada, in April 1993. For the first time many us who study and write on serial murder were together at the same time and place, agreeing or agreeing to disagree on a number of issues.

- The reviewers, Robert E. Bagby, Ph.D., Eastern Kentucky University (Retired); Rudolph DeLaTore, Los Angeles Valley College; Vincent J. Petrarca, Salve Regina University, Newport, Rhode Island; D. Kim Rossmo, Simon Fraser University, Canada; Hannah Scott, University of Alberta, Canada; James Stinchomb, Miami-Dade Community College (Retired).

- All the students at the University of Illinois at Springfield who took my serial murder course and who were frustrated with all of the questions and few of the answers. By asking all those questions, we learned from each other.

- Bob Ladendorf, for his interest and continued support through his personal clipping service he has provided to me.

- The National Crime Faculty at Bramshill Police College in England, who were gracious hosts to my wife Kim and me in May 1996.

- And Kim, my best friend and partner, for her sociological research and steadfast support for my research and writing. Without her, all this would have never been published.

ABOUT THE AUTHOR

Steven A. Egger is Dean of the School of Health and Human Services and Professor of the Criminal Justice Program at the University of Illinois at Springfield. He was formerly project director of the Homicide Assessment and Lead Tracking System (HALT) for the state of New York. HALT was the first statewide computerized system to track and identify serial murderers and it has become the model for the development of a number of other statewide systems.

Dr. Egger has been conducting research on serial murder since 1983. He holds B.S. and M.S. degrees from the School of Criminal Justice, Michigan State University. He has a Ph.D. in criminal justice from Sam Houston State University, where he completed the first dissertation on serial murder. He has worked as a police officer, homicide investigator, police consultant, and law enforcement academy director. His other research interests include the epistemology of criminal investigation, crime and the elderly, and the future predator.

He is the author of *Serial Murder: An Elusive Phenomenon*, Westport, CT: Praeger, 1990, editor of a series of monographs entitled "Criminology and Crime Control Policy" for Praeger, and editor for the new series "Issues in Criminal Justice Controversy" under contract to Allyn & Bacon. He has lectured on serial murder in England, Canada, and the Netherlands.

Dr. Egger and his wife, Kim, are currently working on an encyclopedia of serial murder.

Future Prey

There is a crime
We know not where,
For many crimes
Are there and here
And here and there.
Few care.

Victims no longer feel.
For many others,
The crimes are not real.

Many of the crimes
Are past tense
And seem to have
No sense of sense.

For those victims yet to be found
Many have perished without a sound.
The cycle of horror goes round and round.

Such visions of violence and death
Are only nightmares of our young.
Later acted out in real.
Life snuffed in the deal.

All for power, lust and greed.
Chartering our lives us prey
For the future predator deed
Is there, and here and everywhere.

Steven A. Egger

The fundamental act of humanity is to refuse to kill.
—Elliott Leyton, in *Hunting Humans:*
The Rise of the Modern Multiple Murderer
(1986, p. 33).

PART I

THE SERIAL MURDER PHENOMENON

In Chapter 1 we introduce the reader to the crime of serial murder, summarize the work, and identify the five major myths about serial killers. The various theories that attempt to explain why the serial killer kills are discussed and reviewed in Chapter 2. Chapter 3 provides a multitude of examples of known serial killers as well as unsolved serial murder investigations in America and across the globe. The concept of the "less-dead" victims of serial killers is introduced and explained in Chapter 4 in a discussion of serial murder victims. In Chapter 5 we discuss how the mass media reports on serial killers and generates a number of myths and inaccuracies regarding the phenomenon.

CHAPTER 1

◄═►◄◄◄═►

SERIAL MURDER

I agree that the serial murder problem out there is a tragic and horrendous problem, which plagues society and all that is human and decent. But I am not now, nor have I ever been, a serial nor even a uni-murderer.

—Kenneth Bianchi, convicted serial killer, writing in a letter
to CNN refusing an interview (Griffiths, 1993)

INTRODUCTION

This book is about serial murder. It is about what Kenneth Bianchi claims that he is not. The aim is to tell the reader all that we know about serial murder, or all we think we know. As the reader will quickly learn, the phenomenon of serial murder tends to be very elusive. The author teaches an undergraduate course on serial murder at a state university in central Illinois. At the beginning of the course students are told that they will know less about serial murder when they complete the course than their neighbors, friends, and acquaintances. The students become less uncomfortable with this fact when they begin to understand the extent of false information and mythology that serial killers generate in the mass media. The point is that most people learn about serial murder from television, the newspapers, or in movie theaters. This media information is frequently in the form of hype and unfortunately contains a number of myths, inaccuracies, and outright falsehoods.

Serial murder is not a new crime in America. It has been with us for quite some time. Herman Webster Mudgett, alias Henry Howard Holmes, killed 27 women in the late 1880s in his "Murder Castle," in Chicago, Illinois, considered by some to be "America's first serial killer" (Wilson and Seaman,

1992, p. 8). Mudgett was hanged in 1896. However, this is not a book about the history of serial murder. Rather, it is a book about serial murders being committed in the present as well as serial murderers of the recent past, but primarily for about the last 20 years, when the phenomenon was first identified as a unique and very different kind of homicide.

We have very little tolerance for homicide. When we can see some logic or rational reason for the killing, our tolerance for such an act is somewhat mollified. If we lose a family member, loved one, or a friend as a result of a homicidal act, knowing the motive for such an act seems to reduce our anger or temper our grief. In most homicides, the killing occurs because of an interpersonal conflict in which the killer and the victim have a prior relationship. We find very little sense or rationality for an act of killing where the relational distance is great between the killer and the victim and the killing appears to be between strangers.

To kill a stranger not only defies our understanding of the rationality for such an act but tends to increase our fear level because of the apparent randomness of victim selection. We are a violent society and we tend to kill our friends, loved ones, and acquaintances. To kill a stranger, unless during the commission of another crime, is a definite threat to our society and places us all at risk. A killer who intentionally chooses a stranger for his victim is threatening our very social order.

Unfortunately, most of the mass media provide information in relationship to the "bottom line." What will sell newspapers? What will cause viewers to turn the dial on their TV set to a specific channel or network? Who will attend this movie? The profit motive drives all of these industry questions. Editors and producers add hype and myth to the topic at hand when information is not appealing enough or sexy enough to lure the reader or the viewer. This has certainly been true of talk-TV programs, made-for-TV movies that are "based on the actual facts," and movies. In the past, TV producers and newspaper journalists have been the culprits who have provided us with myths surrounding the crime of serial murder. However, with *Silence of the Lambs*, Hollywood is now the current mythmaker. Since Hannibal Lecter (brilliantly portrayed by Anthony Hopkins) began staring out from movie screens in 1991, most people discussing serial murder think of this horrific and entertaining killer as the typical serial murderer. The sequel to this very profitable movie will undoubtedly only continue to perpetrate a number of serial killer myths.

Defining Serial Murder

Serial murder was originally referred to as *lust murder* in early 1980 (Hazelwood and Douglas, 1980). The term *serial murder* was first used sometime in 1982 or 1983. The criminal investigative pioneer Pierce Brooks, who conceptualized the Violent Criminal Apprehension Program currently being run by the Federal Bureau of Investigation (FBI), may have been first to use the term *serial*. However, others, such as retired FBI agents, claim to have used the term first. No one is certain who coined the term, but it has been with us ever since.

There have been numerous efforts to define the phenomenon of serial murder. The national media began to define serial murder in early 1984 by comparing it to mass murder. *Newsweek* differentiated between serial and mass murder by describing only the former as an act in which the killer explodes in one homicidal rampage (Starr et al., 1984). Darrach and Norris (1984) noted in *Life* that "unlike traditional mass murderers, who suddenly crack under pressure and kill everybody in sight, serial murderers kill and kill and kill, often for years on end" (p. 58). Nevertheless, until about 1989 the news media continually referred to serial murder as mass murder, even though the two are decidedly very different.

Mass murder occurs as one horrific incident in which a killer annihilates a number of victims. Mass murderers are people like Richard Speck, who killed seven nurses in Chicago, Illinois, on July 13, 1966, or James Oliver Huberty, who walked into a McDonald's restaurant in San Ysidro, California, and killed 20 patrons before turning a gun on himself.

Serial murder is very different from mass murder, although there is some disagreement regarding the definition of serial murder. For the law enforcement community, *serial murder* usually means sexual attacks and the resulting death of young women, men, or children committed by a male killer who tends to follow a physical or psychological pattern. Although many researchers agree that serial killers kill a minimum of three to four victims, a more reasonable approach would be to consider two similar homicides as a serial murder until proven otherwise. When law enforcement apprehends a serial killer, he or she may be just beginning a harvest of victims. In other cases a killer may be killed by a resisting victim or die of natural causes before adding to his victim count.

Over the past few years the author has worked to develop a serial murder definition with utility to those law enforcement officers investigating multiple homicides. The following definition developed by the author has seven major components that may be used as flags to alert investigators to the possibility that a serial murderer is operating in their jurisdiction:

> A serial murder occurs when (1) one or more individuals (in many cases, males) commit(s) a second murder and/or subsequent murder; (2) there is generally no prior relationship between victim and attacker (if there is a relationship, such a relationship will place the victim in a subjugated role to the killer); (3) subsequent murders are at different times and have no apparent connection to the initial murder; and (4) are usually committed in a different geographical location.

Further, (5) the motive is not for material gain and is for the murderer's desire to have power or dominance over his victims. (6) Victims may have symbolic value for the murderer and/or are perceived to be prestigeless and in most instances are unable to defend themselves or alert others to their plight, or are perceived as powerless given their situation in time, place, or status within their immediate surroundings, examples being (7) vagrants, the homeless, prostitutes, migrant workers, homosexuals, missing children, single women (out by themselves), elderly women, college students, and hospital patients.

The author will use this definition throughout the book. However, alternative definitions are being used by others. The FBI uses a briefer definition of a serial murderer as "someone who has murdered three or more victims, with a cooling-off period in between each of the homicides" (Griffiths, 1993). Brooks et al. (1988) define serial murder as "a series of two or more murders, committed as separate events, usually, but not always, by one offender acting alone. The crimes may occur over a time ranging from hours to years. Quite often the motive is psychological, and the offender's behavior and the physical evidence observed at the scene will reflect sadistic, sexual overtones" (p. vii).

Besides drawing a distinction between serial and mass murder in definitions, it is also necessary to identify the serial murderer as a unique actor who can be differentiated from other murderers. Other definitions developed provide this distinction to lesser and greater degrees. Some have argued that the apparent lack of rational behavior and the compulsive premeditation distinguishes the serial murderer from other killers (Norris, 1989). Others argue that the stranger-to-stranger relationship between killer and victim, who are primarily of similar status, provides this distinction (Holmes and DeBurger, 1988).

Why Do They Kill and Kill Again?

I felt a kind of madness and ungovernability in perverted sexual acts. I couldn't control my actions, because from childhood I was unable to realize myself as a real man and a complete human being.

—Andrei Chikatilo, November 21, 1990
(Russian serial killer, convicted of 52 homicides)

Much of the early research on serial murder focused on the sexual component of this crime to explain the motivation of the killer. Psychologists have referred to this sexual component in a number of ways: those "who suffer from a deviation or perversion of the sexual impulse" (de River, 1949, p. 99); "kill because of an underlying basis of sexual conflicts" (Revitch and Schlesinger, 1981); and "usually have few normal social and sexual relationships. In fact, they often have had no experience of normal sexual intercourse" (Lunde, 1976, p. 53). Some criminologists also focus on the sexual component by stating that "the serial killer, motivated by sex and sadism . . . favors immediate gratification, regardless of the consequences" (Levin and Fox, 1985, p. 225).

Other researchers disagree and argue that the sexual component is either overstated or is simply an instrument of the killer and not the motivating factor behind the act. For these researchers, the focus of study is on the power relationships or the issue of control. The motivation is then enhancing the killer's sense of control and domination over his victims. The motivational dynamics of serial murder seem to be consistent with research on the nature of rape, which is considered to be a power-and-dominance crime (Egger, 1985b). This similarity becomes even more evident when one considers that it may take only a small increase in the fury of the rapist or the struggle of the victim to change a violent rape into a murder.

Leyton (1986) identifies relative and absolute deprivation as the provocation for the serial killer's frustration. Focusing on a cultural perspective, Leyton rejects the arguments of excitement or victim conquest and views these killers as reacting to their denied ambitions.

Wilson and Seaman (1983) view the serial killers' violent acts as a result of philosopher Sartre's magical thinking, that is, thinking that cannot possibly accomplish its objective. However, in the case of the serial murderer, such thinking is apparently nothing more than a lack of self-control and an unwillingness to delay gratification. These characteristics of the serial killer, although possibly valid, do not increase our understanding of the killer's motivation.

Norris (1989) offers a *serial killer syndrome*, comprised of 22 patterns of episodic aggressive behavior as factors of predisposition for the killer. He does not, however, offer empirical documentation or references for the development of this syndrome. To many, this syndrome as an explanation of the serial killer's motivation is seriously lacking.

The term *psychopath* is frequently used by psychologists and psychiatrists to describe the behavior of the motiveless serial murderer. The term *sociopath* is also often used in this context. Both terms are obsolete. The *Diagnostic and Statistical Manual of Mental Disorders*, published in 1968 by the American Psychiatric Association (APA), referred to *sociopathic personality* (code 52). The fourth revision of this manual (revised, 1994) refers to such behavior as *antisocial personality disorder* (Code 301.7). In laymen's terms, persons suffering antisocial personality disorder are not considered mentally ill or grossly out of touch with reality. Nevertheless, they are unable to experience love or empathy, due to family rejection and needs frustration. They lack a sense of moral guilt and are not able to postpone drives for immediate gratification. They will rape and murder as easily as they will lie and cheat.

Many social science researchers have found trauma, abuse, and neglect in the childhood of serial killers (Reinhardt, 1962; Hazelwood and Douglas, 1980; Ellis and Gullo, 1971). The neglect and wretched states of social and psychological deprivation consistently identified in the childhood of serial killers would certainly indicate a strong correlation between such a childhood and serial killing. However, such a childhood has been identified in a number of people who have not become serial killers. Correlation does not mean cause. For if such a correlation was revealed as the central causal factor of the serial murderer, the United States would have thousands and thousands of serial killers, given the current disturbing statistics on child abuse and neglect in this country. Such a terrible childhood may contribute to the serial killer's makeup, but it is apparently only one factor in the etiology of serial killing.

Hickey (1985) has noted that there is a strong and common belief that pornography, drugs, alcohol, or insanity are the direct causes of serial murders. Although these factors may contribute to serial murder, there is no empirical or direct evidence that they are the direct causes of serial murder behavior.

It may simply be (as the author is beginning to believe) that the serial killer's search to gain control over his or her own life by violence and sex and to control and dominate others is the central and causal factor in the development of the serial killer. Explanations of the serial killer's behavior are offered in Chapter 2.

Who Are the Serial Killers?

The most infamous serial murderers with whom people will be familiar are Ted Bundy, who was convicted of three homicides in 1979 and 1980 in Florida and is believed to have killed at least 28 women between 1974 and 1978; the "Hillside Stranglers," Kenneth Bianchi and Angelo Buono, who killed at least nine women in the Los Angeles, California, area in 1977 and 1978, after which Bianchi killed two women on his own in Bellingham, Washington, and was caught; John Wayne Gacy, who killed 33 young men in the Chicago area between 1972 and 1978; Arthur Shawcross, who killed 11 women in 1988 and 1989 in and around Rochester, New York, shortly after being paroled from prison, where he was serving a sentence for killing an 8-year-old girl in 1972 (he was also suspected at the time of killing a 10-year-old boy); Wayne Williams, who was found guilty in 1982 for killing two young men following the "Atlanta child murders" investigation in Atlanta, Georgia; Richard Ramirez, the "Night Stalker," who was found guilty in 1989 of 13 murders, five attempted murders, 11 sexual assaults, and 14 burglaries in California; Henry Lee Lucas, convicted of eleven murders in Texas, West Virginia, and Michigan and still suspected by law enforcement agencies in 27 states of killing another 162 people; and Aileen Wuornos, who killed seven men in central Florida in 1990 before she was arrested.

SOLO PREDATORS

There are a number of serial killers who operate as loners: stalking, luring, and killing their victims with no assistance from others and with no witnesses to their horrific deeds. Ted Bundy and John Wayne Gacy are two well-known solo serial killers. A brief life history of these notorious serial killers may tell us something about serial killers who kill alone.

Ted Bundy

Theodore Robert Bundy was born out of wedlock on November 24, 1946. In 1951 his mother married John C. Bundy, who adopted Ted and had his last name changed to Bundy. Ted suspected that he was illegitimate but was never told of it by his parents. Many suspect that learning the circumstances of his birth had a decided effect on his behavior, but there is no direct evidence of this.

Bundy's heroes were politicians and he was active in political campaigns. His goals in life were to become a lawyer and to work in politics. He received a bachelor's degree in psychology and he attended law school. During the early 1970s he committed a number of larcenies and burglaries in the Seattle area but was never caught (Michaud and Aynesworth, 1983).

Between 1974 and 1978 Bundy is believed by law enforcement authorities to have committed over 25 murders of young women and girls in five states. He was convicted of three homicides in Florida and executed in 1989.

John Wayne Gacy

John Wayne Gacy was born on May 17, 1942, in Chicago, Illinois. As a boy Gacy always talked about wanting to be a policeman. He was closer to his mother than to his father. His father drank a lot and would call him a sissy and a mama's boy.

Gacy attended two vocational high schools but dropped out of the second school his sophomore year. He was married in Chicago and lived in Springfield, Illinois, and Waterloo, Iowa, where he was convicted of sodomy for forcing homosexual relationships with young boys and sentenced to an Iowa prison. While in prison, his wife divorced him.

Gacy was paroled to Chicago in 1970. His killing of boys and young men began in January 1972. In December 1978, Gacy became a suspect in the disappearance of a 15-year-old boy in Des Plaines, Illinois, a northern suburb of Chicago. Gacy was arrested, confessed to the killings, and was convicted of killing 33 young men and boys. He was executed in May 1994.

TEAM KILLERS

We went out as friends. We had our arguments, as far as arguments we worked 'em out. Me and Ottis never been in a fist fight. Friendship is further than anythin else.

—Henry Lee Lucas, October 1984

There are a number of cases where murders are committed by two or more offenders working together. Such group serial murder is certainly not a rare occurrence. Jenkins (1989) identified 12 cases out of 52 serial murder cases (23%) where 10 or more victims were attributed to a separate team of killers. For example, Henry Lee Lucas was assisted in most of his killings by Ottis Toole, his homosexual partner; Kenneth Bianchi assisted Angelo Buono, his cousin, in their killing spree in Los Angeles County, California; Douglas Clark involved his girlfriend, Carol Bundy, in a number of bizarre and sadistic murders of prostitutes; Roy Norris and Lawrence Bittaker cruised the beaches in southern California in their "Murder Mac," a customized van, in which they killed a number of their victims. Jenkins (1989) found that a common factor of these teams of killers was their attempts to control victims through "absolute sexual domination" (p. 11).

Some serial killers may prefer to operate in pairs, to make the abduction or killing of the victim an easier task. Hickey (1991) who surveyed 203 serial killers, found that "37% appeared to have at least one partner in committing their homicides. Of all offenders who started killing since 1975, 35% were found to have at least one partner" (p. 81).

England's case of the "Moor Murders," a gruesome series of three child murders committed by Ian Brady and Myra Hindley, would indicate that group serial murder is not unique to the United States. Brady was a stock clerk and Hindley was a typist. Shortly after meeting, they became lovers and Brady began teaching Hindley about his favorite interests: Nazism and the philosophy of the Marquis de Sade. Brady and Hindley abducted their victims and forced them to pose for pornographic pictures before they were killed and in one case recorded the screams of a 10-year-old girl before they strangled her.

Henry Lee Lucas and Ottis Toole

Possibly the most prolific team of serial killers was Henry Lee Lucas and Ottis Toole. In 1960 Lucas was convicted of killing his mother and sentenced to 20 to 40 years in Michigan. He was paroled in 1970, then rearrested in 1971 for attempted kidnapping and sentenced to four to five years. Paroled in 1975, he married a woman whom he abandoned in 1977.

In 1976, Lucas teamed up with Ottis Elwood Toole, a homosexual living in Jacksonville, Florida. Until 1983, Lucas traveled across the country with Toole and Toole's niece and nephew. They are believed to have killed a number of people during this time. Toole returned to Florida in 1983 and was arrested for arson in Jacksonville, Florida, found guilty, and received a sentence of 20 years in prison.

In l983, Lucas was arrested in Texas. Shortly after his arrest, Lucas began confessing to the killing of scores of people across the country. Law enforcement agencies began to take some of his confessions seriously when his statements were matched with the facts, evidence, and location of unsolved murders. Lucas was convicted of a total of 10 charges of homicide in Texas and West Virginia. He received the death penalty for one of these convictions and is currently on Texas death row awaiting execution. Toole is incarcerated in Florida at a maximum security prison. Even today, Lucas, and, in many cases, Toole, are currently considered suspects in over 100 homicides.

The Hillside Stranglers

Another killing team was dubbed the "Hillside Strangler" by the media before they were identified. This was the serial killer team of Kenneth Bianchi and his cousin Angelo Buono. Bianchi had always wanted to be a police officer. After his move to California he continued to apply for police work but was not hired. He lived with his half-cousin Angelo Buono in Glendale, a suburb of Los Angeles, where Buono ran an auto upholstery business out of his home.

Bianchi and Buono abducted, tortured, and strangled 10 young girls between October 1977 and February 1978 in the Los Angeles County area, abducting most of their victims by posing as police officers. Bianchi left California and traveled to Bellingham, Washington, where in January 1979, he sexually assaulted and strangled two young girls in an unoccupied house in Bellingham and then left them in the trunk of their car on a little-used street in the city. He quickly became a suspect, and under hypnosis claimed to have a multiple personality and confessed to both the Bellingham killings and the "strangler" killings in Los Angeles, implicating Angelo Buono as an accomplice.

Bianchi was found to be faking his multiple personality and pled guilty to the killings in Washington and the killings in Los Angeles. He testified against Buono in return for being spared the death sentence. Buono was found guilty in nine of the 10 murders and was sentenced to life imprisonment. Bianchi was returned to Washington for incarceration.

THEY ARE ALL AROUND US

To better understand serial murder, it is important to address a number of issues. First, serial murder is generally referred to as a stranger-to-stranger crime. If this is so, what does it mean? In addition to the better-known cases of solo and team killers noted briefly above, we need to look more broadly at this phenomenon. Who are they? What do these killers look like? How many are there? These and other general topics are discussed in Chapter 3.

SERIAL MURDER VICTIMS

> *When they were being killed, there wasn't anything going on in my mind except that they were going to be mine. . . . That was the only way they could be mine.*

— Edmund Kemper, March 1974

Research on serial murder has focused on finding similarities among these murders. The victims of serial killers have largely been ignored. The serial killer seems to prey on people who are vulnerable or easy to lure and dominate. Little else is known regarding the victims of serial murderers other than they are almost always a stranger to the murderer. They appear to be selected because they crossed the path of the serial murderer or their physical appearance held some symbolic significance for the killer. Vulnerable victims may be in a particular area where the killer is hunting or their appearance may trigger the selection. Or the opportunity and the victim's availability in a specific location may contribute to their fatal selection.

The high-risk lifestyles of victims (such as homosexuals, cult members, released mental patients, skid-row alcoholics, and prostitutes) certainly contributes to their victimization. The killer seems to pick victims who they have power over and who they can dominate. The serial killer does not care about his victims or have any feelings of remorse. The issue of victims is covered more fully in Chapter 4.

INVESTIGATION OF SERIAL MURDER

Serial killers are frequently not captured until they have killed a number of victims. This is a law enforcement problem and not due to some special skills that allow the killer to elude the police. *Linkage blindness,* the crux of this law enforcement problem, is a term coined by the author in 1984 to refer to a communication problem among law enforcement agencies in this country. The problem also exists in other countries. Linkage blindness, a major weakness in law enforcement's ability to respond to and identify the serial killer, occurs because:

- Police do not exchange investigative information on unsolved murders to police agencies in different jurisdictions.
- Police do not exchange investigative information on unsolved murders in different command areas within the same jurisdiction.

- Police do not share or coordinate investigative information on unsolved murders very well with one another.
- Very little networking of information and sources relating to unsolved murders occurs among the police.

The author has documented the problem of linkage blindness in a number of serial murder cases (Egger, 1990a). Although it is not the only problem associated with the investigation of serial murder, it is the major problem in a police response to serial murder. Other investigative problems relate to and originate from this important problem. The problems of investigating serial murder are presented in Chapter 11 with reference to the linkage blindness that occurred in the John Wayne Gacy, Henry Lee Lucas, Kenneth Bianchi, and Ted Bundy cases, and are presented as case studies in Chapters 6 through 9 with a brief comparative and cross-case analysis in Chapter 10.

In attempting to determine the best response to serial murder by law enforcement, the author has been documenting different responses for a number of years. Chapter 12 documents 14 police responses to serial murder. These responses are primarily from the United States, but in some instances examples of police responses in England are utilized, primarily because information on police and crime is frequently shared between these two countries more readily than most. Canada is also cited in these various responses since it shares a large common border and is an English-speaking country.

Throughout this book the author attempts to disabuse the reader of a number of myths of serial murder that are unfortunately promulgated with great abandon by mass media journalists and entertainment industry writers. Any attempt at objectivity or factual reporting of a serial murderer operating among our populace is colored with journalists and fictional writers competing for the public's interest in these killers, who are shown as killing strangers at random on our city streets, in our parks, or on university campuses. Factual reporting of this crime and the reliability of these facts is marred by the hype and horror of newspaper column space and 30-second sound bites of prime-time TV programs.

MYTHS OF SERIAL MURDER

Silence of the Lambs, first shown in 1991, was a very popular movie and has probably done more than any other single movie, book, or television program to promote the mythology of serial murder. Other movies about serial killers, thriller novels, the recent increase in true-crime accounts of serial killers, and the media treatment (sometimes almost a frenzy) of such recent serial killers as Ted Bundy's execution in Florida; Richard Ramirez, the "Night Stalker" and self-professed Satanic worshiper from California; Arthur

Shawcross, who killed at least 10 prostitutes in the Rochester, New York, area from 1988 to 1990; and Jeffrey Dahmer, who needs no introduction, have promoted a number of myths regarding serial murder. Media reporting of unsolved serial murder cases such as the "Green River Killer," San Diego killings, and the "Gainesville Slayer," finally identified as Danny Rolling, have added to these myths. The fact that serial murder is a growing media industry is addressed in Chapter 5.

There are basically six major myths about serial killers that are for the most part engrained in the public's understanding of serial murder. These myths are listed below.

SIX MAJOR MYTHS ABOUT SERIAL KILLERS

1. All serial killers had terrible childhoods, were beaten by their parents, and were sexually abused.
2. Serial killers are "mutants from Hell," who do not look or act like the average person in appearance and mannerisms.
3. Serial killers prey on anyone who crosses their path and do not spend time selecting their victims.
4. Serial killers have an uncanny ability to elude the police for long periods of time.
5. Profile of the serial killer: the serial killer is a sex-starved man-beast who is driven to kill because of a horrible childhood and the way society has treated him. He has had an unusual relationship with his mother. He travels alone across large geographic areas of the country and has an in-depth knowledge of police criminal investigative procedures, which allows him to elude the local, state, and federal law enforcement. He is an insane and cowardly maniac who preys on the weak and helpless.
6. The Federal Bureau of Investigation investigates all serial murderers since most of them cross state lines.

Like all myths, these include a little of the truth. Myths do not really help us very much in dealing with a serial killer. In many ways, myths make our ability to understand and catch these killers all the more difficult. The driving force behind the writing of this book is to clarify issues related to serial murder and provide a better understanding of how serial murder is investigated. Clarifying some of these issues and an analysis of investigation should give the reader a better idea of where we go from here.

The last part of the book deals with the future. In Chapter 13 we address the future of the phenomenon. Chapter 14 deals with the future of serial murder investigation. In Chapter 15 we look at the Jeffrey Dahmer case and what it means for future serial killers and how we will have to deal with them.

CHAPTER 2

⮞◦◆◦⮜

WHY DO THEY KILL AND KILL AND KILL?

I am beyond good and evil. I will be avenged. Lucifer dwells in all of us.
—Richard Ramirez, the "Night Stalker,"
upon being sentenced to death for 13
murders, November 7, 1989

Of all the carnivores, only two lack built-in inhibitions against killing members of their own species—rats and man.
—Konrad Lorenz

SERIAL KILLERS ON THE COUCH: EXPLANATIONS

The killing of a stranger is not seen as motivated principally by previous interpersonal friction in the killer–victim relationship, but rather, must be seen as the outcome of some other interpersonal motive. While the ability to identify and capture serial killers is the critical short-term objective of law enforcement, it is becoming more and more important to understand why these killers behave as they do. As they are identified, apprehended, and studied, some description of these murderers has developed. Older references in the literature tend to reflect a Freudian orientation to this phenomenon.

Some researchers tend to classify theories that explain behavior into very broad categories. Those examining serial murder might classify theories of the behavior and motivation of the killers as falling within three general areas: sociological, psychological, and cultural. Others would add the biological category. The problem with placing serial murder behavior into specific categories is that the behaviors found in serial killers that have been identified and studied do not necessarily fall within neat and tidy theories—or groups of theories, for that matter.

Some researchers will study the serial killer from their own specific frame of reference. In other words, a sociologist will examine and concentrate on those behaviors or characteristics which in total tell us something about the serial killer in the aggregate. Sociologists attempt to use data and empirical evidence from a large group of subjects (serial killers) to explain what these subjects are "like."

Psychologists and psychiatrists are in the business of studying individuals, and much of their research is reported in the form of clinical case studies. Data from clinical studies of larger populations of subjects are frequently reported in journals and research reports. Psychiatrists differ from psychologists by holding a medical degree, and their research frequently combines the biological and social science information on the subjects of their study. Cultural explanations of serial murder behavior are provided by anthropologists, sociologists, social psychologists, and a number of other social science disciplines who look to the broader issues of historical development, media influence, trends, marginal members of society, and so on. Biological explanations of serial murder generally deal with genetics (XYY chromosomes), neurology (brain abnormality or dysfunction), and biochemistry (chemical imbalance in the brain).

All of these disciplines have contributed to our understanding of serial murder. However, many theories and explanations of serial murder behavior combine one or more of these disciplines, and these theories do not fit tightly within a discipline or theoretical framework.

SOURCES OF SERIAL MURDER THEORIES AND EXPLANATIONS

The research on serial murder behavior is based on five basic sources of information. Each of these sources of information is historical in nature; that is, we observe, view, and analyze these sources after the fact. We attempt to determine the motivation or explanation of the killings based on what the killer has accomplished. We do not try to determine a theoretical basis for the killing until after the killer is in custody. (Analysis of behavior prior to the capture of the killer is used to catch the killer and is referred to as psychological profiling, investigative profiling, or just simply profiling. This investigative approach is covered in Part III.) Once this information is available, we begin to look at the background of the killer in a variety of ways to determine why the killer has killed repeatedly.

1. Specific homicide scenes
2. A pattern or series of murders that have been identified
3. Serial killer's confessions

4. Victims of serial murder

5. Published research on serial murder

The scene of a killing will tell us something about the killer or killers. Where the killing took place, how the victim was killed, how the victim was left to be found, whether the victim was hidden from view or displayed for all to see, and what methods were used to subdue or torture the victim are all characteristics or descriptions of the kill site that will allow researchers to deduce explanations about the killer's motivation.

A pattern or series of murders that have been identified as committed by an identified serial killer may give us greater insight into the mind of the serial killer. In this case the researcher has a larger view of the killer's acts from which to begin to understand the motivation for such killings. The similarities and possibly differences of these murders and how they were carried out provide a clearer picture of these crimes.

The confessions of the serial killer probably provide most of the information used in developing an explanation for his killings. The killer states first to police, and frequently later to the news media, book writers, and researchers, what he has done. In practically all instances the killer is asked "why?" The killer may not know or realize why he has committed these horrific acts, or he may well understand why he has killed (at least in his own mind). The acts themselves and how they were accomplished are important for the police to know in order to charge the killer with his crimes.

The "why" is not required for criminal prosecution, but it is something everyone is interested in knowing. We are all curious. How much of the killer's confessions regarding his motives is fact and how much is fiction? The killer may be honestly telling why he thinks he killed or he may be telling the police and others what he thinks they want to hear, based on his perception of what serial killers do, his audience's perception of the serial killer, or both. This is definitely a problem for those researchers attempting to determine the killer's motive from his confession.

Victims of serial killers may provide a clue to the researchers. What type of person has the killer selected as his victims? Are they simply those that crossed his path and provided the opportunity for a "kill" or abduction? Do these victims have some symbolic significance for the killer? Were they selected, abducted, or killed in similar locations? These are some of the questions that might be answered from victim information that would lead to a theory about the killer's motivation.

Published research on serial murder forms the basis of a number of theories and explanations of serial murder behavior. This is the basis of scientific knowledge. Scientists refer to earlier research and then try to make the same observations under the same conditions, attempting to replicate earlier experiments or experiment with different variables to prove or disprove a hypothesis. This work builds toward the development of theories and the testing of these theories against facts. However, human behavior is not something that can be placed in a test tube and manipulated with different ingredients to reveal changes or differences. Social scientists attempt to collect and quantify behavioral data so that they can be tested against a hypothesis or used to develop a theory, which can then be tested against further observations of behavior. Quantifying behavioral information requires that the behaviors be classified into variables and frequencies of variables. It does not make for an exact science.

Although a small amount of published research has been developed on serial murder since the mid-1980s, much of the research on serial murder has not been empirically based and the data that have been collected have been limited in scope. This is the problem in researching the phenomenon of serial murder, little empirical research exists. This is primarily because the information on these murders and the murderers is not readily available. It is not collected systematically by government agencies. Serial murder falls within the much larger category of homicide within the Uniform Crime Reports collected by the federal government from federal, state, and local police jurisdictions. Without any official reporting mechanism, researchers have had to build their own databases from a variety of sources.

In addition to research published in journals and monographs, there is a great deal of information published in newspaper accounts, electronic media, true-crime books, and government publications which may or may not be reliable or valid. For that matter, research published in journals or monographs may also be of questionable reliability or validity. The point is that all of these data should be held suspect. But it is all we have and all we are likely to get for quite some time.

Another way of viewing sources of information about serial murder behavior or in determining how we know what we know or think we know about serial murder behavior is to consider yourself an observer of the serial killer's behavior. Since we cannot in any practical way observe the actual killings, we must limit ourselves to what can be observed prior to the apprehension of the killer and after the apprehension of the killer.

Prior to the killer's apprehension we can observe:

- The victims
- The crime scenes
- The areas surrounding the crime scenes
- The scenes of the abductions
- The areas surrounding the abductions

After apprehension we can observe:

- The background of the killer
- The physical characteristics of the killer
- What the killer says about the killing

We can then aggregate these observations of the killings and the killer with other killings and killers from which we can then attempt to make observations across cases.

COMMON CHARACTERISTICS OF SERIAL KILLERS

A number of researchers of serial murder derive common behavioral characteristics or similarities of these killers from single case studies, small groups of case studies, or from data and information on a number of killers in order to suggest theories about their behavior. These characteristics are derived from a variety of places, falling within the five major sources of information described above.

Singular case studies are where a great deal of our information on serial killers was determined in the early research into this phenomenon. To some extent, individual cases studies are still being conducted today; however, more and more of our information on serial murder behavior from case studies is based on the combination of small groups of case studies. In addition to the more serious research using a case study approach, much of the true-crime literature relies almost entirely on the case study approach, either in the form of singular cases or in brief descriptions of a number of cases. It is up to the more serious researcher and student of this material to discriminate between *The Misbegotten Son*, a study of serial killer Arthur Shawcross by Jack Olsen (1993), who is well known for his painstaking research in writing crime books, and the more recent books written about Jeffrey Dahmer, many of which reached the bookstores within weeks or a few months of the national reporting of this case from Milwaukee, Wisconsin.

Information available on serial killers can also be found in a number of "encyclopedias" of serial killers, mass murderers, spree killers, and the like (e.g., Lane and Gregg, 1992; Newton, 1990). In addition, there are a number of books that claim to provide the reader with all the information available on general categories of murder, which list and briefly describe these murders and the murderers. (e.g., Linedecker, 1990). Few, if any, of these books provide us with completely reliable or valid information on serial killers. For the most part, and like the true-crime books, the authors and editors of these books have been under pressure to publish quickly to meet the public's continuing interest and fascination with serial murder (see Chapter 5 for a more detailed discussion of serial murder as a media growth industry).

EMPIRICAL WORKS

Holmes and DeBurger (1988) and Hickey (1991) have provided us with a great deal of information on the behavioral characteristics of serial killers using databases of serial killers that they themselves have assembled, as well as the author's work (Egger, 1990a), which synthesized some of their research and others much more limited in scope.

It should be noted here that the empirical efforts of Holmes and DeBurger and Hickey are very difficult, given the problems of collecting this information noted above. Data and descriptive information on the serial murderers or their victims is almost always missing. Reaching back more than 10 to 15 years to collect information on earlier killers only increases problems for the researcher.

Holmes and DeBurger (1988) deal with behavioral backgrounds of serial killers and then concentrate on a typology or classification of serial murder (see Chapter 3). Their data set is composed of material on 110 serial murderers, from which they provide examples. Analysis of these serial murderers (apparently, all males) revealed that there were three central core characteristics in the behavioral background of the serial killer (adapted from Holmes and DeBurger, 1988, pp. 63, 49–50):

1. "The basic sources of the repetitive homicide pattern are psychogenic." The serial killer's psyche includes norms, values, beliefs, perceptions, and propensities that result in the killing. Sociogenic factors provide a context for the propensities of this behavior but are not considered an immediate cause or source for the killing.

2. "Motives that impel and justify the repeated acts of homicide have an intrinsic locus; they are structured and rooted within the mind of the murderer." The killing is the expression of the killer's desire to kill, and in most cases the motive is not for material gain, political power, or other external rewards.

3. "The serial killer's homicidal behavior is expressive of the interlocking motives and propensities that predominate in his mind and personality. His behavior is therefore oriented toward psychological gain." Given the killer's psychological drive to kill, the more murders committed, the greater the buildup of psychological gain. Although the orientation of some serial killers may appear to be seeking material gain, this gain is for creature comforts and pleasure and is mainly psychological in nature.

Holmes and DeBurger (1988) argue that whereas serial murder is psychogenic, social and cultural elements in this society tend to enhance the probability of serial killings. They cite such factors in our society as redundant violence, exemplified in our entertainment industry, an emphasis on thrills, violence seen as a normal way of dealing with problems, anonymity and depersonalization in urban society, and great spatial mobility as all serving the homicidal propensities of the serial killer. Meloy (1989) refers to this as a psychosocial approach to serial murder in which psychogenic factors are central to the mind of the murderer but greatly influenced by the sociocultural context.

Hickey's (1991) research is based on his collection of 203 serial murderers (34 females and 169 males) who killed between 1795 and 1988. Although this is a large database of serial killers, the information presented from these data are not specific to the behavioral characteristics of the serial killer, since Hickey's focus is on the victims. Further, Hickey breaks down his sample into gender as well as different types of male serial killers. However, it must be remembered that Hickey's primary unit of analysis is on victims and many of his data are historical, in some cases reaching back over 180 years.

While Hickey (1991) does provide us with a close look at female serial killers, his data set includes only 34 cases, and historical research on female serial killers tends to provide more general information on female killers than on men because of their notoriety in newspapers, crime books, and historical documents. The data on male serial killers are not presented in total, nor does the author discuss many behavioral characteristics of this total sample. Rather, he identifies subsets of these data when discussing specific types of male killers or when highlighting various important characteristics.

Hickey's analysis of female serial killers deals primarily with the emergence of these types of killers and their selection of victims. In discussing the motives and methods of these killers, Hickey does shed some light on their behavioral characteristics. With limited biographical data on each killer, he did find a number of these killers to have histories of child abuse, extreme poverty, and unstable relationships. Given Hickey's taxonomy of motives developed from his data, he states that their motives "appear to center on financial security, revenge, enjoyment, and sexual stimulation" (1988, p. 122). Of the 34 female killers described, he listed the motive as "money sometimes" in 53% of cases. Since Holmes and DeBurger and others believe that the primary motive or driving force of the serial killer is psychological, this category could be attributed to achieving creature comforts. However, the second-highest category of motive among these female killers is listed as "money only" in 41% of the cases. A number of researchers would exclude these cases since they deal with material motives. However, a number of these killers may be "black widow" killers, who kill their husbands or relatives for insurance compensation. Hickey notes that some of these killers' motivation for money may simply be their attempt to meet an unfulfilled need, and for others, psychological needs and economic needs are one and the same. Hickey (1988) also found that only 15% (or five) of these female killers had a criminal history. Further, he found that the primary method of killing for this group was with the use of poison, and almost half used poison exclusively.

Hickey's empirical data on male serial killers' behavioral characteristics is first described based on all the males in his data and then according to various subgroups of killers. For all males he found these killers not to be highly educated and generally not to hold professional or skilled jobs. Further, they did not commonly use firearms as their sole means of killing. He found mutilation in over half of the cases and strangulation or suffocation in one-third of the cases. Hickey notes that the act of killing must be viewed as a process, since a number of these serial killers have tortured, beaten, and mutilated their victims prior to death.

Hickey also addresses the issue of motivation for all males. While sexual motivation was the most commonly listed among these offenders, only one-fifth gave it as their sole reason for killing. Enjoyment was listed frequently, and money was listed by one-third of these killers; however, rarely were these motives listed as the sole reason. He notes that many of the stated motives in his study "may actually have been methods by which they achieved ultimate power and control over other human beings" (Hickey, 1988, p. 151).

Hickey's subgroups consisted of solo killers (killers killing by themselves) who killed women ($N = 42$), who killed men (N not given, but apparently only a few), who killed children (about 5% or $N = 8$), who killed primarily the elderly ($N = 12$), who killed families (few cases after 1940), and who killed both men and women ($N = 13$). Hickey provides a separate analysis of team killers ($N = 32$, with 76 offenders, 12 cases involved one or more female offenders).

Solo killers who kill women represented 25% of the male sample and was the largest subgroup. Although not the sole method, 59% of this group used strangulation and suffocation in killing some or all of their victims. Torture was used in 21% of the cases and mutilation was used in 54% of the cases. Hickey argues that this subgroup can be referred to as "lust killers" because of the sexual nature of their criminal assaults. He further argues that the primary motive of this group was control. In comparison to all other male serial killers, they were more prone to rape their victims, carry out bizarre sexual acts on their victims, have a frequent history of sex-related crimes, and have spent time in prison or mental institutions. Hickey found that one-third of this subgroup experienced an unstable home during childhood.

In the remaining subgroups, Hickey found that those who killed men, children, and the elderly involved a strong sexual component. Team killers were also found to have this same motivational component. It is interesting to note that Hickey found, "*In only a few cases* of team offenders who targeted children *were there any hints of Satanism, rituals, or other cult-like activities"* [emphasis added] (Hickey, 1991, p. 188).

CASE STUDIES

A number of researchers and authors have used combined case studies in their analysis, while others have used a number of case studies or interviews as an empirical basis for their analysis. Others have based their analysis on a very small number of case studies, and in some instances analysis and conclusions have been based on singular case studies. In an earlier work, Holmes and DeBurger (1985) utilize information from five case studies, from which they make certain generalizations regarding mobility and types of killers. In their later work (1988) they provide a case study of Ted Bundy, including the results of an interview with Bundy. However, the Bundy case study is used primarily as an example of a serial killer, most certainly a famous one, and how he corresponds to empirical research presented earlier in their book. This case study is not used as the basis of their conclusions regarding serial murderers. Hickey (1991) used brief case studies to provide examples of his subgroups and to highlight various characteristics of the subgroup.

In their analysis and interviews of 36 sexually oriented murders, Ressler et al. (1986) concluded "that the motivation for murder is a complex developmental process that is based on needs for sexual dominance at the destructive expense of the victim" (p. 284); also that "the victim and offense must be seen as having symbolic meaning to the offender, reflecting violent sadistic fantasies" (p. 285).

Apsche (1993) used a singular case study of Gary Heidnik to reach certain conclusions regarding serial murder. Between November 1986 and March 1987 Gary Heidnik kidnapped six women in Philadelphia and held them as sex slaves in the cellar of his home to produce his offspring. One of these women died while hanging from the cellar rafters and was dismembered by Heidnik. A second victim was electrocuted by Heidnik, who then disposed of her body in New Jersey. Heidnik was found guilty on two counts of first-degree murder, five counts of rape, six counts of kidnapping, four counts of aggravated assault, and one count of deviate sexual intercourse.

Apsche analyzed the background and behavior of Heidnik through interviews with him and other information collected regarding his criminal trial. In his analysis of Heidnik, Apsche was attempting to develop a new diagnostic category for the serial killer. Apsche argues that the characteristics found in Heidnik were very similar to those of other serial killers. He found an insatiable obsession or an almost instinctual drive that pushes these killers to fill their empty lives with an overactive fantasy life leading to ritual murder. Apsche argues that serial killers are very manipulative and attempt to control the world around them. Apsche found serial killers to have a strong feeling of inadequacy and to never have felt the intimacy of bonding with their parents when they were children. Although Apsche's research relies a great deal on the research of others (Ressler et al. 1988; Norris, 1989), he also argues that suicide or attempted suicide is found in many serial killers and that they all attempt to get help. He argues that these killers "appear to want to stop what is about to happen yet they always regain control of themselves to prevent their discovery" (Apsche, 1993, p. 18): Heidnik, for example, attempted suicide a total of 13 times. Apsche calls for much more research into the mind of the serial killer. He notes that his efforts in attempting to understand the serial killer are only a first step.

Abrahamsen (1985), who interviewed David Berkowitz (Son of Sam), described him as "a human being inexorably driven to destroy himself and others" (p. xii). Abrahamsen found Berkowitz to have total indifference to the fate of his victims and to have an urge to kill (and confess when the time was ripe). Berkowitz as his own detective became, in a sense, the victim as well as the victimizer through his own confessions (p. 215). Such a description could easily have been given of other well-known serial killers, such as Denny Rolling, John Wayne Gacy, or Dennis Nilsen.

Other researchers have analyzed serial killers from a combination of sources and found similar behavioral characteristics of these killers. de River (1958) categorized those we now refer to as serial killers as "lust killers" who suffer from a deviation or perversion of the sexual impulse" (p. 99). They are "cold, calculating and egotistically sadistic" (p. 120). Guttmacher (1960) states that many of these sadistic killers vent their hostile impulses through cruelty to animals but that their real hatred is not against animals, it is against their fellow human beings.

In discussing these compulsive homicides, Revitch and Schlesinger (1981) argue that the majority of these crimes have an underlying basis of sexual conflicts and that most of the sex murders belong to this group. According to Lunde (1976), serial murderers are sadist murderers who are apt to repeat their crimes. He describes the sadist murderer as one who kills, mutilates, or abuses his victims to achieve sexual pleasure and may choose victims with specific occupations or characteristics. Lunde (1976) states, "They usually have few normal social and sexual relationships. In fact, they often have had no experience of normal sexual intercourse" (p. 53). The sadist murderer is one of the most common types of killers of strangers and of all types of murderers, the most likely to repeat his crime, according to Lunde. Brittain (1970) describes the sadistic murderer as one "excited by cruelty, whether in books or in films, in fact or fantasy" (p. 202). Levin and Fox (1985) state that, "the serial killer, motivated by sex and sadism, is hardly deterrable. His sociopathic disposition favors immediate gratification, regardless of the consequences" (p. 225).

Even when they look at the same data, there is no consensus among behavioral scientists regarding why so many Americans kill each other (Rose, 1979). Banay (1956) notes that the reasons given for the act of homicide by the killers are misleading since the true cause is masked by other "logically" understandable explanations. Banay concludes simply that there is no logic in murder (p. 193).

Emanuel Tanay, a forensic psychiatrist, notes that the serial killer does not give any visible signs of derangement, even under the most expert examination (Tanay, undated). Tanay interviewed Theodore Bundy and found no overt psychopathology in examining him. Helen Morrison, who reportedly spent a number of hours with John Wayne Gacy, believes that the serial killer is a new personality type (Berger, 1984).

PSYCHOPATHS OR SOCIOPATHS?

Serial murderers are frequently described as psychopaths by social scientists and by the mass media. Psychopaths have a personality disorder involving a range of affective, behavioral, and interpersonal characteristics. Primary personality characteristics of the psychopath include a lack of empathy, guilt, or remorse for those who suffer from the results of their actions, and a callous disregard for the feelings, rights, and welfare of others (Cleckley, 1964). These persons are typically egocentric, selfish, glib, deceitful, callous, impulsive, manipulative, sensation seeking, irresponsible, and act as if they had no conscience. They resist any social convention or norms and ignore social and interpersonal obligations. Because of this they frequently come into contact with the criminal justice system (Hare et al., 1992).

The worst murderers in the world are frequently referred to as psychopaths. They are not the most numerous, but they provide the sensations and commit the motiveless crimes that shock and puzzle society today. The word *psychopath* is frequently used by psychologists and psychiatrists to describe the behavior of the motiveless serial murderer. They have also used the term *sociopath*, although this term is more frequently used by sociologists to emphasize the social interaction of the behavior.

Cleckley (1964) identifies a number of marks or attributes of psychopaths, whose behavior is not readily understood in terms of mental deficiency, neurosis, or psychosis. These primary attributes include unreliability, insincerity, pathological lying, and egocentricity; poor judgment and impulsivity; lack of remorse, guilt, or shame; an inability to experience empathy or concern for others or to maintain affectionate attachments; impersonal and poorly integrated sex life; and an unstable lifestyle with no long-term plans. Beyond such general attributes the psychiatric and psychological literature does not allow us to develop a set of the common serial murderer characteristics. This is due to its individual case approach used by psychologists and psychiatrists to study such people and their classification. John Liebert, a psychiatrist at the University of Washington, has stated: "We have some basic clinical knowledge of serial murderers that allows us to rule people out. What we don't have is how to rule them in" (Berger, 1984).

Levin and Fox (1985) found the terms *sociopath* and *psychopath* used interchangeably to describe serial murderers repeating acts of brutality and sadism due to a lack of conscience or guilt. For Levin and Fox (1985) these terms

> apply to those individuals who are not mentally ill, not grossly out of touch with reality, but who are incapable of experiencing normal amounts of love and empathy. Though psychologists don't know for sure, they speculate that some people become sociopaths because of rejection, the sociopath lacks a sense of responsibility, guilt, or morality and is unable to have lasting and meaningful relationships. He has trouble postponing impulsive behavior, is immature, and is unaffected by the rewards and punishments which might ordinarily inhibit immoral action. This type of individual is often implicated in behaviors ranging from cheating and lying, on the one hand, to rape and murder, on the other. (pp. 71–72)

Joel Fort, a psychiatrist who testified at the trial of serial murderer Edmund Kemper in Santa Cruz, California, defined the sociopath as having "a morality that is not operating by any recognized or accepted moral code, but operating entirely according to expediency to what one feels like doing at the moment or that which will give the individual the most gratification or pleasure. It includes an absence of conscience" (Godwin, 1978, p. 300).

For example, Luke Karamazov, convicted serial killer, is described by Hilberry (1987) as "on the whole . . . well satisfied with his own composure, his lack of feeling [for his victims]" (p. 88). Hilberry quotes Karamazov as stating, "I had a certain detachment, if you can visualize. There has to be some part of me left out" (p. 88).

As previously noted in Chapter 1, the *Diagnostic and Statistical Manual of Mental Disorders* (DSM) first published in 1952 by the American Psychiatric Association referred to a *sociopathic personality* (code 52). The terms *psychopath* and *sociopath* were replaced in DSM-III (APA, 1980) with the term *antisocial personality disorder*. The fourth and revised edition of this manual, commonly referred to as DSM-IV, again refers to such behavior as antisocial personality disorder (APA, 1994, code number 301.7).

The case of Kenneth Bianchi illustrates the utility of such a diagnosis using DSM-III-R (APA, 1987). Bianchi was diagnosed "antisocial personality disorder 301.70," a diagnosis which requires that at least 3 of 12 criteria be met prior to the age of 15 years. His history indicated that he (1) persistently lied from an early age, (2) had school grades that were consistently below his estimated intellectual ability; and (3) chronically violated rules at home and at school. This diagnosis further requires at least four of nine manifestations of the disorder after the age of 18 years. In Bianchi's case, he displayed (1) an inability to maintain consistent work behavior, (2) failure to accept social norms with respect to lawful behavior, (3) an inability to maintain an enduring attachment to a sexual partner, and (4) a failure to honor financial obligations. DSM-III-R adds two additional requirements: a pattern of continuous antisocial behavior in which the rights of others are violated, and that the behavior noted cannot be attributed to severe mental retardation, schizo phrenia, or manic episode (APA, 1987).

In the classroom, after reciting how Bianchi met these requirements, I ask my students to measure their own general behavior against these characteristics, excluding the last two requirements of the diagnosis. It is obvious from their reactions that quite a few (if they are being honest with themselves) have or have had similar behaviors during periods of their life. The point is that DSM-IV (APA, 1994) does not provide us with a set of characteristics or criteria from which to predict homicidal or serial homicidal behavior. Once the serial killer is identified, we can, with hindsight, find the character trait or flaw. As Hickey (1991) and others have noted, offenders do not always come from the same background or mold. Each evolves from very different events and situations that they encounter, and they react or respond to these events and situations very differently. J. Reid Meloy, a noted psychiatrist, has argued that the criteria for this diagnosis are "too descriptive, inclusive, criminally based, and socioeconomically skewed to be of much clinical or research use" (1988, pg. 6). Hare (1993) and others have argued that the antisocial personality disorder criteria in DSM-III-R are primarily a measurement of antisocial and criminal behavior and do not measure the affective and interpersonal characteristics of the personality disorder commonly referred to as psychopathy.

David Canter of the University of Surrey provides a different and perhaps more practical perspective on the use of the terms *psychopath* and *sociopath*: "They [serial killers] may be labeled psychopath or sociopath; both are curious terms that imply a medical, pathogenic origin yet in fact describe someone for whom no obvious organic or psychotic diagnosis can be made. The seemingly informed technical term is therefore more an admission of ignorance than an effective description" (Canter, 1994, p. 263).

Thus the utility of the terms *psychopath, sociopath,* and *antisocial personality disorder* is that they provide us with a set of typical characteristics or a lack of certain characteristics. The terms allow us to assign a group of attributes to certain individuals. The terms and their descriptors may tell us who does not fall within these categories but not those who specifically fit the labels. These terms advise us that such individuals lack a conscience and have no sense of empathy for their victims. The terms do not, however, allow us to predict such behavior. The terms may have a socioeconomic bias that causes those using the criteria to overlabel certain types of people. And finally, as David Canter has noted above, these terms may simply be an admission that we in fact don't know why these people act as they do.

Giannangelo (1997) argues for a new and separate classification in the *Diagnostic and Statistical Manual of Mental Disorders* for the behavior of a serial killer. He argues that such a classification, which he labels *homicidal pattern disorder*, should be listed under "impulse-control disorders not elsewhere classified" (APA, 1994, p. 269). Giannangelo (1996) describes homicidal pattern disorder as having the following characteristics (p. 98):

1. Deliberate and purposeful murder or attempts at murder of strangers on more than one occasion.
2. Tension or affective arousal at some time before the act.
3. Pleasure, gratification, or relief in commission or reflection of the acts.
4. Displays personality traits consistent with diagnosis of at least one cluster B personality disorder (antisocial, borderline, histrionic, narcissistic).
5. Understands the illegality of actions and continues to avoid apprehension.
6. Murders are not motivated by monetary gain, to conceal criminal activity, to express anger or vengeance, in response to a delusion or hallucination, or as a result of impaired judgment (e.g., in dementia, mental retardation, substance intoxication).

In short, the terms *psychopath, sociopath,* and *antisocial personality disorder* allow us to define our label and to characterize those who seem to fit the label but not to explain their behavior. It allows us to put the serial killer into a group or category. It provides a way of classifying the serial killer. For those who are asking the question, "why?", however, the problem remains. The group, category, or classification goes no farther toward an answer. It remains an enigma, indeed, an elusive phenomenon.

INADEQUATE SOCIALIZATION

Theories regarding inadequate socialization or childhood trauma are frequently cited in the homicide literature and often referred to regarding serial murderers. Storr (1972) states that human cruelty (which describes the acts committed by serial murderers, i.e., torture, mutilation, dismemberment, etc.) is "a phenomenon which can only be understood if we take into account the fact that many people suffer from persistent feelings of powerlessness and helplessness which date from a very early period in childhood" (p. 76).

The intense rage of the serial killer may be a mirror of the horror suffered in childhood. This rage reflects an intense hatred bred in childhood and which can now be targeted on victims. Reinhardt's (1962) case studies of multicides (mass and serial murders) found a prevalence of neglect and early years spent in wretched states of social and psychological deprivation. "They gave preponderant evidence of never having experienced normal communication with a dependable, understanding part of the social world about them. They had no workable system of social or personal frames of reference" (p. viii).

Willie (1975), who concurs with Reinhardt, found the most common feature of the family backgrounds of the murderer to be the violent punishing practices inflicted on the child, and that there "appears to be no other factor which is as specific in the family backgrounds of homicidal offenders" (p. 168).

FBI agents Hazelwood and Douglas (1980) state that, "Seldom does the lust murderer come from an environment of love and understanding. It is more likely that he was an abused and neglected child who experienced a great deal of conflict in his early life and was unable to develop and use adequate coping devices (i.e. defense mechanisms)" (p. 4).

In their extensive reading of the case histories of murderers, Ellis and Gullo (1971) found that "whenever sufficient material is given on the murderer's background, it is consistently found that (1) his upbringing particularly in relation to being treated kindly by his parents and his being emotionally close to them and to his other family members, left much to be desired; and (2) from an early age, he acted peculiarly, especially in his interpersonal relations with others, and began to get into some kind of school, social or vocational difficulties" (p. 158).

Serial murderers are frequently found to have unusual or unnatural relationships with their mothers. Lunde (1976) notes: "Normally there is an intense relationship with the mother. Her death is often one of those fantasized during adolescence. Later on, she may become one of the victims" (p. 53). "Many serial murderers have had intense, smothering relationships with their mothers—relationships filled with both abuse and sexual attraction" (Starr et al. 1984, p. 105).

In his classic 1927 study of murder, Bjere (1981) states:

> Time after time during my studies among murderers I was struck by the fact that just the most brutal criminals—men who, however different their psychological natures may have been in the beginning, and who had a stereotyped incapacity to conceive their fellow creatures as anything but dead matter or as the means to the satisfaction of their animal lusts; in other words men who for a long time had been cut off from any sort of association with humanity—were nevertheless frequently attached to their mothers by bonds which seemed even stronger than those which one ordinarily finds between mother and son. (p. 81)

SEX AS A MOTIVE

The killer's sexual preference or orientation is not a consistent correlate when known serial murderers are examined. As West (1987) notes, "there is no reason to suppose that the likelihood of becoming homicidal is associated with a particular sexual orientation" (p. 194). For example, DeSalvo, Bundy, and Kemper preferred females as sexual partners and as prey, whereas Gacy, Nilsen, and Corll preferred males in these roles.

The author has argued that sex is only an instrument used by the killer to obtain power and domination over his victim (Egger, 1990). Although the sexual component is frequently present in a serial murder, it is not the central motivating factor for the killer but an instrument used to dominate, control, and destroy the victim.

Helen Morrison, who has reportedly interviewed a number of serial murderers, argues against the sexual theme of serial murder. She states: "The incidence of sadomasochistic sex is very high. The incidence of mass murders is not, at least in the sheer number of perpetrators" (McCarthy, 1984, p. 1). Storr (1972) also discounts the sexual nature of sadomasochism or cruelty. He argues that "sado-masochism is less 'sexual' than is generally supposed, and is really a 'pseudo-sexual' activity or preoccupation, much more con-cerned with power relations than with pleasure" (Storr, 1972, pp. 74–75). The emphasis on power relations or control was, for Levin and Fox (1985), an important characteristic of serial murderers. They state: "Domination unmiti-gated by guilt is a crucial element in serial crimes with a sexual theme. Not only does sadistic sex—consensual or forcible—express the power of one person over another, but in serial homicides, murder enhances the killer's sense of control over his victims" (p. 72).

VARIATIONS ON POWER AND CONTROL

Levin and Fox (1985) contend that the serial murderer is trying to achieve a feeling of superiority over the victim and to triumph or conquer by destruc-tion; further, that "as the serial killer becomes more and more secure with his crime, however, he may also become increasingly more sadistic and inhu-mane" (p. 67), and that "the pleasure and exhilaration that the serial killer derives from repeated murder stem from absolute control over other human beings" (p. 68). The psychological need to control and the wish to command the fate of those around them is, for Fox and Levin (1985), often evident in serial murderers. However, in their study of 36 sexually oriented murderers, Ressler et al. (1986) found every indication that their motivation was a com-plex developmental process based on needs for sexual dominance based on violent sadistic fantasies.

Sewell (1985) analyzed the case of Ted Bundy from the literature dealing with Bundy and Sewell's own involvement as an investigator of the Chi Omega sorority house murders committed by Bundy at Florida State University. The purpose of Sewell's analysis was to apply Megargee's "algebra of aggression" (Megargee, 1982) to Bundy's behavior. Megargee's multidisciplinary approach to criminal behavior contends that "an individual automatically weighs alternatives and chooses a response to a situation which maximizes his/her benefit and minimizes potential pain distress" (Sewell, 1985, p. 15).

Sewell (1985) argues that the behavioral characteristics of Ted Bundy provide a clear application of Megargee's algebra of aggression:

> Bundy's overall violent response exemplified an instigation to aggression which was grounded in his rage against women and magnified by his need for excitement, attention, and ego gratification. His habit strength drew on his repeated successful acts of violence . . . to obtain control of the victims and the unsuccessful attempts by a number of states to charge him with these crimes. A number of situational factors added to his predisposition towards violence as an acceptable response. (p. 47)

Sewell concludes that "it would appear that Bundy chose a violent response as an acceptable reaction to many situations" (p. 24).

SIMILARITIES TO RAPE

As the author has noted elsewhere (Egger, 1985), the motivational dynamics of serial murder seem to be consistent with research on the nature of rape. Power would appear to be a vital component in either crime. Although this is conjecture without an empirical foundation, the similarity of these acts becomes evident when one realizes that "it may take only a small increase in the desperation of the assailant or the resisting victim to convert a violent rape into a murder" (West, 1987, p. 180).

Canter (1994) has also recently noted this similarity in his research. Canter states that "men I have spoken to who have admitted a series of rapes have often also admitted that they would have killed subsequent victims if they had not been caught. Rape has the same roots as murder. The difference between rape and murder lies in the form and degree of control the offender exerts over his victims" (p. 257). The implication from Canter's statement is that the motivations of these two violent acts may be similar. However, the motivational dynamics of either violent act are certainly complex and their similarities may only explain a certain level of action, in this case the form and degree of control, not necessarily the inner thoughts and drives of the violent actor.

In discussions with FBI agent Roy Hazelwood (who has since retired), he readily agreed that there was a similarity between rape and serial murder. He acknowledged that they were repetitive and there seemed to be a number of similarities between the two crimes. He agreed with the author that there was a power component to each and that further study was needed to determine if motivational factors were similar in these crimes.

It is certainly true that the crime of rape can be found in the criminal histories of numerous serial murderers. In some cases the rapes are found to have been committed months and sometimes years before the act of murder is committed. In other cases, the killer may vary his crimes, raping some of his victims and killing others. The crimes of James Edward Wood illustrate a varied serial pattern of rape and murder as well as a number of robberies.

JAMES EDWARD WOOD'S TRAIL OF CRIME

1961: Auto theft, Idaho Falls, Idaho.

November 23, 1967: Stabs two women in Bossier City, Louisiana and rapes one of them.

1967–1971: In prison in Angola, Louisiana.

1971–1975: Robbery suspect in Missouri, Arkansas, Texas, and Louisiana.

December 24, 1976: Kills woman in Shreveport, Louisiana.

July 1977: Armed robbery in Baton Rouge, Louisiana.

1979: Suspect in two murders in Louisiana; convicted of rape in Ruston, Louisiana.

1979–1986: In prison in Angola, Louisiana.

March 1987: Robbery suspect in Oklahoma.

October 24, 1992: Rapes Alton, Ill. woman.

October 25, 1992: Rapes and shoots Jamie Masengill in Bridgeton [Missouri].

October 27, 1992: Robs restaurant in suburban Denver.

November 28, 1992: Rapes 15-year-old [girl] in Pocatello, Idaho.

March 13, 1993: Robs sandwich shop in Pocatello.

March 27, 1993: Robs Tyhee County Store in Pocatello.

June 9, 1993: Rapes 14-year-old [girl] in Pocatello.

June 19, 1993: Rapes prostitute near Salt Lake City after robbing a restaurant.

June 23, 1993: Robs restaurant in Idaho Falls.

June 27, 1993: Robs Poppa Paul's Cafe in Pocatello.

June 29, 1993: Kidnaps Jeralee Underwood, 11 [year-old], in Pocatello.

June 30, 1993: Murders Jeralee in Idaho Falls.

July 6, 1993: Caught by police and confesses.

—Reprinted from *St. Louis Post Dispatch,* February 27, 1994, p. 4, with permission.

BIOLOGICAL PREDISPOSITION

There is a developing body of literature which suggests that certain biological characteristics may cause a person to commit violent acts or may contribute to violent actions. These characteristics may be certain abnormalities in the brain caused from trauma, brain damage, or genetic traits from birth. For example, Adrian Raine, professor of psychology at the University of Southern California, Los Angeles, recently completed a series of psychological studies of Danish men, schoolboys in York, England, and murderers on California's Death Row which all point specifically to mild brain dysfunction in early life as playing a crucial role in determining whether a young boy turns into a violent man. Raine's research results strongly imply that birth complications can lead to mild brain damage that may go unnoticed throughout childhood, yet predispose a boy to violent behavior in adulthood. Raine suggests that these studies in the three cities show that birth complications could have produced the prefrontal dysfunction, which then goes on to lead to low levels of arousal, which result in a tendency to commit violent crime. Raine states: "We suspect that under-aroused people seek out arousal to increase their levels back to normal. One way to do this as a kid is to join a gang, burgle a house or beat somebody up" (Connor, 1994, p. 19).

Jonathon Pincus, a noted neurologist, believes that it is a combination of factors, including brain damage and psychiatric impairment, that produces illogical thinking and paranoia in the serial killer. The other factor which he believes is always present in these killers is physical and/or sexual abuse. Brain damage alone will not cause violence in a person but when brain damage, abuse, and psychiatric impairment are all present, "those factors interact, and produce a very violent person" (Griffiths, 1993).

The serial murderers that Pincus has seen have been a bit less obviously neurologically impaired than those who aren't serial murderers and less psychiatrically impaired than those who aren't able to function in society at all. All had been abused sexually and physically. Pincus suggests that "a number of them [serial murderers] have had episodic disorders of mood that have made them unable to control their impulses at a particular time" (Griffiths, 1993). The fact that serial murderers have a mood disorder may explain, according to Pincus, why these murderers don't kill all the time and kill only when their mood swings dictate such behavior.

Richard Restak, neurologist and neuropsychiatrist, disagrees with Pincus. He argues that serial murderers have not been found to have episodic dyscontrol—that these killers are often stalkers who follow their victims. Restak argues that society has difficulty understanding and putting a person like a serial killer into a framework. "Circular arguments start from the idea anybody will have to be crazy in order to do this, and this person did it, and therefore they must be disturbed. . . . It's easy to say they must be insane, or they must be suffering from some mental disorder. But it's also a way of eliminating, or I should say refusing to look at the outer limits of human freedom, and even human, evil if you will" (Griffiths, 1993).

Restak thinks that to a lesser extent, psychiatry and neurology are being drawn in again and asked to explain behavior in a court of law that the public have difficulty understanding. Rather than explaining behavior from a Freudian perspective, which juries, judges, and the public spurned and rejected, the idea of brain damage is being proposed and discussed. Restak argues that "behavior doesn't necessarily imply brain damage at all" (Griffiths, 1993).

Restak sums up the current state of psychiatric and neurological knowledge of the serial killer by stating:

> I think we're at the beginning, we're going to study different brain functions with pet scans, and new computer-assisted electro-cephalograms, and things like that, but I don't think we're going to turn up some type of magic bullet, or magic key that's going to explain this. . . . we've learned more about the brain in the last ten years than we did in the previous two hundred. So you could say that about any particular behavior that you want to look at, serial killers as well as anything else . . . but I don't think we are going to predict or prevent, because not every person that fits a certain profile goes on to become a serial killer. The current state about knowledge of the brain of serial killers is at a very elemental level. (Griffiths, 1993)

Richard Kraus, a rural psychiatrist from New York, has taken a somewhat different approach to studying the biology of the serial killer. Kraus studied Arthur Shawcross, a serial killer who was convicted of killing 11 women in the Rochester, New York, area between 1988 and 1989. Kraus's examination of Shawcross revealed some unusual results. Kraus (1995) states:

> In this case, there was no predisposing family history of alcoholism, violence, criminality, or psychiatric disorder and no evidence of parental abuse, neglect, abandonment, or cruelty. However, at age seven years, this "bright, well-dressed, neat" child (as he was then described) was beginning to exhibit solitary aggressive conduct disordered behaviors which set him apart from his family, alienated him from his peers, and probably contributed to his becoming a loner. In the years that followed, his life style became that of repeated aggressive and antisocial behaviors, with convictions for burglary, arson, manslaughter, and finally, the serial homicides of 11 women. (p. 2)

In examining Shawcross's medical history, Kraus found a number of serious accidents. When he was 9, Shawcross suffered leg paralysis and was hospitalized for one week. At age 16 he suffered a skull fracture and cerebral concussion. When he was 20 he was accidentally struck in the head with a sledgehammer and was involved in an auto accident the same year. In each of these instances he suffered a cerebral concussion. The following year he fell from a ladder. While in prison his record shows numerous complaints of passing out, headaches, and similar problems. Shawcross received a 10% medical disability for numbness in his left hand related to a military injury when he was in Vietnam (Kraus, 1995).

Shawcross stated that his homicides were due to an "uncontrollable rage . . . it wasn't everyone, just certain ones [who] were more aggressive . . . the first one, she bit me . . . some tried to rob me . . . some belittled me . . . some didn't care . . . one threatened to tell my wife" (about his infidelities) (Kraus, 1995, p. 11).

Kraus found that Shawcross was not too impaired to understand the nature and consequences of his acts and to know that what he did was wrong. But Shawcross did have a "hair-trigger" temper and would lose control when provoked or under stress (p. 12).

A battery of psychological tests on Shawcross revealed a primary diagnosis of antisocial personality disorder. Laboratory examinations revealed that Shawcross had a 47, XYY karyotype chromosome. Kraus found a great deal of controversy in the research literature on this XYY chromosome condition and whether or not it was suggestive of abnormality in some men. Further lab tests also revealed that he had 10 times the normal level of krytopyrroles, which according to Kraus's research "correlated with marked irritability, rages, terrible problems with stress control, diminished ability to control stress, inability to control anger once provoked, mood swings, poor memory, a preference for night time, violence and antisocial behavior." (Olsen, 1993, p. 506).

In summary, Kraus (1995) found that

> these clinical findings revealed a matrix . . . of genetic, biochemical, neurological, and psychiatric impairments, which at least partially explain the "actual inner workings" of this serial killer. . . . Such a matrix of findings in one individual can reasonably be expected to result in behavioral disturbance. While biological influences do not control behavior or predetermine outcomes, this case demonstrates that criminal tendencies do have biological origins. (p. 27)

ANTHROPOLOGICAL VIEWPOINT

Wilson and Putnam (1961) state: "If man is deprived of meanings beyond his everyday routine, he becomes disgusted and bitter, and eventually violent. A society that provides no outlet for man's idealist passions is asking to be torn apart by violence" (p. 233). Wilson and Seaman (1983) carry this line of thinking one step farther by attempting to examine the thoughts of those who commit murder. While the argument for unmotivated resentment as a prerequisite for such violence is extended and developed further, the authors also attach an explanation for what they label as "motiveless viciousness" (p. ix). "Such violence, as frequently committed by the serial killer, is the result of Sartre's magical thinking, that is, thinking that cannot possibly accomplish its objective" (Wilson and Seaman, 1983, p. xii). However, such an etiological argument seems specious given the fact that such thinking is apparently nothing more than a lack of self control and an unwillingness to delay gratification. Explanations of this nature are indeed almost trite and frequently found in much of the more mainstream true-crime literature.

Leyton (1986) argues that multiple murders are a "kind of sub-political and conservative protest which nets the killer a substantial social profit of revenge, celebrity, identity and sexual relief" and "and is viewed by them as a mission or crusade" (p. 26). For Leyton, these killings are "a kind of rebellion against the social order (p. 26); "a protest against their [the killers] perceived exclusion from society" (p. 27).

Leyton (1986) concludes by rejecting arguments of sexual excitement or of conquest over the victim. He argues that motivation is, rather, a solution of those problems resulting from denied ambition. Multiple murderers act "to relieve a burning grudge engendered by their failed ambition" (p. 298).

Leyton expands on a frequently cited explanation for homicide. Leyton, an anthropologist, identifies relative deprivation, which he also extends to absolute deprivation, as the provocation for the multiple murderer's frustration. From a cultural perspective, the multiple murderer (Leyton includes both mass and serial murderers) is then "a profoundly conservative figure who comes to feel excluded from the class he so devoutly wishes to join. In an extended campaign of vengeance, he murders people unknown to him, but who represent to him (in their behavior, their appearance, or their location) the class that has rejected him" (p. 23).

PROBLEMS WITH EXPLANATIONS

There are indeed a number of different theories that claim to explain the behavior of the serial killer. In *Serial Killers*, Norris (1989) presents a list of behavior patterns which he offers as the epistemology of the "serial killer syndrome" (p. 212). These 22 patterns are symptoms of episodic aggressive behavior, which for Norris provides a profile of predisposition. Norris contends that these patterns or profiles are the "combined symptomatology of hundreds of serial killers" (p. 242). It would seem that the reader must accept such a statement as fact based on Norris's assertion of having interviewed "more that a dozen serial killers" (p. 210) and that the remaining data for such a synthesized symptomatology stem from interviews of secondary data sources. Such acceptance is indeed difficult, given the total lack of empirical documentation, footnote, or references in Norris's work.

Few, if any, of the theories of serial murder described above have been tested empirically against a large number of serial killers. Frequently, psychologists and other researchers who have interviewed serial killers have approached their interviews with a structured format or protocol intended to verify an already developed theory of the behavior. Frequently, when those interviewed have produced information inconsistent with already established theories, the information obtained is not considered important or relevant.

We are locked into a single-factor approach or the belief that there is a common profile for the serial killer and that each serial killer has certain common characteristics. The mass media tend to drive this approach by constantly asking for a "profile" of the serial killer. It is quite possible that by failing to consider those characteristics of the serial killers that do not distinguish these killers from other nonkillers, we are missing an important and critical ingredient in the behavior of serial murder. If these nondistinguishing characteristics of serial killers are present in concert or combination with other factors, this combination may be what drives the desire of these killers to kill and kill again. More research is undoubtedly necessary.

CHAPTER 3

THEY ARE ALL AROUND US

It has been widely stated by psychiatrists and lay writers that in our culture every killer must be psychopathic. That implies a rosy view of our society. It leaves out the terrible aspects of normallty (however defined) in a violent age. We flatter ourselves if we believe that our social conditions are so far above reproach that only mentally ill adults and children can commit violence.

—Fredric Wertham, *A Sign for Cain* (1966, p. 17)

Violence is good for those who have nothing to lose.

—Jean-Paul Sartre, *Le Diable et lebon Dieu*

INTRODUCTION: WE ARE STRANGERS TO ONE ANOTHER

We are creating *strangers* of each other. As we become strangers we begin to see others more as objects and less as human beings. Our connections with others become tenuous and fleeting. Interpersonal relationships become short-lived and unique occurrences. A sense of alienation continues to grow within ourselves tempered only by the strong need and desire to maintain our social status, advance our careers, or assure a relatively comfortable existence.

As we walk past a homeless man huddled over a grate in the sidewalk, we don't see the man. He is not a human being, only one of "them." Certainly not one of us but one who is different, probably dangerous, and certainly not worthy of society's attention. Were our eyes to see this man as a human being, they would tear with emotion. However, as we walk on, our eyes remain dry, furtively focusing on those around us in anticipation of an attack.

The vestiges of our humanity have been driven inward, hidden in our inner selves. This is not only due to our alienation but from a driving and ever-present fear of the stranger. In anticipation of falling prey to the stranger or from the memories of prior victimization, we remain a part of society, yet apart from most of its members. Only those close family members and the few we call friends continue to have meaning for us. Essentially we are alone: one among the many.

Our self perception places great value upon our success as an individual. We survive, maintain our lives, and continue on. The others with whom we are required to interact demand only slight, impersonal interaction. We negotiate with others for mutual profit. We try to delude ourselves that we have control over our own lives. However, as we move about among strangers, we have little control over these strangers. As we become the ever-increasing prey for these strangers, we are reminded that predators are all around us. We feel truly isolated and very alone.

WHO ARE THEY?

Who are these serial killers? To answer that question we should first look briefly at some of the better known serial killers in our society.

Jeffrey L. Dahmer's deadpan stare is known to most people with a TV set or a subscription to *Time, Newsweek,* or *People*. In July 1991, Dahmer was charged by Milwaukee police with the death of 16 young men and was charged with the death of one young man in Ohio. He confessed to killing and dismembering his victims, and at his trial, Dahmer pled guilty but insane. The judge decided that Dahmer was sane and he was sentenced to 15 consecutive life sentences in Wisconsin, a state that prohibits the death penalty. He was killed in prison.

Arthur Shawcross pleaded innocent to the murders of 10 women. His lawyers argued that he was legally insane. He was found guilty of second-degree murder, however, and was sentenced to a minimum of 250 years in prison in New York. He pled guilty to killing an eleventh victim (Olsen, 1993).

Richard Ramirez was dubbed the "Night Stalker" by the press. He claimed to worship Satan. He was convicted of 13 murders and 30 felonies by a California jury. He is incarcerated in San Quentin Prison in California (Linedecker, 1991).

Theodore Robert Bundy is referred to elsewhere and is well-known to most people.

Shortly after his arrest on suspicion of killing an 84-year-old woman, Henry Lee Lucas confessed to killing 60 people. He is referred to elsewhere in this work.

Wayne Williams pleaded innocent to the killing of two black youths in Atlanta, Georgia. An Atlanta jury found him guilty of two counts of murder. He was sentenced to two consecutive life terms in Georgia (Isaacson, 1982). Police at the time believed that Williams was responsible for the killing of 24 youths in what was referred to as the "Atlanta child killings." Prosecutors linked Williams to these other murders and effectively closed the files on 29 youths who had been murdered or were missing (Curriden, 1992).

Police in Des Plaines, Illinois, found most of the young men killed by John Wayne Gacy, Jr., in a crawl space under Gacy's house. Gacy is referred to elsewhere in this work.

Donald Harvey's co-workers called him the "Angel of Death." It seemed that whenever he was working, someone died in the hospital. Harvey was charged with killing hospital patients in Ohio and Kentucky. He was convicted of 37 murders, seven aggravated murders, and one felonious assault. He pled guilty to avoid the death penalty. He claims to have killed 87 people (Griffiths, 1993) and is believed by others to have killed between 54 and 58 people (Hickey, 1991, p. 138).

"Hillside Stranglers" Angelo Buono and Kenneth Bianchi were accused of killing 10 young women in the Los Angeles, California, area. Bianchi was convicted of two killings in Bellingham, Washington, after his claim of a multiple personality was found to be a hoax. Bianchi is discussed elsewhere in this work.

Patrick Wayne Kearney pled guilty to killing 32 young men in the Los Angeles area between 1975 and 1978 in what was referred to as the "trash bag murders" because the victims were dismembered and dumped in trash bags. He was sentenced to two concurrent life sentences (see Godwin, 1978; Newton, 1988).

For 13 months in 1976 and 1977 the "Son of Sam" shot 13 young men and women in eight different incidents in New York City. Six of these victims died. David Berkowitz, a 24-year-old postal worker, was charged with these crimes. Claiming that a dog told him to kill, he pled guilty to killing five women and one man. He was sentenced to 25 years to life (see Abrahamsen, 1985).

Juan Corona was found guilty in January 1973 of slaying 25 migrant farmworkers in California. The prosecution argued that these were homosexual murders, but a motive for these killings was never firmly established. He was sentenced to 25 consecutive life terms. An appeals court ordered a new trial and he was again convicted for all these murders (see Kidder, 1974; Lane and Gregg, 1992).

Albert DeSalvo claimed that he was the "Boston Strangler," but police lacked evidence to bring him to trial for the 13 female victims that had been killed between mid-1962 and early 1964. He was tried for unrelated assaults, convicted, and sentenced to life imprisonment. He was stabbed to death in his cell in 1973 (see Frank, 1967; Rae, 1967; or Lane and Gregg, 1992).

Westley Allan Dodd was the first person in over 30 years in this country to be executed by hanging. He was convicted in 1993 for the kidnapping, rape, and murder of three small boys. Prior to these murders he claims to have molested young boys virtually nonstop for 15 years (Griffiths, 1993). Dodd is quoted as saying that if he were ever freed, "I will kill and rape again and enjoy every minute of it" (Griffiths, 1993).

Lawrence Bittaker and Roy L. Norris began committing a series of rapes, torture, and murder of teenage girls during the summer of 1979 in California. They had met in prison the previous year. They dumped their last victim, naked and mutilated, on the lawn of a suburban house so that they could see the reaction of the press. They were found guilty of five murders and 21 other felonies, including rape, torture, and kidnapping. Norris received 45 years to life in prison and Bittaker received the death penalty (see Markman and Dominick and Bosco, 1989).

Known by the media as the "Sunset Strip Killer," Douglas D. Clark, together with his partner Carol Bundy, abducted and murdered six young prostitutes and runaways from Hollywood's Sunset Boulevard during the summer of 1980. Clark was found guilty of all six murders and sentenced to death. Bundy, who testified for the prosecution, received two sentences of 27 years to life and 25 years to life to run consecutively. Clark continues to deny all involvement in the murders (see MacNamara, 1990). Clark claims that Bundy (no relation) did all the killings and was attempting to duplicate Ted Bundy's crimes (Michael Reynolds, personal communication, February 5, 1991).

At 17 years of age, Jerome Brudos forced a young girl at knife point to pose in the nude. As a result he spent nine months in a mental hospital. Nine years later, between 1968 and 1969, he began killing young women in his garage under a special mirror he had installed to feed his fantasies. He was convicted of three murders and is serving three life sentences at the Oregon State Prison (see Rule, 1983).

On August 21, 1992, Benjamin Thomas Atkins confessed to killing 11 women in the Detroit, Michigan, area. During his lengthy confession he "explained to police in detail how he raped and strangled the 11 women in Highland Park and Detroit from the fall of 1991 to the spring of 1992" (Detroit Free Press, May 23, 1993). The bodies of his victims, all black women suspected of drug use and prostitution, were found nude or partially clothed in abandoned buildings. Atkins was found guilty on 11 counts of murder and one count of rape and sentenced to life without parole (Detroit Free Press, May 23, 1993).

Richard Angelo, referred to as the "Angel of Death" by the press, worked as a supervising nurse in the intensive care unit and coronary care unit of Good Samaritan Hospital in Long Island, New York. He had conducted experiments on field mice with the drugs Pavulon and Anectine and in 1987 began using these drugs on patients to put them into cardiac arrest. In some cases he would revive these patients, in other cases the patients would die. When a surviving patient complained, an investigation was initiated and 33 bodies were exhumed. Angelo was convicted of second-degree murder and manslaughter for injecting four patients with a deadly drug and was sentenced to 50 years to life. He is suspected of killing as many as 25 patients (see Linedecker and Burt, 1990).

Florida law enforcement officials believe that Christine Falling murdered six young children. She was found guilty of murdering three children, all under her care as she worked as their babysitter. When she is released she wants to babysit for young children again. She stated to CNN, "I just love kids to death" (Griffiths, 1993).

Gerald Gallego and his wife Charlene went on a killing spree, abducting young women in search of the perfect sex slave and murdering them. Charlene lured women to the car that Gerald was driving, and often held a gun on the women while Gerald raped them. This team of killers murdered at least 10 young women between 1978 and 1980 (see Biondi and Hecox, 1988).

John Joseph Joubert IV says that he had a fantasy of cannibalism since he was 6 or 7 years old. He was convicted of killing three young boys near Omaha, Nebraska, in 1983. He is believed to have killed others. He is on death row at the Nebraska State Prison (see Pettit, 1990).

Robert Berdella confessed to killing six men in Kansas, Missouri, in the late 1980s as part of a plea bargain to avoid the death penalty. All his victims were killed by injections of an animal tranquilizer after he had tortured them and used them as his sex slave for a number of days. The bodies were then dismembered by Berdella. One of his victims escaped and police found skulls and a number of pictures of the victims in his apartment. He died in prison of a heart attack in October 1992 following a lengthy series of interviews with British TV journalists (see Clark and Morley, 1993).

There are four serial killers who play bridge together on California's death row. They have been convicted of killing a total of 49 people. One of these card players is William Bonin, know as the "Freeway Killer," who killed 14 young men and boys between August 1979 and June 1980. Another player, Randy Kraft, was convicted in 1989 of killing 24 young men. Authorities believe that he may have killed as many as 63 people. The third card player is Lawrence Sigmound Bittaker, who with Roy Norris committed five murders. The fourth card player is Douglas Clark (referred to earlier as the "Sunset Strip Killer"). He was convicted of killing six prostitutes and runaways during the summer of 1980 (see MacNamara, 1990).

Kenneth Allen McDuff was on death row for the murders of three teenagers in Fort Worth, Texas, in 1966. His sentence was commuted to life in 1972, and in 1990 he was paroled. Less than two years later he was suspected of killing at least six women in Texas. The body of one of McDuff's victims was discovered just three days after he got out of prison. He was profiled on *America's Most Wanted* TV program in May 1992 and a caller spotted him in Kansas City, Missouri, where he was arrested. He was convicted in

1993 of killing a pregnant convenience store clerk in Temple, Texas. He is still a suspect in the disappearance of several women in the Temple, Texas, area. He was sentenced to death and is on death row once again (see Fair, 1994).

Roy and Faye Copeland, a farm couple from rural northern Missouri, celebrated their fiftieth wedding anniversary in separate jail cells shortly after they were arrested for killing five transient farmworkers with a 22-caliber rifle and burying them on the farm (see Miller, 1993b). Roy recently died of natural causes in a Missouri prison.

In 1964, when Edmund Kemper was 15 years old, he killed his grandparents and was committed to a California state hospital for the criminally insane. In 1969 he was released as "cured." He then murdered six young female hitchhikers and murdered his mother, all over an 11-month period. After the murder of his mother he drove to Pueblo, Colorado, where he called the local police and confessed to the murders (see Cheney, 1976; Leyton, 1986).

David Martin Long told police after his arrest, "I've got something inside my head that clicks sometimes. It just goes off "(Sare, 1986, p. 1). Four of these lethal "clicks" resulted in the violent deaths of five women whom Long killed with an ax.

Wayne Nance killed at least four people in Montana between 1974 and 1986. He is suspected by police of killing others. Nance was referred to as "Montana's baby-faced serial sex murderer." Unlike most of the killers described here, Nance was acquainted with his victims. One of them was the mother of his high school classmate (see Coston, 1992).

Charles Ng, together with Leonard Lake, tortured and killed at least 11 women in their survivalist bunker near Wilseyville, California, between 1981 and 1983. They are believed to have killed at least 14 additional women during this time. Lake committed suicide shortly after his arrest in June 1985 for theft. Ng, who was with Lake at the time, escaped and fled to Canada. The car that Ng and Lake were in led police to the killers' hideaway, a torture–murder bunker in Calaveras County. Ng was arrested in Canada in 1985 and in September 1991 extradited to California, where he was arraigned on 11 counts of murder. Lake's diary was found in the bunker by police. He wrote: "God meant women for cooking, cleaning house and sex and when they are not in use they should be locked up" (Associated Press, September 29, 1991; see also Harrington and Burger, 1993).

And the list goes on, and on, and on, and on. Currently, the author's files contain data on hundreds of these serial killers. The list keeps growing.

WHAT DO THEY LOOK LIKE?

Unlike serial killer Hannibal Lecter in the film *Silence of the Lambs*, serial murderers do not look like killers, nor does their appearance reflect an ultimate

evil. Unfortunately, serial killers appear on the streets of our cities, in suburban neighborhoods, and on our highways as the average person. Once a Ted
Bundy, Henry Lee Lucas, or John Wayne Gacy is identified, some are quick to
comment on the killer's appearance. "He has an evil eye." "He sure looks like
a serial killer." "I wouldn't want to meet him in a dark alley late at night."
However, without a criminal identity, in most instances the serial killer looks
likes everyone else.

Even though a number of people retrospectfully reinterpret the background and appearance of a serial killer, once he or she is caught, many others marvel at the fact that these killers look like the "boy next door," just your
"average Joe," or "just like any other normal person." Jeffrey Dahmer certainly doesn't look like a killer. Nor do many other serial killers described
briefly in this chapter. This seems to dumbfound a number of people. At the
very least, the normal outward appearance of the serial killer remains a fascination for many people.

SOME ARE VERY QUIET AND HARD TO SPOT

When Joel Rifkin confessed to murdering 17 prostitutes in the New York City
area, a high school classmate said that he was "quiet, shy, not the kind of guy
who would do something like this." When David Berkowitz was convicted of
six "Son of Sam" murders committed in 1976 and 1977 in New York City, a
former friend from the Army stated, "He was quiet and reserved and kept
pretty much to himself." Berkowitz's boss said, "That's the way he was here,
nice—a quiet, shy fellow." Juan Corona was convicted of 25 murders of itin-
erant farmworkers in California in 1971. Following Corona's conviction a
friend described him as being a very quiet person: "That's the kind of man he
is—kept to himself and never said much, for the most part." When Jeffrey
Dahmer confessed to killing and dismembering 17 people in Milwaukee and
Ohio in 1991 a friend of one of Dahmer's victims said: "He [Dahmer] didn't
have much to say about anything, just 'Hi, nice to meet you.' He seemed
quiet." And when Westley Allan Dodd was arrested and later executed in
1993 for the kidnapping, rape, and murder of three small boys, one of his
neighbors stated, "Wes seemed so harmless, such an all-around, basic good
citizen" (Griffiths, 1993).

SOME TAKE YEARS TO CATCH

In July 1994 the Federal Bureau of Investigation announced that for the past
eight months they had been posting messages on the Internet, seeking assistance in its efforts to locate a suspect who has detonated 14 bombs around
the United States since 1978, killing three people and injuring 23. The most

recent bombings occurred in June 1993, when a medical geneticist in Tiburon, California, and a Yale University computer science professor were severely injured by mail bombs.

This is the first known use of the Internet, recently referred to by the media as an information superhighway, in a major criminal investigation. In mid-December, the FBI began posting a request for tips in the "Unabom" case on the Internet's World Wide Web via a server at the NASA/Ames Research Center in Moffett Field, California.

In September 1995, the *New York Times* and *Washington Post* (after long soul searching and a number of meetings with federal officials of the U.S. Justice Department) published the Unabomber's 35,000-word Manifesto. In January 1996, David Kacyznski found papers written by his brother Ted very similar in nature to the Unabomber's Manifesto.

On April 3, 1996, after a nearly two-month stakeout and a search of a home in Lombard, Illinois, federal law enforcement agents arrested Ted Kacyznski as a suspect in the Unabom case. During this arrest agents found explosive chemicals and bombmaking material in Kacyznski's remote mountain cabin in Stemple Pass, Montana, where he had lived for the past 25 years. Kacyznski's trial by federal authorities is pending.

A NUMBER OF SERIAL KILLERS HAVE NOT BEEN CAUGHT

There are currently a number of unsolved homicides believed to be the work of serial killers. Unsolved murders that appear to be serial can be found in most states in this country. The following cases are only a few examples of these unsolved serial murders.

California

When the bodies of four women were found in the East San Gabriel Valley and nearby Chino, California, in the fall of 1993, authorities said that the killings did not appear to be linked. The victims were all black and in their thirties, they had been strangled and their bodies thrown in business parks or along the roadside. But investigators said the similarities were happenstance and not the work of a serial killer. They said that the bodies of eight slain women had been found dumped in Los Angeles in November alone. The San Gabriel Valley murders were just part of an abnormally high monthly tally of dumped bodies, officials reasoned. But after the body of a fifth woman was found in the San Gabriel Valley on December 30, 1993, the Los Angeles County Sheriff's Office and the Pomona Police Department indicated that three of the deaths were considered to be linked and two other victims might be connected (*Los Angeles Times*, January 7, 1994, p. B3).

On May 30, 1993, Los Angeles police began seeking public help in finding a Jeep driver who they said had killed three black men and wounded a fourth in a series of shootings since January of that year. The attacks occurred within a three-block radius in the Harbor City area near San Pedro. The suspect was described as a white man, 25 to 35, with red hair, driving a Jeep, possibly red in color. The killings occurred on January 31, February 14, and April 15, 1993. The last attack, in May, resulted in the wounding of a 38-year-old man. No one has ever been charged with these shootings (*Sacramento Bee*, May 30, 1993, p. B3).

Texas

Four unsolved murders were probably committed by the same killer outside League, Texas. The skeletal remains of Heidi Villareal Fye, 25, a waitress reported missing on October 10, 1983, were found on April 4, 1984. The body of Laura Lynn Miller, 16, reported missing September 14, 1984, was found February 2, 1986. The remains of Jane Doe and another unidentified victim known as Janet Doe were found on February 2, 1986, and September 8, 1991, respectively. Local police believe the four women were victims of an "organized serial sexual offender" but have not been able to link the murders to any suspects (*Houston Chronicle*, May 12, 1994, p. 20).

An investigation into a suspected serial killer's activities in Houston and surrounding areas over the past several years was recently reopened in Houston, Texas. A task force may be revived to study the violent deaths of 13 women in Brazoria, Galveston, Fort Bend, and Harris counties since 1986. A suspect was identified in 1987, but no charges were filled against him. The same suspect was arrested on May 18, 1994, for aggravated kidnapping of a woman. If the task force is revived, local police indicated that the FBI may join the investigation (*Houston Chronicle*, May 28, 1994, p. 34).

New York

A number of unsolved killings of prostitutes and alleged drug addicts in Rochester, New York, is raising fears that another serial killer is at work—just two years after Arthur Shawcross (see above) was convicted in a series of slayings in that area. Since September 1992 the bodies of four women with a history of prostitution and drug abuse have been found within a few miles of one another near the Lake Ontario State Parkway in northwestern Monroe County. The bodies of another 10 women with similar histories have been found elsewhere in the Rochester area since 1989. Police are searching for two others who are missing.

Following the 1990 conviction of Shawcross, who killed mostly prostitutes, police and sheriffs set up a program where all missing persons cases are pursued aggressively. "Now we chase every lead," said Captain Lynde

Johnston. "We immediately get dental records and other things to help with identifications. We treat them all like potential homicides" (*Newsday*, July 4, 1993, p. 45). Police still have no suspects in these murders. Although they avoid the term *serial killer*, investigators have repeatedly drawn parallels to the investigation of Arthur Shawcross, who was sentenced to life in prison for killing 11 women, many of them prostitutes and drug addicts, in the Rochester area between 1988 and 1989.

Nor was the "Pennsylvania Train Station Sniper" (also referred to as the "25-Caliber Killer") ever caught by the New York City police. The teletype shown below was sent out by the police on July 9, 1985.

ATT—BALLISTICS UNITS—HOMICIDE
UNITS—DETECTIVE UNITS—CRIME
ANALYSIS UNITS

PENN STATION TASK FORCE, comprised of members of the Long Island Rail Road Police Dept., AMTRAK Police Dept., and New York City Police Dept. is attempting to identify the person responsible for seven (7) "Sniper Shootings" (including one homicide) which have occurred in and around the Penn Station Rail Road Station at 7th Ave. and 32nd Street, Manhattan, New York.

The first shooting occurred on 4/28/83 at 2225 Hrs. The victim was a F/W age 50 and lived in a women's shelter for the homeless at 257 W. 30th Street, Manhattan. The victim was shot from the second story ledge of the shelter and through a partially open window.

The second shooting occurred on 4/28/83 at 0030 Hrs. The victim was a security officer for the hotel (no distinctive clothing worn) and was in a basement corridor. The victim was a M/W age 25. location was approx. two blocks away from the women's shelter.

The third shooting occurred on 6/29/83 at 222 Hrs. The victim was a M/W, artist, 29 Yrs. of age. He was shot from a second story ledge and through a partially open window. The location is adjacent to the women's shelter (Loc. of 1st victim).

The fourth shooting occurred on 7/31/83 at 0335 Hrs. The victim was a F/W 55 Yrs. of age who resided in the same building and room as victim number one. She was also shot in the same manner as victim Nbr. one.

The fifth shooting occurred on 12/4/83 at 1730 Hrs. The victim was a railroad worker at the Penn Station. He was a M/W 38 Yrs. of age. He was shot while walking on the platform, lower level of the station. Victim was not wearing any distinctive clothing. The location of the Sta. is three blocks from the women's shelter.

The sixth victim was shot on 12/20/83 at 2110 Hrs. The victim was a M/W 61 Yrs. of age. He was a RR worker and was shot in the same location as the fifth victim.

The Seventh and "last" victim was a M/W 29 Yrs. of age. He was a RR worker and was shot and killed on 2/21/84 in the same Loc. as victims five and six except that he was approx. 60 feet further west on the platform.

All areas of the train station, hotel and women's shelter are accessible through a sub terrain network of tunnels which run beneath the RR station.

All shooting have been ballistically matched to the same 25 caliber weapon. The ammo used in the shootings were either "Aguila" or R&P 25 caliber rounds. In each shooting all injuries were either to the chest, neck or head areas of the victims.

Anyone with similar shooting, please contact the task force.

—New York State Police Teletype, July, 9, 1985

Louisiana

The body of a 30-year-old woman, clad in nothing but pink socks, was discovered by two crawfishermen shortly after dawn Sunday, February 21, 1993, in a ditch alongside a two-lane blacktop road in a rural stretch of St. Charles Parish near New Orleans, Louisiana. She had been there for several days and had been strangled. The next morning, another strangled, naked female body was discovered 700 feet down the road. The St. Charles Parish Sheriff's Office determined that the second body had been there less than 12 hours. Both victims were known prostitutes. These murders were linked to a murder in September and then, sheriff's investigators discovered that New Orleans had 10 similar cases.

"We haven't linked all these murders to one suspect," Sergeant Sam Fradella of the New Orleans police said of the unsolved Louisiana cases. "The murders are similar; the victims are similar. But we can't call this a serial killing. We're handling each one as an independent murder." (*Newsday*, July 4, 1993, p. 45).

Indiana, Kansas, Missouri, and Texas

What is now referred to as the "I-70 robbery-murders" began April 8, 1992, with the slaying of a shoestore clerk in Indianapolis. Three days later, the owner and a clerk at a Wichita, Kansas, bridal shop were slain. The killings continued on April 27, 1992, with the slaying of a ceramics store clerk in Terre Haute, Indiana. Eight days later, a Western footwear shop clerk in St. Charles, Missouri, was killed. Another murder occurred May 7, 1992, outside Kansas City in Raytown, Missouri, where a curio shop clerk was killed. Five of the six midwestern victims were women. The sixth victim was a man with long hair tied in a ponytail. All were shot in the head. In addition, none of the stores had security alarms, and all were robbed of the little money available. All these serial killings have been linked by ballistics tests, which revealed that the same 22-caliber weapon had been used in all homicides. Authorities recently begin examining three similar killings in the Dallas–Fort Worth, Texas, area, which appear to be similar in nature (police detective Plummer, personal communication, St. Charles, Missouri).

Washington and Oregon

Since 1982, King County, Washington, authorities have sought the Green River killer, blamed for the deaths of up to 49 women in Washington and Oregon. In 1986 the following teletype was sent out to all U.S. law enforcement agencies:

ALL POLICE DEPARTMENTS
(CITY, COUNTY, STATE, NATIONWIDE)
MSG H22KING COUNTY POLICE
OCTOBER 17, 1986

THE KING COUNTY POLICE DEPARTMENT—GREEN RIVER TASK FORCE, SEATTLE, WASHINGTON, has been investigating a series of female homicides which occurred from approximately July 1982 through March 1984. It is the opinion of the FBI's Behavioral Science Unit, as well as others familiar with serial murders, that this killer will not stop until he is caught, or moves from the area. Since there have been no murders in King County attributed to this killer since approximately March 1984, it is highly probable he has moved and is killing elsewhere. It has also been documented that serial murderers have changed their modus operandi to avoid detection.

Receiving agencies are requested to advise the King County Police Dept— Green River Task Force of any serial murderers and their modus operandi who have operated in their jurisdiction since March 1984. It should be emphasized that information is being solicited on serial homicides in your area, not just those whose modus operandi is similar to that of the serial murder who operated in King County. In evaluating whether a "Serial Murderer" has operated in your area, it may be useful to note that a "Serial Murderer" generally refers to a number of murders by a single person over a period of a month—or, occasionally year. Each killing is usually a discrete episode, but there is usually a common motive, method, and/or type of victim.

A reply is requested regardless of whether the response is positive or negative. All replies should be directed to the attention of Anthony M. Caruso, or Frank Atchely, Green River Task Force, (206) 433-2013.

Washington

A list of 29 unsolved killings and the disappearance of 12 women in King, Snohomish, and Pierce counties in the state of Washington since 1985 were given to the press in 1993. 1984 was the year when officials say that the Green River killer stopped murdering young women in the Seattle area. Many of these 41 cases were prostitutes or young, streetwise teenagers. This was the first public acknowledgment that a killer or killers is killing in the Seattle area since the Green River Task Force was disbanded in 1990 (UPI, January 22, 1993).

Florida

It would appear that one or more serial murderers may have been killing recently in Florida. In January 1993, Marion County Sheriff's spokesmen reported that 18 female victims of murder had been killed in Florida between late 1991 and January 1993 and dumped in remote areas. All of these victims were believed to be prostitutes, and no arrests had been made for these killings. In describing these murders the spokesman indicated that nine were found in Brevard County, four in Volusia County, three in Lake County, and one each in Marion and Pasco counties. He also reported that four of the victims had been found in the state of Indiana and three had been found in Tennessee. However, the spokesman downplayed the possibility of these murders representing the work of a serial killer (*St. Petersburg Times*, January 8, 1993, p. 6B).

Massachusetts

The district attorney's office and the police spent years investigating the killings in the late 1980s of 11 women in the New Bedford, Massachusetts, area. The women all had connections to drug use and prostitution in the Weld Square area. All of these women had small children. Most were strangled to death and abandoned along the major highways that ring New Bedford. A man was charged in one of those killings, but the case was dismissed for lack of evidence. The killings have not continued and remain unsolved (see Smith and Guillen, 1991, for an excellent analysis of a serial murder investigation and its problems).

Connecticut

In Connecticut, investigators created a task force to seek the killer responsible for the strangling of two Waterbury prostitutes in 1988 and 1989. The task force disbanded without a conviction.

Pennsylvania, Kentucky, Tennessee, Mississippi, and Arkansas

Between October 1983 and April 1985, eight female victims, some of them red-haired prostitutes, were found strangled and left along highways in five states bordering the Ohio and Mississippi rivers. The case is open and no likely suspects have ever been identified (*Tennessean*, April 25, 1984, p. 1).

Michigan

Michigan police have never identified the "Oakland County child killer." Two young boys and two young girls were killed in 1976 and 1977. A task force formed to catch the killer was finally disbanded when all leads were exhausted (see McIntyre, 1988).

California and New York

During the period October 1966 through October 1969, California was the scene of a series of baffling murders committed by an unknown person who signed himself variously as "r-h, "Z," "the Zodiac," "a Friend," "a Citizen," and "Red Phantom." He killed six people and wounded two others. He wrote to the San Francisco police and taunted them. The Zodiac Killer was never identified (see Graysmith, 1976).

Twenty-one years later, a serial killer calling himself the "Zodiac Killer" struck New York City. A gunman shot and seriously wounded four people in the Brooklyn and Queens boroughs of the city between March and June 1990. The fourth victim died three and a half weeks after being shot in the back. Letters from someone, signed "the Zodiac," have been received by newspapers. In these letters the writer knew things about the killing that only the killer could know, according to the police. The writer claimed that he was going to kill one person for each of the 12 signs of the zodiac, which is used by astrologers to predict the future. This killer is not believed to have killed again in New York City, and a task force of 50 detectives formed in June has not made an arrest in this case (*Newsday*, June 20 to July 8, 1990).

Kansas

Between October 1989 and March 1990, four Native Americans were found killed in Lawrence, Kansas. Leaders of the Arapaho and Cheyenne tribes suspect that these deaths are the work of a serial killer and have asked the Federal Bureau of Investigation to investigate the killings. Local authorities claim that the homicides are unrelated (August 16, 1990, *Wall Street Journal*, pp. 1, 5).

Maryland

In Suitland, Maryland, a suburban community adjacent to the District of Columbia, five young black women were killed within two months. Their bodies were found between December 13, 1986 and January 13, 1987 in a wooded park in Suitland. All the victims were sexually assaulted and stabbed to death. No one has been charged with these murders (*Schenectady Gazette*, February 12, 1987, p. 2).

FEMALE SERIAL KILLERS

"So, I would have to say that to the families. I mean, that guy's gonna...'You stupid bitch, you killed my husband.' Or whatever, you know, or my brother or somethin'. And I'd just have to say to 'em, listen, what they were gonna do to me. I would be probably turning around if I had survived it and say, 'You stupid bastards. You almost killed me, you almost raped me, you almost beat the shit out of me.' ...So I can't really say they were sweet."

—Videotaped confession of Aileen Wuornos,
female serial killer, January 16, 1990

Not a great deal has been written about the female serial killer. The author formerly wrote the following about gender and serial killers: "One characteristic of the serial murderer not addressed in the literature is that there are very few instances in which a serial murderer is a female. Instances of female mass murderers can be found but relatively few serial murderers have been identified. This sexual differentiation may lead researchers to study maleness and its socialization as an etiological consideration. However, the lack of this obvious distinction has apparently precluded such study" (Egger, 1990a, p. 22). Given Hickey's (1991) research and recent reports of women serial killers (e.g., Wuornos, Falling, and Puente), it would appear that this gender distinction is at least not as pronounced as the author has indicated. Most certainly women are capable of killing serially; they just don't do it as often as men.

Hickey's (1991) analysis of 34 female serial killers revealed that at least some of the time, most were likely to use poison to kill their victims. He refers to female serial killers as the "quiet killers" (p. 106). Many of the serial killers in Hickey's data set could be described as either "black widows" or nurses: the former killed their husbands and the latter victimized their patients. Hickey (1991) notes correctly that this group of serial killers seem to be almost invisible to the news media and are frequently able to kill over long periods before they are noticed by law enforcement.

Most known female serial killers appear to have been motivated primarily by financial gain, although the psychopathy is undoubtedly much more complicated. Like their male counterparts, most of them have come from broken homes, been sexually abused by parents or relatives, or experienced other emotionally traumatic experiences in their youth. In a number of cases, female serial killers have had a relationship with their victims before they killed them. In other words, their victims were not strangers to some of these killers. It should also be noted that a number of female killers considered to be serial in nature have killed partly for their own material gain. It could even be argued that material gain was their sole reason or motive for killing. The presence of a relationship prior to killing their victim and a motive for material gain does not, of course, fit the author's definition of a serial murderer provided in Chapter 1. For instance, female killers Marybeth Tinning, Velma Barfield, and Dorothea Puente (discussed in the following pages) could all be considered as killers who killed for material gain, whether for insurance money, to cover other crimes, or for the social security checks of the victims. Certainly in these three cases the killers knew their victims.

In the case of female serial killers, the reader will have to make a judgment as to whether some of the female killers described briefly below should be considered serial killers. When looking at female serial killers it may be that there are a number of exceptions to the author's definition of serial murder or that female serial killers demand a separate serial murder definition. In fairness to others who would expand the author's definition to include material gain and a prior relationship (see Hickey, 1991) and in keeping with the author's desire to continue to study serial murder with an open mind, killers not strictly meeting the author's definition are included.

Aileen Wuornos had to agree to go with her victims for the purpose of having sex with them in order to kill them. Wuornos, who was incorrectly called this country's first woman serial killer by the FBI, killed seven middle-aged men in north-central Florida between November 1989 and the summer of 1990. The following is part of her confession to Florida Police.

⸺⸺◆⸺⸺

I just . . . I have to say it, that I killed 'em because they got violent with me and I decided to defend myself. I wasn't gonna let 'em beat the shit outa me or kill me, either. And I'm sure if they found out I had a weapon on me, which was very easy to find, 'cause I always had it in plain view where I could grab it quick, and if after the fightin' they found it, they would've shot me. So I just shot them. I really can't believe I'm in here tellin' you guys this. But I'm glad because I feel very guilty. Uh . . . I don't think I should live. I think I should die. I'm not gonna commit suicide. I'm gonna get right with Lord and live a normal life until I'm to die or I die a normal death, but I don't think I'm . . . I should live. I think I should die because I killed all those people. Well, I think it was like self defense, myself, but no one can judge that but God. . . . And then when I shot him the first time, he just backed away. And I thought . . . I thought to myself, well, hell, should I, you know, try to help this guy or should I just kill him. So I didn't know what to do, so I figured, well, if I help this guy and he lives, he's gonna tell on me and I'm gonna get for attempted murder, all this jazz. And I thought, well, the best thing to do is just keep shootin' him. The stupid bastard woulda killed me so I kept shootin'. You know. In other words, I shot him and I said to myself, Damn, you know, if I didn't . . . shoot him, he woulda shot me because he woulda beat the shit outta me, maybe I woulda been unconscious. He woulda found my gun goin' through my stuff, and shot me . . . this dirty bastard deserves to die anyway because of what he was tryin' to do to me. (Transcript of Aileen Wuornos confession, January 16, 1991, p. 7)

⸺⸺◆⸺⸺

Wuornos was sent to Florida's death row on January 31, 1992, for the shooting death of one of her victims.

After the fifth infant died while under the care of babysitter Christine Falling, the Florida Health Rehabilitative Services formed a task force to investigate the deaths. Bob Wray was asked by this task force to interview Falling to determine any psychological reason for these deaths. Falling confessed to Dr. Wray that she had killed these infants.

Statement of Bob Wray to CNN Correspondent Richard Roth

Well, she really couldn't say why she did it. The first child and I believe the third and the last child she alleged that she heard voices telling her to kill them. Two of the infants she didn't say that she heard any voices at all. On two of the people she alleged that she had some kind of weird sensation, as though she was taken over. And she killed them literally being in another personality. The other one or two times, which of course overlapped, she just said she had sort of automatic movements. For example, the first child, she said she just automatically moved her hands from the waist to the neck and as she was looking the child in the face she saw this poor child change from red to purple and she kept choking this child until it didn't twitch anymore. And the others are probably somewhat the same, although that's the only one I remember that she went into that kind of grim detail in describing. One of 'em I think the fourth child was actually her step niece. She was in the car with the child's mother. The child's mother, her step sister, went into a store, she strangled the child right there in the car. And when the mother came out and they drove down the street the mother noticed the child was not moving and discovered she was dead. (Griffiths, 1993)

In some cases it is difficult to label a person as a serial killer when they have not been convicted of a number of murders. Genene Jones is considered by many to be a serial killer, although she was only convicted of one killing. She was found guilty of the murder of 14-month-old Chelsea McClellan at a pediatrics clinic in Kerrville, Texas, for which Jones received the maximum sentence of 99 years. As the child's nurse, she had injected the child with the drug Anectine. Genene was further sentenced to 60 years in prison for "injury to a child" for injecting a child with heparin. Jones is still suspected by authorities in Texas of being responsible for at least 13 other deaths of infants under her care at Bexar County Hospital between February 1981 and January 1982 (Brown and Edwards, 1992; see Scott, 1992; Elkind, 1990; Moore and Reed, 1988).

Marybeth Tinning is another woman who most people consider to be a serial killer, although she was only convicted of one murder. In total, Tinning had nine children and she is suspected of killing most of them. When her adopted child was brought into the hospital emergency room in

1981 (after a number of her children had died of sudden infant death syndrome), the doctors were suspicious and performed an autopsy. However, the child was found to have died of pneumonia and no evidence was found to prove otherwise. When her last child was born in 1985, she, too, died. Tinning was charged with her death, found guilty of depraved indifference to human life, and received a prison sentence of 20 years to life. During the trial Tinning admitted to killing two of her other children by smothering them to death. She was never charged with these other deaths (see Egginton, 1989).

Margie Velma Bullard Burke Barfield was tried for only one of her murders, when she poured rat poison into her fiancé's beer in 1978. However, she also confessed to poisoning her mother in 1964 and an elderly man and woman whom she had cared for as a nurse and housekeeper in 1977. She is suspected by many people of committing many more murders. Barfield was convicted in 1978 of the first-degree murder of her fiancé and became the first woman to be executed since 1962 when she was executed by lethal injection on November 2, 1984, by the state of North Carolina (see Newton, 1990; Scott, 1992).

In early November 1988, a volunteer social worker who had placed a client in Dorothea Montalvo Puente's boardinghouse in downtown Sacramento, California, near the state capitol begin to look for her client. The client's social security checks had been cashed regularly, but the social worker had not seen her client since August of that year. Sacramento police found seven bodies buried in Puente's yard. She was arrested after fleeing to Los Angeles. The results of the police investigation lead to Puente being charged with nine deaths. Prosecutors maintained at her trial that she was killing her tenants so she could cash their social security checks.

On August 26, 1993, Puente was convicted of killing three of her tenants during the 1980s. At her trial the jury deadlocked on six other murder counts. The jury also became deadlocked during the penalty phase and the judge declared a mistrial. Under California law, since she was convicted of serial killing, she was sentenced to life in prison without the possibility of parole. Unlike many other serial killers, Puente still maintains her innocence. She admitted to cashing the checks of some of her tenants but claimed she had not killed anyone. One explanation Puente gave for the seven bodies in her yard was that all the victims died of natural causes. Much was made in the press and by her defense attorneys of the grandmotherly appearance of Puente and of the fact that she had given much to her boarders and to the Mexican-American community in Sacramento. These arguments may be the reason that jurors deadlocked on whether or not she should receive the death penalty (see Wood, 1994; Norton, 1994; Blackburn, 1990).

CATEGORIES AND TYPES OF SERIAL KILLERS

An examination of the spatial dimensions of serial murder reveals a multitude of geographic and chronological patterns that provide us with little similarity among victims or offenders. These events may occur within hours or in some cases, months or years apart. The only source, in most cases, is the memory of the murderer himself through confessions or patterns of kills identified by police or the news media. Nevertheless, some limited typologies and/or categories of serial murder were found in the literature.

Serial murderers are generally considered to be very mobile, moving from city to city and state to state. Robert Keppel, chief criminal investigator for the Washington State Attorney General's Office, who investigated the Theodore Bundy case and was involved in investigating the Green River killings in the Seattle area, characterizes serial murderers as tending to be highly mobile, ready to move quickly to another town after committing several killings that might lead to their detection (Lindsey, 1984). Theodore Bundy is reported to have left victims across the country from Seattle, Washington to Pensacola, Florida. Killings by Henry Lee Lucas are suspected by law enforcement agencies in 27 states. Levin and Fox (1985) found serial murderers to have become more geographically mobile, like society in general.

Many serial murderers traveled continually. Where the average person might put 10,000 to 20,000 miles a year on his car, some serial murderers have traveled 100,000 to 200,000 miles a year by automobile (Sonnenschein, 1985). However, it should be noted that not all serial murderers are as mobile, and may commit their killings within a relatively small geographic area. For instance, John Wayne Gacy committed his killings in and around the suburbs of Chicago. Robert Hansen committed his killings within the Anchorage, Alaska, area, even though he buried his victims in rural areas outside Anchorage.

Ressler et al. (1984) found that a number of serial murderers have been fascinated with law enforcement. They found several who had posed as law enforcement officers, held positions as security guards, and some who actually worked as auxiliary police. Some serial murderers are so fascinated by detective work that they school themselves in police procedures and investigative techniques. For example, Theodore Bundy worked for the King County Crime Commission in Washington; Wayne Williams often photographed crime scenes; John Wayne Gacy had a police radio in his home; and Edmund Kemper frequented a bar near police headquarters and questioned off-duty officers about the murders he had committed. Robert Keppel states that "a lot of them [serial murderers] seem to know something about police routine and are kind of police buffs" (Lindsey, 1984, p. 7).

When one refers to the serial murderer, it is frequently understood that such a person is mobile, as indicated above. Cecil Wingo, chief investigator for the Harris County, Texas, medical examiner, describes serial murderers in geographic terms. He has coined the terms *megastat* and *megamobile*. The megastat commits killings over time in a single static urban environment. The megamobile is mobile, moving over great stretches of geography as he kills (Egger, 1984a, p. 352). Holmes and DeBurger (1988) use the terms *geographically stable* and *geographically transient*. They define the former as one who typically lives in a particular area and kills his victims within the general region of his residence, and the latter as one who travels continually throughout his killing career (pp. 6, 7). Holmes and DeBurger further differentiate between these two types, stating that for the geographically stable serial murderer, "very frequently, the motive is sexual in nature and the predator may slaughter a selected group of victims" (p. 6). This assertion is, however, based on only three cases (John Wayne Gacy, Albert Fish, and Wayne Williams). Hickey's (1985) geographic typology of serial murder is a more fully developed attempt. He identifies three different types: the traveling or mobile, the local, and the place-specific. Hickey states:

> Mobile murderers are those individuals, almost exclusively male, who move from city to city and across state lines, killing victims at random, or seeking out a specific type of victim. These killers tend to appear friendly and helpful to their victims and usually take considerable precaution against being caught, i.e. Edmund Kemper. (p. 9)

> The local serial murderer stays in close proximity to his city or community. Again, almost exclusively male, these killers usually have a specific type of victim, i.e. prostitutes in the Green River Killings or the young males in the Atlanta Child Murders. (p. 10)

> The place-specific serial murderer [is a] killer who repeatedly murders in the same place. This type of killer usually operates in nursing homes, hospitals or in private homes. Either male or female these murderers kill for reasons of financial security, "mercy" killing, hatred of a particular group of people such as infants, handicapped or the elderly as well as motives of violence and sex . . . i.e. Ed Gein; John Gacy; Herman Webster Mudgett. (p. 10)

Hickey's (1985) typology is based on a historical literature review in which he reports to have identified "117 men and women in the United States who can be identified as serial murderers. An additional 47 serial murderer cases were collected from foreign countries" (p. 3). Hickey, however, provides no specific references for these cases, nor are his selection criteria identified.

Legal classifications of murder (first degree, second degree, etc.), and classifications based on assailant–victim relationships, tend to ignore many of the dynamic aspects of the event in the study of serial murder. The classification of murder regarding its motive appears to have provided a somewhat more productive method of examining serial murder in the literature. In her classic study of motive, Jesse (1924) provides six "natural" groups of motive: 1. gain, 2. revenge, 3. elimination, 4. jealousy, 5. lust of killing, and 6. conviction (p. 13). Jesse (1924) describes her fifth group by dividing it into lust-murders where the satisfaction is the actual killing, without any sexual connection with the victim; and lust-murders committed at the same time or directly after the sexual act as part of the sexual gratification.

Megargee (1982) classifies aggressive acts into instrumental or extrinsic motivation, in which the aggressive or violent behavior serves as a means to some end, and angry or intrinsic motivation, in which the injury to the victim is an end in itself. It is his first classification which concerns us here, as the motive of sexual gratification is frequently identified in cases of serial murder.

Guttmacher (1960) refers to purely sadistic homicides as lust-murders. Karpman (1954) describes the perpetrators of lust-murders as nearly always psychotic and as sexually impotent. de River (1958) defines lust-murder as when death has occurred through torture brought about to relieve sexual tension. The lust-murderer only gains sexual gratification through physical injury or torture of the victim (p. 99). Lust-murder is further described by de River (1958) as being accompanied by acts of perversion such as vampirism, cannibalism, and necrophilia (p. 40). Nettler (1982) refers to this as intentional lust-murder or sadistic murder.

Hazelwood and Douglas (1980), early pioneers with the FBI who examined serial murder, describe two types of lust-murderers. The organized nonsocial is seen as a totally egocentric amoral person who can be superficially charming and manipulative of others. His or her crimes are committed with method and "expertise." The disorganized asocial type is described as a "loner" with feelings of rejection who has great difficulty in interpersonal relationships. His killings are less cunning and done on impulse. They generally select female victims, although male victims are not unknown.

Nettler (1982) provides a further description of the lust-murderer: "For such men, the act of killing a woman is itself sexually stimulating. . . . Many have intercourse, in varied fashion, with the corpse before and after mutilating it. . . . The distinctive significance of sadistic killers is that they commit 'butcher murders' without being psychotic. By legal standards they are in touch with reality. They do not kill under the direction of a delusion" (p.131). Revitch and Schlesinger (1978) refer to lust-murders as compulsive homicides that are stimulated through a combination of social pressures, resulting in weakening of authority and controls. However, a lust-murder does not necessarily mean serial murder, which often appears to be random and motiveless.

HOW MANY ARE THERE IN THE UNITED STATES?

What are the extent and prevalence of serial murder? How many serial murderers are there? How many people do they kill? Is serial murder on the increase? The literature provides no decisive answers to any of these questions. Is serial murder a contemporary phenomenon or a recently discovered problem with a history? The research provides us with a somewhat clearer answer to this question.

Serial murder, as indicated earlier, is generally a stranger-to-stranger crime. Thus one must look to this category of homicide to attempt to determine the number of serial murders, since no evidence is found of monitoring or tabulating this phenomenon in the literature. In the past, homicides have typically been separated into three categories: about one-third have been between intimates—family members or lovers; one-third have been between acquaintances, and one-third have been between strangers. In the 1960s the rate in the last category began to rise dramatically, while the other two have remained relatively stable (Meredith, 1984). Franklin E. Zimring, director of the University of Chicago's Center for Studies in Criminal Justice, says that this classification needs to be examined much more carefully. He states: "That's as specific as police agencies get with that category [between strangers], and it's not enough. We need to know who these strangers are and why the rate is going up" (Meredith, 1984, p. 44).

In analyzing victim–killer relationships of homicides in England between 1957 and 1962, Morris and Bloom-Cooper (1964) find that it was, "abundantly clear that homicide 'out of the blue,' in which the victim is struck down without reacting in any way, is exceptionally rare" (p. 325). This has certainly changed, at least in the United States. Riedel (1987) found that the proportion of violent incidents in the United States involving intimates and acquaintances had dropped between 1956 and 1976, while the proportion involving strangers had risen. Godwin (1978) finds a dramatic increase in stranger-to-stranger killings, and he argues that these types of slayings are becoming more and more prevalent, quadrupling in the 1970s (p. 7). Gilbert's (1983) analysis of homicides in San Diego found that between 1970 and 1980, nearly 50% of all homicide victims did not know their killers. During this period there was a 60% increase in all reported violent crimes, and the criminal homicide rate increased from 7.8 to 10.2 per 100,000 population (FBI, 1981).

The Centers for Disease Control (1982) analyzed all homicides reported to the Federal Bureau of Investigation between 1976 and 1979. Results of this analysis revealed that during this period 13% of the homicides were committed by strangers and in 29% of the offenses, the offenders, were unidentified. In analyzing the same data for circumstances of the homicides, 20% were found to be indeterminable. In most instances, serial murders would be found within these categories since they are frequently stranger to stranger, or the circumstances of these murders may not yet be determined.

In 1993, 24,526 criminal homicides were reported nationally to the FBI, a rate of 9.5 per 100,000 population. If we look back from 1993 at an 18-year period, both the total number and the rate of murders have increased. In 1965 the total was 9,850, and in 1993 it was 24,526, a 149% increase. The rates per 100,000 population for the same period was from 5.1 to 9.5, or an 86% increase (FBI, 1994). So when population increases are taken into account, the murder rate still shows a dramatic increase in the last 18 years. If we look at 5- and 10-year periods, we still see a dramatic increase. The 1993 rate was 9% higher than in 1989 and 20% higher than in 1984.

Even though the murder rate has decidedly increased, this does not tell us whether serial murder has in fact increased with the overall trend. If we knew the total number of serial murders or the rate of serial murder at a point in time, we could extrapolate from that point, assuming an increase consistent with the total murder increase. Unfortunately, we simply do not have good data. Serial murders or serial murderers are not counted in official crime statistics, and even if they were, we would be missing an unknown percentage given the nature of the crime. In other words, a number of them would not be counted because they had not been identified or linked as such by law enforcement authorities. So we are in a quandary.

An estimate of the number of serial murders for a given period of time is very problematic. Possibly the best evidence available to begin to try to determine the extent and prevalence of serial murder comes from two major sources: identified trends within the overall murder count over time and totals based on newspaper reporting of serial murder.

Homicide trends in stranger-to-stranger murders or where the relationship between the killer and victim is unknown do provide some evidence which suggests an increase in serial murder. This, of course, does not give us a magic number, but it does provide an indication of the magnitude of the problem. As indicated earlier, the circumstances or relationships of victim and offender related to homicide has changed dramatically since the 1960s. In the past the vast majority of murders have been between persons who had formed some type of relationship or acquaintance. This is no longer the case. In 1965 only 5% of the murder circumstances were unknown. In 1992 this increased to 28%. In 1992, murders by strangers and unknown persons represented 53% of all murders in the United States reported to the FBI (FBI, 1994). "In 1965, nearly 1 out of 3 (31%) murder victims was killed by a person or persons within his or her family. In 1992, however, the figure fell to only 12% . . . supporting the trend of murders becoming less family-oriented" (FBI, 1994, p. 285). The FBI and others generally attribute to the nation's drug trade this increase in murders whose circumstances are unknown or in stranger-to-stranger killings. Although this may be the conventional wisdom to account for some of these murders, it is also reasonable to consider at least part of this increase to be the result of serial murderers.

The *Vital Statistics of the National Center for Health Statistics*, published annually, documents cause and nature of death in the United States, but their statistics are not collected to reveal motive or relationship between victim and offender, nor do police agencies collect or maintain data and information of this type. Darrach and Norris (1984) found that at least 120 serial killers had been captured or singled out by the police in the last 20 years; however, the authors did not indicate how this number was derived, nor do they provide any documentation for this claim.

It would appear that the mass media is currently the only other source (in addition to examining overall trends within murders reported to the FBI) from which to quantify serial murders in this country. Serial murders come to the attention of the print media when a serial murderer is apprehended and the killings are revealed or a series of murders occur within a relatively small geographical area and their multiplicity becomes evident over time. Press attention and column space thus provide a source for identifying and accumulating a more aggregate picture of this phenomenon. Fox and Levin (1983) utilize this data source in examining multiple murders, and they state: "Because of the newspaper publicity associated with extreme acts of aggression, we believe that our selection procedure uncovered most of the acts of multiple murder committed during the time period under investigation" (p. 3). The information collected from this data source (42 mass murderers between 1974 and 1979) was also apparently used by Levin and Fox (1985) in their book on mass murder. Dominick (1978) found that newspapers devote a great deal of column space to a few sensational crimes, especially on the more spectacular homicides. Without extensive survey research to provide an inventory of serial murders from each law enforcement jurisdiction, newspaper research is the only means currently available to collect these data. The problem with this approach is that many unsolved murders are potentially serial in nature. Without the serial murderer and a confession, numerous unsolved murders will remain separate distinct homicide events and thus will receive little, if any, attention in major newspapers.

A great deal of cross-checking and backtracking is necessary to research serial murderers through newspaper content analysis. Two strategies can be utilized in the initial search: a search for an identified serial murderer or a search for identified serial murders. The former, used by Egger (1984a) in a preliminary search of the *New York Times Index* from January 1978 to June 1983, revealed a total of 54 serial murderers who had reportedly killed four or more persons and been identified by the paper during this period.

Any attempts to determine the number of serial murder victims is fraught with the same problems of determining the number of serial murderers. In addition, known victims of homicide will probably not be potentially identified as serial murder victims unless their demise has occurred in a relatively small geographical area such as in the Green River murders in the Pacific northwest area, or their assailant has been apprehended and confesses to the murders, as in the cases of Lucas, Gacy, Bianchi, and other serial murderers. Also, the victims of serial murder are sometimes not found, or if found, it may be next to impossible to determine their identity. Alfred Regnery, former administrator of the Office of Juvenile Justice and Delinquency Prevention, U.S. Department of Justice, contended that many missing children are the victims of serial murderers and stated: "Because the bodies of the victims are not always found, we have no idea what the real number is" (*Houston Post*, November 11, 1983, p. 1). Robert O. Heck, a U.S. Justice Department official, has stated that each year more than 4,000 bodies are found abandoned on lonely hillsides, in city dumpsters, or beside rural roads and are never identified (Lindsey, 1984). However, Heck's statistics are only an estimate and have no empirical basis, for there is no mechanism for collecting such information. In discussing the number of serial killers, Levin and Fox (1985) state: "Indeed, one can only speculate that many of the more than five thousand unsolved homicides in the nation each year are the work of a few very effective killers" (p. 186).

Whether or not the incidence of serial murder is increasing is a question frequently addressed in the contemporary literature, with a great deal of focus on the increase of stranger-to-stranger or motiveless homicides. Those who contend that there is such an increase apparently base their argument largely on the increase in the number of apparently motiveless killings over the 1960s and 1970s (Nelson, 1984). Law enforcement officials assert that history offers nothing to compare with the spate of such murders that has occurred in the United States since the beginning of the 1970s. These officials will concede that more murders than are generally recognized could have occurred in the past. They may have gone unnoticed because detectives in widely scattered jurisdictions did not connect the crimes. However, officials still maintain that the increase of murders with no apparent motive is definitely increasing.

In a paper presenting the results of a two-year study on serial or series murder, Ressler et al. (1984) state: "The beginning of such stranger, motiveless murders was first noticed by the media in the mid-sixties when the 'Son of Sam' killer, David Berkowitz stalked victims in New York and gunned them down with a .44 pistol without apparent motive. Since that time there has been a considerable upswing in these types of murders and in the past decade the rate has climbed to an almost epidemic proportion (p. 1). To illus-

trate the scope of this problem, Ressler et al. (1985) cite a newspaper indexing report on the occurrence of mass murders and serial murders in the years
1982, 1983, and through July 1984. They conclude that the figures from this
report, "dramatically illustrate the increase in mass murders as well as the
category of serial murders" (p. 3). While the information presented from this
newspaper indexing report by Ressler et al. does tend to show an increase in
serial murders, with 10 in 1982, 27 in 1983, and 12 in the first seven months
of 1984, there are severe limitations to these data. The total murders in the first
seven months of 1984 may reflect a decrease if seasonal variation of serial
murders is discounted. This total of 12 murders in seven months reflects an
average of only 1.7 per month, compared to 2.25 per month for the previous
12 months and 0.83 for 1982. If the incidence of murders is linear, the total
number of serial murders for 1984 would be less than 22. While linearity of
serial murder occurrences is, of course, not assumed, the limited time frame
of 31 months is not sufficient, given the data presented, to conclude that serial murder is increasing, implying a definite trend in this phenomenon. True,
the data reflect an increase within the 31-month period, based on 12-month
increments or a portion thereof. This does not, however, represent a trend.
Even more problematic is the fact that the data presented by Ressler et al.
represent only those data reported as occurrences of serial murder and subsequently reported in the newspapers indexed in the report.

The U.S. Justice Department has hesitated to refer to serial murder as
an epidemic, but the volume of cases of serial murder has certainly brought
more attention to the phenomenon. Roger Depue, former FBI director of the
National Center for the Analysis of Violent Crime, stated: "It isn't just a matter of being more aware of [serial murders]. The actual number seems to be
increasing "(Starr et al., 1984, p. 100).

Others who argue that serial murder is increasing attribute the increase
to the violence on television or the growth of sadistic pornography. Pierce
Brooks, a recognized homicide expert, argued that the increased mobility of
Americans is partly to blame for the rise in serial homicides. Brooks stated:
"We are becoming more of a society of strangers" (Berger, 1984).

Zahn (in Inciardi, 1980) also notes that there is a definite increase in
stranger murders and in cases where the offenders remain unknown (p. 124).
Zahn further states that "with careful monitoring of these types of homicides
that are occurring, differing allocations to solve the problems associated with
these types might occur" (p. 128). The problem, however, is that there is no
such monitoring on a national scale. The *Uniform Crime Report* and preliminary content analysis of newspaper accounts reveals that the occurrence of
serial murder is a persistent and possibly increasing phenomenon in our society. It is possible, however, that serial murder is stable in rate and that any
"increase" is the result of rising awareness and reporting procedures of the

media. Newspaper stories of serial murder are not particularly reliable because they depend on editorial decisions frequently meant to sensationalize the phenomenon to increase circulation. No resources are being allocated to examine the extent or prevalence of this phenomenon. The number of serial murders or the extent to which they are increasing has not been documented.

As Kiger notes: "Without accurate quantitative assessments of the extent of serial murder we will be unable to develop informed typologies, theories, and policy decisions. Indeed, we run the risk of creating a social problem, the magnitude of which may be greatly exaggerated" (Egger, 1990a, p. 36).

FBI and CNN Disagree on the Numbers

The FBI Behavioral Sciences and Investigative Support Unit at the National Center of the Analysis of Violent Crime attempts to keep track of serial murderers. According to an official summary provided by this unit to *CNN Special Reports*, there have been 331 serial murderers and almost 2,000 confirmed victims of serial murder between January 1977 and April 1992. But an independent examination of the FBI's supporting data commissioned by CNN found a much different picture. The FBI data had been collected from major newspaper wire services and other publications. After removing a number of duplicated cases, the total number of serial killers listed in the FBI's own supporting data was only 175. After adding in serial murderers missing from these data, the total number of known serial killers during this period was 191 and the actual number of confirmed victims totaled 1,007. So this independent analysis resulted in reducing the number of serial killers by 140 (42%) and reducing the number of victims by almost 1,000 (almost 50%) (Griffiths, 1993).

A spokesperson for the FBI admitted to CNN that the numbers were: "Very squishy. Very unreliable numbers. It's hard for anybody to come up with accurate numbers" (Griffiths, 1993). During the same TV special, first aired on CNN in early 1993, the FBI also estimated the number of active serial killers at any one time in the United States. One agent stated, "25, 35 or 40 serial killers active at a given time is not out of the ballpark" (Griffiths, 1993). Another agent estimated "probably fifty to a hundred out there in society" (Griffiths, 1993).

A New Phenomenon?

There is a general impression that serial murder has emerged only in the last few years. However, this perception cannot be supported. Hickey's (1985) historical literature review refutes the notion that serial murderers are a product of contemporary society. Hickey (1985) found 117 serial murderers as far back in U.S. history as early in the nineteenth century and concluded: "First, the data unequivocally contradicts the assumption that serial murderers are a recent phenomenon. Regardless of their typologies, serial murderers can be traced back 200 years. Secondly, the emergence of serial murderers to the public view is made possible by our advancing technology, but they probably have always existed and operated in the United States" (p. 11).

An Increase in Serial Killers?

Riedel (1992) found a large percentage of homicide cases in the United States between 1976 and 1978 in which the victim–offender relationship was unknown and increasing (24 to 30%) over the three-year period. Riedel and Zahn suggest that this trend may indicate an increase in stranger homicides.

Dietz (1986) states: "Claims to the contrary notwithstanding, there is no empirical evidence that the frequency of serial killers is increasing or is higher in the United States than in other countries" (p. 486). He argues that although detection of serial killers may be increasing, rates are not known, and the study of trends or comparisons is not yet possible.

Smith (1987) describes a number of serial killers from southern and southeastern Asia, Europe, and England. Smith concludes by stating: "One thing appears certain, serial killing represents a world-wide problem which isn't going away" (p. 4).

Norris (1989) argues that the number of serial killers has increased since 1960. Masters (1985) also finds a "rash of cases" (p. 251), beginning in the early 1960s. He concludes that these murderers "are becoming less rare and may well come to represent a type of 'motiveless' criminal who belongs predominantly to the twentieth century" (Masters, 1985, p. 251). Wilson and Seaman (1983) concur, finding such crimes rare prior to 1960. However, few serious researchers would appear to support Linedecker's (1991) claim of fewer than 12 serial killers in the United States between 1900 and 1950.

Norris (1989) agrees with the earlier estimate of Holmes and DeBurger (1985): "In 1983 alone, according to the FBI, approximately five thousand Americans of both sexes and all ages—fifteen people a day and fully twenty-five percent of all murder victims—were struck down by murderers who did not know them and killed them for the sheer 'high' of the experience. The FBI calls this class of homicides serial murders and their perpetrators recreational or lust killers" (p. 15). However, this reference to the FBI in 1983 apparently refers to Norris's analysis of the *Uniform Crime Report*, not to statements by FBI officials. Norris provided neither reference citations within the text nor a list of references or a bibliography.

Leyton (1986) states in his book, *Hunting Humans: The Rise of the Modern Multiple Murderer*, that in the early 1980s the multiple-murder rate in the United States was on a "meteoric rise" (p. 22) when the homicide rate was beginning to abate. In a footnote to this statement, Leyton readily admits the unreliability and unavailability of statistics for multiple-murder and the further weakness of these numbers due to those not captured and the reliability of reporting police jurisdictions. This footnote certainly tends to weaken Leyton's own argument for a "meteoric rise" or a dramatic increase in multiple murders. (Others mentioned herein who provide the same basic argument for an increase could also be held accountable to Leyton's footnote, to a greater or lesser extent.)

INTERNATIONAL: A GLOBAL PHENOMENON

Q: Did you ever think of the pain you were causing your victim? When you were killing boys, didn't you ever stop to think of your own son?

A: It never entered my mind.

—Transcript of Russian Judge Leonid Akubzhanovof's interrogation of serial killer Andrie Chikatilo, convicted of killing 52 girls, boys, and young men (Krivich and Ol'gert, 1993, p. 270)

Serial murder is not unique to the United States. Hickey (1985) found 47 serial murderer cases in foreign countries (p. 3). Franklin (1965) provides numerous examples of European murderers, which today would be referred to as serial, such as Bela Kiss (early twentieth century Hungary); Henri Desiré Landru (1919, France); Peter Kurten (1929, Germany); Marcel Petiot (1941, France); Gordon Cummins (1942, England); and John Reginald Christie (1950, England). Of course, the most famous serial murderer was "Jack the Ripper," who operated in the late nineteenth century in London, England.

The following are examples of foreign serial killers. This section is not intended to be exhaustive but rather to provide the reader with information about some of the better known serial killers outside the United States. Following this brief summary of serial killers in foreign lands are some examples of identified serial killings or suspected serial killings where the killer has not yet been identified.

Russia

Andrei Chikatilo (quoted above), a former university professor, know as "Citizen Ch." or the "Monster of Rostov" by the Russian press, confessed to killing and mutilating 22 boys, 14 girls, and 19 women (a total of 55 victims) between 1978 and 1990 in or near the city of Rostov-on-Don in Ukraine, Russia. Chikatilo's first victim was a 9-year-old girl in December 1978. However, it was not until June 1982 that one of the killer's victims was discovered, a 13-year-old girl who had left her village to buy cigarettes, bread, and sugar. It was not until October of that year that police saw a similarity between three of Chikatilo's victims and organized a special work group of investigators to solve these three killings. Chikatilo became a suspect in these murders in 1984 and 1987, when he was placed at or near the scene of some of the murders. There were no witnesses to these murders and practically no physical evidence, except for semen samples. Chikatilo was placed under surveillance in 1990 and arrested on November 20 of that year. Nine days later he began confessing to his horrible crimes. He was described by Russian police as having no remorse for his victims and only pity for himself. He was convicted of killing 52 people in October 1992 and was executed on February 14, 1994 (see Conradi, 1992; Cullen, 1993; Krivich, 1993; Lourie, 1993).

India, Turkey, Thailand, and Nepal

Charles Sobhraj doesn't call what he does murder; he calls it "cleaning." By his own confession, he has cleaned many times. During one year, 1976, and for no obvious motive, he befriended and then sadistically killed at least eight travelers on the drug trails through Thailand, Turkey, and India. After his conviction for one of these killings he escaped from a Delhi high-security prison and may have orchestrated his own recapture to avoid being sent to Thailand, where he would almost certainly receive the death penalty for his murders. He is currently serving life imprisonment in an Indian prison. Thailand and Nepal still have a number of outstanding murder charges against Sobhraj (see Thompson, 1979, for a fascinating account of the crimes and travels of Sobhraj; and Lane and Gregg, 1992).

South Africa

On August 27, 1994, Norman Afzal Simons, 29, who is suspected of being a serial killer dubbed the "Station Strangler," was charged in Cape Town, South Africa, with killing 10 more people, bringing to 12 the number of murder charges he faces. This serial killer is believed to have killed 21 boys and a young man over an eight-year period in and around Cape Town. In June 1995, Simons was convicted of murdering a young boy.

South African police had assembled a team of three police psychiatrists to help track him. These psychiatrists were helping a team of detectives compile a psychological profile of the killer. Simons is referred to as the "Station Strangler" because several of his victims were attacked near railway stations. Most of the victims were children, who were found buried in shallow graves after being sodomized and strangled near Cape Town since 1986. A note found on one of his victims read, "one more, many more in store" (Reuters, August 10, 1995).

Australia

Australian police have recently arrested a suspect in the "backpacker murders." In late June 1994, truck driver Ivan Milat was arrested. He has protested his innocence and fired his lawyer during a court appearance at which he was again refused bail. Two women backpackers, the latest of the seven backpackers to be slain in an Australian forest, were the first to be found. The forest had been chosen as the site of the Australian national orienteering championships on September 20, 1992. Without the orienteers assisting the police in looking for the missing women, they would still be two names on the missing persons list.

On October 5, 1993, the next body was found close to where the first two victims were found. He had been missing in December 1989, after setting off to hitchhike with his girlfriend to a conservation festival in Melbourne. The girlfriend's body was later found nearby. For the next two months police coordinated a search of the forest with more than 400 volunteers. They found the remains of three more young bodies who had been stabbed and shot to death.

After the discovery of the last of the seven bodies, the Australian government offered a $500,000 reward and a local paper added another $200,000 to the reward. Milat was ordered to stand trial in early December 1994 after a seven-week pretrial hearing. His trial began in October 1994 (Milliken, 1994).

United Kingdom

England has had its share of serial killers with Yorkshire Ripper Peter Sutcliffe, London's Dennis Nilsen, and, of course, the infamous Jack.

Peter William Sutcliffe was first arrested for carrying a hammer in 1969 and was convicted for going equipped for theft. During that same year he was accused of attacking a woman in the red light district of Bradford, England, with a weighted sock; however, he was not charged with this crime. There is no record of Sutcliffe's criminal activities for the next four years. He was married in 1974, and approximately 11 months later he began a series of 20 attacks on women for which he was eventually charged. He tried to kill two women during that year and in October, killed a third in Leeds. He used a hammer in each attack and police began to suspect a serial killer. The British media dubbed those attacked the work of the "Yorkshire Ripper," after Jack the Ripper, the infamous serial killer who killed during the Victorian era of England in London. In November 1975 another woman was murdered, and by March 1978 Sutcliffe had killed a total of eight women and had tried to kill five others.

Between 1975 and 1981, Sutcliffe (sometimes referred to as the "Harlot Killer," as most of his victims were prostitutes), who was working as a truck driver, is believed to have killed 13 women and injured seven others who survived his attacks. Others credit Sutcliffe with four other murders and seven additional assaults (Yallop, 1982). He was arrested in the company of a prostitute on January 2, 1981, for theft of a car license plate; however, at the time of the arrest the arresting officers weren't really sure who they had in custody (David Baker, the arresting officer, personal communication, May 31, 1994). Following his arrest, Sutcliffe confessed to being the "Yorkshire Ripper."

It was not until after his arrest that Sutcliffe had ever seen a psychiatrist. He was diagnosed as suffering from paranoid schizophrenia. Sutcliffe stated during his trial in London: "They [the police] had all the facts for a long time. ...But then I knew why they didn't catch me; because everything was in God's hands" (Davies, 1981). He was convicted of 13 homicides and sentenced to life in prison (see Doney in Egger, 1990a; Burn, 1985; Jouve, 1986).

Prior to his arrest, Dennis Nilsen had never been incarcerated or suspected of a crime. He had worked as a police officer for a year for the London Metropolitan Police Force. It was only when Nilsen complained to his landlord of blocked drains in his flat in north London that he became of interest to the police, who soon found the drains clogged with body parts of Nilsen's victims. When confronted with this evidence, he quickly confessed to his crimes. He had murdered 15 men in his flat between 1978 and early 1983. All of his victims were drifters, homosexuals, or prostitutes. Only seven of the victims were ever identified. Nilsen kept his victims in his flat for days and sometimes weeks, posing them and holding one-way "conversations" with them. He was found guilty on six charges of murder and sentenced to 25 years to life in prison (see Masters, 1985).

Recently, the neighbors of Frederick and Rosemary West were surprised to learn that they had lived on Cromwell Street in Gloucester with a serial killer in their midst for quite some time. In late February 1994, police began a search for human remains that would last 114 days and result in the unearthing of 12 female corpses from two houses in the western English city of Gloucester and a field nearby. West, 52 years of age, was charged with 11 of the murders, including those of his first wife, Catherine, and two daughters. His present wife, Rosemary, was charged with nine murders. Two other adult accomplices were charged with sexual assault on some of the deceased murder victims.

The remains of nine women were found buried in the garden, cellar, and under a bath at 25 Cromwell Street, central Gloucester. The search then moved to a second house at 25 Midland Road nearby and a country field outside the city close to where West once lived. Police finished searching 25 Midland Road late in May 1994. The last body found, exhumed from the field earlier, was that of a pregnant woman.

Frederick West died while awaiting trial. The criminal trial of his wife Rosemary began in 1995. She was charged with 10 murders and two rape offenses (Associated Press, February 6, 1995). She was found guilty on all charges on November 27, 1985 and sentenced to life imprisonment.

Bad management of health services that were seriously short of funds enabled nurse Beverly Allitt to attack children she was caring for, according to a health workers' union representative. Warning signs were apparently overlooked or ignored. Allitt was known to have incurred self-inflicted injuries and feigned illness while a student at the hospital. Her frequent absences should have been investigated, and her family doctor asked if she was suitable for appointment as a nurse.

Information about Allitt was either unavailable to hospital management or lost in the hospital bureaucracy. By several criteria she was unfit to begin work as a nurse. Hospital authorities made "a serious error of judgment" when they recommended Allitt for employment. Allitt, 25, was sentenced to 13 life sentences for the attacks, including four murders. She is detained at Rampton special hospital in Nottinghamshire, England.

Robert Black is now referred to as Britain's worst child killer, but in 1982 he was a truck driver and not under suspicion for anything. His birth certificate has a blank space under the column headed "name and surname of father." Black's mother didn't know who the father was. Eighteen months after his birth, Black was placed in foster care to a widow who died when he was 13 years old. At age 16 he was convicted of indecent assault on a 6-year-old girl, and by the age of 20 he had a large collection of child pornography.

During the summer of 1982 a videotape showing a young schoolgirl reading poetry to her classmates was seen by millions of television viewers across the United Kingdom. The police were trying to jog the public's memory, believing that someone somewhere could hold a vital clue to the whereabouts of the missing child. A few days later the schoolgirl was found brutally murdered and was probably already dead when she was seen and heard on television. The police then made another plea to the British television viewers: "Help us find her killer." This was the beginning of a murder investigation (referred to as an "inquiry" in Britain) that would become the biggest manhunt ever by police in Britain. The investigation lasted nine years, utilizing unparalleled personnel resources and cost an estimated 5 million British pounds to conduct (*The Independent*, May 20, 1994, p. 3). The investigation involved both Scottish and English police and initially, four separate police forces.

In March 1986, after the third young victim was found dead (four weeks after she was reported missing) 70 miles from her home near Leeds, 15 police forces attended a Scotland Yard conference on a series of child murders and abductions across the country. The Nottingham police force then joined what was to become the largest computerized murder investigation ever in the United Kingdom.

In July 1990, a 6-year-old girl was abducted by Black, who dragged her inside his van. A neighbor who saw the incident took the van's license number and alerted the police. When police located and stopped the van, they rescued the young girl and arrested Black. The victim's hands had been tied behind her back, two pieces of plaster were stuck over her face, and a bag had been placed over her head.

Black was convicted of abduction and assault in August 1990. He was subsequently found guilty of kidnapping, murder, and improper burial of three young girls, ages 5, 10, and 11. He was also found guilty of kidnapping a fourth girl. These crimes were committed by Black between 1982 and 1986. On May 19, 1994, Black, 47, began serving a minimum of 35 years in prison for these murders. Police believe that he may be responsible for between 13 and 17 other murders of young children.

SERIAL KILLERS OUTSIDE THE UNITED STATES WHO HAVE NOT BEEN CAUGHT

The United States is not the only country where police have difficulty catching serial killers. The following cases are examples of unsolved and apparently serial murders outside the United States.

United Kingdom

Detectives of the South Yorkshire police force in England are hunting the killer of an unidentified woman found beaten and naked in a ditch. The police fear that she could be the fifth victim of a serial killer. The body, with clothes and jewelry missing, was found wrapped in a blanket.

Chief constables and senior detectives met on August 9, 1994, to discuss possible links between the murders of four women who were all strangled during the last nine months in an area known as the Midlands, north of London. Three of the women were prostitutes. They all had jewelry removed and their bodies were left naked or seminaked in isolated areas. Police believe that the fourth victim could have been mistaken for a prostitute. The killings, being referred to by the British press as the "Midlands Ripper slayings" are being compared to the Yorkshire Ripper case because the first four victims were prostitutes or believed to be prostitutes who regularly worked red light districts.

One of the victims, who was discovered in May 1994, was a 19-year-old mother of a young boy who was found naked in a shallow grave in the Peak

District in Derbyshire. She disappeared from the Sheffield red light district of Broomhall and was last seen getting into a dark-colored hatchback. However, this fourth victim was later excluded from this series of killings (personal communication, anonymous South Yorkshire police officer, September 21, 1994).

The police jurisdictions of Leicestershire, West Midlands, Lincolnshire, and Lancashire have not formally linked their investigations. These murders remain unsolved (August 10, 1994, *The Daily Telegraph*, p. 3).

Canada

The unsolved murders of six women in southern Ontario, Canada, show that some were stalked, kidnapped, and driven to remote areas, where they were murdered between early spring and late summer, from 1982 and 1992. While a sixth victim wasn't abducted, there are similarities between her murder and the other five. Over the years, detectives have cautiously, and privately, admitted the possibility that several of these killings could be linked. *Toronto Star* newspaper reporters found that as many as four other murders could also be connected to this possible series.

The bodies of five of the women were discovered in lovers' lanes, wooded areas down back roads frequented by teenagers. No effort was made to conceal the bodies. In at least three of the slayings the clothing of the victims was folded neatly and their shoes placed side by side at the murder scenes. Most of the victims were transported many miles from where they were abducted. Five of the victims either vanished or were killed on a weekend; the sixth was murdered on a Friday; five of the crimes took place at night, the sixth in the early evening. Two of the women were stalked after getting off a bus; a third was apparently waiting for a bus; a fourth was hitchhiking at the end of a bus line. The killer or killers kept personal effects from some of the victims—clothing, a shoe, jewelry. The detectives who worked on the six murders said that the similarities pointed out by the *Toronto Star* reporters might warrant further investigation.

Staff Sergeant Les Graham, head of Halton's Criminal Investigation Bureau, said police had looked at connections but came up with nothing. "One thing's for sure, the killer had to know the location of that lovers' lane before taking her there" (Pron and Duncanson, 1994).

In all six murders examined, the women were out at night alone. Of the six victims, one was strangled, a second was believed to be strangled, two were stabbed, and one was bludgeoned. The cause of death was not established for the sixth. Despite the similarities, police forces involved have made no concerted effort to establish a task force or to pool information (Pron and Duncanson, 1994).

Poland

Fear recently swept Warsaw in June 1993 as law enforcement officers hunted a deranged killer and hundreds of people telephoned police to turn in their neighbors. The man is believed to have bludgeoned six women in recent attacks, killing one and leaving three hospitalized, unconscious, and in critical condition. Each of the women was hit on the back of the head with a blunt instrument. Several of the victims were struck as they entered darkened staircases of their apartment buildings in the city center.

Until the attacks were made public by the Warsaw police, there was no campaign to warn women about two similar waves of assaults April 9 and May 18, 1993, when seven women were attacked. According to newspaper reports, two of these victims died (Staff, June 18, 1993) Callers turn in neighbors, *Los Angeles Times*, p. 26).

Sweden

In July 1993 police in Stockholm announced they were investigating a string of homosexual murders and warned gay men to be on their guard against a possible serial killer. Detectives are working on seven separate and as yet unresolved murder cases involving gay male victims dating back to 1990. Although police are not linking all the killings, they say that several bear strikingly similar hallmarks (1993, July 9, Stockholm gays warned, *The Gazette* (Montreal), p. C11).

In addition to South Africa, Australia, and the United Kingdom, serial killers have recently been reported operating in Germany, China, Japan, Austria, France, Russia, Nigeria, Bosnia, Italy, and Hungary. Few countries in the world have escaped the horror of the serial killer.

It would appear that serial murder is very definitely an international problem. Although the United States has reported many more serial killers than other countries of the world, more and more serial killers are being identified across the globe. In particular, areas of the former Soviet Union are acknowledging the presence of a number of killers either currently or in the relatively recent past.

CHAPTER 4

—◆◆—

VICTIMS: THE "LESS-DEAD"

I were just cleaning up the streets.
—Peter Sutcliffe, the Yorkshire Ripper

SERIAL KILLING OF THE LAMBS IN OUR DREAMS:
CONCEPT OF THE "LESS-DEAD"

The perverted, dominating, horrific mega-intellect of serial killer Dr. Hannibal Lecter (played by Anthony Hopkins) packed movie houses across the country. For those who fell under the spell of Jonathan Demme's *Silence of the Lambs*, many failed to feel the slaughtering of their senses as Dr. Lecter's hypnosis took its toll. As rookie FBI Agent Starling revealed in her recurring nightmare of the spring slaughter of her innocence symbolized by the death of lambs on her uncle's farm during her youth, her submission to this psychopathic interrogator reflected movie audience's voyeurism into the ultimate evil.

It was not only the brilliance of Anthony Hopkins that transformed this serial killer from a cruel, sadistic animal to an antihero. Acting skills notwithstanding, the public is preprogrammed to identify with or even laud the role of the serial killer in our society. The victims of serial killers, viewed when alive as a devalued strata of humanity, become "less-dead" (since for many they were less-alive before their death and now they become the "never-were") and their demise becomes the elimination of sores or blemishes cleansed by those who dare to wash away these undesirable elements. Just as the psychopathic serial killer depersonalizes his victims, society dissociates these victims from the human race, due to the irritant symbols they represent. Victims become those that "had it coming" or whose fate is preordained. We publicly abhor this violence while privately excusing the killer's acts as utilitarian or derived from motives explained by a terrible parentage or childhood trauma.

Victims become much less important, and the multiple nature of the killer's acts and his ability to elude the police becomes the central focus of this phenomenon. Many who view with nostalgia the rapidly disappearing patriarchal society will view these acts as a reassertion of male potency and domination. Others will vicariously view these acts as a personal safety valve for their own aggressive impulses to do violence. Some will secretly value the killer for his ability to outdo the typical murderer who slays his wife or her husband. For many, the serial killer is a symbol of courage, individuality, and unique cleverness. Many will quickly transform the killer into a figure who allows them to fantasize rebellion or the lashing out at society's ills. For some, the serial killer may become a symbol of swift and effective justice, cleansing society of its crime-ridden vermin. The serial killer's skills in eluding police for long periods of time transcends the very reason that he is being hunted. The killer's elusiveness overshadows his trail of grief and horror.

The debt to our humanity increases as we clamor to read the "page-turners" of Thomas Harris, Stephen King, and David Lindsey. This debt increases geometrically as our view of the multiple victims of these killers relegates them to the status of the "less-dead." The interest on this debt continues to be compounded with our heightened curiosity in the horror and gore of real serial killers such as Ted Bundy, Richard Rameriz (better known as the "Night Stalker"), and John Wayne Gacy or the unsolved serial killings such as the "Green River Killer" or the more recent terror spread by Danny Rollings in Gainesville, Florida. It is only when the "less-dead" are perceived as above the stature of prostitutes, homosexuals, street people, runaways, or the elderly that our own at-risk vulnerability becomes a stark reality. Until such time, the killer's aberrant behaviors are embued with a rationality or logic of our class consciousness. Even when we begin to take on an identity with the killer's prey, we shirk such feelings and intellectualize the precipitant behavior of victims and their lifestyles as the centrality of their demise.

The serial killer is not in fact our hero but the mirror image of our potential selves. He becomes just like us, except his avocation happens to be killing. We develop a twisted infatuation with the fact that he has killed and killed and killed again. We marvel at his ability to commit the unthinkable, even though we ourselves have harbored such thoughts. To commit this act time and time again, to satiate the killer's continuing taste for death, has resulted in society's own insatiable fascination with these acts.

Once caught, the serial killer doesn't look "abnormal" on our television screens or on the front page of our newspapers. We label him insane or a "whacko," but deep down we see him as very much like ourselves. Yet he is different. It is this difference, yet similarity, that captures our attention. His less-dead victims become less and less real. Their similarity to our own lives and their demise, which should indeed alert us to our own risk, loses clarity and focus as our self-manufactured reality defines our status as the antithesis to the serial killer's prey.

As theater audiences unknowingly submitted to the hypnotic strength of Dr. Lecter's presence, they reached a point in their subconscious where they began to think of this psychopath as "cool." The woman, fulfilling the male role of the hunter (portrayed by actress Jodie Foster), becomes a troubled soul in need of Dr. Lecter's superhuman expertise. The evil of the doctor has become cool and thus natural, and we seek to identify with such naturalness. We begin to ask ourselves, "How are we different from this person?" or "How are we alike?" Such stimulation of our id forces buried homicidal thoughts to the surface of our personality. We marvel at one who brings such thoughts to a personal reality. We become avid spectators to such continuous reality in which these thoughts are acted out again and again with such amazingly creative and horrific violence.

After all, victims are only the grist for such courageous acts, the result of our actor's heroism. Our hero, the super serial killer, is admired. It is not Anthony Hopkins' acting but the reality it represents. We are frequently reminded to revile this creature by an almost unreal morality, yet we continue our admiration for his deeds. Our recreational focus is on these homicidal acts as we become willing patients to Dr. Lecter's clinic of horrors.

The doctor's treatment results in a self segregation from the reality of pain and death as the empathetic pathways of our combined humanity are anesthetized to a virtual numbness. The phenomenon of serial violence, in particular serial homicide, is indeed rising. This is not the result of a few abnormal outliers in our demography but is due to an aggregate psychopathology in the very essence of our being. Human beings are devolving into an ultimate immorality. Our humaneness is rapidly dissipating into an enjoyment, an addictivelike drive, toward our fate.

Our ability to feel compassion for serial murder victims is brutalized by the excessive brutality provided by a slick Hollywood sheen. The wide-screen realism and appeal of a Hannibal Lecter is but a metaphor of our future morality. A morality where less-dead victims are dropped from perceived reality and Orwellian thought becomes a Disneylike fantasy. Descriptions of the horrific acts of serial killers lose their uniqueness as they begin to articulate a truer reality. Human skins to clothe and hide the remnants of our innocence will become unnecessary. Vestiges of our humanity will be lost in the fantasies of childhood, soon forgotten in a world inured to violence and death. We are seeking the ultimate experiences of evil, and the bleating of the lambs in our dreams will become our future nightmares as we become the less-alive and deaf to the cries of the victims.

SERIAL MURDER VICTIMS

In most cases the victims are selected solely on the fact that they crossed the path of the serial murderer and became a vehicle by which hypo-arousal occurred for his pleasure (Egger, 1984a). Victims are self-selecting only due to their existence at a place and point in time. This is apparently the only known precipitating factor. The definition of serial murder used by the author strongly suggests some commonalties among victims. Levin and Fox (1985) appear to concur with this definition regarding victims. They state, "Serial killers almost without exception choose vulnerable victims—those who are easy to dominate" (p. 75). "The serial killer typically picks on inno-cent strangers who may possess a certain physical feature or may just be accessible" (p. 231). Levin and Fox (1985) provide examples of these vulnera-ble and frequent victims of the serial murderer, such as prostitutes, hitchhik-ers, children, derelicts, and elderly women (pp. 75–78).

Karmen (1983) in discussing susceptibility and vulnerability of victims states: "The vulnerability of an individual or group to criminal depredations depends upon an opportunity factor as well as an attractiveness factor. Extreme risks are run by people who appear at the 'right time' and the 'right place,' from the offender's point of view. Hence certain lifestyles expose individuals and their possessions to greater threat and dangers than others" (p. 241). Karmen (1983) provides examples of these high-risk lifestyles: homosexuals cruising downtown areas and bathrooms, cult members soliciting funds on sidewalks and in bus stations, and released mental patients and skid-row alcoholics wandering the streets at odd hours (pp. 241–242). The same could possibly be said for hitchhikers, lost or run-away children, migrant workers, and single and often elderly women, col-lege students, or hospital patients (refer to the author's definition in Chapter 1).

In discussing homosexuals as victimizers and victims, Maghan and Sagarin (1983) note that "the offender's rage against society is deflected and targeted on those who are victimized as the offender is. Victimization appears to produce a rage that feeds an offender mentality, and offenders then choose victims who are the most vulnerable, closest (spatially and socially), and offer the greatest opportunities" (p. 160).

If Karmen's (1983) discussion of vulnerability and Maghan and Sagarin's (1983) discussion of victim–victimizer are combined, an extrapolation is possible in examining the victims of the serial murderer. If a number of serial murderers were victimized in childhood, as case studies and research suggests, and vulnerable due to their childhood situation, they may in fact have chosen victims like their earlier selves or from the same general lifestyle from which to victimize. Karmen (1983) states: "One common thread that emerges from most victim/offender studies is that both parties are usually drawn from the same group or background" (p. 242). However, it must be noted that there were no serial murder, victim–offender empirical studies found in the literature other than anecdotal material or conclusions based on very few serial murder cases. Therefore, no valid conclusions can be drawn from the literature regarding victim–offender relationships in this context. The literature does suggest, however, that many of these killers have been abused, neglected, and victimized in their childhood and appears to indicate the possibility that a number of serial killers do victimize earlier versions of their youth.

Some blame the mobility of U.S. society for making victims more available to serial murderers. "It's not unusual for people, especially if they're drug users, to just up and leave home," says Commander Alfred Calhoun of the Ouachita Parish Sheriff's Office in Monroe, Louisiana. "Many become victims because they're hitchhiking or wandering in deserted places" (Gest, 1984). Robert Keppel contends that since many serial murderers are charismatic, they can convince their victims to go with them for some reason. "They pick people they can have power and control over, small framed women, children and old people" (Lindsey, 1984, p. 7).

Psychiatrist Helen Morrison contends that the "look" of the victims is significant. She states, "If you take photos, or physical descriptions of the victims, what will strike you is the similarity in look." Morrison also theorizes that some nonverbal communication exists between victim and killer: "There's something unique in that interaction" (McCarthy, 1984, p. 10). Morrison believes that the victims of serial murderers were symbolic of something or someone deeply significant in the murderers' lives. Some psychologists have specifically said that the victims represent cruel parents on whom some murderers feel they cannot take revenge directly (Berger, 1984).

Morrison says that the serial murderer does not distinguish between human beings and inanimate objects (Berger, 1984). This characteristic may be similar to that of contract killers, whom Dietz (1983) describes as depersonalizing their victims (p. 115). Lunde (1976) found dehumanization of the victims, or perception of them as objects, by sexual sadist murderers. He argues that this "prevents the killer from identifying with the victims as mothers, fathers, children, people who love and are loved, people whose lives have meaning" (p. 61).

Society's Throwaways: A Low Priority for Law Enforcement

Unfortunately, there is a great deal less pressure on the police when the victims of a serial murder come from the marginal elements of a society or a community. The public becomes much less incensed over a serial murderer operating in their area when they have little or no identification with the victims. In this case, the victims seem far from real and little attention is paid to their demise.

As can readily be seen from press accounts in newspapers and television news reports, victims and survivors receive little attention in mass media accounts of crime. Unless victims are well-known celebrities or people of power and wealth, the central focus of the media is on the crime and the offender. Victims are of little interest, and survivors are, for the most part, ignored or quickly forgotten.

It would appear from the data available on serial murder investigations that the most frequent victim of a serial killer is the female prostitute. From the killer's view these women are simply available in an area that provides anonymity, comfort from easy detection, and adequate time in which to make a viable selection. It is highly probable that the serial killer selects prostitutes most frequently because they are easy to lure and control during the initial stages of what becomes an abduction. Potential witnesses of this abduction see only a pickup and transaction prior to paying for sex. They are programmed to see what they expect to see when a woman gets into a car with a "John." And who will miss one less prostitute plying her trade on the streets?

A search was made by the author of major newspaper reports of prostitutes as victims of serial murders either unsolved or under active investigation occurring between October 5, 1991, and October 5, 1993. During this two-year period a total of 198 prostitutes were identified as victims of serial killers involving 21 different and distinct serial murder patterns, an average of more than nine prostitute victims per serial murder. No other group of victims was found that frequently among identified serial murder victims during that period. For the female prostitute, lifestyle certainly plays a part in her being at-risk prey for a serial killer.

Most victims of serial killers are vulnerable, being perceived as powerless or prestigeless by most of society. A lack of power or prestige readily defines them as easy prey for the serial killer. A careful selection of vulnerable victims does not mean that the serial killer is a coward, only that the killer has the "street smarts" to select victims who will not resist, will be relatively easy to control, and will not be missed. For the killer, such a selection protects him from identification and apprehension. In many cases, selection of a prostitute assures him that the killings may never be revealed. Or if such a victim's remains are found, she will be difficult for the police to identify, given her lifestyle and lack of close ties to her family, relatives, or the community.

THE KILLING FIELDS: WHERE DO THEY HUNT?

Hunting grounds of the serial killer will vary a great deal among killers; however, many serial killers tend to select their victims from the same general areas, where they feel comfortable, have control over those frequenting the area, or are assured that the area is patrolled infrequently by local police. They hunt in areas where they will not be noticed or appear different from others. They seek anonymity.

There would appear to be a number of favored hunting grounds for the serial killer. Each different area that serial killers search for their prey reflects different types of victims sought out by the killer. The red light areas of the larger urban areas are probably the most favored hunting grounds for the serial killer, given the large number of prostitutes who fall victim to the serial killer. Here the killer can blend in with all the other "Johns" and have relatively little fear of drawing attention from witnesses taking special notice of him. Many serial killers have lured and abducted their victims from business establishments that provide short-term services to people in transit, such as convenience stores or service stations near interstate highways. These locations would appear to provide very attractive hunting grounds to the serial killer given the almost guaranteed anonymity where stranger-to-stranger interaction is commonplace and witnesses remember little of their brief time spent there. One unique and attractive characteristic of these points of prey, from the killer's perspective, is that stranger-to-stranger interaction is the norm and to be expected. No one takes any notice.

INVESTIGATIVE VALUE OF VICTIM INFORMATION QUICKLY DISMISSED

Our criminal law in this country defines a criminal offense as an offense against the state, and it is the state rather than the victim, who prosecutes the charged offender. The criminal justice system focuses on the crime and the criminal offender. Little formal attention of recognition is paid to the victim other than providing evidence to strengthen the state's efforts in prosecuting the offender. The needs, comfort, and convenience of victims (in the case of serial murder, the surviving relatives and loved ones of the victims) very rapidly lose importance or priority. Attention is drawn to the crime and offender, and crime victims or survivors become insignificant in a system emphasizing crime control and prosecution.

Criminologists have turned their attention to crime victims only recently. Much of this research has focused on lifestyle and victimization, victim characteristics, and victim precipitation (the ways that victims contribute to their own victimization). Seldom have criminologists studied victims' or survivors' responses or ways to provide assistance to them.

Ironically, the criminal investigation literature depicts a similar disinterest in the victims or survivors. Once physical evidence or information gathered begin to point toward a suspect or a type of suspect, the victims or survivors quickly become only names on a police report for entry into a master name index file to be retrieved later only if they are considered valuable in the prosecution of a defendant.

In the investigation of a number of homicides believed to have been committed by the same person, victim information may be the most important information collected by criminal investigators. For in many serial murder investigations, physical evidence from the crime scene is usually scarce or practically nonexistent. In most of these homicides (as noted earlier), the victims and killer had not been acquainted prior to the victim's fatal encounter with the killer. In other words, the victims may be the only major source of information upon which the investigation can proceed and be further developed.

As Ford (Egger, 1990a) has indicated, in the investigation of gay murders committed in the Indianapolis, Indiana, area in the early 1980s, the Central Indiana Multiagency Investigative Team initially discounted the value of a victimological approach to the investigation. Ford argues that this early exclusion of a valuable investigative strategy was a major problem for the team's effectiveness.

Early attention by investigators to the targeted victims are essential in a serial murder investigation, which typically reveals a very elusive killer. Sufficient analysis of targeted victims and their networks will inevitably yield greater insight into the victim's role in the crime setting and permit inferences regarding the decision-making process in the selection of intended victims.

Ford argues that an applied victimological approach requires five general tasks to be accomplished to assemble social characteristics of victims and circumstances of the crimes (adapted from Egger, 1990a, p. 116):

1. Identify category or type of victim.
2. Delineate victim social networks.
3. Determine personal factor determining risk.
4. Describe situational factors affecting risk.
5. Identify routine victim activities and expected behaviors related to contact with predator.

Ford, a sociologist and the only nonsworn member of this Indiana investigative team, argues for the importance of analyzing the ecology of possible contact settings (between killer and potential victims), to help narrow the focus of the investigation to promising areas for locating witnesses, including surviving victims.

Much of the research on serial murder has concentrated on finding similarities among these murders. With few exceptions, the victims of serial killers have been all but ignored. However, one of the greatest similarities among serial killers is their consistent choice of victims. As indicated in the serial murder definition offered earlier, many of the victims of serial murderers are vagrants, the homeless, prostitutes, migrant workers, homosexuals, missing children, single women out by themselves, elderly women, college students, or hospital patients. In other words, the serial killer preys on people who tend to be vulnerable or those who are easy to lure and dominate. Part of these victims' vulnerabilities may be the locations that they frequent, or the fact that they are powerless, or that they are considered the throw-aways of our society. Many are frequently not missed or reported missing by others. A good example of this would be the recent arrest of Joel Rifkin in New York on June 28, 1993. Police chased and stopped him for not displaying a license plate. They found a decaying female corpse in the back of his pickup truck. After a lengthy interrogation, Rifkin confessed to killing 17 prostitutes during the past three years. Based on this confession, the police investigation then concentrated upon finding and identifying Rifkin's victims. This was indeed difficult since there were few records of these victims being reported missing. In instances where these victims had been found, they were yet to be identified when Rifkin was arrested. No one had missed these victims until Rifkin stumbled into the hands of a New York state trooper.

Little else is known regarding the victims of serial murderers other than they are almost always a stranger to the murderer. In a preponderance of known cases, the victims seem to be young females presumably chosen to satisfy the dominance craving of the mostly male serial murderers. The victims are sometimes young males, as in the cases of John Wayne Gacy, Elmer Wayne Hanley, and Jeffrey Dahmer. It has been estimated that 50% of unidentified bodies in county morgues or medical examiner's offices across the country are young children or adolescents (C. Wingo, personal communication, July 1983). Unfortunately, we don't know how many of these bodies represent victims of serial murder.

In a number of cases it would appear that the victims were selected solely because they crossed the path of the serial murderer and became a vehicle for his hypo-arousal and pleasure (Egger, 1984a). Victims may be self-selecting only from their existence at a place and point in time. This and possibly the physical appearance of the victim, which may hold some symbolic significance for the killer, are apparently the only known precipitating factors for their selection. The definition used by the author identifies prestigelessness, powerlessness, or membership in a lower socioeconomic group as common characteristics of serial murder victims. Levin and Fox (1985) seem to agree that "serial killers almost without exception choose vulnerable victims—those who are easy to dominate" (p. 75). "The serial killer typically picks on innocent strangers who may possess a certain physical feature or may just be accessible" (p. 231).

Predatory stranger offenses may be particularly dependent on the avail ability of vulnerable victims at a particular geographic location. Also, victim precipitation, the extent to which the victim's actions contribute to his or her demise, is considered a major cause or, certainly, a contributing factor of homicide by many criminologists. However, the extent to which victim precipitation occurs in serial murder can only be speculated on, since very little information is usually available regarding the interaction between the killer and the victim prior to the point of fatal encounter.

There are a number of high-risk lifestyles that place one in a victim-prone status: homosexuals cruising downtown areas and bathrooms, cult members soliciting funds on sidewalks and in bus stations, and released mental patients and skid-row alcoholics wandering the streets at odd hours (Karmen, 1983). In some instances it may simply be that a person is out by himself or herself. Females out by themselves are particularly vulnerable, given the high proportion of female serial murder victims. Prostitutes are almost certainly at risk. For women there appears to be strength in numbers in reducing the risk of a serial murderer attack.

In many cases, serial murderers may be attacking mirror images of themselves. If the correlation of sexual child abuse and neglect are contributing factors in the production of a serial killer, the killer may be choosing victims who resemble his earlier self or from the same general lifestyle. Many victim–offender studies indicate that both parties are usually drawn from the same group or background (Sagarin and Maghan, 1983).

Some blame the mobility of American society for making victims more available to serial murderers. We are indeed a very transient culture. Robert Keppel, chief investigator of the Attorney General's Office in Washington, contends that since many serial murderers are charismatic, they can convince their victims to go with them for some reason: "They pick people they can have power over and control over, small-framed women, children and old people" (Lindsey, 1984, p. 7). Many psychiatrists believe that the victims of serial murderers were symbolic of something or someone deeply significant in the murderers' lives. Some psychologists have said that the victims specifically represent cruel parents against whom some murderers feel they cannot take revenge directly. The alternative for the serial murderer is to take revenge against a cruel parent indirectly by killing others who resemble or represent this parent.

Typically, the serial killer doesn't think much about his victims, have any empathy for loved ones of the victims, or reflect any feelings of remorse. When asked about his victims, Ted Bundy responded, "What's one less person on the face of the earth anyway?" When Australian serial killer James Miller, charged with the murder of seven young girls and women, was asked during his trial he stated, "They weren't worth much. One of them even enjoyed it" (Wilson and Searman 1983, p. 81).

A number of researchers have found that children and young women are the prime targets for serial killers. These groups are certainly considered to be victim prone, primarily due to their vulnerability. Children are frequently the victims of serial killers. Hickey (1991) found 62 serial killers, 31% of those he studied, who had killed at least one child. As indicated earlier, young females comprise a majority of the serial murderer's victims. It is still a man's world, at least for the serial killer.

CHAPTER 5

⟨=◆=⟩

SERIAL MURDER: A GROWTH INDUSTRY

> *It's something you can't get anywhere else. I mean if you like the truth, if you like something a little different, a little bit more fresh, a little bit more bloody, well we got the meat.*
>
> —Hart Fisher, author and artist of the comic book, *Jeffrey Dahmer: An Unauthorized Biography of a Serial Killer,* discussing the popularity of his comic book (Griffiths, 1993)

INTRODUCTION

Serial murder is important to the press, the electronic media, screen writers, and movie producers as well as comic book artists. It sells newspapers and draws viewers to TV screens and movie theaters. It sells books and fills movie theaters. The true-crime section of most large bookstore chains are always kept well stocked by the publishers of this genre.

In media reporting of a possible serial murder, one of the first things that journalists ask about is whether a profile has been done on the killer. In most fictional accounts, there is either an FBI agent or a local psychiatrist who has developed a profile of the serial killer. Serial killers in police procedurals and the more elaborate mystery genre are now being written with a required formula format requiring that when a serial murder is suspected, the author better have a profiler somewhere in the first 70 pages of the novel. Unfortunately, these fictional accounts are far from the reality of a serial homicide. In the first place, a series of murders may run to double digits before someone begins to suspect that all these murders were committed by the same killer. Second, when multiple agencies are involved, it normally takes time for these agencies to agree to work together on the homicides. A novel closer to reality would develop a character who profiles the killer late into the story, and the resulting profile may or may not assist the detectives in identifying the serial killer.

The myth and infallibility of the psychological profile has been further promoted by adaptation of the book *Silence of the Lambs* (Harris, 1988) into a very successful film starring Anthony Hopkins and Jodie Foster. David Canter, pioneer profiler in England, has noted the generation of this myth by stating: "The character of Hannibal Lecter, the gruesome and brilliant multiple murderer created by the novelist Thomas Harris and interviewed by a novice FBI agent, draws on the interviews that were conducted by real FBI agents with murderers and rapists, but the fictional creation has as much to do with reality as the fictional Dr. Jekyll and Mr. Hyde of a previous century" (Canter, 1994, p. 65).

Many theorists of serial murder believe that the killer's reason for killing is to achieve a sense of power over his or her victims. In effect, the serial killer's search for power receives an intensified and additional fulfillment through the mass media's celebration of his horrific acts. This fulfillment in the form of a celebration continues through a sensationalized criminal trial in which the killer's attorney invariably attempts to show that the killer was insane at the time of his killings. Subsequent fame, or more correctly, notoriety, continues through TV movies of his life and crimes. Much earlier in this transformation process from an evil and deranged killer to a celebrated antihero, the "instant" true-crime paperback providing the reader with graphic description of the serial killer's crimes can be found on the "just published" shelves of major bookstore chains across the country. In effect, serial killers achieve renown by being celebrated by the media and true-crime writers. It would appear that more and more men and women are becoming students of the darker side of the soul and that the exploits of the serial killer exert a singular power and fascination that attracts us like an addiction, never to be satisfied. Unfortunately, fodder for such fascination continues to be forthcoming in our society.

We no longer have public executions or flaying, but macabre films such as *The Texas Chain Saw Massacre* or *Natural Born Killers* (the author walked out after the first 4 minutes of this film, which depicted six or seven horrible slayings in the same amount of time). For those who would pay to view a public execution or a private showing of a "snuff flick," it may be that viewing of fictional accounts of serial killers on the big screen or from our TV sets showing news pictures of their crime scenes while news readers recite the police accounts of these horrific acts, satisfy our thirst for suspense, entertainment, or thrills that for many is lacking in the single-murder who-done-it or a drive-by shooting in our urban slums. After the credits roll across the screen or the crime scene fades to a commercial, viewers are left with the warm feelings of being a "survivor."

For some, violence and the mass media feed off one another. Park Dietz, a criminal psychiatrist, stated: "The psycho killer public relations industry depends on real offenders for its fodder, and the real offenders draw ideas, inspiration and hope of historical importance from their public relations industry" (Griffiths, 1993).

In his content analysis of newspaper crime coverage in the United States from 1893 to 1988, Marsh (1989) provides a number of findings relevant to journalist coverage of serial killers. The result of his findings were, in part (p. 511):

- The vast majority of newspaper crime coverage pertains to violent and sensational crimes.
- The overemphasis of violent crimes, and failure to adequately address personal risk and prevention techniques, often result in exaggerated fears of victimization in certain segments of society.

In other words, reporting of crime—in particular, serial murder—does not generally reflect an accurate picture of this phenomenon in society. Serial murder headlines or serial murder lead-ins to TV news programs attract readers and audiences. They don't inform.

"MUTANTS FROM HELL"

It is very self-serving and comforting to think of serial killers as different from us. We seem to think, "They are different and that must be why they do what they do. Certainly not something we could do!" Our thoughts are fallacious, however. These "monsters" or "mutants from hell" may in fact actually reveal the very human forces of life rather than the diabolical and mysterious riddles of these "unique," atavistic creatures. They terrify us not because they are from hell but, rather, because they are extreme examples of the potential of humanity. This is seen in the popularity of the serial killer phenomenon in the 1980s and 1990s in the United States and elsewhere. Serial killers long for recognition and an end to their tormenting nightmares of childhood. Society counters with a hunger for the sight of their handiwork and the splatter of blood.

THE PROFILE THAT ISN'T

Like any news medium, TV news reporting provides its viewers with summaries of facts, theories, concepts, and situations. Reporters are constantly striving to simplify and provide brief explanations to complex problems, whether in the reporting of the war in Bosnia or of a serial murderer. Reporters have a limited amount of air time to make their point before the next story or commercial.

Television reporters and, to a somewhat lesser extent, newspaper jour-nalists are infatuated with the term *profile*. To them, this term belongs in any report of crime where the criminal is yet to be arrested. A profile is a summa-ry of the offender for the public. It is the culmination of criminological research on why these people commit crime. It is shorthand for the criminal's background, his motivation, the type of victims he selects, and how the police will eventually catch him. Experts who shy away from use of this term receive little attention. They take too long in answering reporters' questions and generally don't have all the answers—and reporters want answers.

The problem with this simplistic approach by the mass media is that there are no simple answers and that even complicated answers frequently provide only half-answers. Also, many of the answers are simply someone's theory of why someone did something or why something happened. Although reporters may treat these opinions as fact, it must be remembered that they are only someone's opinion, and opinions are frequently wrong.

SOUND-BITE ANSWERS

Not only do reporters and journalists want profiles that are easily understood by their readers or audience, but they want them to sound nice. They want comments that are slick and polished, that provide wide appeal. The 30-sec-ond sound-bite is what the mass media are seeking constantly. If it is good enough, it can be used to advertise the upcoming story and give the reporter more air time and exposure. For the TV reporter or journalist, a good sound-bite means that his career is on an upward spiral.

THE FBI AND SERIAL MURDER MYTHOLOGY

The FBI, a large bureaucratic mechanism, tends to function as a monopolist organization when it comes to serial murder. Notwithstanding the fact that only a small number of FBI agents have ever conducted a homicide investi-gation, the FBI is portrayed by much of the press and electronic media as experts on the phenomenon of serial murder and the central police force that is tracking and arresting these killers all over the United States. Many of the true-crime books published have FBI agents in them hunting down the serial killer or providing uncanny and accurate psychological profiles of the killer for the local police. The perpetuation of this myth is carefully manipulated through the media promotion of individual technocrats skilled in psychologi-cal profiling or the crime analyst experts pouring over VICAP forms at the Behavioral Science Unit of the bureau in Quantico, Virginia.

Crime journalists have become so expertly "trained" in FBI mythology that their questions revolve around the point in time that the experts from the FBI are called into the case. Terms such as *organized nonsocial, unorganized asocial, lust murderers, sexual homicide,* and *psych profile* become part of their argot without these reporters realizing such terms originated from the bureau itself and have little empirical basis.

As implied earlier, media manipulation and the resulting media perception that the FBI are experts in homicide investigation, and more specifically serial murder investigation, builds a large basis of power for the bureau. Such a power base forces the media focus of any major homicide investigation away from local law enforcement agencies investigating the homicides to the agents assisting those who conduct the actual day-to-day and hour-to-hour investigation.

This power base also means for any writer interested in developing a crime novel or true-crime story of a serial killer to seek assistance from the experts at the FBI. This can be seen in the recent work of David Lindsey in *Mercy,* Thomas Harris in *Silence of the Lambs,* and Patricia Cornwall in *Body Farm.* These works, all best-sellers, provide advocacy for the false notion that FBI agents investigate homicides. For someone to question this fallacious assertion is to bring the equally fallacious retort from any layman that if the victims are killed in different states, the FBI takes over jurisdictional authority.

Far be it for the FBI to disabuse the public of this mythology. To do so would call the cost-effectiveness of VICAP into question and refocus media attention to the more accurate target of local law enforcement's effectiveness or ineffectiveness in identifying and apprehending the serial murderer. Thus FBI agents continue to ride the wave of publicity that surrounds a serial murder investigation. These agents speak as experts to the media, even though their knowledge may be based solely on a training bulletin from the FBI Academy. Some of these agents even have the audacity to characterize the movie *Silence of the Lambs* as an accurate portrayal of a typical FBI investigation into a serial murder.

A VIOLENT CULTURE

American culture as a whole has cultivated a taste for violence that seems to be insatiable. We are a people obsessed with violence, and consequently, our entertainment industry is driven by such violence. The violence of our popular culture reflected in movies, TV programs, magazines, and fact or fiction books in the latter part of the twentieth century has made the shocking realism of this violence a routine risk that we all face. Our own sense of humanity is anesthetized almost to the point of losing consciousness. We sit in front of television and "obliterate" our sensitivity for the victims of the serial killer. We desire to learn more about the killer. The killer becomes our total focus. We want to hear or read about the torture and mutilation deaths of female victims almost as if such acts were an art form. The serial killer becomes an artist, in some cases performing a reverse type of sculpturing by taking the lives of his victims with a sharp knife.

Pick up a paperback mystery or a police procedural. Or choose a mystery. Almost all that sell are about the hunt for a serial killer. We as a society enjoy serial killing, albeit vicariously. Elliott Leyton, a very wise observer of cultures, stated: "If we were charged with the responsibility for designing a society in which all structural and cultural mechanisms leaned toward the creation of the killers of strangers, we could do no better that to present the purchaser with the shape of modern America" (Leyton, 1986, p. 295).

PART II

———⪥◆⪤———

CASE STUDIES OF SERIAL KILLERS

To acquire information on serial murderers, a case study approach was utilized. Case studies are generally the preferred strategy when "how" or "why" questions are being posed, when relevant behaviors cannot be manipulated, and when there is a need to understand a complex social phenomena (Yin, 1984).

Case studies of criminals are common in the psychological literature and have a long-standing tradition (see Abrahamsen, 1973; Bjerre, 1981; Wertham, 1966; Lunde, 1976). Although less well known and with a briefer tradition, past criminological–criminal justice literature does provide a precedent for the case study approach (see Cressey, 1932; Chambliss, 1972; Klockars, 1974; Shaw, 1930; Sutherland, 1937). The research conducted for these case studies differs from earlier criminological/criminal justice research in two respects. First, that research dealt with what could be considered quasi-natural behavior, where serial murder is psychopathological and thought to be idiopathic. In other words, the origin or cause of this behavior is unknown. Second, and more important, the former research focused primarily on etiological concerns, not on questions of crime control or the administration and operation of such control. Nevertheless, case study methodology for which there is ample tradition and precedent is justified and has been utilized here in a modified context and for an applied purpose.

Seeking knowledge of serial murder through this case study approach required an exploratory effort concerned primarily with descriptions verified through a variety of data sources to the extent possible within available resources. Selected case studies of serial murderers were documented as examples for the reader.

A multiple-case (embedded) research design was used. Four cases were selected for documentation and analysis. External validity is frequently cited by critics as a major problem for case studies since they offer a poor basis for generalization. However, case study research does not rely on statistical gener-alization of samples to the universe (as in survey research), but rather, upon analytical generalization of a set of results to some broader theory. Further, Katz (1982) argues that "statistical evidence of representativeness depends on restricting a depiction of qualitative richness in the experience of the people studied" (p. 139).

This multiple-case design utilized a replication logic as opposed to a sam-pling logic. Each case selected was not a "sample" of the total phenomenon. Such a universe has yet to be defined and it is not the objective of a case study to assess the incidence or prevalence of a phenomenon. Each case documented and analyzed served as a separate exploration into the phenomenon of serial murder. In discussing multiple-case studies, Yin (1984) suggests that in following a replication logic, "a major insight is to consider multiple cases as one would consider multiple experiments" (p. 48). However, it must be remembered that this research design is not causal or predictive as is the case with classic experimen-tal studies, but rather, exploratory and developmental in nature.

The selection of four serial murderers for documentation and analysis was based on four major criteria: ease of access to information, currentness of murder-er's arrest or conviction, geographical representativeness, and murderer mobility. The fact that a great deal had been written on a murderer or case was also a significant factor in data collection. Secondly, the fact that the arrest and/or con-viction of the murderer had occurred within recent history was considered impor-tant to the relevance of subsequent conclusions and recommendations of the study. A third selection consideration was the differences in geographical areas of the country in which the murderer operated in order to determine if differences in "linkage blindness" varied by region. The inclusion of both megastat (killing over time in a single area) and megamobile (killing in different geographic areas) serial murderers within the sample was a final consideration since they appear to be two different types of serial murderers.

Serial murderers selected for case study were John Wayne Gacy; Henry Lee Lucas; Kenneth Bianchi and Angelo Buono, Jr.; and Theodore Robert Bundy. A protocol or guide for conducting each case study was utilized to facilitate between-case comparisons. This guide was organized according to Gibbons' (1965) dimensional categories developed for role–career typological research. Modifications were made to these categories to better fit serial murder case study research. The dimension of role–career was eliminated. Recall of events by the murderer was added to the dimensions because a preliminary review of cases revealed that serial murderers appear to have an unusually acute memory. Each dimensional category was considered to be self-defining by its category label or in traditional social science terminology. (The reader should note that an additional case study is provided on Jeffrey Dahmer in Chapter 15. The Dahmer case study is not included here since a great deal of information will probably never be known about this serial killer, and to include the case study here would take away from the comparison made at the conclusion of these four case studies. The Dahmer case study is presented in Chapter 15 in a very different format from the organization utilized here.) This dimensional category schematic was used as a guide in collecting data on each case study:

1. Social environment
2. Family background
3. Peer-group associations and personal relationships
4. Contact with defining agencies
5. Offense behavior
6. Self concept
7. Attitudes
8. Recall of events

Part II concludes with the results of a cross-case analysis of the four case studies in Chapter 10.

CHAPTER 6

——◆——

JOHN WAYNE GACY: CASE STUDY

As I walked into death row in Menard Penitentiary, John Wayne Gacy began spitting out a long stream of profanity at me between the bars. His utterance became almost a scream as it ended with "expert!" I turned to face the man I had read about and written about but never met. My answer to him was straightforward, "No, John, I'm not the expert. You are the expert. An expert serial killer." From the other cells came laughter and catcalls. It seemed not even the condemned liked a serial killer.

—Author's notes, Menard Penitentiary, Illinois,
April 14, 1993

SOCIAL ENVIRONMENT

John Gacy grew up in a working-class neighborhood on the northwest side of Chicago, Illinois. Little is known about his childhood. By the end of grade school he reportedly daydreamed a lot and had become resistant to his teachers. His sister described him as a normal person like everyone else. The only unusual thing that she could recall about her brother's younger years was that he occasionally had blackouts. The problem, she said, was diagnosed when he was 16 as a blood clot on the brain that was thought to have resulted from a playground accident five years earlier. He was treated and apparently cured (*New York Times*, January 10, 1979, p. 14).

The episodes of blackouts, however, continued into his adult life. He sometimes complained of shortness of breath and pains in his chest. His problem in childhood had been diagnosed as syncope, a brief loss of consciousness caused by transient anemia, leading to probable psychomotor epilepsy later. He was once given the last rites hurriedly by a priest after a seizure. The cause of his malady was never determined with certainty and his friends tended to regard it as heart trouble.

He was always interested in being a police officer. He was always playing policeman as a boy. Gacy went to a vocational high school, where he
took business courses. His grades ranged from good to excellent. He was
enamored with uniforms, according to his brother-in-law. Both his sisters
stated that he was active in a civil defense organization that allowed him to
go to accidents and fires with a flashing blue light on his car. The following
year he transferred to another vocational high school and after two months
dropped out of school and moved to Las Vegas, Nevada, where he worked a
brief time for a mortuary before returning to Chicago.

He worked for a shoe company in Chicago and in 1964 was transferred
to Springfield, Illinois, to manage the company's retail clothing store. He
moved to Waterloo, Iowa, in 1966 to manage three fried chicken restaurant
franchises, owned by his father-in-law. His father-in-law reportedly considered him a "braggart and a liar" but had encouraged the move so as to be
near his daughter and grandson (Sullivan and Maiken, 1983, p. 261). His fal-
sified résumé at that time indicated that he had managed several stores in
Springfield, Illinois, and held a college degree in accounting and business.

Gacy was very active in the Junior Chamber of Commerce in Waterloo.
He recruited many new members and was the chaplain for the organization.
He was referred to as "Colonel" by the local paper, which published a picture
of him describing his organizational activities. From then on he liked to be
referred to as "Colonel."

Gacy frequented the bar at a local motel and a night spot that featured
strippers in Waterloo. According to his friends, he was constantly bragging
about his sexual prowess with women. Gacy never showed any affection
toward his wife in public and on several occasions reportedly offered her as a
sexual favor to other men in return for fellatio on himself.

Gacy's wife stated that he was a "police freak" (Sullivan and Maiken,
1983, p. 263). He had an intense curiosity about emergency vehicles, which
he would sometimes follow at high speeds with his portable red light flashing. Gacy liked to be known as having influence with the police, and several
times a month he would take free fried chicken to police and firefighters.

Upon his release from prison in Iowa in 1970, Gacy returned to
Chicago to live with his mother in an apartment on the northwest side of
the city. He got a job through a family friend in a downtown Chicago
restaurant and worked as a cook. The restaurant was a gathering spot for
city police and politicians. It was here that he met Chicago policeman James
Hanley, whose name Gacy later modified as his street alias. Gacy briefly
dated a waitress from the restaurant, but was soon seen associating with
homosexuals.

Four months after he had returned to Chicago, Gacy reportedly bor-
rowed money from his mother and bought a house in Norwood Park

Township, an unincorporated area northwest of Chicago. Shortly thereafter he formed his own construction company, operated out of his home, specializing in remodeling work at retail stores and subcontracting work on larger construction projects.

Gacy was active in politics in the Chicago area. He was precinct captain in the township. In 1976 he organized a fund raiser attended by over 500 people for then President Carter's reelection campaign. He was also involved in organizing the annual Polish Constitution Day Parade in Chicago. His second wife stated that she felt that Gacy had often used his local political involvement to buy his way out of trouble.

Gacy's neighbors described him as a likable man who frequently volunteered to perform as a clown for children at charitable events. One neighbor stated that he seemed short-tempered at times and that he often threw large parties. His former babysitter said that many people, mostly teenagers who worked with him, were "always going in and out of the house" (*New York Times*, December 3, 1978, p. 11). The head of Norwood Park's Democratic organization stated: "The John Gacy I'm reading about in the newspapers is not the same John Gacy I knew. He was always available for any job: washing windows, setting up chairs for meetings, playing clown for the kids at picnics and Christmas parties, even fixing somebody's leaky faucet or rehanging a crooked door. I don't know anyone who didn't like him" (*Newsweek*, January 8, 1979, p. 24). He was characterized by many as a civic-minded building contractor. He claimed that he made $200,000 a year prior to his arrest. He was known to be an excellent cook but an untalented construction worker.

Gacy was described by those who employed him as a very gregarious man who had a lot of energy in getting the job done. He was obsessed about keeping track of his time and kept notebooks that recorded what he did minute by minute, even logging such trivia as the precise moment he mailed a letter (Berger, 1984). He kept an extremely neat and clean house, doing his own housekeeping.

He stated that he began dating at 16 and had his first sexual intercourse at age 18. He claims that his first homosexual experience was after his first wife's pregnancy. He said that he got drunk with a friend who performed fellatio on him. Gacy told his second wife in 1972 that he was bisexual. She was convinced that he was rapidly becoming homosexual. Less than two years after they were married, Gacy announced to her on Mother's day that this occasion would be their last sex together. It was. His wife stated later that she frequently found her bikini underpants in the garage. Gacy had been bringing young men to the garage late at night, sometimes spending hours with them (Sullivan and Maiken, 1983, p. 73).

FAMILY BACKGROUND

John Wayne Gacy was born on March 17, 1942, at Edgewater Hospital in Chicago, Illinois. His parents were John and Marian Gacy, who were both factory workers. He grew up in a working-class neighborhood in northwest Chicago. He had two sisters, one two years older and one two years younger.

He was reportedly heavily influenced by his mother. As a newborn, Gacy was given daily enemas by his mother for no apparent reason (Berger, 1984). When his mother found a bag full of her underpants under the porch of their house where John played, she made him wear a pair of her underpants to embarrass him. When his father learned of this, he whipped John with a leather strap.

Although Gacy was reportedly a hard worker, he rarely pleased his father. When he failed to meet his father's standards, his father called him stupid. His father was of Polish parents, a hard worker, a perfectionist, a stern parent, and a good provider, according to Gacy's younger sister. John's father was also a drunkard, who beat his wife and had a Jekyll and Hyde personality according to his children. Apparently, John's father got drunk almost every night. When Gacy tried to help his mother when she was being beaten by his father, his father called him a mama's boy or a sissy. His father reportedly never showed his own emotions, except once when Gacy was sentenced to prison in Iowa on a sodomy conviction. His father cried at that time.

Gacy left home during his second year of high school. His father, who had loaned him the money to buy his first car, had gotten tired of all his driving around and had removed the distributor cap on his car. Gacy became angry and moved to Las Vegas, Nevada.

After returning to Chicago in 1964 and being transferred to Springfield, Illinois, by the shoe company he worked for, he met a woman whom he dated for nine months and then married in 1965. His wife gave birth to a boy and then a girl. According to neighbors, Gacy was a loving and attentive father to his children. While in Springfield he was viewed as a hard worker who was heavily involved in the Junior Chamber of Commerce.

Following Gacy's move with his family to Waterloo, Iowa, and his subsequent conviction for sodomy, his wife divorced him. After a divorce hearing in Waterloo in September 1969, he told friends in prison that as far as he was concerned his children were dead. After returning to Chicago, Gacy tried to arrange visitation rights to his children by writing his former wife. She never answered his letters, and he told his mother to get rid of the pictures of his former wife and children and just to consider them dead. Gacy's father died while he was in prison on December 25. He would sometimes cry later on Christmas day remembering his father. Gacy told a friend that the prison officials had not told him about his father's death until a month later. He stated he was still very angry about that.

Gacy's sister stated that John had always been the sort of brother and son who could not do enough for his family, who stayed in close touch by telephone, and who visited once or twice a year. The family knew of his sodomy conviction in Iowa, she said, but considered it an incident in his life that he paid for (*New York Times*, January 10, 1979, p. 14).

After purchasing a house in Norwood Park, he moved there with his mother in 1971. According to a former employee of Gacy's, he, as well as several other males, lived with the Gacys in 1970 and 1971. The former employee admitted that he had slept in John Gacy's bedroom while living there.

In May 1971, Gacy became reacquainted with a high school girlfriend who had two children and was going through a divorce. They began dating and were married in July 1972 after Gacy's mother moved to an apartment. Gacy reportedly didn't like his mother answering the telephone and talking to his potential business clients as "John's mother" (Sullivan and Maiken, 1983, p. 278). After his mother left, Gacy invited his wife's mother to move in with them. After a year, Gacy later complained, he needed a court order to evict his mother-in-law. Gacy's relationship with his second wife deteriorated rapidly, when shortly after their marriage he began to associate more and more with young boys. After declaring his bisexuality less than two years after their marriage and stating that he would no longer have sex with her, Gacy and his wife lived separately in the same house. They were divorced on February 11, 1975. The next day one of Gacy's male employees moved into the house. In Gacy's second interview with police he said he had been divorced twice and was now enjoying single life.

PEER-GROUP ASSOCIATION AND PERSONAL RELATIONSHIPS

John Gacy was described as a good, friendly, and generous man by his neighbors in Norwood Park. At Christmas time Gacy gave his neighbors hams or baskets of fruit. He had shown genuine kindness toward their children. However, his boastful personality turned them away. They were invited to the huge parties he held, but many chose not to attend. To some, John Gacy was striving for a social status that he would never attain.

In Springfield, Illinois, he was nominated by the local Junior Chamber of Commerce as "Man of the Year." In Waterloo, Iowa, where he had been convicted of sodomy, there was disagreement over Gacy. His friends said he was a real go-getter, did a good job, and was an excellent Jaycee. Others stated he was a glad-hander type, who would shower you with affection as a way of getting more attention himself. A man who had run against Gacy for presidency of the local Junior Chamber of Commerce and won stated: "He was not a man tempered by truth. He seemed unaffected when caught in lies" (*New York Times*, January 10, 1976, p. 14).

An associate of Gacy's in the construction business characterized Gacy as a workaholic who talked a big line. One of his employees stated that a lot of Gacy's workers quit because "they don't like the aggravation. John is so much of a perfectionist, it gets to where he's nitpicking" (Sullivan and Maiken, 1983, p. 68). Gacy developed a reputation among some of his associates, friends, and employees as a man who didn't always tell the truth. An employee stated, "John is a funny person. He's a bit of a bragger, and he lives in a fantasy world. Now, how much is fact and how much is fiction is up to the individual to decide, but he claims that he does work for the syndicate. He's said he has set up people before" (Sullivan, 1983, p. 70).

Gacy told the police who had him under surveillance that he had attended bisexual parties and that he saw nothing wrong with what went on. He said that he thought people should do whatever they wanted, as long as it didn't infringe on the other person's rights and no force was used. However, he made it clear to the police on a number of occasions before and after his arrest that he was not a homosexual. After he was arrested, Gacy told police that he had his first sexual relationship with a male when he was 22 years old. Police would learn that to the homosexual community, Gacy was thought to be a policeman and was known as a "chicken-hawk," an older man who looks for young men and boys.

An employee who lived with Gacy for two months stated that he had to sleep with his pants on because Gacy was always coming into his bedroom in the middle of the night trying to have sex with him. The employee stated that on one occasion Gacy and he were celebrating Gacy's birthday and John had locked him in handcuffs to show him a trick. Gacy had then stated, "The trick is you gotta have the key" (Sullivan and Maiken, 1983, p. 142). Gacy then began to swing the man around the room on the handcuff chain. They fought and the man recovered the key and freed himself.

On the day Gacy was arrested he apparently knew he would soon be behind bars. He went around saying goodbye to people he considered his friends. To a young man he always bought gas from he stated, "We've been friends. You're like a brother—I can't take much more" (Sullivan and Maiken, 1983, p. 151). Gacy then slipped a bag of marijuana into the youth's pocket. To an employee, Gacy begged him to listen to him, stating, "This may be the last time you'll ever see me" (Sullivan and Maiken, 1983, p. 152). He said goodbye to another employee and his lawyer. He then stated that he wanted to go to the cemetery and say goodbye to his father's grave. Gacy was arrested before he reached his father's grave.

CONTACT WITH DEFINING AGENCIES

John Gacy's first known contact with the criminal justice system occurred on May 2, 1968, in Waterloo, Iowa, when he was given a polygraph examination by the police in response to accusations of two young boys, who stated that he had sexually assaulted them. The polygraph examiner found indications of deception in the tests, although Gacy continued to deny any guilt. He was indicted by a grand jury later that month. He took another polygraph examination in July of that year with the same results, after which he admitted having had homosexual relationships with one of the boys but that he had paid the boy.

In September 1968, Gacy was arrested for paying a boy to beat one of the boys who had accused him of sexual assault and for being implicated in a lumberyard break-in. On September 12 at his court appearance, he was ordered by the court to submit to a psychiatric evaluation at the psychiatric hospital of the State University of Iowa. During Gacy's 17 days at the hospital, he was observed by the staff, given psychiatric interviews, and tested physically and psychologically. In his report to the court, Eugene F. Gauron stated:

> Gacy would twist the truth in such a way that he would not be made to look bad and would admit to socially unacceptable actions only when directly confronted. He is a smooth talker and an obscurer who was trying to white-wash himself of any wrongdoing. He had a high degree of social intelligence or awareness of the proper way to behave in order to influence people.
>
> The most striking aspect of the test results is the patient's total denial of responsibility for anything that has happened to him. He can produce an "alibi" for everything. He alternately blames the environment, while presenting himself as the victim of circumstances and blames other people while presenting himself as a victim of others who are out to get him. Although this could be construed as paranoid, I do not regard it that way. Rather, the patient attempts to assure a sympathetic response by depicting himself as being at the mercy of a hostile environment. To his way of thinking, a major objective is to outwit the other fellow and take advantage of him before being taken advantage of himself. He does things without thinking through the consequences and exercises poor judgment. (Sullivan and Maiken, 1983, pp. 271–272)

Gacy's discharge summary noted that he did not seem to have remorse over his actions. He was evaluated as competent to stand trial. The diagnosis of the psychiatrists was that Gacy was an antisocial personality and unlikely to benefit from known medical treatment.

Gacy pled guilty to the charge. The probation officer recommended in his presentence investigative report that Gacy be placed on probation. The judge disagreed and sentenced Gacy on December 3, 1968, to 10 years' imprisonment.

In prison, Gacy told other inmates that he had been charged with showing pornographic films to teenagers. He was assigned to food service, and the prison food improved while the kitchen was kept spotless. He became involved in the Jaycees as director of the prison chapter, served as chaplain, and played Santa Claus at Christmas. He was awarded the "Sound Citizen Award" by the chapter and helped build a miniature golf course on prison grounds. Gacy applied for early release under supervision but was denied his request by the parole board.

Following his denial, Gacy completed his high school education and began taking college-level classes. He became more heavily involved in the Jaycees. In March 1970 a psychiatric evaluation of Gacy was ordered by the parole committee. The prison psychiatrist diagnosed Gacy as a "passive aggressive personality," recommending him for parole, stating, "The likelihood of his again being charged with and being convicted of antisocial conduct appears to be small" (Sullivan and Maiken, 1983, p. 276). After spending 21 months in prison, Gacy was paroled on June 18, 1970, to Chicago, Illinois.

Police records show that on two occasions before June 1971, he had engaged in homosexual activity, thus violating his parole (Sullivan and Maiken, 1983, p. 277). However, Gacy never received a formal parole violation. In August 1975 and December 1976, Chicago police questioned Gacy about the disappearance of two young men. Police officers placed Gacy's home under surveillance for two weeks in January 1976 during the investigation of the disappearance of a 9-year-old boy. There were also accusations of kidnap and rape placed against Gacy in December 1977 and March 1978 in Chicago (*New York Times*, January 8, 1979, p. 16).

On December 12, 1978, Gacy was contacted by telephone by the Des Plaines Police Department regarding the disappearance of a 15-year-old boy outside a pharmacy in that city the day before. Gacy had been to the pharmacy twice the previous evening, giving the owner advice on rearranging his display shelves. He had left his notebook at the pharmacy and returned a second time that evening to pick it up. The missing boy worked at the pharmacy and shortly after Gacy left the pharmacy, the boy told another employee he was going outside to talk to a contractor about a job. He never returned.

The Des Plaines police pursued the missing report on the boy in a nonroutine fashion after preliminary investigation showed that he was probably not a runaway. Gacy became a suspect in his disappearance after they examined his police record and learned of his sodomy conviction in Iowa, his charge of battery in Chicago in 1978, and his charge of aggravated battery and reckless conduct in a Chicago suburb in 1972. He was interviewed at his home on December 12 and asked to come to the police station to fill out a witness form, since he admitted seeing, but not talking to, the missing boy. Gacy stated that he would come to the station later that evening. He was put under surveillance and eluded the officers. He called the Des Plaines police at 11:00 P.M. that night, asking if they still wanted to see him. They indicated that they did wish to see him and he stated that he would be there in an hour. A vehicle registered to Gacy was reported by Illinois State Police to have been stuck in a ditch off the northbound lane of the Tri-State Tollway approximately 13 miles south of Des Plaines at 2:29 A.M. that morning. Gacy arrived at the police station that morning at 3:20 A.M., but the officer he was to have seen had left. He was told to come back in the morning.

The following morning Gacy came to the station and was interviewed. When asked to make a written statement regarding his activities at the pharmacy, he complied. He was then asked to wait for the police lieutenant's return. In the meantime the police and the Cook County State's Attorney's Office obtained a search warrant for his house based on probable cause of unlawful restraint. Gacy remained at the police station while the police searched his house looking for evidence of the missing boy.

The search of Gacy's house revealed a high school ring, a number of erotic films and pornographic books, a switch blade knife, a starter pistol, handcuffs, a wooden two-by-four 3 feet long with holes cut in either end, a hypodermic syringe, an empty small brown bottle believed to have contained chloroform, and a customer photo receipt from the pharmacy where the missing boy had disappeared. Two driver's licenses were also found. The police cut a section of carpeting believed to be stained with blood and they discovered a trap door in a closet which led to a crawl space beneath the house. The ground in the crawl space was covered with what appeared to be lime and showed no evidence of recent digging. The officers noticed a strong odor in the house but could not determine its origin.

Gacy's pickup truck and his car were confiscated. He signed a Miranda waiver form on his lawyer's advice and was released by the Des Plaines police at 9:30 P.M. that evening. Gacy was placed under 24-hour surveillance by the police, but he managed to elude his surveillance officers on three separate occasions on December 15, 1978. He drove at high speeds and often in a reckless manner. During this time, officers arrested a friend of Gacy's in Chicago for reckless driving. Gacy and another friend were passengers in the vehicle.

On December 16, Gacy began to converse with his police surveillance team as they followed him around the Chicago area. The officers ate with Gacy at restaurants at which he stopped. On one occasion at a Chicago restaurant Gacy stated to the officers, "You know, clowns can get away with murder" (Sullivan and Maiken, 1983, p. 90). Gacy repeated this statement to another police surveillance team the same day.

The police began to determine a pattern to Gacy's travels around the Chicago area. He was leading his surveillants to places where the Des Plaines detectives had just checked out, apparently to learn what the investigators had found out. On December 17, Gacy invited his surveillance team to his house for dinner. Following dinner he tried to elude the officers. On December 19, Gacy accused surveillance officers of trying to tape their conversations. Gacy also told the officers that he was prepared with bond money if arrested and that he expected to be allowed to call his attorney if they arrested him. Later that day a surveillance team was invited by Gacy to his house for a drink, during which they attempted to read the serial numbers on his television set, which they suspected had belonged to a missing boy. They again detected a strong unidentified odor in the house. On December 20, Des Plaines police and the state's attorney's office learned that on December 22, Gacy's lawyer would be filing a lawsuit against the police for harassment.

On December 21, 1978, Gacy had a late night conference with his lawyers which lasted until 8:00 A.M. that morning. Gacy was then followed around Chicago meeting various friends, who told the officers that Gacy was saying goodbye to them. Police observed Gacy giving one of his friends a plastic bag which they believed contained marijuana. Gacy was arrested later that day on a marijuana charge. The same day, one of the officers who had been in Gacy's house determined that the strong odor he had smelled there was the same odor that he had smelled many times at the county morgue. That evening another search warrant was obtained to search Gacy's house again.

Early the following morning, December 22, 1978, Gacy began confessing to a number of murders of young boys after the police discovered dead bodies buried in the crawl space of his house during their search. Gacy stated that the body of the missing boy they had been searching for had been in the attic of his house when police had first interviewed him at home. Gacy had taken the body in his car later that evening to the Des Plaines River bridge of the Tri-State Tollway and dumped it into the river, which was why he had been late in coming to the Des Plaines police station the following morning.

That morning officers took Gacy to the Des Plaines River bridge and he showed them where he had dumped the body of the missing boy and four other boys he had killed. Gacy was then taken to his home, where he showed the officers where he had buried one of his victims in his garage. On December 22, 1978, Gacy was charged with the murder of the missing boy for whom the Des Plaines police had been searching. He was denied bail and was transferred to the medical wing of the Cook County Jail.

By December 29, 1978, police had recovered 26 bodies from under Gacy's house and one from his garage. On January 3, 1979, Gacy was interviewed by police and state's attorney's lawyers in the Cook County jail. At this time Gacy elaborated on his earlier confessions and was questioned regarding the identification of his victims. The following week, Gacy was indicted by a Cook County grand jury on seven counts of murder and one count each of deviate sexual assault, aggravated kidnapping, and taking indecent liberties with a child. At his arraignment on January 10, Gacy entered pleas of not guilty to all charges and was ordered to undergo a behavioral–clinical examination to determine his fitness to stand trial. On February 16, 1978, Gacy was found mentally fit to stand trial by the examining psychologist. The psychologist, A. Arthur Hartman of the Cook County court forensic unit, stated that Gacy was "very egocentric and narcissistic with a basically antisocial, exploitative orientation. One reflection of this is his development of a technique of 'conning' (his own term) or mis-leading others in his business or personal dealings. He has a severe underlying psychosexual conflict and confusion of sexual identity" (Sullivan and Maiken, 1983, p. 252). Hartman's diagnostic impression of Gacy was of a "psychopathic (antisocial) personality, with sexual deviation and a hysterical personality and minor compulsive and paranoid personality elements" (Sullivan and Maiken, 1983, p. 252).

The Cook County State's Attorney's Office had requested an evaluation of Gacy by Frank Osanka, a sociologist from Lewis University in Glen Ellyn, Illinois. Osanka reviewed all the files on Gacy, including taped interviews, but did not interview Gacy. He concluded:

> The explanation of episodic psychotic states simply cannot explain multiple murders, committed essentially at the same location, in essentially the same methodological manner, hiding the remains in essentially the same methodological manner, over a period of eight years by a man labeled acceptable and successful by his neighbors and in his business. [Gacy] suffered neither with a mental illness nor mental defect which prevented him from appreciating the criminality of his behavior or from conforming his conduct to the requirements of the law. (F. Osanka, personal communication, March 8, 1980)

Gacy's defense lawyers employed a psychiatrist who concluded that Gacy was insane at the time of his alleged crimes. The psychiatrist, R. G. Rappaport, stated that Gacy had a "borderline personality organization with the subtype of psychopathic personality and with episodes of an underlying paranoid schizophrenia" (Sullivan and Maiken, 1983, p. 253). Rappaport supported his diagnosis of psychopathic personality by attributing the following characteristics to Gacy: "unusual degree of self-reference, great need to be loved and admired, exploitative, charming on the surface and cold and ruthless underneath, noticeable absence of feeling of remorse and guilt, and a history of chronic antisocial behavior" (Sullivan and Maiken, 1983, p. 253).

The Cook County State's Attorney's Office employed psychiatrists from the Issac Ray Center at St. Luke's Medical Center in Chicago to examine Gacy. Psychiatrists found:

> For at least the last fifteen years, Gacy had demonstrated a mixed personality disorder, which included obsessive-compulsive, antisocial, narcissistic, and

hypomanic features. He abused both alcohol and drugs. The crimes he committed resulted from an increasingly more apparent personality disorder dysfunction, coupled with sexual preoccupations within an increasingly primary homosexual orientation.

Narcissistically wounded in childhood, by a domineering and at times brutal father figure and inability to physically participate in athletics, Gacy continued to fail to master psychosocial milestones, in part because of a series of apparent psychosomatic disorders. Increasingly obsessed with his sense of failure (constantly emphasized by his father), he dedicated himself to a career of productive work, which brought him positive feedback. Simultaneously, however, his rage at his presumed powerlessness, due to a pervasive, defective self-image, began to merge with sadistic elements in a slowly unfolding homosexual orientation. This began to center upon young men with whom he re-enacted the projected helplessness and sense of failure that he himself continued to experience. His sadistic, homosexual conquests were much more gratifications through the exercise of power than erotic experiences motivated by unmet sexual needs. Murderous behavior became the ultimate expression of power over victims rendered helpless. With each murder victim he was presented with undeniable evidence of his crimes (a dead body), yet he continued with the same patterns of behavior. Ultimately he came to justify murder as socially acceptable because of the degraded nature of his victims (human trash) and his increasingly egocentric conviction that he would never be apprehended because of his own cleverness in concealment and a disordered belief that his murderous behavior was of assistance to society. (Sullivan and Maiken, 1983, pp. 255–256)

On April 23, 1978, a Cook County grand jury indicted Gacy on an additional 26 murders, for a total of 33. All charges against Gacy were consolidated for purposes of criminal trial. A compromise on a change of venue for his trial was reached between prosecution and defense. Jurors were selected from the community of Rockford, Illinois, in late January 1980, and the trial was held in Chicago, beginning February 6, 1980.

Gacy's criminal trial lasted six weeks. His lawyers' strategy and defense, and the major issue at the trial, was that John Wayne Gacy was insane at the time he committed the crimes and could not control his conduct. The final rebuttal witness for the defense, Helen Morrison, a psychiatrist, diagnosed Gacy as having mixed or atypical psychosis. Despite his high IQ, she said Gacy had not developed emotionally; his entire emotional makeup was that of an infant. She concluded that Gacy suffered from mixed psychosis at least since 1958. When asked under cross examination if she thought that Gacy would have killed his victims if there was a uniformed officer in the home with him at the time, she replied that she did. On March 11, 1980, Gacy was found guilty on all indicted charges and two days later was sentenced to death. Fourteen years later, on May 10, 1994, John Wayne Gacy was executed by the state of Illinois.

OFFENSE BEHAVIOR

Little specific information is known regarding the circumstances of the deaths of Gacy's 33 victims between 1970 and 1978. Although Gacy confessed to these killings, he provided very few details of these murders. It is from the surviving victims of Gacy's assaultive crimes that most of his criminal behavior has been determined. Police officials and psychiatrists have then hypothesized or extrapolated from this behavior to his homicidal acts.

Gacy's first known criminal offenses occurred in Waterloo, Iowa, when he was 24 years of age. In Waterloo, Gacy was a member of the merchants' patrol, a cooperative security force which guarded their business establishments at night against break-ins. Gacy took his male employees from the restaurants he managed with him on patrol and broke into businesses, stealing auto parts and funds from vending machines. Gacy would monitor the police radio to determine if police patrols were nearby.

Gacy also organized a social club in the basement of his home. Young boys employed at the restaurants he managed would be allowed to play pool and drink alcoholic beverages for monthly dues. Gacy had many of the boys perform fellatio on him when they won at pool, by intimidating and coercing them or by convincing them that he was conducting scientific experiments for a commission on sexual behavior in Illinois.

In the summer of 1967, Gacy took a young 16-year-old boy to his home to watch some films, shoot pool, and have a few drinks. His wife was in the hospital, having given birth to their second child. When the boy refused to perform fellatio on him, Gacy attacked him with a knife and cut the boy on the arm. Gacy quickly apologized and insisted that the boy stay and watch some pornographic films. After showing the films, Gacy chained the boy's hands behind his back and then tried to attack him sexually. The boy resisted and Gacy began choking him. The boy pretended to black out. Gacy revived him and agreed to take the boy home.

During 1967 and early 1968, Gacy frequently forced a 15-year-old boy, who was a part-time employee, to submit to oral sex. Gacy often got the boy intoxicated on alcohol before these acts. He told the boy that he was conducting experiments and usually paid the boy. After being indicted for sodomy, Gacy paid one of his employees to assault one of the boys who had gone to the police with his parents and had, according to Gacy, spread lies about him.

According to police records, within eight months after Gacy was released from the Iowa prison, he had twice violated his parole. In November 1970, Gacy had a homosexual encounter with a 20-year-old male in his mother's apartment. In February 1971, Gacy was arrested on a complaint of disorderly conduct filed by a 19-year-old male who claimed that Gacy had attacked him sexually. Gacy filed a similar complaint against the boy, and the charges were dismissed.

In late fall of 1971, Gacy struck an employee in the head with a hammer. When the employee asked why Gacy had hit him, he replied he didn't know but that he had a sudden urge to kill the man.

In June 1972 a 24-year-old man told police that he had been picked up by Gacy who offered him a ride. Gacy identified himself as a county police officer, showing the man a badge and telling him he was under arrest. Gacy then told the man if he performed oral sex on him, he would let him go. Gacy drove the man to a building in Northbrook, Illinois, where the man resisted Gacy. Gacy then clubbed him and pursued him in his car, knocking the man down. The man finally escaped to a gas station nearby. The complainant later identified Gacy as his assailant and police arrested Gacy on June 22, 1972. Gacy told police that the complainant was threatening him and trying to extort money from him. After finding marked money given by Gacy on the complainant, police dropped the charges against Gacy.

Prior to Gacy's arrest by the Des Plaines police, Gacy had been arrested by Chicago police on July 15, 1978, for battery. The victim, a 27-year-old male, had been walking at 1:30 A.M. in the morning when a man driving a black car stopped and asked him if he wanted to smoke some marijuana with him. The male got into the car and shortly thereafter the man held a rag over his mouth and he lost consciousness. The victim awoke at 4:30 A.M. that morning with burns on his face and rectal bleeding. The victim later identified the car he had gotten into and gave police the license number. After several court postponements of the case, it was still pending when Gacy was arrested by Des Plaines police.

Gacy's employees, one after another, had disappeared. One boy had disappeared after only a week in Gacy's employ. Another boy had been found drowned in a river 60 miles south of Chicago. Gacy sold the car of a former employee to another employee, stating that the owner had left for California. When asked about the constant turnover of employees, Gacy would respond that the boy had gone back home or that he had fired him. The transitional nature of his business meant that victims would appear and disappear with little notice. It was reportedly very common for Gacy to have offered money to his former employees for oral sex.

One of Gacy's employees told police that he had been down in the crawl space under Gacy's house on two occasions. Once he had helped Gacy spread lime. On another he had dug some trenches. Gacy had told him he was going to lay some tile because of all the moisture. When the employee had started digging away from the area Gacy had plotted out, Gacy became very upset.

Gacy was known to have marijuana in his house. He used the drug frequently and often provided some to his employees. He was also reported to abuse alcohol. He was apparently not habituated to either marijuana or alcohol. When the police found human bodies buried in the crawl space of his house, they also found other evidence of his criminality: a TV set and radio belonging to one of the missing boys, a foot-long vibrator with fecal matter on it, and pieces of plywood stained with blood.

From the autopsies and examination of bodily remains, forensic patholo- gists deduced that most of Gacy's victims had been Caucasian males in their teens or twenties. In most cases the cause of death was impossible to deter- mine. Clothing and clothlike material was found in the throats of some of the victims, indicating that they had suffocated to death. Gacy claimed that none of his victims had been tortured and that they had all been strangled.

Gacy stated that all but one of his victims had been killed by looping a rope around his neck, knotting it twice, and then tightening it, like a tourni- quet, with a stick. Many of the victims had been handcuffed at the time. He stated that others would put the rope around their neck themselves, antici- pating that Gacy would show them an interesting trick. On more than one occasion, Gacy claimed to have killed two boys in one night. He reportedly read the Twenty-third Psalm from the Bible to one of his victims as the boy died. Gacy stated that one of his victims was a masochist. He had chained the youth to a two-by-four with his wrists and ankles together. Gacy stated, "Since he liked pain, I did the ultimate number on him." When asked how he got the idea of the restraint board, he answered, "From Elmer Wayne Henley, the guy in Texas" (Sullivan and Maiken, 1983, p. 197).

He stated that he had lost count of the number of victims he had buried in the crawl space under his house. He had either soaked their bodies in acid or put lime on them and buried them under a foot of earth. He told police that he buried one of his victims in his garage, and the last five victims had been dropped into the Des Plaines River off a bridge southwest of Chicago.

In addition to some of his male employees, Gacy had preyed on homo sexuals and male prostitutes who frequented Bughouse Square, a park in north Chicago. He would cruise the area in his car late at night picking up youth. Gacy often convinced boys he picked up that he was a policeman. Gacy stated that he had sex with 100 people he had picked up in this area and that he had paid all of them. He had a schedule. Between 1:00 and 3:00 A.M. he had sex. All but two of his victims had died between 3:00 and 6:00 A.M., according to Gacy. He referred to most of his killings by stating that his "rope trick" had been performed. One of Gacy's intended victims had sur- vived the rope trick by physically forcing Gacy to release the stick. The sur- vivor had not reported the incident because he believed Gacy to be a police officer. Gacy told police that his first killing was in January 1972 and that his second was in January 1974. He said he killed no one while his mother-in- law lived with him. Police determined that Gacy had killed five people in less than a month in June 1976. He stated that he had killed for two reasons: the victim raised the originally agreed upon price for sex, or he posed some sort of threat, such as telling the neighbors about his sexual activities (Sullivan and Maiken, 1983, p. 225).

Gacy's murders appear to have been well planned and thought out in advance. He eliminated most of the traces of his victims and disposed of their remains in a methodical manner. He even prepared the graves of his future victims in advance.

SELF CONCEPT

Gacy was very concerned about his sexual identity with other people. While he had been engaged in homosexual relationships since his early twenties and probably prior to that, he always talked about being bisexual because he did not want anyone to consider him a homosexual. He was certainly aware of his own homosexual desires when he told his second wife that they would no longer engage in sexual intercourse. After his arrest in Des Plaines and during his confession, he wanted his captors to know that he was bisexual, not homosexual. He stated, "After all, I do have some pride" (Darrach and Norris, 1984, p. 60).

Gacy told police that the pornographic books taken from his house were not his. He stated that he would not spend money on this type of reading material and used the books only to stimulate some of his victims.

Gacy seemed to rationalize everything he did. After the fact, his actions were always inflated to others, or if they might be seen in a negative light, he would twist the truth so that he would be viewed as having committed no wrongdoing. With others he seemed to have an excuse and ready action for everything. Gacy told his family that he had been mentally ill. On Christmas eve 1978, he wrote to his family, "Please forgive me for what I am about to tell you. I have been very sick for a long time (both mentally and physically). I wish I had help sooner. May God forgive me" (Sullivan and Maiken, 1983, p. 199). Whether he truly viewed himself as he portrayed John Gacy to others is difficult to determine. His psychological and psychiatric evaluations indicate that he did.

Gacy appears to have seen himself as an important person and a good businessman. He always discussed his management and sales experience in Iowa in glowing terms. It was also frequently inflated beyond his actual experiences in business.

He had always wanted to be in control of a social situation or an organized activity. He was the boss of his business and would frequently mention it in conversation. In the Junior Chamber of Commerce in both Springfield, Illinois, and Waterloo, Iowa, he sought leadership roles and always held some official position. He was later characterized by friends and others as one who would manipulate situations and people to his advantage and try to place them under his control. The county attorney in Waterloo, Iowa, attributed Gacy's prominence in the community to a "unique ability to manipulate people and ingratiate himself" (Sullivan and Maiken 1983, p. 264).

He wanted to be considered a celebrity figure. Whenever he considered it appropriate he would claim to be part of a criminal syndicate in Chicago. In Iowa he seemed to enjoy being addressed as "Colonel" by his friends. He is remembered by many in Iowa as always talking about money and his connections. He was very proud of his political activities. According to his first wife, his political work was extremely important to Gacy. He displayed his political trophies prominently in his home, including an autographed picture from President Carter's wife.

Even after being arrested and jailed for his murders, he acted importantly. He asked the jail chaplain to have the Chicago archbishop visit him. He also falsely claimed to have received a social visit from the Cook County sheriff (Sullivan and Maiken, 1983, p. 238). People later realized that he had frequently lied about his previous status and accomplishments. However, he had seemed to have believed his own falsehoods.

ATTITUDES

In Iowa, Gacy had his car equipped with spotlights and a siren. His membership in the merchants' patrol allowed him to patrol in uniform with a shotgun. Gacy was always interested in ambulances, fire engines, and police cars. His first wife stated that he would follow these vehicles when they were speeding to an emergency. While under police surveillance, he had taken great pride in eluding the police. In Chicago he convinced the homosexual community that he was a policeman. He frequently carried a police badge, and a number of police badges were found in his house. He was remembered as a boy, as wanting to be a policeman. His attitudes toward law enforcement officers and what they represented seemed to place him above them, yet he identified with them as people who could control others. His prison inmate friends noticed that he closely identified with the guards because he, himself, enjoyed being boss.

Following his arrest, Gacy seemed to feel no remorse or concern for his victims. During his confession, he spoke continuously about his murderous actions, reflecting no emotion. He discussed his victims with the police in an almost clinical fashion with no show of remorse. He stated he killed his victims "because the boys sold their bodies for 20 dollars" (Sullivan and Maiken, 1983, p. 173). Gacy gave his police audience the impression that he felt he had only been ridding the world of some bad kids. Helen Morrison, a psychiatrist who examined Gacy, quoted him as saying that "all the police are going to get me for is running a funeral parlor without a license" (Berger, 1984, p. 11).

Little has been written regarding Gacy's religious beliefs. He came from a Polish Catholic heritage, but this activities in the church appeared to be for social or political gain only. He was the chaplain for all three chapters of the Junior Chamber of Commerce to which he belonged. His reading the Twenty-third Psalm to one of his victims may have been a way of expiating himself of any sins he was committing or simply as added torture to the victim.

John Gacy enjoyed the limelight that his crimes had brought to him. In his first formal confession to a group of police officers, Gacy spoke as if holding court, frequently leaning back in his chair and talking with his eyes closed. He had overcome his fatigue and spoke with a renewed air of confidence. Just as he wanted, the room belonged to John Gacy (Sullivan and Maiken, 1983, p. 176).

It is reported that following his arrest, Gacy kept a scrapbook on his case (*Newsweek*, November 26, 1984, p. 106). He would complain about how his old friends were now treating him and how the press was libeling him. However, to those around him, he appeared to be enjoying all the attention. Regarding his former associates and friends, he wrote: "When things were good and I was giving, everyone was on my bandwagon, but as soon as I am accused and suspected, they run and hide. May God have mercy on them. If it wasn't for God's will, I would have never given or helped so many people. Oh, I am no saint or anything like that, just one of God's children. I do not take the right to sit in judgment on others or myself" (Sullivan and Maiken, 1983, p. 237). Gacy felt the press had taken everything he had said and misinterpreted it or that it had been taken out of context.

RECALL OF EVENTS

When first asked by the police how many people he had killed, Gacy responded: "I told my lawyers 30 or 35 but I don't know, there could be 35, 45—who knows" (Sullivan and Maiken, 1983, p. 183). Gacy never spoke of his victims by name, other than the ones the police already knew about or suspected when he was first arrested. He said he couldn't remember their names. He provided relatively sketchy information regarding his actual killings, stating that he couldn't remember. Gacy was tested on an alcohol-electroencephalogram by psychiatrists prior to his trial. The psychiatrists found the results of the test and the fact that Gacy blacked out within an hour after drinking six ounces of whiskey as significant. The psychiatrists concluded that in Gacy's repetitive murder pattern, there is "a psychological mechanism or repression, in which he attempts to spare whatever conscience he had from awareness of and responsibility for his actions, could explain the 'patchy recollection.' [However] the defendant's degree of intoxication could be so extreme that recollection of some or all of the details of what transpired could in fact be missing—e.g., 'a blackout'" (Sullivan and Maiken, 1983, pp. 254–255).

In his opening statement to the jury, a state's attorney's lawyer for the prosecution referred to Gacy's wife's assertion that he had a memory like an elephant. Examples of this assertion are Gacy's pinpointing of the precise location on the river bridge where he had dumped some of his victims and the detailed recollections offered in some of his statements to the police. Gacy's lack of memory or his patchy memory of his crimes, contrived or real, is still debatable.

THE DEMISE OF JOHN WAYNE GACY

As indicated in the previous pages, Gacy was executed in 1994. For all those years Gacy continued to maintain his innocence. Joseph Kozenczak, who chronicled the investigation that led to Gacy's confession and subsequent conviction in *A Passing Acquaintance* (Kozenczak and Herickson, 1992), states that at the time of his book, Gacy had been on death row for 11 years and that most of his major appeals in the courts had been denied (p. 187).

During his time on death row, Gacy kept busy maintaining his innocence. He continually referred to himself as another victim. In his correspondence with the author, Gacy stated that "nearly 80% of what is known about me is from the media, it is they who made this infamous celebrity fantasy monster image, and now they have to live with that as I have not granted any interviews in over ten years to media people" (personal correspondence, March 6, 1991). Toward the end of his stay on death row, Gacy did grant media interviews, in which he still maintained his innocence.

In his one and only letter to the author (further correspondence seemed fruitless, although I did write him again about a month prior to his execution and received no answer), Gacy included a two-page "fact sheet" entitled "They Called Him the Killer Clown: But Is JW Gacy a Mass Murderer or Another Victim?" The sheet was sent to all who corresponded with Gacy between the late 1980s and his execution in 1994.

John Wayne Gacy was consistent in maintaining his innocence. One writer who interviewed him in February and March 1994 found him to be obsessed with his innocence (Wilkinson, 1994). In 1991, Gacy's obsession was published in book form. The book was called *A Question of Doubt: The John Wayne Gacy Story*, by John Wayne Gacy, C. Ivor McClelland, editor. The book was spiral bound on 8 ½- by 11-inch paper and totaled 216 pages. In the preface to this first-person account of Gacy's first contact with the Des Plaines police through his trial, conviction and sentencing, he states: "He is the man waiting to be strapped to a gurney with an IV of lethal injected drugs coursing through his system—*who has never told his story.*" Gacy concludes the preface by stating: "These are the first words that John Gacy has spoken. This is *my side of the story*—the story of THE THIRTY-FOURTH VICTIM" (Gacy, 1991, p. ii). Very few people will ever consider John Wayne Gacy a victim.

CHAPTER 7

—◆—

HENRY LEE LUCAS: CASE STUDY

SOCIAL ENVIRONMENT

Henry Lee Lucas has been described as always having lived at a very low economic level. The house he lived in until age 14 is described as a two-room shack that had no electricity until 1951. The house had no flooring and was furnished with only the bare necessities. Lucas mentions the fact that he frequently stole the food that his family ate.

Lucas was in the first-grade for the first three years of his schooling. His first grade teacher remembers him as "a very humble little boy who was a little slow and a little dirty" (anonymous, personal communication, 1985). He finished the fourth grade at age 14. He never finished the fifth grade, and his last known exposure to formal education was some vocational training while in prison.

When not "doin' all the work for the family" (interview, July 7, 1984), Lucas spent his childhood playing with knives and terrorizing animals. He claims to have learned how to have sex with animals from his mother's live-in boyfriend. He experimented by killing cows, sheep, goats, dogs, and cats.

His goal in life was to travel. "I wanted to travel and have adventure" (interview, June 5, 1984). Lucas made numerous attempts to run away from home and at age 14 was successful. He would travel thousands of miles and never return. He states, "I ain't got no roots" (interview, June 22, 1984).

His focal concern in life was survival. He has stated, "I don't leave witnesses" (interview, June 5, 1984). For Lucas, having no witnesses guaranteed his survival. To survive, he kept moving and he kept killing. He was always on the move when not incarcerated. He stated: "Remaining in one place causes me to have thoughts of escape. It becomes more of a pressure—not bein' able to get up and go" (interview, July 18, 1984). He boasted of sometimes traveling 24 hours a day, keeping himself awake with amphetamines, marijuana, and PCP. For years he lived among the rootless, the searching, the homeless, and the roamers of this country, living out of his car, stealing, murdering hitchhikers and stranded travelers. All but three of his victims were strangers.

Lucas spent a great deal of his life behind bars. Although he does not talk kindly of his keepers in prison, his discussions of prison life never reach the intensity and hatred with which he describes his home life. For Lucas, prison was where he got his degree in criminality. He states: "It was a learnin' to do crime" (interview, June 24, 1984). He says he spent many years in the Michigan prison as a records clerk. During this time, Lucas says he studied crimes committed by the inmates and learned how to commit them. He describes living at Jackson Prison in Michigan as like living in a big city.

Because Lucas spent most of his life in institutions of correction since age 14, he never really learned to live by the rules of society. If the rules benefited him, he went along. If they did not, he broke them.

The last year of his travels seemed to signal his capture, for he was apparently trying to settle down. For almost a year he continued to return to Stoneburg, Texas, from his murderous trips. He and Becky, then 15 years old, lived there in a trailer as man and wife until he killed her and dissected her body in a farmer's field the day after his forty-sixth birthday in 1982.

FAMILY BACKGROUND

Lucas has been described by a psychiatrist as having a poorly developed moral sense due to undesirable ancestry. Lucas's family consisted of his father and mother, a brother, three half-brothers and four half-sisters. He was reportedly closest to one of his half-sisters, who lived in Tecumseh, Michigan. He lived in a two-room cabin with dirt floors located in a mountainous area of Montgomery County, Virginia. The first 14 years of his life were spent growing up there, living with his mother, a man he remembers as his father (records indicate that the man was not his real father), his older brother, and his mother's boyfriend.

As Lucas described his parents: "They lived together, but my father didn't have no legs and he stayed drunk and my mother, she drank and was a prostitute. And, that's the way I growed up, until it was time to get out on my own" (interview, June 22, 1984). Lucas remembers that his father was either drinking or trying to sell pencils, his mother was either gone or having sex with different men, and his brother was gone most of the time. His mother was the head of the family and dominated everyone.

He describes his mother as a Cherokee Indian of muscular build, weighing 150 to 160 pounds. He states that his mother "didn't work, she'd rather sell her body. [She] believed just in sex. Didn't try to provide for anyone" (interview, October 25, 1984). Lucas stated that the worst thing he remembers about his family was being forced to watch his mother having sexual intercourse with various men.

He states that his father never argued with anybody and he had a good relationship with him. Lucas remembers his grief at his father's death in 1949, and his mother claiming, "Good riddance." Lucas remembers his brother as stronger and bigger. He claims that his mother would not allow him to play with his brother. Reported to have once suffered a nervous breakdown, his brother joined the Navy when Lucas was 14.

Authorities describe Lucas's mother as a woman who drank heavily and was a bootlegger. Her daughters remember her as always cleaning homes and restaurants to support them. She was 51 years old when she gave birth to Lucas. Her granddaughter remembers her as a dirty old woman who was not nice to be around.

The man Lucas calls his father, Anderson Lucas, had worked for the railroad and lost his legs when he reportedly fell under a train. He was described by one caseworker as being illiterate and as having a bad reputation as a bootlegger.

From as early as he can remember, Lucas was apparently confused as to his own gender. "I grew up from 4 years old, best I can remember, 'till about 7 years old as a girl. I lived as a girl. I was dressed as a girl. I had long hair as a girl. I wore girl's clothes" (interview, June 22, 1984). His half-sister in Maryland still keeps a childhood picture of Lucas with long curls dressed in girl's clothing.

In the first grade at age 7, Lucas had his hair cut after his school teacher complained about its length. Lucas claims that his mother's attitude toward him changed after this and that she beat him, forced him to carry heavy objects, to steal, cut wood, carry water, and take care of the hog.

Lucas remembers no good times in his childhood because if he had fun, he "would get beat for it" (interview, June 22, 1984). He has a scar on the back of his head which he claims resulted from his mother striking him with a two-by-four piece of wood. He reports that he was unconscious for 11 hours following this beating and that his skull was fractured.

Lucas refers to his childhood as one of constant abuse or neglect:

> I don't think a human being alive that can say he had the childhood I had. Bein' beaten ever day. Bein' misused ever day. Havin' to cook my own food, havin' to steal my own food. Eatin' on the floor instead of the table. Bein treated like what I call the hog of the family. It's a lot harder than what people can imagine. Growing up with hatred, without any kind of friendship, without any kind of companion to be around or anything. The best thing was leavin' home. (interview, November 30, 1984)

His accomplices in crime could be described as his substitute, self-made family. He was very close to Ottis, a pyromaniac as a child, a homosexual, and an admittedly sexually sadistic killer. Lucas states that in their sexual relationship, he was the passive participant. He treated the two children, Becky and Frank, like his own children. Ironically, he exposed these two children to his killings as his mother had allegedly exposed him to her sexual relationships. Lucas states, "I would avoid actually killing anyone in front of them, and a lot of times they would sneak around to see what I was doin' and I would catch 'em and I would scold 'em for it" (interview, February 2, 1985). For Lucas, the fact that these young children witnessed some of his horrific deeds was not all that important.

PEER-GROUP ASSOCIATIONS AND PERSONAL RELATIONSHIPS

In describing her brother, Lucas's half-sister states, "He always seemed like he wanted someone to love. He never seemed to be able to keep a friend for some reason" (anonymous, personal communication, 1985). He was described as being reticent to initiate any conversation with other boys and girls while in school. In retrospect, those who knew Lucas as a boy characterize him as either socially inept or hostile.

Due to an empty eye socket and subsequent implant of an artificial eye, his appearance apparently caused children to shun him or avoid direct contact with him. This restriction of peer relationships was intensified by his mother, who Lucas claims would not allow him to play with other children, including his own brother.

The lack of any significant peer relationships combined with his treatment at home resulted in an overwhelming hatred, which Lucas refers to frequently.

> I've hated since I can first remember, uh, back when I was a little kid I've hated my family and anything. Anytime I went out, uh, to go play [with other children] or some show, or something, I never could get anybody to go with me. I never could make friends and I just hated people. Nobody would accept me 'cause of my left eye. [I] looked like garbage! No girls would go out with me. No boys would have anything to do with me. They just wanted to stay away from me. (interview, June 22, 1984)

Lucas says that upon leaving home, "[I] didn't believe in association with anybody" (interview, August 14, 1984).

With the exception of a young woman Lucas wanted to marry prior to his mother's death, Lucas claims to have had few relationships in his life. For Lucas, the true relationships in his life have been Becky Powell, Ottis Toole, a lay minister in Stoneburg, Texas, who provided him with housing, and the lay sister who visited him in the Williamson County jail. In describing his attempts to establish relationships, he states: "I tried married life and it didn't work. I tried to go back with my family and that didn't work. I went to Florida, met Ottis and just started travelin'" (interview, June 22, 1984).

He states that Becky "More fit into my kind a life. She accepted everything I done. I could tell her things. She understood. This took off the pressure that was there. Before, I had the urge to destroy anything within my reach. Becky took some of the pressure away." In describing his relationship with her, he says, "Yeah, uh it's, uh weird. My love for her was like a daughter—you know, a father to daughter. I never thought of her as sexual." He stated that he only had sexual intercourse with her three times, to satisfy her. "I loved her, but I don't think she felt love," he said (interviews, June 22, 1984, and February 8, 1985).

Psychiatrists who have talked to Lucas characterize him as poorly socialized with an exaggerated need to feel powerful and important, who views others to be manipulated. They describe his mind-set as putting trust in no one except himself. Lucas's relationships are described by psychiatrists as solely for self aggrandizement and exploitative in nature, in which he will ultimately be in control.

CONTACT WITH DEFINING AGENCIES

Lucas's first documented contact with law enforcement officers was at age 14 or 15. His first contact with correctional personnel was in 1952 when incarcerated at Beaumont, Virginia. During this period he was assigned to a correctional case worker. His first documented contact with correctional psychologists was when he was in prison in Michigan. His first known psychiatric diagnosis occurred in July 1961 involving his transfer to Ionia State Hospital.

While Lucas appears to enjoy playing detective in "solving" his crimes, which he refers to as "my cases," he appears to have little regard for law enforcement in general. He states, "The police didn't know who done it. They never would have knowed who done it. They'd never know who done it unless I'd told 'em." He frequently reiterates, "Unless I tell 'em, they'd never clear these cases." He characterizes many of the hundreds of law enforcement officers who have interviewed him by stating, "I've seen better kids play cops than that!" (interviews June 5, 1984, June 22, 1984, and July 18, 1984).

All officers who traveled to Georgetown to interview Lucas on homicides were thoroughly briefed by the Texas Rangers on ways to handle Lucas and specific procedures to follow. Lucas was shown a live picture of the victim or a number of pictures including the victims. He was told the state, jurisdiction, and the date of the incident. If Lucas remembered the victim, he describes the crime in great detail. He has a phenomenal memory for details. In 113 separate instances, Lucas has led law enforcement officers back to the scene of his homicides unassisted.

Lucas describes his interviews with police officers: "I have to give 'em every detail . . . how it happened, where it happened at, the description of the person, what was used, uh every type of, uh where the body was left, parts of bodies missing. I have to tell them what parts are missing, if they've been shot, I have to tell them that. If they were stabbed, cut, whatever. They don't give me no details" (interview, June 5, 1984).

From January 1, 1952, when he was incarcerated in juvenile detention in Richmond, Virginia, to June 11, 1983, when he was arrested in Stoneburg, Texas, Henry Lee Lucas spent over 21 years living under the control of various correctional authorities. In other words, 70% of his life during these 30 ½ years was spent under someone else's control. Lucas contends that he was beaten and even shot by "law enforcement" while in prison. He threatened to kill himself while in prison in Michigan and is reported to have attempted suicide by cutting his left wrist. Prison authorities did not consider this a serious suicide attempt. He states that he was trying to change and get help in prison by talking to doctors and prison officials. During his first confession in Stoneburg, Texas, Lucas claimed that he had begged prison officials in Michigan to help him and got no assistance. Between the times he was diligently reporting to his parole officer in Maryland following his first release from prison in Michigan, he was traveling across this country and leaving the dead remains of his victims in a number of states.

Lucas consistently maintains that he requested that he not be released from prison when paroled in 1975. He claims the day that he was discharged, he killed four people. Five murders committed by Lucas have been confirmed by the Texas Rangers during the remainder of 1975. One of those murders was committed on the same day that he was married.

The results of psychological testing while Lucas was incarcerated reveal that he reads at the sixth-grade level, spells at the fifth-grade level, and understands mathematics at the fourth-grade level. Institutional psychological examinations conducted in Michigan show Lucas to have a total average of 65 on the Standard Achievement Test and an IQ of 89 as determined by the Army General Classification Test. He placed in the sixtieth percentile on the revised Minnesota Paper Form Board. Lucas was further administered the Minnesota Multi-phase Personality inventory, the Figure Drawing Test, and the Rosenzweig P. H. Study. A summary of the interpretation of these tests written by psychologists on July 14, 1961, is as follows:

> While contraindicating any underlying psychotic process as well as incapacitating neurotic qualities, tests results are suggestive of a basically insecure individual who has a relatively well crystallized inferiority complex and who is grossly lacking in self confidence, self reliance, will power and general stamina. There is also some evidence of a preoccupation with sexual impotence, the same which is believed to exist as only another reflection of his deflated impression of personal qualities in general. According to Rosenzweig P. H. Study he was found more value oriented than he is need oriented, but due to his lack of will power and self confidence he does not characteristically engage in behavior which is aimed at an implementation of his values. The anxiety and hostility caused by threats to the ego are usually directed intropunitively toward himself or inpunitively toward the frustrating situation. *He does not have the courage to blame others for mistakes or misfortunes or to engage in aggressive social behavior* aimed at alleviating some of his discomfort [emphasis added] (Ionia State Hospital, July 14, 1961).

The clinical psychologist providing the interpretative summary above qualified his diagnostic impression due to the absence of pertinent and general background information on Lucas. In fact, prior to writing the above, he had never seen Lucas. He stated that his report should be a working hypothesis.

The following psychiatric diagnoses completed on Lucas while incarcerated were provided to law enforcement officials in 1984 in the form of narrative reports:

- *July 14, 1961*—Psychiatric Clinic Ward, Jackson Prison (2nd admission)—DSM-II 301.81 *Passive-aggressive personality* with a significant inferiority complex and general lack of confidence, self reliance, will power and perseverance—DSM-II 295.0 *Schizophrenia, simple type, chronic, severe*. Transfer to Ionia State Hospital recommended, prognosis fair (Ionia State Hospital, July 14, 1961).
- *August 10, 1961*—Ionia State Hospital—DSM-II 295.90 *Schizophrenia, chronic undifferentiated type* sex deviate, sadist (Ionia State Hospital, August 10, 1961).
- *January 28, 1965*—Ionia Staff Conference on Lucas—"The patient's affect during the staff interview was definitely inappropriate. He is *potentially dangerous*" [emphasis added] (Ionia State Hospital, January 28, 1965).
- *November 17, 1971*—Center for Forensic Psychiatry—DSM-II 301.81 *Passive aggressive personality*. Found competent to stand criminal trial for kidnapping. "It is not felt that there is much outside an incarceration setting which would be effective in modifying the defendant's

presently erratic social behavior" (Center for Forensic Psychiatry, November 17, 1971).

A psychologist for the defense testified at Lucas's murder trial in San Angelo, Texas, that Lucas was a chronic schizophrenic who belonged in an institution. Three other psychiatrists for the prosecution disagreed, finding Lucas sane enough to stand trial (*Houston Chronicle*, April 7, 1984, p. 1). "I need medical help, there's no doubt about it," was the layman's diagnosis offered by Lucas himself (interview, February 8, 1985).

Lucas was transferred to the McLennan County jail in Waco, Texas, on April 12, 1985, by authority of the state attorney general and the McLennan County district attorney, who had convened a grand jury in Waco to investigate two homicides that Lucas had confessed to in the county and the conduct of the Lucas Task Force coordinated by the Texas Rangers. On April 14, 1985, the *Dallas Times Herald* charged in a five-page article that Lucas committed very few of the murders he had confessed to and that law enforcement agencies across the country had fed Lucas information on homicide cases so that he could confess to them. The paper also charged that in many instances the Lucas Task Force was aware that Lucas was confessing to murders he did not commit. The Texas attorney general publicly stated that Lucas probably did not commit all the murders to which he had confessed. The Texas Rangers and numerous law enforcement agencies across the country have disputed the charges made by the newspaper and the attorney general.

The grand jury completed its investigation in late June 1985 and issued a no bill on Lucas for the two homicides he had confessed to in McLennan County. It should be noted that the officers who took the confessions from Lucas never testified at the grand jury. Members of the Lucas Task Force did testify at the grand jury only after insisting strongly that they be allowed to testify. No charges against the task force were issued by the grand jury.

Upon completion of the grand jury, Lucas was transferred to the Texas Department of Corrections death row facility near Huntsville, Texas. Lucas stated at this time that he no longer wished to talk to law enforcement. Lucas sued the Texas Rangers, charging that they had drugged him to elicit confessions, did not provide him with an attorney during questioning, and did not advise him of his rights prior to questioning. Ironically, by state law, the attorney general had to defend the Rangers against these charges. The charges were never upheld.

Lucas still talks to people in his death row cell and conducts interviews. On advice of his attorney, he sees no law enforcement personnel, and corrections officials have also been advised not to allow police officers to talk with Lucas. He still proclaims his innocence. He has had a number of extensions on his pending execution.

OFFENSE BEHAVIOR

While his first deviant act, labeled as such, was theft, Lucas killed animals for his sexual gratification in his early teens and began using alcohol at age 9. He also became fascinated with knives in the first grade. They would become one of the tools of his "trade." The knife was his favorite weapon since it was silent and quick, its target the throat and chest area of his victims.

Lucas stole numerous automobiles during his criminal career. Also, many of his killings were the result of burglary, theft, and armed robbery. His most frequent target for robbery was the 24-hour convenience store.

His criminal career was diffuse, intermittent, yet involving ever-increasing forms of aggression. His first homicide was a 17-year-old girl in Virginia in 1951. His second was his mother, nine years later. For Lucas,

> It was just an impulse thing that if I wanted to kill somebody, I'd go and kill 'em. I wouldn't plan it, how I was gonna do that. Then I would sit and plan how to get rid of the body. Whether I would just dump it out on the road or whether I would leave it partially clothed or would leave anything around the body or whether I'd leave the body cut up, how I would leave the body, ya know. (interview, February 8, 1985)

In describing his killing, Lucas states:

> We killed them every way there is except one. I haven't poisoned anyone. . . . We cut 'em up. We hanged 'em. We ran 'em down in cars. We stabbed 'em. We beat 'em, we drowned 'em. There's crucifixion—there's people we filleted like fish. There's people we burnt. There's people we shot in cars. . . . We strangled them by hand. We strangled them by rope. We strangled them by telephone cord. We even stabbed them when we strangled them. We even tied them so they would strangle themselves. (*Avalanche Journal*, June 3, 1984, p. 1)

All methods have been confirmed by the task force except hanging and crucifixion. Lucas talks about some of his victims being used for target practice. Synopsis of two confirmed homicides by the task force reveal one victim being shot while standing at a car wash and another shot while hanging up clothes in her backyard. They were shot as Lucas and his accomplices drove by in a car.

Lucas claims that he and Ottis Toole were members of a death cult, which resulted in many of his murders. A religious book on Lucas (Call, 1985) and a religious pamphlet on Lucas (Larson, 1984) provide details of his activities in this cult. Law enforcement officials have, however, been unable to substantiate any of Lucas's claims regarding the existence of such a cult.

Lucas admits to being a necrophiliac, although the term had to be explained to him. He stated, "In most of my cases, I think you'll find that I had sex with them after death, uh the other way I'm not satisfied" (Terry interview, August 11, 1983).

Lucas states, "I've had people in houses, I've had people in stores, I've had people in banks" (interview, June 5, 1984). During his confinement in the Williamson County jail in Texas, he continued to stick to the number 360 victims.

One reason Lucas gives for his killings is, "I didn't leave no witnesses. I've never left witnesses" (interview, June 5, 1984). A witness for Lucas, in addition to his felony murders was whoever was on the street or in the area. He states, "After the first few, ya know, I just felt the next one was covered. I'd just kill that one so they couldn't say I was there. If I came into contact with somebody, I couldn't afford to let 'em live" (interview, February 2, 1985).

Lucas claims to have been drinking prior to most of his killings. His argument with his mother in 1960, which led to her death, began in a tavern. He has reportedly used numerous amphetamines, PCP, LSD, and marijuana. He states that the drugs he took kept him relaxed and kept him awake so he could travel a lot. "Drugs allowed me to stay on the road, to get out of the victim's neighborhood" (interview, June 5, 1984). For Lucas, being on drugs increased his degree of awareness.

Lucas and accomplices used many vehicles in their travels. Several old cars were purchased in Jacksonville, Florida. When a car they were using broke down, they would hitchhike or steal a car. Sometimes they would briefly use the cars of their murder victims.

He was constantly and almost ceaselessly moving about the country, taking care not to be seen, to leave behind clues and rarely repeating in the same area the ways in which he murdered. Lucas talks of a "force" that kept him moving and traveling with no specific destination. For Lucas, it was as if he had heeded the advice of Harry King, "the Boxman," who stated: "The only way you can beat the law is by moving all the time. The law is easy to beat as long as you keep moving. But you have to continuously move" (King and Chambliss, 1984, p. 91).

Many of his victims have been subjected to what the task force refers to as overkill. Lucas explains this by referring to the "force," which causes him to mutilate and dissect the bodies of many of his victims. He and his accomplices claim to have carried the head of one victim through two states.

Very little physical evidence has been found to link Lucas to the crime scenes of his murders. A partial latent fingerprint was found in a robbery murder he committed at a motel in Louisiana. Victims' hair has been found in cars used by Lucas. Blood has been found at crime scenes which match his blood type. Lucas's blood type is ABO-A, AK-1, HP-2, and he is a nonsecreter (Regional Organized Crime Information Center, 1984). This blood type is found in less than two-tenths of 1% of the population. Also a composite drawing made by a police artist from witnesses' descriptions of an abduction closely resembles Lucas.

Lucas contends that he constantly changed the way he killed in order to confuse law enforcement. By the time one of his murders was discovered, he might be two or three counties away, killing in a different way. Sergeant Bob Prince, a Texas Ranger in charge of the task force, states, "Lucas has 16 homicides within a 50-mile radius of Georgetown [Texas]. If you laid these cases out on a table and asked investigators not familiar with Lucas to evaluate them, the officers would undoubtedly talk about numerous different killers instead of just one" (interview, November 30, 1984).

SELF CONCEPT

Lucas speaks frequently of being driven by hatred. He attributes this hatred to the way he was brought up by his mother. "When I first grew up and can remember, I was dressed as a girl. And I stayed that way for two or three years and then after that I was treated as, uh, what I'd call the dog of the family" (interview, June 5, 1984). This, the beatings by his mother, and being forced to watch her in sexual intercourse caused, according to Lucas, a deep embedded hatred that he couldn't get rid of.

He was killing and experimenting sexually with animals at age 9, and states that he "never thought about killing anyone till I was 14 years old. Everything I had was destroyed" (interview, June 22, 1984). When asked if he ever really thought about himself, Lucas replied, "Once in 1970. I knew what I was gonna do" (interview, February 2, 1985). He says he thought someone would eventually shoot him before long. He says he didn't care.

Many detectives who have questioned him report that Lucas is not reliable. He has admitted to crimes and then denied them. He has confused places and dates. In some respects he brags about his murders. "Well, most of your other people leaves evidence. I don't. I've never left evidence in any of my cases" (interview, June 22, 1984). During a subsequent interview, Lucas claimed to have specifically left evidence on purpose.

Lucas states that he was trying to "show people I can do anything I want to. Outsmart everybody else. It's your responsibility to catch me. Anything I wanted to do, I could do. Outsmart a burglar alarm. Get around electric alarms. No kind of safety device I can't get out of" (interview, August 14, 1984).

He is apparently impotent. In discussing sexual relations he always refers to not getting anything out of it. He attributes this to a stab wound to his groin while in prison requiring surgery. After that, he states, "I could only get a feeling but no liquid" (interview, June 22, 1984). He sees himself as sterile.

Lucas states that at one time he had a problem, "but I wasn't sick." In reference to his past killings, he states: "From 14 years old all I can say is I killed. I just lived a criminal life." As to his specific killings he says: "To me, it's as if I haven't killed anyone, yet I have. . . . It's like bein' two people. I could see myself commit 'em, the crime, but I couldn't feel myself committin' it." Lucas states further: "It's like living in two different worlds. You want to do what is right, and yet, ya can't do it" (interviews, February 2, 1985, and March 22, 1985).

Attitudes

Although frequently claiming to the contrary, Lucas seems to enjoy his "celebrity" status. For a change, he has something others want—information. Lucas is now in the limelight, no longer going unnoticed. When he speaks, a great many people are willing to listen.

Lucas now claims remorse for his victims. However, a big smile crosses his face when he is identified as having committed a homicide and he clears another of his "cases." The smile on his face is either because he had gotten away with a murder for so long or that he had, as he calls it, "solved his case."

To value human life seems beyond his capability. When asked why more of his victims weren't males, he replied: "That's somethin' I very seldom do, unless it's an emergency and have to do it." For him, the victim was an object, "only one that ever bothered me was Becky." As for his mother, "No, 'cause I didn't kill her, she died of a heart attack after I hit her with the knife." He doesn't see any responsibility for his mother's death since she was beating him with a broom when she was killed. He views it as self defense (interviews, August 14, 1984, and February 8, 1985).

Lucas does not like to admit that some of his victims were young children. He blames most of these deaths on his accomplice, Toole. He claims to have believed that a 4-year-old victim was 15 years old. He seems to have traveled from one victim to the next. "I'd go from one to the other and wouldn't think about the last one I'd killed. I never had no feeling for that person at all" (interview, August 14, 1984).

Most of his female victims were, for him, prostitutes. "Most of the girls I've met on the highway has turned out to be prostitutes. [They] has been either out sellin' theirselves to truckers or people on the highway and I, uh have always since I was a little kid hated prostitutes" (interview, June 22, 1984).

Lucas claims to have studied law enforcement. On the one hand, he shows concern for law enforcement problems; on the other, he shows disdain for law enforcement agencies. Lucas states, "I've turned a lot of law enforcement, as far as people know it today, upside down. It took years of practice, years of understanding criminal law" (interview, June 22, 1984).

When asked how he has changed since his arrest, he responded, "I've changed from what I used to be. I was a killer. Let's put it plain out. The type of life I lived. I mean that thing was nothin but crime. I didn't do nothin else. It got so killin' somebody meant nothin' to me" (interview, March 22, 1985).

When asked why he has changed, he responded: "Seein' what I've done. It's my own personal feelins. What I've seen what I've done. Stuff like 'at. That's caused me ta change. Since I've learned about the families. I've learned about the sufferin' they went through. How much sufferin' I've caused. It hurts! It would cause anybody to change. Seein' the misery 'cause of what I've done. I'd never dreamt of that before" (interview, March 22, 1985).

RECALL OF EVENTS

His memory is described as including an excruciatingly intense wealth of detail. Law enforcement authorities have found Lucas to have a remarkable recall for road numbers, mileages, and landmarks. They have frequently taken Lucas into the countryside and let him direct them to the crime scene. In one instance in Texas, Lucas was driven past a commercial building when he said that he and an accomplice had killed a man and woman in an armed robbery of "that liquor store over there." The officer noted that the building was not a liquor store but later learned that it had been when the proprietors were killed in a robbery. In another instance, a rural crime scene was so remote that the officer could not find his way back to it. Lucas led the officers directly to the crime scene.

When questioned about his memory, Lucas stated, "Yeah, I can't recall how I do it, really. . . . There's so many of 'em, they just seem to come back clear as crystal. It's like something in a movie, like watching a movie over and over" (interview, March 22, 1985). Lucas is confessing to his murders because, "The Lord told me to" (interview, June 5, 1984). As for his phenomenal memory, he states, "That was done by Jesus Himself. That was from a light comin' into my cell and uh, asking me to come forth with my confessions. And, uh, I have been able to uh, go back to the bodies, and give complete descriptions of the bodies through Him. And that's the only way I can do it" (interview, June 5, 1984).

A more plausible explanation of his recall ability is referred to by psychologists as hypernesia, an unusually exact or vivid memory. His ability to remember his victims can also be attributed to an eidetic memory, causing mental images that are unusually vivid and almost photographically exact.

CHAPTER 8

———❖———

KENNETH BIANCHI: CASE STUDY

SOCIAL ENVIRONMENT

Kenneth Bianchi had numerous problems in his childhood, due to a number of maladies and illnesses, many of which were reported to be psychosomatic in nature. His mother was reportedly very overprotective. In his teens Bianchi was a frequent purchaser of hard-core sex material in Rochester, New York, adult bookstores. He would sometimes borrow the family movie projector and show films to friends at their homes. He told his mother he was showing family movies. Bianchi smoked marijuana a few times but had never been seriously habituated. His first sexual experience was probably in his early teens.

His teenage marriage right after high school lasted only eight months. After the annulment of his marriage, Bianchi attended Monroe Community College in Rochester, taking police science and political science courses. His grades were generally high C's. Bianchi dropped out of college and took qualifying tests for the Air Force, registering high on the electronics tests. He did not, however, enter the military. He worked as a bouncer at a bar for awhile, and then obtained a job with an ambulance service.

After his mother remarried, he decided to travel to California. Bianchi's mother had arranged for him to stay with Angelo Buono, his 47-year-old half-cousin, who ran an auto upholstery business out of his home in Glendale, California, a Los Angeles suburb.

In early 1977 Bianchi moved in with a girl from Bellingham, Washington, who would later bear him a son. Finances were tight, but Bianchi bought a Cadillac. He couldn't afford the payment on the car, but instead of returning it, he simply ignored the bills until it was repossessed. In May 1977, Bianchi's girlfriend went to Las Vegas with a friend and was allegedly raped during her stay. She did not report the incident to the police or to Bianchi. It wasn't until later, when Bianchi had caught venereal disease from his girlfriend, that he learned of the rape. When his girlfriend was examined by doctors, they discovered that she was pregnant.

In March 1978, three and a half weeks after Bianchi's son was born, his girlfriend broke up with him and moved with her baby back to her home-town of Bellingham, Washington. In May of that year the couple decided to try their relationship again and Bianchi moved to Bellingham, Washington. His girlfriend was breast-feeding their son and Bianchi limited his sexual relations with her during that time. He stated later that he went out with other women during this time. He had also apparently been masturbating frequently during this time. After his arrest, police found a briefcase belong-ing to him which contained hard-core pornography, several stained pairs of undershorts, and a heavily stained towel.

When Bianchi arrived in Bellingham he was hired by a uniformed pri-vate security firm. Bianchi left his security job in the summer and went to work for a department store for higher wages. Bianchi was reportedly popu-lar with some of the security firm's clients, and the firm rehired him in a supervisory position.

Reportedly throughout high school Bianchi had been obsessed with becoming a police officer. As noted, Bianchi took police science courses at Monroe Community College. However, he was repeatedly rejected when he applied and reapplied for police positions in New York and California. In Los Angeles he participated in police ride-along programs twice later in 1978. He was never satisfied with any of the jobs that he had. He wanted police work. His security job in Bellingham was the closest he would come to police work. Prior to his arrest, he had reportedly held 11 jobs in the last seven years (*New York Times*, April 24, 1979, p. 16).

FAMILY BACKGROUND

Kenneth Alessio Bianchi was born in 1951 to a young teenage girl in Rochester, New York. After Bianchi's mother became pregnant, she married a man who was not the father. She was allegedly an alcoholic. The Monroe County, New York, adoption report stated: "She [Bianchi's mother] appears to be a pathetic creature of limited intelligence" (Schwarz, 1981, p. 123). After his birth, his mother placed Bianchi in a foster home. When he was a few weeks old, a private adoption proceeding was initiated by Francis and Nicholas Bianchi. He was legally adopted by them in 1952 and given their last name when Bianchi reached his first birthday.

Bianchi's adoptive parents were both born in 1919 and were of similar backgrounds; first-generation Americans raised in Italian Catholic families. They both left high school in their second year for full-time jobs. Nicholas had a stuttering problem as a child which he never fully overcame. In December 1941, they were married. Francis learned shortly thereafter that she could not bear children and had to undergo a radical hysterectomy. Ten years later when Ken was adopted, she very quickly became an overprotective mother to him. Between December 1951 and May 1952 she took him to the doctor eight different times, but nothing was found wrong with him other than a minor respiratory infection that was responding to treatment. Shortly after the adoption, the Bianchis' moved to a larger apartment with a fenced-in yard so that their son wouldn't wander into the street.

Doctors had evaluated the Bianchis' for the adoption agency. The adoption agency report described the doctor's evaluations: "He [the doctor] thinks she [Francis Bianchi] will always be excitable but doubts that this will affect the baby in any way. He thinks that her love for him will compensate any emotional upset, as her love is true and not artificial. Her attitude and emotional stability may improve after she is through the menopausal period which was induced by the operation" (Schwarz, 1981, p. 127).

The family moved to Los Angeles in 1956 because of Ken's asthma. In January 1957, Ken fell from a jungle gym at the school playground and struck his nose and the back of his head (Schwarz, 1981, p. 127). Ken also began to have petit mal seizures, and when he was upset he would roll his eyes. His mother thought that he had epilepsy but the doctors felt that his various problems were psychological, and this angered her. Doctors thought the eye rolling was a habit that Ken had developed. In 1958 the family moved back to Rochester, where Ken was later admitted to Rochester General Hospital because of the frequency with which he urinated in his pants. His mother had done everything she could to stop Ken from urinating in his pants. She had gone so far as to spank him before he went to the bathroom to ensure that he urinated enough not to dribble in his pants later.

Ken was diagnosed as having diverticulitis, a horseshoe kidney, and transient hypertension. Although these were physical findings, the doctor also stated that Ken had many emotional problems. The hospital report stated that there was no problem with Ken until his mother would visit him in the afternoon. Then Ken would complain about everything for his mother's benefit. Hospitalization was a trying experience for Ken and the attending doctor wondered if his social or home environment could be considered at all adequate. The hospital staff and investigating social workers suggested that Ken and his mother see a psychiatrist, but his mother refused.

Ken's third-grade teacher described his mother in a parent–teacher conference report as a very nervous person who was easily upset. The teacher said that as a result, Ken was also nervous and wet his pants.

Ken's parents had been reported numerous times to the Rochester society of the Prevention of Cruelty to Children, Inc. because of concern over Ken's emotional state. On September 15, 1962, the society issued a report on their investigation of the Bianchis. This report apparently focused on Ken's mother. She was found to be "deeply disturbed, socially ambitious, dissatisfied, unsure, opinionated and overly protective . . . guilt ridden by her failure to have children [and who had] smothered this adopted son in medical attention and maternal concern from the moment of adoption" (Schwarz, 1981, p. 130). The report also focused on Ken's mother's frequent attempts to have him tested because of constant urination. Each test involved the probing of his genitals.

Ken's mother would frequently keep him home from school for fear he would develop an illness and cause his urination problem to worsen. Ken was seen at DePaul Clinic in Rochester in 1962. Part of the clinic report stated:

> The boy drips urine in his pants, doesn't make friends very easily and has twitches. The other children make fun of him and his mother is extremely angry at the school because they do not stop the other children. The mother sounded as if she were very overprotective of this boy. When the boy fell on the playground in kindergarten early in the school year, she kept the boy home the total year. She indicated that she has become so upset because people keep telling her to take her child to a psychiatrist. She does not think he needs a psychiatrist and she went into great detail about how the doctors these days are just out for money and she does not trust any of them.

> The mother is obviously the dominant one in the family and impresses one as a quite disturbed woman. Mrs. Bianchi tends to displace her anger especially on doctors and hospitals and project the blame for the boy's problem onto other sources. (Schwarz, 1981, pp. 132–133)

The DePaul report also more specifically addressed Ken's behavior:

> Dr. Dowling reports that Kenneth is a deeply hostile boy who has extremely dependent needs which his mother fulfills. He depends on his mother for his very survival and expends a great deal of energy keeping his hostility under control and under cover. He is eager for other relationships and uses a great deal of denial in handling his own feelings. For example, he says that his mother and father are the best parents in the world. . . . To sum up, Dr. Dowling said that he is a severely repressed boy who is very anxious and very lonely. He felt that

the only outlet whereby he could somehow get back at his mother was through psychosomatic complaints. Dr. Dowling felt that without this defense of the use of his somatic complaints he might very well be a severely disturbed boy. (Schwarz, 1981, p. 133-134)

Bianchi would testify at Angelo Buono's trial in 1983 that he had lied about his mother while he was being examined by psychiatrists in 1979. He stated that his statements about child abuse were "exaggerated and extended" (*Los Angeles Daily News*, August 18, 1982, p. 1). Bianchi had told psychiatrists that his mother had held his hand over a flame as punishment for playing with matches. Bianchi claimed that he was encouraged by his attorney to lie about his mother to bolster a potential insanity defense plea.

Bianchi reportedly did not spend much time with his father, who worked a great deal of overtime during Ken's childhood. When Bianchi was 14 years old his father suddenly died at work. Ken reportedly underwent a prolonged period of grief for his father.

Shortly after Bianchi graduated from high school in 1971, he got married. He quarreled with his wife constantly and after eight months she left him and filed for an annulment. Bianchi later referred to the marriage as being "dumped on" (Schwarz, 1981, p. 40).

PEER-GROUP ASSOCIATION AND PERSONAL RELATIONSHIPS

The prosecutors at Buono's trial characterized both Bianchi and Buono as having sex-oriented, manipulative personalities (*Los Angeles Daily News*, October 17, 1983, p. 1). Bianchi had read a lot of hard-core pornography. Buono had reportedly been involved in a number of perverted sexual acts. Bianchi had very obviously manipulated his girlfriend from Washington. He had convinced his girlfriend that he had cancer and would go to his appointments for chemotherapy without her. He had apparently stolen some medical records and altered them with his own name. Although not appearing manipulative, Buono certainly gave his wives the strong impression that he had wanted to control them totally.

When Bianchi was arrested, his live-in girlfriend stated: "The Ken I knew couldn't ever have hurt anybody or killed anybody, he wasn't the kind of person who could have killed somebody" (Barnes, 1984). His boss at the security firm where Bianchi had worked considered him an excellent security guard (Levin and Fox, 1985, p. 148). A number of Bianchi's friends in Bellingham offered to be character witnesses for him. Almost everyone who knew him believed him to be innocent.

A Canadian border guard who worked with Bianchi in the county sheriff's reserves program in Bellingham described Bianchi: "He was a little off. Always talking about psychology and stuff, but in a way that made you know he didn't know what he was talking about. Nice guy, though. Wouldn't want him as a cop. I wouldn't have trusted his backing me up. Not aggressive enough. Just a nice guy. A bit of a nut, but not the kind to murder anyone" (Schwarz, 1981, pp. 117–118).

Bianchi met his live-in girlfriend in Los Angeles in 1976. They lived together on and off for about two years. In the summer of 1978 they argued often and the girl moved to Bellingham, Washington. Bianchi moved there shortly thereafter and they resumed living together. After Bianchi's confessions to the murders in Washington and California, the girlfriend became convinced that Bianchi had a multiple personality. She stated, "How else could he have killed those women and then come home to me as though nothing had happened? Maybe he could have fooled me once or twice, but for three years!" (*Bellingham Herald*, January 1, 1980, p. 1).

A former girlfriend of Bianchi's testified at Buono's trial that she had lived with Bianchi in 1976. She said that she had broken up with him in late 1976 and that for more than a year Bianchi had continuously harassed her by stealing items from her apartment, cutting up her sandals with a razor blade, ripping up her nightgown, and pounding on the outside walls to her apartment.

CONTACT WITH DEFINING AGENCIES

Bianchi had joined the sheriff's reserve in Bellingham. He had been the first private security officer accepted by that organization. He had been scheduled to attend a meeting of the reserve on the night the two girls disappeared in Bellingham. Bellingham police learned that he did not attend the meeting that night. When police found out that Bianchi had been out in a security vehicle that night and that he had been made aware that the keys were missing from the home that the missing girls were supposedly house-sitting, they became suspicious. Then the police learned that Bianchi had called a nearby neighbor and told her not to go near the house that night because of alarm work being done on the house. Nothing appeared to be wrong in the house, although someone had been there recently. When the strangled girls' bodies were found in their car the following day, the police immediately arrested Bianchi. Bianchi surrendered willingly to the police, stating that he had killed no one.

Kenneth Bianchi had become a suspect very quickly in the Bellingham case. Bianchi consistently and calmly maintained that he was innocent even though police had found long blond hairs probably belonging to one of the victims and pubic hairs matching those of Bianchi in the Bellingham house where the victims were supposed to be house-sitting. His attorney requested the assistance of psychiatrist Donald Lunde. Bianchi told Lunde about his love-filled, joyous, and tranquil childhood. Bianchi's recollection did not match medical and psychiatric records from his childhood. Lunde was forced to conclude that Ken was repressing much of his past and possibly might not remember the stranglings (Levin and Fox, 1985, p. 149).

By now his attorney was not only skeptical of Bianchi's alibis, but of his sanity. Bianchi resisted his attorney's argument to enter an insanity plea. John Watkins, an expert in hypnosis was called in to try to restore Bianchi's memory. During one of the hypnosis sessions, Watkins discovered the emergence of a second personality, called "Steve Walker." Bianchi's second personality, who appeared sadistic and boastful, proudly talked about his killings in Bellingham and Los Angeles. He stated that Angelo Buono, his cousin, had killed with him in Los Angeles. Based on Watkins's discovery of this second personality, Bianchi's attorney concluded that Bianchi was not legally sane at the time of the murders. After videotapes of Watkins's interviews with him were shown to Bianchi, he agreed to allow his attorney to plead not guilty by reason of insanity.

Because of this change of plea, the judge in Bellingham called in Ralph Allison, an expert on multiple personalities and altered ego states, as an independent advisor to the court. Allison hypnotized Bianchi and was also confronted with Bianchi's second personality, Steve, who boasted of the murders. Allison took Bianchi back to his childhood through hypnosis and learned that the second personality or altered ego had been invented by Bianchi when he was 9 years old. Allison concluded to the court that Bianchi was a dual personality, not aware of his crimes and incompetent to stand trial.

The prosecutor who disagreed with the conclusions regarding Bianchi's dual personality requested that Martin Orne, a psychiatrist with the University of Pennsylvania Medical School, be called in to examine Bianchi. Rather than attempting to authenticate Bianchi's multiple personality, Orne devised tests to determine the authenticity of Bianchi's hypnotic trance. Orne told Bianchi before hypnotizing him that it was rare in cases of multiple personalities for there to be only two personalities. When Bianchi was hypnotized, another personality surfaced, called "Billy." On another occasion while hypnotized, Orne asked Bianchi to talk to his attorney, who was not actually in the room. Bianchi complied with Orne's request, even shaking the hand of his attorney, who was not there. When Bianchi's attorney was asked to come into the room, Bianchi stated, "How can I see him in two places?" (Barnes, 1984)

Based on the third personality, which had been suggested by Orne prior to hypnosis, the fact that a hypnotized person ordinarily does not question the existence of two of the same people, and other tests, Orne concluded that Bianchi was faking hypnosis and thus faking his multiple personalities. Books on psychology had been found in Bianchi's home, including one on hypnotic techniques. This seemed to support Orne's conclusion; however, there was no real proof that Bianchi was faking a hypnotic trance and the existence of a multiple personality.

While checking into his background in Los Angeles, investigators found a copy of Bianchi's transcript from Los Angeles Valley College. The transcript had an incorrect date of birth and listed courses that had been taken before Bianchi had moved to Los Angeles. The original transcript revealed that the transcript had originally belonged to Thomas Steven Walker. Further investigation revealed that Bianchi had placed an advertisement in the *Los Angeles Times* requesting applications for a counseling position to send in their résumé and college transcript. When Walker sent in his transcript, Bianchi substituted his own name on the transcript and used the transcript to further his own career.

Although an alter ego could presumably mimic a real identity, like Steve Walker, Bianchi first saw Walker's name as an adult, whereas "Stevie Walker" had appeared under hypnosis when Bianchi regressed back to the age of 9. Although it is possible that two Steve Walkers appeared in Bianchi's life by coincidence, it was more likely that Bianchi was faking hypnosis (Levin and Fox, 1985, p. 153).

On June 1, 1979, psychiatrist Saul Faerstein examined Bianchi at the request of the judge. At the end of his report to the judge, Faerstein discussed Bianchi's motivation and long-standing interest in the police:

> I would like to add one note of speculation which may shed some light on the motivation for these crimes. From his earliest years, Kenneth Bianchi admired and dreamed of becoming a law enforcement officer. He drew the figure of a policeman in a childhood Draw-A-Person test. He studied police science at junior college. He applied to law enforcement agencies for jobs in New York, California and Washington, but he was always rejected. Perhaps he saw his goal as the achievement of some victory over his mother whom he saw as another authority figure. All these rejections by law enforcement agencies made him bitter. In the long string of murders he committed, he demonstrated that he had mastered the science of law enforcement and that he was a better policeman than any policeman on the force. He left no clues. He went undetected for over a year. So in the process of achieving his victory over the female authority figure by killing her surrogates, he also vanquished the male authority figure by eluding the police, sheriffs, and detectives. (Schwarz, 1981, p. 218)

Since the multiple personality was no longer believable, Bianchi's lawyer negotiated a plea with the prosecutors in Bellingham, Washington, and Los Angeles County, California. He would enter a plea of guilty to the murders in Bellingham and to five of the murders in California if he would not be given the death penalty. In return, Bianchi would testify against his cousin, Angelo Buono, in California.

Angelo Buono was arrested in Los Angeles on October 18, 1979, for 10 of the "strangler" murders, shortly after Bianchi entered a plea of guilty in

Washington. The only substantial evidence against Buono was Bianchi's testimony. Buono was also charged with a number of nonmurder felonies and misdemeanors, including sodomy, pimping, pandering, and conspiracy to commit extortion and oral copulation involving an outcall prostitution scheme Buono and Bianchi were accused of operating in 1977. In March 1980, two young women reportedly told a Los Angeles County grand jury that they had been engaged in a prostitution and extortion operation with Buono and Bianchi in 1977. Buono was arraigned on these nonmurder indictments on March 27, 1980. Buono was appointed private counsel by the court since the regular public defender's office in Los Angeles County could not defend Buono, due to a conflict of interest—they were representing Bianchi. Buono was eligible for court-appointed representation since prior to his arrest while under police surveillance he had given his home and business to his neighbor through a quit-claim deed. The first part of Buono's preliminary hearing in the summer of 1980 dealt with the nonmurder charges. The second part dealt specifically with the 10 counts of murder. The hearing was closed to the press and media at the request of Buono's attorneys and was granted by the presiding judge. On June 20, 1980, Buono was allowed by the judge to fire his court-appointed attorneys. The judge appointed new attorneys to defend Buono, and the second part of the hearing was delayed for 10 days. On March 16, Buono was bound over for trial after the longest preliminary hearing ever held in Los Angeles County (involving 120 days of testimony).

Shortly after his arrival in California, Bianchi wrote a letter to Dr. Allison, one of the psychiatrists who had examined him in Bellingham, stating that he had not personally killed any of the strangler victims. When the Los Angeles district attorney's office confronted Bianchi with this change in his story, he reportedly said that he had not told them initially that Buono did all the killings because he was afraid they would not believe him if he did not also implicate himself (*Los Angeles Times*, October 22, 1980, p. 1). In early October 1980, Bianchi's jailers seized some papers in his cell, including a 43-page document entitled "an open letter to the world," in which Bianchi denied participation in any murder. On October 2 just prior to this letter being seized, a woman who had been visiting Bianchi in jail was arrested in Los Angeles for attempting a "copycat" version of the two murders in Bellingham, Washington, that Bianchi had confessed to committing. She was charged by Bellingham authorities with the attempted strangling of a woman, who she had lured to a downtown hotel in Bellingham. The woman was also accused of sending a series of tape recordings to law enforcement authorities with a message that Bianchi was the wrong man and that more murders would be committed by the real killer. The woman had told law enforcement officers and the press that Bianchi could not have committed the strangler murders because he was in bed with her on the nights that the victims had been abducted and killed. She claimed that she had met Bianchi in 1977. Police, however, had learned that the woman's first contact with Bianchi was by mail in January 1980. Police believe that all of this woman's actions were coordinated by Bianchi during her visits to him in jail in an effort to free Bianchi of all charges. The woman was later convicted of attempted murder in Bellingham and sentenced to life in prison.

Prior to Buono's trial scheduled for July 1981, the Los Angeles County district attorney filed a motion for dismissal of charges against Buono, due to Bianchi's lack of credibility as a witness. The judge, in an unusual move, denied the motion, and the prosecution of Buono was moved into the hands of the office of the attorney general of California.

When the trial began in November 1981, it took five months to choose a jury, due to the highly publicized nature of the case. The trial lasted a total of two years and two days and was the longest trial in the history of the United States. The prosecution's key witness was Kenneth Bianchi, who testified for a total of 80 days. Bianchi described how the abductions took place, how the victims were tortured and killed, and how the victims' bodies were discarded. His testimony, however, changed frequently. At one point he stated, "The strangulations I don't remember. I remember the women were alive and picked up and . . . dead and . . . dropped off" (*Los Angeles Times*, July 1, 1982). As to what happened in between these times, he stated he did not know. At other times he was particularly graphic in his descriptions of the killings, but the descriptions changed with his further testimony.

On March 14, 1982, the California Supreme Court ruled that witnesses whose memory had been enhanced through hypnosis could not testify in criminal trials. This ruling effectively barred some witnesses for the prosecution from testifying who would have linked Buono to some of the victims. The ruling, however, did not bar Bianchi's testimony since the presiding judge had ruled that Bianchi had "voluntarily and consciously faked hypnosis" (*Los Angeles Times*, March 15, 1982, p. 3).

Late in the trial in June 1983, the woman who had attempted the "copycat" killing in Bellingham testified for the defense. She had been found guilty of attempted murder in Washington. She stated that she and Bianchi had conspired to frame Buono for the strangler murders. She and Bianchi had planned to testify falsely that Buono had confessed to the murders and told them he had an accomplice other than Bianchi. She stated further that Bianchi had directed her to go to Bellingham and commit a murder to show that the accomplice was still at large (*Los Angeles Times*, June 22, 1983, p. 1).

After 345 days and the testimony of over 400 witnesses, the case went to the jury on October 20, 1983. The jury found Buono guilty of 9 of the 10 counts of murder. The "not guilty" verdict was for the first victim. In this case the body of the victim had not had the ligature marks of the other nine victims, and microscopic fibers from the chair in Buono's house were not found on her body as they had been with the other victims. The verdicts of the jury included a finding of "special circumstances of multiple murder," which in California dictates that there are only two possible sentences to be given: life imprisonment without parole eligibility, or death. Following his conviction, it was revealed that at one time prior to the trial Buono's attorney had been offered a life sentence with possible parole for his client by the Los Angeles County District Attorney's Office if Buono would plead guilty. Buono had rejected the offer.

Buono requested that he be allowed to defend himself during the penalty phase of the trial. After the presiding judge determined that Buono's understanding of the law applicable to the penalty phase was too limited, he denied the request. The jury recommended life imprisonment without parole possibility. On January 9, 1984, the judge sentenced Buono to life imprisonment without the possibility of parole. He is currently incarcerated in Folsom State Prison in California. Bianchi was returned to the state of Washington to be incarcerated in Walla Walla State Prison until his first parole hearing in a little less than 27 years. If freed by Washington, Bianchi would then face five consecutive life sentences in California. In late 1984, Bianchi legally changed his name. Later that year he changed it again, to Nicholas Fontana. Bianchi has been denied parole on a number of occasions since his convictions.

On May 6, 1994, the U.S. Court of Appeal in San Francisco rejected Bianchi's challenges to his legal representation and guilty plea in the Washington killings. The court stated that it was not clear whether Bianchi was hypnotized during psychiatric examinations. But even if he was hypnotized, the court said, there was no proof that his memories of the murders were the product of hypnotic suggestion. The prosecution's case against him was strong, and he avoided a possible death sentence by pleading guilty. The court also said that Bianchi's claims of ineffective assistance by his court-appointed lawyer were far outweighed by the evidence against him (*San Francisco Chronicle*, May 7, 1994, p. A21).

OFFENSE BEHAVIOR

Within two months, 11 females between the ages of 12 and 28 had been found strangled in Los Angeles County, California. Seven of the victims had been raped. Eight were found within a six-mile radius of the city of Glendale. Two of the victims, ages 12 and 14, had last been seen together at a local shopping center in Glendale. Their bodies were found a week later near Dodger Stadium. Six of the victims were known to have been heavily involved in the nightlife of Hollywood Boulevard. One had been seen frequently in an area where prostitutes gathered at Hollywood and Vine streets.

One was a local runaway well known on the streets of Hollywood. One had worked as a waitress in Hollywood. One had moved to Hollywood after being convicted of prostitution in the state of New York. One was a Hollywood resident and a chronic hitchhiker and the last was frequently seen in the area trying to get into show business.

The nude body of the first victim was discovered alongside Forest Lawn Drive near Forest Lawn Cemetery. She was a 19-year-old part-time prostitute. She had been manually strangled. Almost two weeks later a second victim was found on a roadside in Glendale. The 15-year-old girl was nude and had ligature marks around the wrists, ankles, and neck. She had been raped and sodomized.

Between October 18 and November 29, 1977, eleven victims were found dumped by their assailants in a similar manner. The victims were all found nude, strangled, and left in remote areas of the county. The majority had been sexually assaulted. Most of them bore ligature marks similar to those of the second victim.

On December 14, 1977, a twelfth female victim was found strangled and nude in a residential area east of Silver Lake (*Los Angeles Times*, December 15, 1977, p. 1). An autopsy revealed that she had not been sexually assaulted. The victim had been employed by an outcall "modeling" service and known to have worked as a prostitute. The victim had been reported missing shortly after 10:00 P.M. on December 13 after she had failed to make her customary check-in call at 10:00. The victim had been sent to what turned out to be a vacant apartment in Los Angeles. Her abandoned auto was found nearby. It was learned later that the original call for modeling services had been placed from a telephone booth in the Hollywood branch of the Los Angeles City Library.

Almost two months later a thirteenth victim was found. The victim, a 20-year-old female who lived in Glendale, was discovered nude and strangled in the trunk of her car, which was found in a ravine near a highway in the Angeles National Forest. She had been seen last near her home in the afternoon of February 16, 1978 and discovered at 9:45 A.M. the following morning. This was the last victim of what was now being referred to as the "Hillside Strangler."

On January 11, 1979, Kenneth Bianchi had lured two girls in Bellingham to an unoccupied house by offering them a house-sitting job. He met them there and forced them into the house at gunpoint. He bound them with rope, sexually assaulted them, and then strangled them. He then put them in their car and drove it to a deserted cul-de-sac, where he left the car. He was quickly linked to the girls' disappearance and arrested. When Bianchi's home was searched, a number of stolen items were found that had been taken from houses where Bianchi had been assigned as a security guard.

Thus almost a year after the last "Hillside" victim had been found, following a double murder in Bellingham, Washington, and Kenneth Bianchi's arrest and subsequent confession, the task force in Los Angeles would learn that 10 of the 13 victims attributed to the "Hillside Strangler" had been killed by Angelo Buono and Kenneth Bianchi. According to Levin and Fox (1985), by one account Bianchi and Buono reportedly were sitting around Buono's house one day when they began talking about what it must feel like to kill someone. They decided to try it. Except for the first victim who was killed in an automobile, the other nine victims had been kidnapped and taken to Buono's home in Glendale, where they were tortured and killed. One had been injected with a cleaning fluid and gassed with a hose from the oven in the home. Another was tortured and burned with an electric cord before her death. Bianchi's girlfriend, who lived with him during the time the murders were committed, said that Bianchi had been gone a lot at night during this time.

The killers had reportedly first asked each of the victims to go to the bathroom, to avoid their urinating involuntarily right after death (Los Angeles Times, November 15, 1983, p. 6). The victims were each tied by their arms, legs, and neck to a special chair in Buono's spare bedroom. Each was then raped, sodomized with various instruments, and strangled to death. Nine of the bodies were then tossed on roadsides and hillsides in Los Angeles and Glendale. The last victim was put into the trunk of her car, which was then pushed down a ravine.

Bianchi told police that he and Buono would frequently flip a coin to see who would rape the victims first before they were murdered. He also stated that many of the victims had plastic bags placed over their heads before they were slowly strangled to death by tightening a rope around their necks. He stated that on one occasion he took Polaroid pictures of Buono raping one of the victims (Los Angeles Times, March 2, 1982, p. 1).

Buono had promoted Bianchi as a casting director and location scout for Universal Studios. Bianchi had played this role with a number of women. However, in most cases the victims had apparently been lured into going with Buono and Bianchi because the two had been posing as police officers. Witnesses stated they had seen Buono with a badge and handcuffs. Police proved that Buono had owned a police-type badge by an impression left in a wallet found in his home. Bianchi was known by a number of people to have police badges. Also police learned that Bianchi had reportedly obtained an official Los Angeles county seal from an aide to a county supervisor. The blue and white Cadillac that Bianchi drove while in Los Angeles was impounded by police with this seal still affixed to the windshield. The daughter of the late actor Peter Lorre identified Buono and Bianchi as the men who posed as vice-squad officers and tried to force her into their car on a Hollywood street during the fall of 1977 (Los Angeles Times, July 22, 1981).

Buono reportedly kept one woman a virtual prisoner in his home for three weeks in the summer of 1977. She testified at the trial that she was beaten by both Buono and Bianchi. She and another woman were apparently forced into prostitution by the duo. While neither were allowed to testify to the specific acts of prostitution, since these charges were pending against Buono and were to be tried separately by court ruling, police investigation reportedly has shown that the women did commit acts of prostitution under Buono and Bianchi's direction (*Los Angeles Times*, March 11, 1982, p. 8).

Following Buono's arrest he talked of demolishing his home where the murders were believed to have taken place. A search of his home at this time revealed that Buono's house was completely bare of any fingerprints. Forensic experts testified at the trial that fibers found on two of the victims matched fibers found in Buono's house. Following Buono's trial and his sentencing, those who prosecuted the case stated, "We still don't know how they did the strangulations and how they worked together" (*Los Angeles Daily News*, January 14, 1985, p. 10).

SELF CONCEPT

Bianchi had bragged about his killings as "Steve Walker," one of his other alleged personalities. He had also talked of hating women under this alter ego. The clues to Bianchi's self concept appear to be so conflicting and contradictory that determining Bianchi's self-image becomes an empirically based guarantee for failure. Although Darcy O'Brien's (1985) book, *Two of a Kind*, presents a reconstruction of many of the killings that Bianchi and Buono committed, a reconstruction is not an accurate rendition of what was said and done but only the author's best guess of what transpired. For this reason, O'Brien's material has not been used, but no criticism of the book is intended.

ATTITUDES

When Kenneth Bianchi pled guilty to the two murders in Bellingham, Washington, he stated: "I can't find the words to express the sorrow for what I've done. In no way can I take away the pain I have given others, and in no way can I expect forgiveness from others" (Schwarz, 1981, p. 239). Bianchi was sobbing and crying as he made this statement. Some would contend that he was truly a sick man with a multiple personality and truly sorry for what he had done. Others would argue that he was crying out of frustration because he had been caught. Psychiatrists still disagree over Kenneth Bianchi.

RECALL OF EVENTS

Bianchi was able to remember minute details about his victims. He gave only limited details of the actual killings and frequently changed his recollection of these events. Buono never spoke of the killings and consistently maintained his innocence.

CHAPTER 9

—◆—

THEODORE ROBERT BUNDY:
CASE STUDY

SOCIAL ENVIRONMENT

Not a great deal has been revealed of Bundy's early childhood. His fourth-grade teacher stated that "Ted was neither good nor bad, happy, well adjusted and always eager to learn" (Larsen, 1980, p. 92). He talked of being a policeman or a lawyer when he grew up. According to Robert Keppel, a detective from Seattle who spent a great deal of time delving into his background, information was sketchy on Bundy's early years, "mainly because the crucial people we talked to—his cousin, his mother—have this particular image of him where he could do no wrong" (Larsen, 1980, p. 99). Keppel reports that Bundy displayed babyish tendencies up to the fifth grade in school. He was a loner who didn't want to get involved with too many people at a time. He could do superior work in school when he wanted to and liked to foster the impression that he always did superior work. Keppel describes his character at this time as too good for any sort of discipline.

Bundy had been born out of wedlock and his mother later married when he was 4 years old. The Bundys were not well off financially, but neither were they poverty stricken. Upper lower class would best describe their socioeconomic level when Ted Bundy was growing up. Following his mother's marriage, the family reportedly moved several times over a four-year period in Tacoma. While Bundy was adjusting to his new father, he was also dealing with family moves around the city. Bundy comments on this period in his life by saying, "Life was not as sweet, but not a nightmare" (Winn and Merrill, 1980, p. 105). This was a difficult and sometimes lonely period of readjustment for Bundy.

On the surface Bundy's teenage years could be characterized as fairly typical for a young man growing up in Tacoma, Washington, in the 1950s and early 1960s. Following junior high school, he participated in little league baseball and high school football. He was a Boy Scout and ran unsuccessfully for the student council in high school. He was a member of the high school cross-country team. However, these activities were tried only once and then Ted moved on to something else.

During high school he felt at ease in only two environments: the ski slopes and the classroom. Bundy found a lot of enjoyment in skiing and is believed to have stolen his expensive ski gear. Although he was considered a scholar by many of his fellow students, Bundy graduated from Wilson High School with only a B- average.

At age 13 he was reportedly very naive about sex and would shy away from any discussion of the subject. In high school Bundy never appeared interested in girls. He had one date in his three years of high school. Bundy would later argue that he was "particularly dense, or insensitive, not knowing when a woman's interested in me. I've been described as handsome and all this shit or attractive. I don't believe it. It's a built-in insecurity. I don't believe I'm attractive" (Michaud and Aynesworth, 1983, pp. 55–56). Bundy's best friend in high school describes him as being a very sensitive person.

He was considered a very private and introverted person. His IQ was tested at 122. He earned above-average grades but was not considered an outstanding student. Bundy's neighbors remember him during this time as serious, nice, and polite, not a troublemaker and rather quiet.

Bundy had three goals in life; to become married and have a family life, to be a lawyer, and to get involved in politics. His heroes were Senator J. William Fulbright, Nelson Rockefeller, and later, Governor Daniel Evans. Upon completing college he dreamed of going to law school and remarked, "but money's a real problem" (Winn and Merrill, 1980, p. 4). Within the next three years he would attend two different law schools and for a brief period become very active in politics.

During the summer of 1965, after graduating from high school, he worked at a warehouse in Tacoma and purchased his first car, a 1933 Plymouth coupe. That fall he entered the University of Puget Sound in Tacoma. He purchased a 1958 Volkswagen during his first year of college. Bundy would state later, "I just love Volkswagens!" (Larsen, 1980, p. 111) He transferred to the

University of Washington in Seattle to major in Asian studies in the fall of 1966. In the summer of 1967, Bundy attended the Stanford Chinese Institute in Stanford, California. In the fall of 1967 he changed his major to urban planning and sociology and withdrew from the University of Washington with several incompletes in the winter quarter of 1968. He traveled to Aspen, Colorado, to California, and to Philadelphia to visit his grandparents. Upon returning to Seattle in the spring of 1968, Bundy committed numerous crimes of shoplifting and burglary and then became involved in politics as a volunteer in a campaign for the Republican nominee for lieutenant governor.

During his campaign activities Bundy began using more alcohol and often got drunk. He became the nominee's official driver and made a number of political contacts and acquaintances. According to Bundy, it was during this period that he lost his virginity, at age 22, by being seduced by an older woman after he had gotten intoxicated (Michaud and Aynesworth, 1983, p. 62).

He traveled to Philadelphia in early 1969 and attended Temple University, taking classes in urban affairs and theatrical arts. Bundy returned to Seattle in the summer of 1969 and rented a room near the University of Washington. He reentered the university in the summer of 1970 and graduated in the spring of 1972 with a degree in psychology. In 1972 he applied to a number of law schools. While he was given high character references from his college professors, his academic record and his law school aptitude test scores were not impressive. He was rejected by the law schools. Bundy became very active in Governor Dan Evans' reelection campaign in 1972. In February 1973, Bundy reapplied to the University of Utah College of Law with a glowing character reference from Governor Evans and was accepted. He decided at the last minute, late in the summer, not to attend law school that fall and lied to the school that he had suffered serious injuries in an auto accident.

In late 1974 and early 1975, Bundy attended night classes at the University of Puget Sound Law School. He was not happy with the school and dropped out. In the spring of 1974 he applied again to the University of Utah and was accepted. He attended law school there through the fall semester of 1975. Later, after being convicted of aggravated kidnapping, he stated that the two greatest goals in his life were to return to law school and get active in the church.

Bundy met his first real girlfriend at age 20 while at the University of Washington in 1966. She was from a wealthy family in San Francisco. It was at her urging that he had attended Stanford in the summer of 1967. That same summer, his girlfriend broke up with him. Bundy's second romance began in September 1969, when he met a divorcee with a young child who was living in Seattle. After three months they talked of marriage. Bundy changed his mind, but the relationship continued. He was involved sexually with his second girlfriend and after a while began experimenting by tying her up with nylon stockings prior to intercourse. On one occasion after tying her up, he started strangling her during intercourse. She stopped him and the experiments ceased.

Ted Bundy worked at a number of jobs to pay his way through college: at the Seattle Yacht Club as a busboy, at a Safeway store stocking shelves, at a surgical supply house as a stockboy, as a legal messenger, and as a shoe salesman. His summer jobs included working at a sawmill and a power company in Tacoma. In 1968, Bundy was the office manager for the Draft Rockefeller Headquarters in downtown Seattle. In 1971, he was a work-study student at Seattle's Crisis Clinic, where he met Ann Rule, a volunteer, who would later write a book about him, *The Stranger Beside Me*, published in 1980. In 1972 he worked on Evans' political campaign taping opponents' speeches, posing as a political science graduate student doing research and reported directly to the governor. He also worked as a counselor at a psychiatric outpatient clinic for four months that year. In October he began working as the assistant director of the Seattle Crime Prevention Commission and conducted some research on rape and white-collar crime. He resigned from this position in January 1973, when he was not selected for the director's position. The same month Bundy obtained a consulting contract with King County to study recidivism among misdemeanor offenders in the county jail. In April 1973, Bundy was given a political job as an aide to the chairman of the Washington State Republican party.

Ted Bundy appeared to be living by the rules of society. He had held jobs in law enforcement–related positions. From his early childhood he had been interested in a career in law enforcement. In April 1973, he had caught a purse snatcher at a shopping mall in Seattle. He had been involved in politics and had held responsible positions within the Republican party. During his teens he had saved a young girl from drowning. However, Ted Bundy had committed a number of thefts by shoplifting and breaking into homes. In 1973 he had also become a voyeur, walking the streets of Seattle late at night.

By the early 1970s Bundy was considered a sharp dresser and a compulsively neat and orderly person. He was seen as a young man with charming ways, good looks, and a steady social life when he wanted it. When he was arrested in Utah for evading a police officer in August 1975, he was attending law school, working part-time as a university security guard, and about to join the Mormon church.

FAMILY BACKGROUND

Born Theodore Robert Cowell on November 24, 1946, to his mother Eleanor Louise Cowell, at the Elizabeth Lund Home for Unwed Mothers in Burlington, Vermont, he lived with his grandparents, his mother, and her two sisters in the Roxborough section of northwest Philadelphia until 1950. In 1950 his mother had his last name changed to Nelson and she moved with her son to Tacoma, Washington, to live with relatives. In May 1951, his mother married John C. Bundy. Bundy adopted Ted and changed his last name to Bundy.

John and Eleanor had two boys and two girls, half-brother and half-sisters to Ted. His mother worked as a secretary at the University of Puget Sound near home. His stepfather was a cook at an Army hospital south of Tacoma. Ted did not get along well with his stepfather and refused to use him as a role model. He had memories of his grandfather in Pennsylvania, who was closer to being a father figure for him. Ted's mother was the dominant force in the family. Bundy states that she "paid all the bills and never used force or anger" (Larsen, 1980, p. 155). However, Bundy would later comment sarcastically in a Tallahassee, Florida, jail regarding his mail, "and not one letter from my beloved mother" (Larsen, 1980, p. 262). He once stated that he grew up believing that his mother was his sister and that he was a late baby born to his grandparents (Rule, 1980, p. 27). Others dispute this (i.e., Michaud and Aynesworth, 1983).

As a boy, Ted had a paper route. He was a member of the Boy Scouts and was active in the Methodist church with his family. He liked school and did well in his studies according to his parents. Bundy states: " We didn't talk a lot about real personal matters, certainly never about sex or any of those things. My mom has trouble talking on intimate, personal terms" (Michaud and Aynesworth, 1983, p. 51).

It is not known when Bundy learned of his illegitimate birth. He was apparently never told by his parents. Bundy states that he found out he was illegitimate at age 13 when he discovered his birth certificate stating "father unknown." Others report that he learned this when he was 18 from his cousin, who taunted him about his birth. Rule (1980) states that he learned of his birth when he traveled to Burlington, Vermont, in 1969 and checked his birth certificate.

While Bundy consistently maintains that his illegitimacy was not important to him, it did seem to upset him. It further strained relations with his stepfather, frequently to the point of outright defiance. Bundy himself does not make the connection; however, Michaud and Aynesworth (1983) argue that there was a contemporary and abrupt halt to his social development concurrent with the discovery of his illegitimacy. Michaud and Aynesworth (1983) offer evidence of this change, assuming that his discovery of illegitimacy was just prior to high school, by quoting Bundy's comment about entering high school. Bundy stated:

> I'm at a loss to describe it even now. Maybe I didn't have the role models at home that could have aided me in school. I don't know. But I felt alienated from

my old friends. They just seemed to move on and I didn't. I don't know why and I don't know if there's an explanation. Maybe it's something that was programmed by some kind of genetic thing. In my early schooling, it seemed like there was no problem in learning what the appropriate social behaviors were. It just seemed like I hit a wall in high school. (p. 55)

Ted Bundy was married to Carole Boone in a Miami, Florida, courtroom during the penalty phase of his criminal trial after being found guilty on two counts of murder. They would later conceive in a Florida prison and his wife would give birth to a baby girl.

PEER-GROUP ASSOCIATION AND PERSONAL RELATIONSHIPS

Bundy describes his teenage years by stating that "social relationships were not that important. I just felt secure with the academic life" (Larsen, 1980, p. 156). He reportedly insisted on showering privately while in junior high and received a great deal of scorn and humiliation from his peers. During his first year of college, he states that he "had a longing for a beautiful coed. But I didn't have the skill or social acumen to cope with it" (Larsen, 1980, p. 93). Bundy's mother remembers: "He got good grades that first year [but] never got into the social life of the school at all. He'd come home, study, sleep, and go back to school" (Michaud and Aynesworth, 1983, p. 57).

During his second year of college he worked at the Seattle Yacht Club and became friends with the pastry cook. She would sometimes fix snacks for him and he was constantly borrowing money from her. She once loaned him money to go to Philadelphia and gave him a ride to the airport. He was dressed in expensive clothes and had expensive ski equipment. He was going to stop off in Aspen, Colorado, to do some skiing. She called to complain to his mother and learned that his mother did not know what he was doing, that he never called home, and she did not know where he was living.

A co-worker describes Bundy as the office manager of the Rockefeller campaign in Seattle: "Ted had control of what he was doing. He was really poised. He was friendly. He was always smiling. He was terribly charismatic. Obviously, he was someone who had a great deal of compassion in dealing with other people" (Larsen, 1980, p. 5). He was noted for his attractiveness and charm. Levin and Fox (1985) suggest that his reassuring tone was developed and polished while working the hotline at Seattle's Crisis Clinic. Ted was described as charming and he made friends easily at law school in Utah. However, he never was directly involved in the social circles of law students. His social contacts were with lawyers in the area and his law professors.

A former girlfriend stated: "If you know him, you can't help but have a great deal of affection for him as a human being" (Larsen, 1980, p. 5). However, she stated that he was always on his guard against letting anyone get close to him. This girl's father stated that Bundy was "extremely moody on occasion. He can be very nice, pleasant, helpful, and then all of a sudden he'll sour on you. It'll look like he's really thinking hard about something" (Winn and Merrill, 1979, p. 99).

His first extensive involvement with a woman occurred during his first year at the University of Washington in 1966. She was older, came from a wealthy family in San Francisco, and frequently provided funds for their dates together. For Bundy the relationship was intense until she broke up with him in the summer of 1967. Ted's brother recalls that this "screwed him up for a while. He came home and seemed pretty upset and moody. I'd never seen him like that before. He's always in charge of his emotions" (Michaud and Aynesworth, 1983, p. 59). Bundy describes this period as "absolutely the pits for me—the lowest time ever" (Michaud and Aynesworth, 1983, p. 59).

In 1968 he developed a close relationship with a divorced woman from Utah who lived near Bundy with her young daughter. They talked of marriage. The relationship lasted for five years.

Bundy kept in contact with his former girlfriend in San Francisco and by 1973 the relationship was reestablished to the point where the woman thought they were engaged. Bundy then refused to write or call her, stating: "I just wanted to prove to myself that I could have married her" (Larsen, 1980, p. 157). During this period he had maintained his relationship with the woman in Seattle.

According to police research, Bundy outwardly made a good impression, was energetic, skillful, and bright, and moved from job to job gaining his education and upwardly mobile. But he was into petty thievery, used his boyish good looks and charm to exploit and manipulate, and lacked the inner discipline to finish any major task (Larsen, 1980, p. 100). Robert Keppel's profile of Bundy described him as a "self-serving manipulator who lied at will, pinched goods from his employers, and stole his girlfriends' cars" (Winn and Merrill, 1980, p. 128).

After conducting a background check on Bundy and watching him in the courtroom, the prosecutor in Aspen, Colorado, said: "As long as he's functioning as a lawyer everything's real cool with Ted. Then when something reminds him that he's the prisoner, you sense those flashes of anger, hostility. He's always got to be the superstar. But he's only good in the first quarter of whatever game he's in. Then something happens" (Larsen, 1980, p. 206).

To the police in Utah he was a "loner, always short of money, a leech and very moody" (Larsen, 1980, p. 153). While in Utah, Bundy was to some extent leading a double life. He was getting heavily involved in the Mormon church, but to his friends in the neighborhood where he lived he never mentioned this involvement. He was sometimes involved with two female relationships at the same time, as he was in 1973 when he was engaged to two different women. Rule (1980) notes that he was keeping two intense relationships going through visitations and correspondence while he was in prison in Utah.

Bundy's charm would become well known. It was a decisive factor in both of his escapes. His charm would affect his jailers, guards, secretaries, and officials at the Aspen courthouse and the Glenwood Springs' jail in Colorado. For example, after a month of being incarcerated, Bundy was on agreeable terms with almost everyone around the jail in Glenwood Springs. He got along well with those who didn't trust him as well as with those who did.

Bundy was still a loner in some of his social circles. At the Crisis Clinic in Seattle, most of the students had strong liberal views. Bundy, however, was a strong conservative Republican. In Utah, the students and neighbors with whom he drank and smoked marijuana were also of a different political philosophy.

Because he could control and manipulate women, they were important to him and he was frequently in their company. Yet he was apart from them and never let them get too close. Rule (1980) describes two Ted Bundys emerging in 1973: "One, the perfect son, the University of Washington student who had graduated 'with distinction,' the fledgling lawyer and politician, and the charming schemer, a man who could manipulate women with ease, whether it be sex or money he desired, and it made no difference if the women were eighteen or sixty-five" (p. 169).

Contact with Defining Agencies

Bundy was arrested in the early morning of August 16, 1975, by a Utah Highway Patrol sergeant for evading a police officer in a southern subdivision of Salt Lake City. Bundy had briefly tried to outrun the officer in his Volkswagen and would later state that he had been smoking marijuana and was trying to air the car out before being stopped. When he was stopped he was cooperative and seemed almost too relaxed to the arresting officer. He was also placed under suspicion for possession of burglary tools based on the items found in his car when stopped: rope, two gloves, a pantyhose mask, strips of torn sheet, a pair of handcuffs, a flashlight, and a box of black plastic garbage bags. Bundy was released later that morning from the county jail on his own recognizance.

The handcuffs found in Bundy's car caused the Salt Lake County sheriff's office to connect him with an attempted kidnapping that had occurred the previous November in Salt Lake City. The assailant in that case had used handcuffs and had driven a Volkswagen. Two days after his arrest he was charged with possession of burglary tools and the police began to investigate him further. They searched his apartment and took pictures of his Volkswagen. He was placed under police surveillance and frequently tried to elude his watchers, sometimes successfully. He sold his Volkswagen and canceled his gas credit card.

The sheriff's office contacted King County, Washington, whose officers had notified them a year previously that Bundy had been a suspect in an investigation of missing women in the Seattle area and was moving to Salt Lake City. Contact was also made to police in Colorado, since ski brochures from Colorado had been found in the search of his apartment. A small ink mark had been found on one brochure describing a motel in Snowmass, Colorado, where the unsolved murder of a woman had occurred.

On October 1, 1975, Bundy stood in a police lineup. His hair had been clipped short and parted on the other side. The kidnap victim and two witnesses identified him as the kidnap assailant. He was charged with aggravated kidnapping and attempted criminal homicide. Bundy spent eight weeks in the Salt Lake City County jail and posted bond on November 11, 1975. On November 26, 1975, he was bound over for trial at a preliminary hearing and charged with aggravated kidnapping. Bundy was again placed under police surveillance while awaiting trial. Again he tried to elude the police and frequently seemed to be toying with them.

Prior to the trial, Bundy's attorney had requested a psychological evaluation of him. The psychologist found: "Good social presence, ego strength and good self-concept, positive self identity. Bundy was highly intellectual, independent, tolerant, responsible and with normal psychosexual development. He had a healthy curiosity about his father. The worst thing was that he showed some hostility on tests. He is an extremely intelligent young man who is *intact psychologically*" [emphasis added] (Winn and Merrill, 1980, p. 154).

In late February 1976 Bundy was tried in a bench trial. During the trial he frequently changed his appearance. For three days in a row he wore different clothing, changed his hair style, and wore different glasses. The prosecution's case rested primarily on the victim's identification of Bundy and her memory since the attempted kidnapping. Bundy was found guilty and a presentence investigative report was ordered by the judge. Not satisfied with the results of the presentence report, on March 22, 1976, the judge delayed sentencing and ordered Bundy to Utah State Prison for a 90-day diagnostic evaluation.

The diagnostic report issued on Bundy on June 22, 1976, was presented with a series of negatives and positives:

Plus Side

High intelligence, no severely traumatizing influences in childhood or adolescence, few distortions in relationship with mother and stepfather, no serious defects in physical development, habits, school adjustment or sexual development and emotional maturation, adequate interest in hobbies and recreational pursuits, average environmental pressures and responsibilities, and no previous attacks of mental illness.

Minus Side

When one tries to understand him, he becomes evasive, somewhat threatened by people unless he feels he can structure the outcome of the relationship, passive-aggressive features were evident, hostility toward diagnosis personnel. (Winn and Merrill, 1980, p. 163)

Bundy's test results on the MMPI reflected a somewhat different view of the man: "A fairly strong conflict was evidenced in the testing profile, that being the subject's fairly strong dependence on women, yet his need to be independent. Mr. Bundy would like a close relationship with females, but is fearful of being hurt by them. In addition, there were indications of general anger, and more particularly, well-masked anger toward women" (Winn and Merrill, 1980, p. 164).

The final diagnostic report was written by psychiatrist Van Austin. Bundy was not found to be psychotic or suffering from schizophrenia. He was found to exhibit some characteristics of a personality disorder. Some features of an antipersonality disorder were found, such as lack of guilt, callousness, and tendency to compartmentalize and rationalize his behavior. Van Austin concluded: "I feel that Mr. Bundy is either a man who has no problems or is smart enough and clever enough to appear to the edge of normal" (Larsen, 1980, p. 159). The doctor stated further that he could not predict his future behavior since there was much more to his personality structure that was not known.

On June 30, 1976, Bundy was sentenced to 1 to 15 years in prison. He would be eligible for parole in approximately 15 months. He began serving his sentence in the Utah State Penitentiary in July. He was placed in medium security and given a work assignment in the print shop. Prison officials and guards considered him to be a respectful, pleasant, and cooperative prisoner. He had no problems with the inmates since he provided legal advice to them. Later that year a search of his cell revealed escape contraband: a forged social security card, an Illinois driver's license, an airline schedule, and a road map. He was disciplined by 15 days in isolation and then transferred to maximum security as an escape risk.

In January 1977, Bundy was extradited to Colorado to stand trial for murder in Aspen, Colorado. He was incarcerated in the Pitkin County jail in Aspen. The judge in Aspen allowed Bundy to act as his own attorney and to appear in street clothes without restraining devices. Bundy continually asked to have his jail security reduced, saying that it hampered his defense preparation. A deputy at the jail stated, "He's smart and very observant. He's making himself just as personable as he can be to everyone around here. He's fine until he wants something" (Winn and Merrill, 1980, p. 180). In April he was moved to the Glenwood Springs jail 40 miles from Aspen.

In April and May of that year police and other prisoners warned jail officials that Bundy might try to escape. He had been practicing jumping off his bunk in his cell. On June 7, 1977, Bundy escaped from a window of the courthouse in Aspen by jumping through a second-story window. He was caught in a stolen car after spending six days in the mountains nearby.

Bundy resumed preparation for his defense after being captured. He worked actively as his own lawyer with legal advisors appointed by the court. He interviewed forensic experts and his briefs on various motions to the court were considered superior. At a pretrial evidentiary hearing he cross-examined his previous kidnap victim so that his kidnap conviction would not be introduced against him at the trial. Late in the year he was granted a change of venue and his trial was assigned to Colorado Springs.

On December 30, 1977, Bundy escaped from the Glenwood Springs, Colorado, jail and disappeared. It was later learned that he sawed through a light fixture in the ceiling of his cell to escape. He traveled to Chicago, Illinois, to Ann Arbor, Michigan, and on to Tallahassee, Florida.

On February 10, 1978, Bundy was placed on the FBI's 10 Most Wanted List. The text of the FBI wanted poster described him as an escapee from Colorado, wanted in the questioning of 36 sexual slayings which began in California in 1969 and extended through the Pacific northwest into Utah and Colorado. Below three different looking photos of Bundy, the text of the poster read:

> Age 31, born November 24, 1946, Height: 5'11" to 6', Weight: 145 to 175 lbs., Build: Slender, athletic, Caution: Bundy, a college educated physical fitness enthusiast with a prior history of escape, is being sought as a prison escapee after being convicted of kidnapping and while awaiting trial involving brutal sex slaying of woman at ski resort. He should be considered armed, dangerous and an escape risk. (Larsen, 1980, p. 2)

On February 14, 1978, he was stopped driving a stolen car in Pensacola, Florida. Bundy resisted arrest and shots were fired by the police officer. He was subdued and placed in the Pensacola jail. At the time of his arrest he was using a false identification and the police did not know his real identity. His identity was learned shortly after his arrest and he immediately came under suspicion for the murders of two women and the assault of others in a sorority house in Tallahassee that had occurred on January 15, 1978. Police learned that he had been confronted by a Leon County deputy in Tallahassee on February 11 about stolen license plates in his car. Bundy had fled on foot and escaped the officer.

Shortly after his arrest, Bundy was interviewed extensively by Pensacola investigators. According to depositions given later in court by these officers, Bundy came very close to confessing to a number of murders. A few days after his arrest Bundy was transferred to the Leon County jail in Tallahassee, Florida.

In March, police took blood and hair samples from Bundy. During that month the court in Leon County denied Bundy's request to have access to a law library and the news media. In late April, Leon County secured a warrant to obtain impressions of Bundy's teeth to see if they matched bite marks on one of the victims in the sorority house murders. Bundy was again denied access to the press by the Leon County judge. During his previous periods of incarceration in jails in Utah and Colorado, Bundy had been in constant contact with the press either by phone, correspondence, or by various press conferences. Many of his comments were controversial and probably prejudicial to his own case. The circuit court judge stated that he was keeping Bundy from the press to guarantee "fundamental fairness and protect Bundy from Bundy" (Larsen, 1980, p. 272). Bundy, however, corresponded with reporters from all over the country during this period.

On July 27, 1978, Bundy was indicted on two counts of murder, three of attempted murder, and two of burglary in the crimes committed at the Chi Omega sorority house on January 15, 1978. This indictment was read to Bundy by the Leon County sheriff in front of television cameras. The sheriff was later reprimanded for this action by the Tallahassee Bar Association. Four days later, Bundy was indicted for murder in the death of a 12-year-old girl in Lake City, Florida. He pled not guilty to each indictment.

The judge denied Bundy's request to have a lawyer from Georgia represent him. Bundy moved to have the judge disqualified. He also filed a civil suit against the Leon County sheriff's office to improve his living and working conditions in jail. The civil suit was later settled out of court and Bundy's lighting in his cell was improved and he was given periods of exercise. In December 1978, the Florida Supreme Court disqualified the judge in Bundy's case due to the "intolerable adversary atmosphere" between Bundy and the judge (Winn and Merrill, 1980, p. 285). In April 1979, the U.S. Supreme Court upheld Bundy's denial of a lawyer from Georgia and his conviction in Utah. Throughout his pretrial period, Bundy was repeatedly trying to exclude TV cameras from the courtroom proceedings. Each time the judge ruled against him.

On May 31, 1979, it appeared that a plea bargain had been struck between the Leon County prosecutor and Bundy's attorneys. Bundy would plead guilty to three counts of murder and receive three consecutive 25-year sentences. On this date, however, Bundy claimed in open court that his defense counsel was ineffective and reneged on the negotiated plea. He stated, "There's only one hang-up with pleading guilty, and that is that you have to plead guilty" (Winn and Merrill, 1980, p. 296).

Tapes of the interviews with Bundy conducted by police officers in Pensacola after his arrest were played for the judge and depositions were given by the interviewing officers. After testimony from his public defenders, the judge ruled that Bundy had been denied his right to counsel during these interviews and ruled the tapes and depositions inadmissible evidence.

In May the court requested psychological examinations of Bundy to determine his legal competency to stand trial. Emmanuel Tanay, a Detroit, Michigan, psychiatrist, and Harvey M. Cleckley, an authority on psychopathic and sociopathic personality disorders, were selected to examine Bundy. Tanay found:

> The pathological need to defy authority, to manipulate his associates and adversaries, supplies him with thrills. He takes pride in his celebrity status. His dealings with the criminal justice system are dominated by psychopathy. It could be argued he [Bundy] is effective in concealing his criminal activities—more accurate to say that he is of two minds on the issue—he attempts to conceal and reveal his involvement. (Larsen, 1980, p. 299)

Cleckley's testimony on Bundy was very similar to Tanay's. Under the legal definition, both psychiatrists agreed that Bundy was competent to stand trial. Tanay referred to Bundy's rejection of the negotiated plea:

> He has a deep seated need for a trial. It will allow him the opportunity to confront and confound various authority figures; judge, prosecutor and defense attorney. In a certain sense, Mr. Bundy is a producer of a play which attempts to show that various authority figures can be manipulated, set against each other. Mr. Bundy does not have the capacity to recognize that the price for this 'thriller' might be his own life. (Larsen, 1980, p. 299)

In June the court determined that Bundy could not receive a fair trial in Tallahassee and changed the venue of the trial to Miami, Florida. During the trial in Miami, Bundy was involved in the cross examination of witnesses and eventually fired his defense team, proceeding as his own counsel, with the defense team as standby counsel. He continually objected to the presence of TV cameras in the courtroom but was overruled by the judge. On July 24, 1979, Bundy was found guilty and given two death sentences and three 90-year sentences to run consecutively.

On January 7, 1980, Bundy was tried for the murder of a 12-year-old girl in Lake City, Florida. On February 7, 1980, he was found guilty as charged. In open court during the penalty phase of the trial he married a woman from Seattle to circumvent authorities' denial of his request to get married. He received the death penalty and was returned to death row in a Florida prison, one of eight places he had been incarcerated in since his arrest in Salt Lake City in 1975. He was executed by the state of Florida in 1989.

Offense Behavior

It must be remembered that Bundy was convicted only for the murders that occurred in Tallahassee and Lake City, Florida, in early 1978. He has never been convicted for the other murders that he was suspected of having committed in Washington, Utah, Oregon, and Colorado. He did, however, confess to many of these murders just prior to his execution.

Eight abductions of females occurred between January and July 1974 in the Pacific northwest which have been attributed to Bundy by law enforcement agencies. On January 31, a 21-year-old girl was taken from her basement apartment in Seattle. Bloodstains were found on her night clothes. The top sheet on her bed and her pillow case were missing as well as some clothes. She had apparently been killed in her bed, dressed, and taken from her apartment. Twenty-seven days earlier a young girl had been found viciously beaten and sexually assaulted nearby in a similar basement apartment.

On March 12 a 19-year-old girl disappeared without a trace on her way to a jazz concert on the Evergreen State College campus in Olympia, Washington. On April 17 an 18-year-old girl left her residence hall on the Central Washington University campus in Olympia, Washington, to attend a meeting across campus and was not seen again. That same evening two girls had encountered a young man on campus near the library at two different times. On each occasion the man solicited their help in carrying his books, claiming an injury to his arm, and led them to his Volkswagen in a darkened area of campus before they fled.

On May 12 a 19-year-old female student at Oregon State University in Corvallis, Oregon, took a walk across campus and was not seen again. On May 31 a young women disappeared from outside a tavern in Seattle. On June 11, an 18-year-old girl disappeared from a well-lighted alley on the way to her sorority house in Seattle. Shortly before this girl disappeared, a young man on crutches with a cast on one leg was seen nearby having difficulty in carrying his briefcase and was offered assistance by a young sorority girl. The man waited while the girl entered a house on an errand and when she returned, he had disappeared.

On July 14 of that year two more girls disappeared from the Lake Sammamish Recreation area near Issaquah and east of Seattle, Washington. One of the missing girls, who was 23-years old, was last seen around noon in the company of a young man with his arm in a sling who called himself "Ted" according to witnesses. "Ted" told her that his sailboat was in Issaquah and he needed help putting it on his Volkswagen to transport it to the lake.

She agreed to help him and left with her bicycle. This man was seen on five separate occasions that day asking females for assistance with his sailboat. The other missing female, who was 19 years old, was last seen about 4:30 that afternoon on her way to the restroom.

All of these missing females were single, had long hair parted in the middle, and were of similar appearance. The first six disappearances occurred in the late evening. The last two disappeared in broad daylight. All disappearances happened within a 250-mile radius of Seattle, Washington.

Fifty-five days after their disappearance, skeletal remains of the girls missing from Lake Sammamish were found in the foothills of the Cascade Mountains four miles east of the lake near Interstate 90. The remains of a third person were also found but could not be identified.

On October 12, 1974, the skeletal remains of two girls were found by a deer path 130 miles south of Issaquah near the Oregon border, 17 miles from Vancouver, Washington. One girl was identified as a girl from Vancouver last seen in August. The other girl was not identified.

All of the aforementioned disappearances had occurred while Ted Bundy was living in Seattle Washington. He was reportedly very familiar with the area east of Seattle where six of the missing girls' bodies had been found. As Robert Keppel noted, Bundy was a man who understood police jurisdictions and boundaries, who was familiar with their vulnerability—their imperfect exchange of information with each other (Larsen, 1980, p. 101).

Rule (1980) notes that Bundy had been picked up at least twice by juvenile authorities in Tacoma for suspicion of auto theft and burglary. She states: "There is no indication that he was ever confined, but his name was known to juvenile caseworkers. The records outlining the details of the incidents have long been shredded—procedures when a juvenile reaches eighteen. Only a card remains with his name and offense listed (p. 11).

According to Michaud and Aynesworth (1983), who interviewed him extensively in a Florida prison, when Bundy returned to Seattle from Philadelphia in 1968 he became involved in a great deal of property crime. He shoplifted and broke into homes. Apparently, he continued to steal and shoplifted intermittently until he left Seattle in 1974.

Bundy's girlfriend in Seattle had become suspicious of him during the disappearances of the girls in Washington and Oregon. He had a number of unexplained absences during the nighttime. He frequently slept during the day. Bundy would periodically hide in the bushes near her home and jump out and frighten her. She found surgical gloves in his jacket pocket and she observed a package of plaster of paris and crutches in his apartment. She stated that Bundy kept a lug wrench under the seat of her car and a knife in the glove compartment. His girlfriend also claimed that she had once found a bag of women's clothing in his room.

He moved to Salt Lake City, Utah, in September 1974. On the evening of October 18, 1974, a young girl disappeared while walking in the streets of Midvale, Utah, a suburban community near Salt Lake City. Her nude body was found a week later in Summit Park in a canyon of the Wasatch Mountains east of Salt Lake City. She had been badly beaten, strangled with nylons, and raped. The autopsy determined that she had been killed elsewhere.

On October 31, 1974, a young girl disappeared from American Fork, Utah, after leaving a Halloween party. American Fork is approximately 25 miles south of Salt Lake City. On November 8, eight days later in Murray, Utah, which is just south of Salt Lake City and north of American Fork, a young woman was lured to the parking lot of a local shopping mall by a man who then attacked her with a tire iron. She escaped unharmed. The man was driving a light-colored Volkswagen.

On November 11, 1974, a man posing as a police officer approached a young girl in a shopping mall in Salt Lake City in the early evening and stated that someone had been seen prowling near her car. He asked her to check the car, to see if anything was missing. After finding nothing missing from her car, the man then led her to what he said was a police substation. The door was locked and he then asked her to accompany him downtown to sign a complaint against the prowler who had allegedly been arrested by his partner. He showed her his police identification and then led her to a light-colored Volkswagen with scratches and dents and a tear in the back seat. He drove her for a short distance in his car and then abruptly stopped and tried to handcuff her. She struggled and fled the car, at which time he tried to strike her with a tire iron. She resisted and escaped into the street with handcuffs on one wrist, where a passing motorist stopped and picked her up.

A half-hour later in Bountiful, Utah, just north of Salt Lake City, a young man stopped a woman backstage at a high school musical and asked her to come outside to the parking lot and identify a car for him. She declined, stating she was too busy with the musical. Thirty minutes later the man again asked the same woman for assistance in the parking lot and she again declined. The man was seen a few minutes later pacing near the rear of the theater. Toward the end of the musical this same man sat down in the audience near the woman he had asked for assistance earlier. His hair was mussed and he was breathing heavily. A young girl attending the musical with her parents left the theater during the third act to pick up her brother nearby and disappeared. During a search of the high school the following day a handcuff key was found just outside the school's south door.

On November 27, the body of the girl missing from American Fork, Utah, was found near a hiking trial on the north slope of Mount Timpanogos in the Wasatch Mountains. Like the girl found in Summit Park, this girl had been sexually assaulted, bludgeoned on the head, strangled with nylons, and stripped naked. These girls were found within 20 miles of each other.

On January 12, 1975, a young woman disappeared from a ski lodge in Snowmass, Colorado. She was there on a vacation from Michigan with friends and was last seen on the second floor of the lodge. On February 17, 1975, her body was found lying in the snow between Aspen and Snowmass Village. The autopsy revealed that she had received severe head injuries and had been raped.

In March 1975, four of the girls missing from Seattle and Ellensburg, Washington and Corvallis, Oregon, were found on Taylor Mountain southeast of Seattle and 10 miles east of where the Lake Sammamish victims were found. The victims' skulls had been fractured.

In March of that year a young woman disappeared from Vail, Colorado, while on her way to visit a friend at a local bar. In April of that year a young girl disappeared while riding her bicycle in Grand Junction, Colorado. Her bicycle was found under a bridge, her sandals nearby. On April 25 a girl disappeared on her way home from high school in Nederland, Colorado. On April 23 her body was found 15 miles away off a county road. Her clothes had been partially torn off, her skull had been fractured, and her hands were bound.

In 1977 following his conviction and incarceration in a Utah prison, Bundy was transferred to Colorado, where he escaped twice. His escapes from Colorado authorities were well planned. In each case he had conned his captors into loosening security. His first escape, from the Pitkin County courthouse in Aspen, freed him for six days. He was arrested in a stolen car in Aspen after spending most of his time on foot in the mountains. His second escape, from the Glenwood Springs jail, freed him for 43 days, during which time he took the lives of two college coeds and a 12-year old girl over a 1000 miles away.

In early January, when Ted Bundy arrived in Tallahassee, Florida, by bus, he was traveling under a false identity. Each day he changed his appearance by parting his hair differently, wearing different glasses, cutting off his mustache, and then growing it again. He committed a number of property crimes: shoplifting of food, theft of a bicycle, theft of numerous credit cards from women's purses in libraries and restaurants, and breaking into an auto and stealing a TV set, radio, and typewriter.

In the early morning hours of January 15, 1978, Ted Bundy killed. He entered the Chi Omego sorority house in Tallahassee shortly after 3:00 A.M. and within approximately 15 minutes had beaten five different girls as they slept in their rooms on the second floor of the house. Two of these girls he killed by strangling them with pantyhose. They had been beaten viciously about the head and body. One of the deceased had bite marks on her left buttock and one of her nipples had been bitten off. A pantyhose mask was found next to one of the victims. Bundy was seen leaving the sorority house and later identified by a witness at his trial. One and one-half hours later Bundy struck again four blocks away from the sorority house. He attacked and beat a girl as she was sleeping in her apartment. The attack was heard in the adjacent apartment and police were summoned. Bundy escaped and the victim survived. At 5:00 A.M. that morning Bundy was seen in front of his apartment house, four blocks from the Chi Omega house.

From January 21 until his arrest in Pensacola, Bundy was busy committing a variety of crimes. On the twenty-first he stole a student's wallet and used the student's credit cards for the next 10 days. By February 1 he had obtained a birth certificate of the owner of the wallet he had stolen. On February 6 he stole a Florida State University van and the license plates from another car. On February 7 he bought gas with a stolen credit card in Jacksonville. On February 8 he bought gas in Lake City and tried to pick up a 14-year-old girl by posing as a fireman. The girl got the license number of the van. That same night he stayed at a motel in Lake City and left the following morning without paying the bill. That morning he abducted a 12-year-old girl from outside her school in Lake City. Her partially decomposed body was found on April 7, 35 miles from Lake City. On February 11, Bundy locked the door to his apartment, wiped it clean of fingerprints, and left by the fire escape.

The following day he was stopped by a Leon County deputy near his apartment. The deputy observed a license plate in the car next to which Bundy was standing. Bundy fled before he could be questioned further. That day he stole three different cars; the third one he drove west, leaving Tallahassee. On the thirteenth he was caught using a stolen credit card at a restaurant in Crestview and escaped. The next day he was arrested in Pensacola and at a minimum was facing 67 felony counts in Florida for stolen credit cards, forgery, and auto theft. An inventory of Bundy's stolen Volkswagen included a bicycle frame, a portable TV set, stereo equipment, clothing, a sleeping bag, a notebook with student identification, over 20 stolen credit cards, and a number of photos of girls and women.

Bundy's girlfriend from Seattle claims that he called her on February 18 and confessed to the murders he had committed. In her book (Kendall, 1981) under a pseudonym, she quotes him as saying:

> There is something the matter with me. It wasn't you. It was me. I just couldn't contain it. I've fought it for a long, long time . . . it got too strong. We just happened to be going together when it got under way. I tried to suppress it. It was taking more and more of my time. That's why I didn't do well in school. My time was being used trying to make my life look normal. But it wasn't normal. All the time I could feel that force building in me. (pp. 174–175)

I don't have a split personality. I don't have blackouts. I remember everything I've done. Like Lake Sammamish. (p. 176)

Bundy readily confessed to the Pensacola police that he had stolen the TV set and credit cards. He also admitted to stealing three cars in Tallahassee. He stated to three Pensacola detectives that his "problem" had first surfaced in Seattle while walking on a street one night. He stated that there was a girl on the street ahead that aroused a feeling he'd never had before. He wanted to possess her by whatever means necessary and followed her home until she entered the house and he never saw her again (Winn and Merrill, 1980, pp. 301–302). Bundy stated that he had become a voyeur during law school in Seattle walking the streets at night.

Bundy had an affinity for Volkswagens, stating they went a long way on a tank of gas. He preferred Volkswagens because the seat would come out and he could carry things easier that way. When asked what he carried, he used the term *cargo.* Bundy stated that "sometimes the cargo was damaged and sometimes it wasn't" (Winn and Merrill, 1980, p. 302). He stated that he got along on little sleep and used to drive around at night in his Volkswagen. "Sometimes I felt like a vampire," he said, "just driving all night long" (Winn and Merrill, 1980, p. 302). When the investigators tried to elicit the number of victims Bundy might be talking about, he said, "We're talking about three-digit figures (Winn and Merrill, 1980, p. 321).

Prior to Bundy's confessions prior to his execution, law enforcement authorities believe that Ted Bundy committed at least 17 homicides coast-to-coast over a four-year period:

3 victims	Seattle, Washington
2 victims	Issaquah, Washington
1 victim	Olympia, Washington
1 victim	Ellenburg, Washington
1 victim	Corvallis, Oregon
2 victims	Salt Lake City, Utah
1 victim	Utah County, Utah
1 victim	Bountiful, Utah
1 victim	Aspen, Colorado
1 victim	Vail, Colorado
2 victims	Tallahassee, Florida
1 victim	Lake City, Florida

Law enforcement officers now believe that he committed many more. Robert Keppel states: "By my count he's been directly linked to twenty-three deaths in five states" (R. Keppel, personal communication, April 20, 1984).

SELF CONCEPT

Ted Bundy's conversations with friends about his family, the problems his illegitimacy had caused with his siblings, and the problems he had with his stepfather seemed to reveal that the epithet "bastard" had left its mark. However, Bundy would write one day: "In short, when I just came under attack by the legal system, I was 28, a bachelor, a law student, engaged to be married and enjoying the brightest period in my life. I had come to terms with many things and one thing I had come to terms with long ago was the circumstances of my birth" (Winn and Merrill, 1980, p. 104).

Bundy rarely showed his negative self image. In his interrogation by the Pensacola investigators after his arrest in Florida, this image briefly surfaced. When asked about the location of the little girl who was missing from Lake City, he replied simply: "But I'm the most cold-hearted son of a bitch you'll ever meet" (Winn and Merrill, 1980, p. 314). When asked if the little girl was dead, he responded: "Well, you gentlemen knew that you were getting involved with a pretty strange creature. And you have known it for days" (Winn and Merrill, 1980, p. 314).

He seemed to see himself as an active participant in his life, one who was in control of his environment and his destiny. He enjoyed exhibiting his confidence in himself to others. He stated that he had always wanted to be an attorney and now he was fulfilling that wish by defending himself and doing it fairly well. He compared the prosecutor in his trial with all his skill and training against a man with a year and one half of law school (himself), who could let the air out of the prosecutor's tires (Winn and Merrill, 1980, p. 321).

Against the advice of his attorneys, Bundy cross-examined his previous kidnap victim for four hours in court. It was just something he had to do. During the penalty phase of his trial in Miami, after being found guilty, he asked for phone privileges from the judge. He was still fighting back, showing he was in control. He would state to a psychologist, "I don't fear death, I don't fear anyone or anything" (Larsen, 1980, p. 151).

Bundy was thought to have had an inferiority complex when he was younger. When he began dating, he refused to meet the parents of a girl he dated in Seattle. He referred to himself and his first real girlfriend from San Francisco as "Sears & Roebuck and Saks" (Larsen, 1980, p. 157). In his teens he appeared shy with strangers and reserved with his friends. He was looked upon by many as a "loner." It was the same Ted Bundy, however, who would state to his interrogators in Pensacola, "I feel like I'm in charge of the entertainment tonight" (Larsen, 1980, p. 231).

His application to law school was reflective of the image he held of himself. He started his application letter by stating, "My lifestyle requires I obtain knowledge of the law and the ability to practice legal skills" (Larsen, 1980,

p. 37). He concluded the letter by stating that law school would "give me the tools to become a more effective actor in a social role I have defined for myself" (Larsen, 1980, p. 37). Included in his application was a glowing letter signed by Governor Dan Evans of Washington, which Bundy had written himself.

After his escape and capture in Colorado, he wrote a friend that he had no regrets except that he was foolish enough to get caught. He stated that he deserved to be free and that his own knowledge regarding his innocence was sufficient. For Bundy, he was in control and understood himself. To his captors in Pensacola, Florida, he stated: "This story is one that I have always intended to give to you [the police], and a psychologist or psychiatrist. I'm a psychologist and it really gives me insight. I've got the answers and the answers are mine to give" (Winn and Merrill, 1980, p. 314).

Bundy, however, would on infrequent occasions admit that he was not always in control. He stated after his arrest in Pensacola that after his first escape he seemed to have conquered his "problem." After his second escape he said the "problem" recurred and he noted, "I guess I have a fool [himself] for a doctor" (Winn and Merrill, 1980, p. 303). He would state once that fantasies were controlling his life (Winn and Merrill, 1980, p. 301).

Throughout his incarceration and criminal trials Bundy continued to maintain his innocence of any murders. He was constantly trying to reach the media to get this message across. While he seemed to enjoy being a celebrity, he would contradict himself regarding his own self perception. He stated to a detective that it was important how people perceive him. He was not just a fiend—there was more to him than that (Winn and Merrill, 1980, p. 320). But he would write to a magazine editor in Seattle: "I am still too young to look upon my life as history. I am at a stage in life, an egocentric stage, where it matters only that I understand what I am and not what others may think of me" (Winn and Merrill, 1980, p. 280).

Bundy's most appropriate role was as a defense attorney defending himself. It was what he had wanted to do and he was doing it now for himself. He stated that he wanted to bear the responsibility for his acquittal and sustaining of his innocence.

Bundy obviously felt in charge when attempting to strike a deal with his interrogators in Pensacola to escape the death penalty. He would talk but they must do what he wanted, no death penalty and incarceration in Washington. He stated, "I've got to take care of my own survival too. Ted Bundy wants to survive too. I'm not asking to be back on the streets, but I don't have a death wish either" (Winn and Merrill, 1980, p. 312). Some would argue that he did have a death wish. Others would argue that Bundy's actions were to exalt in the thrill of the chase, and his ultimate euphoria was to remain undetected, to do what no other man could do and do it with impunity (Rule, 1980).

Ted Bundy may have conceived of himself with the utmost clarity when he stated to his captors in Pensacola: "I realize I will never function in society again. I don't want to escape, but if I get the chance, I will. I want you to be professional enough to see that I never get the chance" (Winn and Merrill, 1980, p. 319).

Police believe that Bundy first killed in January 1974 in Seattle, Washington. He is suspected of committing rapes and aggravated assaults on young women somewhat earlier. He was incarcerated in eight different jails and prisons between his arrest in 1975 and his conviction for murder in 1979.

A few days before his execution, Ted Bundy began confessing his crimes. He told one interviewer, "I just liked to kill, I wanted to kill" (MacPherson, 1989, p. 198). In an interview with James Dobson, Bundy claimed that pornography was why he had killed. He stated: "I'm telling you from personal experience, the most graphic violence on screen, particularly as it gets into the home; to children who may be unattended or unaware that they may be a Ted Bundy who has vulnerability to that, that predisposition to be influenced by that kind of behavior, by that kind of movie and that kind of violence" (Dobson, 1992, p. 35–36). To another interviewer, Bundy appeared startled at the hatred of those awaiting his execution. He stated, "I don't know why everyone is out to get me" (MacPherson, 1989, p. 196). The state of Florida executed Ted Bundy on January 24, 1989. For many, he still remains a very troubling enigma.

ATTITUDES

At first impression, Ted Bundy appears to be a calm, self-assured, and charming man. He projects an image of a person who is in control and cares little what others think of him. However, his attitudes reflect a somewhat different person.

It is difficult to determine Bundy's value of human life accurately, since he has never confessed to his murderous crimes. Only a few of his comments reflect his attitudes toward his victims, and they are anachronistic. Following his arrest in Florida, he reportedly stated over the telephone to his girlfriend in Seattle, "I want to make it right with all the people I've hurt" (Larsen, 1980, p. 230). However, he would state a short time later that the girl he tried to kidnap in Utah was "lucky she got away" (Winn and Merrill, 1980, p. 302), and as to the location of his 12-year-old victim in Florida, "I'm the most cold-hearted son of a bitch you'll ever want to meet" (Winn and Merrill, 1980, p. 314).

Bundy told Michaud and Aynesworth (1983) in a Florida prison: "I feel less guilty now than I've felt in any time in my life" (p. 300). For Bundy guilt doesn't solve anything, it only hurts you (Michaud and Aynesworth, 1983, p. 300). Other than the alleged statement to his girlfriend in Seattle, Bundy has never reportedly shown remorse for his actions or his victims, which he claims numbered over 100.

Bundy's attitude toward authority is self-evident in many of his recorded statements and occurrences in his early life. In grade school he had been characterized as being beyond any discipline from his teachers. When things went wrong for Bundy he would rationalize the fault to an authority figure or the system, as he did with his failure to achieve success in law school or sporadic attempts at various areas of study while in college.

He took a great deal of pride in outsmarting law enforcement. He would brag about losing the officers who had him under surveillance in Utah. He wrote to Ann Rule: "I have a standing policy from this point forward never to talk to a law enforcement officer about anything except the time of day and the location of the toilet" (Rule, 1980, p. 217). He would frequently castigate his pursuers, "I never underestimate the inventiveness and dangerousness of such men [law enforcement officers]. Like wild animals, when cornered can become very unstable" (Rule, 1980, p. 219). He reportedly told a neighbor in Tallahassee, Florida that he was a lot smarter than the police and could get away with anything he wanted (Winn and Merrill, 1980, p. 331).

Bundy referred to some police agencies as "Mickey Mouse" operations. He saw himself as a threat to his prosecutor in Colorado. He said his self-confidence was threatening to this man, who "should never enter a courtroom" (Rule, 1980, p. 228). He never really accepted the services of his defense attorneys. To him, they were inferior and not at his level of expertise.

He seemed to taunt the police. To the investigators of the Chi Omega house killings, he said: "The evidence is there. Keep digging" (Larsen, 1980, p. 232). He urged the investigators in Utah to search for straws to make the broom. Regarding the investigators in Washington, he would state: "They're not going to find any evidence there, because there is no evidence there to find" (Larsen, 1980, p. 113). In continuing to proclaim his innocence, he would charge police with wasting the taxpayer's money with all their conferences and task forces. The police, for Bundy, had their heads in the sand (Larsen, 1980). He stated that the police and the prosecutor's charges against him were "grossly exaggerated, their accusations purely fictitious and totally without merit" (Larsen, 1980, p. 167).

Following his escapes from Colorado he would frequently poke fun at his former jailers and enjoy describing in detail how he had outsmarted them. While incarcerated he stated: "I'm not going to do what the man tells me to do" (Larsen, 1980, p. 208). For him, judges were his adversary. He would frequently come close to being held in contempt. He would have one judge in Florida disqualified from his case, which pleased him immensely.

Bundy's view of the psychiatrists and psychologists who examined him was that they were determined to produce an analysis that would explain and rationalize his crimes. He was scornful of their tests, which he as a psychologist saw right through. He found their examinations "malicious, slanted and infernal" (Rule, 1980, p. 205).

Ted Bundy's attitude toward religion is a mystery. Although he affirmed his belief in the Church of Latter Day Saints by being baptized a Mormon in Utah, when arrested in Florida he requested a Catholic priest. In his childhood he attended and was active in the Methodist church. He told a psychiatrist that he didn't believe in a life after death (Larsen, 1980, p. 151). In his letters to Ann Rule, however, he often wrote of his belief in God (Rule, 1980, p. 149).

RECALL OF EVENTS

Whether Ted Bundy remembered his killings and his victims in any detail is not known. He alluded to killing over 100 people in six different states, yet he would not speak of his killings. He came close to discussing his murderous acts when speaking with authors Michaud and Aynesworth (1983) hypothetically in the third person. It is only their contention that he was in fact describing his killings. It is quite possible that he was simply fooling them as he had attempted to con everyone else throughout his life.

BUNDY'S LAST CON

As most people are aware, Ted Bundy was executed on January 24, 1989. Prior to his execution (as indicated earlier), he began confessing to his murders. While a number of his confessions were taken seriously by law enforcement officials, Bundy was trying one more con. A con to save his life. He did, in fact, kill a number of people. By confessing to these crimes he was trying to save his life. Many of his victims may never be identified. He also confessed to being driven by pornography as a young man. His motives remain a puzzle to criminologists, crime buffs, the media, and the general public.

CHAPTER 10

⏤━◈━⏤

CROSS-CASE ANALYSIS: SIMILARITIES OF FOUR SERIAL KILLERS

INTRODUCTION

There are number of similarities as well as differences between the four serial murderers Gacy, Lucas, Bianchi, and Bundy, whose case studies were presented in the preceding four chapters. It is those similarities among these serial murderers that may provide us with a better understanding of this violent crime and the people who kill a number of victims in different locations over a period of time. However, in analyzing these serial murderers and identifying the similarities among them, readers are cautioned not to use the results of this analysis as definitive descriptive statements or as a profile of the serial killer. After all, the analysis is based on only four serial murderers, who may not necessarily be representative of the population of serial murderers. As indicated earlier (see Chapter 1), there is no current and reliable empirical data base on serial murderers from which to determine with any degree of accuracy the extent or prevalence of serial murder in this country or any other country. Therefore, the results of this analysis should be viewed as only a starting point from which to begin an empirical description of the similarities among serial murderers. Efforts in the future will require that a number of other case studies be conducted from specifically selected geographical areas of this country and from a variety of serial murderers who appear to be very different regarding such variables as victim selection, methods of killing, gender and age of the killers, periods between killings, geographical locations of the killings, and type of hunting grounds where victims are selected, to mention only a few of the more obvious variables. It should also be remembered that such a research effort would only be based on those serial murderers who have been identified and apprehended. Missing from the data base would be those killers who have not been identified or even suspected of committing a series of murders.

Given the limitations of analyzing the results of only four serial murderer case studies, the information from such an analysis can be compared and contrasted with other research, which has some empirical foundation, to guide future research efforts attempting to determine the most commonly shared characteristics of serial murderers. This analysis is then only the beginning. Hopefully, this analysis will provide guidance for future research efforts.

SOCIAL ENVIRONMENT

All the murderers were born into a working-class or lower-socioeconomic family. Bundy and Gacy moved into a middle-class stratum, whereas the others remained within their original social class. The educational achievement of the subjects ranged from an attempt at law school by Bundy to Lucas's barely finishing the fourth grade.

Bundy and Lucas abused alcohol. Lucas may very well be an alcoholic. Lucas's parents were reportedly alcoholics. There was no history of alcoholism in Bundy's family. Gacy's father abused alcohol but Gacy did not. There is evidence that all the murderers had used marijuana, but none were habituated to the substance.

Bundy, Gacy, and Buono were very neat and orderly in their lifestyle. Bundy's apartment was always spotless. Gacy and Buono kept their houses very clean. Buono was known as a very meticulous worker. Gacy ordered his life to the extent that he kept a log of his activities during the day.

The murderers had first experienced sexual intercourse in their early to late teens. The sexual relationships of Bundy, Gacy, and Buono all involved some form of violence. They had used bondage on their sexual partners. Buono and Gacy were both sadistic and dominant in their sexual roles with others. Gacy, Bianchi, and Buono all read and showed a strong interest in pornography.

Gacy, Bianchi, and Lucas all experienced childhood health traumas. Gacy experienced blackouts, which were never diagnosed accurately. Bianchi experienced urination problems and reportedly had severe respiratory infections. Lucas suffered the loss of his eye in an accident.

Bundy, Gacy, and Bianchi had a strong interest in law enforcement from early childhood. Lucas claims to have studied law enforcement. Bundy was considered a "loner" in high school. Bianchi and Gacy had what was reported to be relatively normal social relationships in high school. Buono and Lucas never attended high school.

FAMILY BACKGROUND

Bundy, Bianchi, and Lucas were illegitimate children. Bundy was adopted when he was 5 years old after his mother married. Bianchi's mother gave him to a foster home and he was adopted before his first birthday. Lucas's real father is unknown. Bundy was apparently the only one of the three who was troubled by the circumstances of his birth.

Bundy, Bianchi, and Lucas all had dominant mothers. Bundy's mother paid the bills and spoke for the family. Bianchi's mother smothered him with protection and provided his sometimes harsh punishment. Lucas was beaten and neglected by his mother, who gave the orders in the family. Gacy was heavily influenced by his mother, whom he tried to protect when she was beaten by Gacy's father.

Gacy, Bianchi, and Lucas all had parents with emotional problems. Gacy's father never showed his emotions unless he was intoxicated, which was almost every night. When his father came home from work he would start drinking until his anger surfaced. He would then physically abuse Gacy's mother. Bianchi's mother was described as a disturbed woman. She apparently experienced a great deal of guilt in her failure to bear children. She was extremely overprotective of Bianchi and became paranoid over his illnesses. Lucas's mother reportedly forced him to watch her in sexual intercourse with a number of men. Until he was 6 or 7 years old she dressed him as a girl.

Gacy, Bianchi, Buono, and Lucas had been married and then divorced. Gacy had been married twice and Buono was married three times. Gacy and Lucas may have had some confusion regarding their sexual identity. Also, both of these murderers came from families with a history of alcoholism. Gacy and Bundy had experienced problems with their fathers.

PEER-GROUP ASSOCIATION AND PERSONAL RELATIONSHIPS

All but Lucas were apparently very manipulative of situations and people. Lucas could also be considered manipulative, but in a much less sophisticated manner, due to his education and the severe economic conditions of his childhood. On the surface, all of these men appeared to most people as seemingly harmless. However, it is apparent in three of these men, Gacy,

Bianchi's "Stevie Walker," and Lucas, that there was a strong emotion of hatred beneath their surface exterior. All of the murderers had been unable or unwilling to establish lasting relationships with others.

CONTACT WITH DEFINING AGENCIES

Three of the men had had juvenile delinquency records, with Lucas's early criminal activities being the most serious and consistent. Gacy and Bianchi have no known juvenile record. All of these murderers appeared to be well informed regarding the procedures and normal activities of the police. Bundy and Lucas appear to have understood problems of interjurisdictional communication among police and killed in different jurisdictions. Bianchi and Buono were very conscious of leaving any physical evidence from their killings. When Bianchi killed on his own, however, it was a different story. Gacy seemed to understand that no one would miss young homosexuals and may have realized the routineness with which police investigated missing teenagers.

All men, except Buono, for whom psychiatric reports may never have been written, were referred to by psychiatrists or psychologists as having antisocial personalities. They have all been labeled as sociopaths or psychopaths. The diagnoses of these men were not always consistent among mental health professions, who in some cases disagreed strongly on an individual murderer. A common theme in the psychological and psychiatric evaluations of these four men was that they were strongly resistant of authority, were obsessed with being able to control and manipulate other people to their own advantage and benefit, and almost never shared their true feeling with others.

When arrested for the last time, only Bundy physically resisted the police. All the other men offered no resistance and submitted to authorities calmly.

OFFENSE BEHAVIOR

Bundy and Gacy used lures to attract their victims. Bundy used a faked injury, and Gacy used offers of homosexual relations for money. Bundy, Gacy, Buono, and Bianchi posed as police officers, using the force of official authority to persuade their victims to accompany them. All murderers carried some sort of deadly weapon most of the time. In all cases, automobiles were instruments of victim abduction. And all had carried the corpses of their victims in their vehicles.

Gacy's victims were all young Caucasian males. Bundy and Bianchi–Buono killed only females, in most cases under 25 years of age and

Caucasian. Lucas and his accomplices have killed a number of males, but 75% of Lucas's victim were females, and over 90% were Caucasian, with a mean age of almost 31, but with a range of 80 years.

All killed over a period of at least a year, except Buono and Bianchi, who when acting together, killed their victims over a four-month period. Lucas first killed as a 14-year-old boy. The others reportedly first killed in their twenties or thirties, except for Buono, who was in his forties.

Many of the serial murderers' victims were particularly vulnerable to assault or abduction because of their lifestyle or perceived powerlessness. Bundy's victims were young girls who moved about by themselves or were alone in the late evening hours. Gacy's victims were in most cases young homosexuals "cruising" for sexual contacts in areas known to be frequented by homosexuals. Bianchi and Buono approached many young girls with a history of prostitution who were used to being accosted on the street. Lucas reportedly killed 42 of his victims who were hitchhiking when abducted. He also abducted many of his victims while they were traveling alone, away from their homes.

Four of the murderers used strangulation as their primary means of killing. Lucas strangled a number of his victims but used a variety of other means, primarily a knife. Bundy and Lucas used overkill on their victims. Long after his victims were dead, Bundy continued to beat them. Many of Lucas's victims were mutilated after death.

While all murderers were very mobile, Gacy and Buono–Bianchi killed in only one location. Bundy and Lucas, however, killed in numerous police jurisdictions in many different states. Taking Buono and Bianchi as one, each of these men killed at least nine people. All have also committed property crimes and other violent crimes.

SELF CONCEPT

All of these murderers seemed to see themselves in control of others through either their manipulative personalities or by physical force. In many cases they failed to recognize any of their own faults and tended to rationalize their behavior by blaming others for their situation. Except possibly for Buono, who seemed to project a macho image, all appeared to be concerned with their masculinity to some degree. Lucas and Gacy had problems with their sexual identity, based on childhood experiences. Lucas has emphasized that his primary accomplice to his killings was a homosexual, differentiating himself from the accomplice. Yet Lucas admits to being the passive partner with his accomplice in homosexual relations. Gacy had stressed to police when arrested that he was bisexual, not homosexual. All men seemed to have been unwilling or unable to delay their own gratification.

ATTITUDES

When arrested and in custody, Bundy, Bianchi, and Lucas tended to reveal their attitudes toward authority, symbolized for them by their captors. Bundy bragged of his escapes to the police, making fun of his previous jailers. He taunted them into digging deeper to find evidence in his killings. He indicated that he might confess to his crimes if they agreed to his conditions, which the police considered unreasonable or impractical. Bianchi, under faked hypnosis, patronized his examiners and showed pure defiance. Lucas acted on many occasions as all-powerful, controlling whether or not he would see people and choosing to whom he would confess. To him, *he* was clearing the cases, not the police. Lucas bragged about turning law enforcement "upside down" (interview, June 22, 1984). Buono was defiant by ignoring almost everyone during his trial.

All but Buono seemed to enjoy their celebrity status and thrived on the attention they received. With Bianchi it was sometimes difficult to tell, but he did not shun the limelight and seemed to enjoy it most of the time. He was known worldwide. While Bundy complained constantly about the presence of the TV camera in the courtroom, he was always seeking contacts with the media during his incarceration. When Gacy confessed to a number of police and lawyers, he was the center of attention and seemed to want to retain this attention through his clinical, almost professional method of discussing his victims and how he killed them. After his arrest, Gacy kept a scrapbook of newspaper clippings about his case.

Bianchi and Lucas are the only ones who have shown any remorse for their killings. When Bianchi spoke in open court in Washington and cried, some felt that he was truly sorry and a very sick man. Others saw his tears as frustration for his circumstances. After being "saved by the Lord," Lucas now claims to see all the grief he has caused the relatives of his victims. However, few who have interviewed him, including the author, believe that he is sincere in his claims. Many doubt that Lucas is capable of feeling remorse for his victims, which include his mother and his common-law wife, whose killings he rationalizes as accidents.

None of the murderers could be considered to have strongly professed to a religious belief, except for Lucas, whose claims are discounted by most people. Bundy was baptized into the Mormon faith in his twenties and regularly attended a Methodist church as a boy. Yet when arrested for the last time in Florida, he asked for a Catholic priest. Gacy's religious activities appear to have been only for his social aggrandizement. Bianchi and Buono were both of Catholic heritage but have reportedly professed no strong commitments to the Catholic faith.

RECALL OF EVENTS

Buono has never discussed his killings and still maintains his innocence. Bundy has only theorized about the person who committed the murderers he is believed to have done. Bianchi has remembered his victims under "hypnosis" but has been reticent to discuss the details of how the victims were killed. Gacy allegedly remembers some of his victims, but may be repressing the memory of his killings or simply isn't capable of remembering due to blackouts resulting from alcohol use. He is remembered by his wife and relatives as having a very good memory. Lucas's memory is a mystery. He has described his victims in graphic detail, which have been verified by the police. He may have an eidetic memory or have hypernesia.

MISSING PERSONS PROBLEM

In the Gacy, Bundy, and Lucas cases, a number of the victims had been reported missing to various law enforcement agencies.

SUMMARY

To summarize this comparison regarding each of these killers, the following was found:

SOCIAL ENVIRONMENT

- All of these killers came from-working class parents who could be considered lower to lower-middle class. Bundy and Gacy were able to move to middle-class status in their respective careers.
- The educational level of the killers ranged from less than a fourth-grade education to pursuit of a law degree.
- Bundy and Lucas are believed to have used alcohol frequently.
- Gacy's father was an alcoholic.
- It would appear that all these killers used marijuana at one time or another.
- Except for Lucas, these killers had the outward appearance of a neat and orderly existence.
- If Bundy is to be believed, all killers had been exposed to pornography.
- Three of the killers experienced some sort of childhood trauma.
- Three of the killers showed a strong interest in law enforcement at an early age.

FAMILY

- All but Gacy were born out of wedlock.
- All but Gacy had very dominant mothers.
- All but Bundy had parents with emotional problems.
- All but Bundy's parents were divorced.

PEER GROUP AND RELATIONSHIPS

- All were very manipulative.
- All were unable or unwilling to establish lasting, long-term relation-ships with anyone other than their killing partners.

CONTACT WITH CRIMINAL JUSTICE SYSTEM

- Three had juvenile records.
- All had studied law enforcement and were well informed about police investigative procedure.
- All had previous contact with psychiatrists and psychologists.
- All, at one time or another, had been diagnosed as psychopaths.
- A common theme can be identified among these serial killers in their interaction with the criminal justice system. They were viewed as resis-tant to any authority figure, obsessed with controlling and manipulating others, and almost never shared their true feeling with anyone.

OFFENSE BEHAVIOR

- All used automobiles in abducting their victims.
- All transported their victims' bodies in automobiles.
- All first killed when they were in their twenties or early thirties.
- All used strangulation as the primary method of killing.
- All had committed property crimes and other violent crimes in addition to murder.

SELF CONCEPT

- All wanted to control others.
- All frequently blamed others for their situation.

ATTITUDE

- All showed a strong disdain for law enforcement.
- Once caught, all enjoyed the celebrity status of being labeled a serial killer.

PART III

THE INVESTIGATION OF SERIAL MURDER

In Chapter 11 the problems of investigating a serial murder are discussed. First, the four ways that a serial murder comes to the attention of law enforcement authorities is described. Then the seven major problems that law enforcement faces in investigating a serial murder are explained.

Chapter 12 presents an extensive discussion and an update of information presented by the author in a previous book (Egger, 1990a) regarding the various law enforcement responses to a serial murder investigation. Fourteen different responses are highlighted and described in detail. The primary rationale for presenting this response taxonomy is that before determining the optimal response to a serial murder investigation, law enforcement agencies must determine what types of responses have occurred in the past in order to evaluate them and determine their best response given the current situation.

CHAPTER 11

⟹◆⟸

PROBLEMS IN INVESTIGATING SERIAL MURDER

DEFINING THE PROBLEM

A serial murder investigation is generally initiated by an agency or group of agencies following the identification of a series or probable series of related homicides. This identification will typically occur as the result of one of four different situations. First, a serial murder investigation may be initiated as an extension of a current homicide investigation when a second unsolved murder or series of unsolved murders are linked to the original case. This linkage may be similarities in victims, crime scenes, attacks, geography, or any number of actions or situations which convince investigators that the homicides have been committed by a common killer. Such was the case in Rochester, New York, where in November 1989 police publicly acknowledged a possible relationship between five of 11 female homicide victims found since 1987. The police were in fact conducting a serial murder investigation at this time. On January 3, 1990, officers conducting helicopter surveillance of the site where a female homicide victim had been found that morning saw a car near the homicide scene. Following the car into Rochester, they learned that it was registered to Arthur Shawcross, who immediately became a suspect due to his previous criminal record. The killings had begun in March 1988, one year after Shawcross had been paroled from prison, where he had served 15 years for the murder of an 8-year-old girl and a 10-year-old boy. Shawcross's interrogation by police led to his confession and subsequent conviction of 11 homicides.

Second, the suspicion from a non–law enforcement source that a serial murder exists may result in enough pressure on an agency or group of agencies for a formal acknowledgment of this possibility to be made, resulting in an active serial murder investigation. Such pressure may come from the news media, from politicians, from advocates of homicide victims, or from the relatives or loved ones of homicide victims. In the case of Donald Harvey, who was convicted of 37 murders in Ohio and Kentucky, it was a local TV station in Cincinnati that pressured police into reexamining a number of deaths occurring at Drake Hospital. Harvey had been a suspect in one death at the hospital and, under questioning, had confessed to the murder. No other murders at the hospital were being investigated when the TV station reported that there were 23 other deaths of a questionable nature that had occurred at the hospital during Harvey's employment there as a nurse. The situation strongly implied that Harvey was responsible for these deaths. A law enforcement investigation of these deaths resulted in Harvey's confession.

Unfortunately, the identification of a serial murder frequently occurs through happenstance or a fluke in which a serial murderer is revealed through routine police work in response to a seemingly unrelated criminal event. A serial murderer may be apprehended for driving a stolen vehicle, and very quickly the police learn they are dealing with a much more violent crime, as was the case when Ted Bundy was pursued in a stolen car in Pensacola, Florida. Following his arrest, the Pensacola police soon learned that they had more than a car thief in their jail. A more recent example of routine police work and an unrelated crime leading to the arrest of a serial murderer and a serial murder investigation occurred on June 28, 1993, in Long Island, New York. In the early morning hours two state troopers spotted a tan 1984 Mazda pickup with no license plates driving on the Southern State Parkway . The driver refused to pull over and the officers pursued the pickup. The chase ended 25 minutes later when the Mazda slammed into a utility pole. The driver was unhurt and was arrested. Following the arrest, the officers noticed a very strong smell coming from the bed of the pickup, where the officers found the badly decomposed body of Tiffany Bresciani, a 22-year-old woman from Manhattan. The driver, Joel Rifkin, would within hours confess to the killing of 16 other women. And, of course, the two police officers who on the evening July 22, 1991 checked out a reported assault and handcuffing of a man had no idea what they would find in apartment 213 on North 25th Street in Milwaukee. These officers found body parts of some of Jeffrey Dahmer's 17 victims.

A fourth situation in which a serial murder is identified is where the criminal event under investigation is considered unique, singular, and nonsequential until the suspect alerts the police to the multiple nature of his or her acts by confessing to a number of homicides. Within two days of Henry Lee Lucas's arrest in Montague County, Texas, for violation of parole and suspicion of killing an 84-year-old woman, he began confessing to the killing of scores of people across the country. He was subsequently convicted of 10 homicides and remains a very strong suspect in over 100 homicides.

Whether a serial murder is identified by the police through investigative linkages, pressure from the outside, a fluke of routine police work, or a serial murderer's confession, the investigation of a serial murder poses numerous issues for the investigating agency or agencies. These issues involve questions of investigative tactics and strategies, the allocation of personnel to the investigation, the necessary expenditure of funds to meet the increased expenses of such an investigation, news-media relations, the management of large amounts of information, inter- and intraagency communication, and the organization of the investigative effort to include control and coordination. A serial murder investigation is a major undertaking. It is frequently complicated by the involvement of multiple jurisdictions, the scope of the investigation, and the resources necessary to carry it out.

SEVEN MAJOR PROBLEMS OF A SERIAL MURDER INVESTIGATION

A review of serial murder investigations conducted in the United States, Canada, and England over the last decade, as well as recent investigations of serial murder in Australia, South Africa, Sweden, Poland, Russia, and Austria, reveal certain problems that are common to these investigations. The *major* problems commonly faced by agencies involved in a serial murder investigation are:

1. Contending with and attempting to reduce linkage blindness
2. Committing to a serial murder investigation
3. Coordination of investigative functions and actions
4. Managing large amounts of investigative information
5. Dealing with public pressure and limiting the adversarial nature of relations with the news media
6. Overlooking the value of victimological information
7. Being aware of the various strategies that have been employed in serial murder investigations, to understand the ramifications of each, and select appropriate methods to identify and apprehend the serial killer

LINKAGE BLINDNESS

Law enforcement investigators do not see, are prevented from seeing, or make little attempt to see beyond their own jurisdictional responsibilities. The law enforcement officer's responsibility stops at the boundary of his or her jurisdiction. The exception is generally only when hot pursuit is necessary. The very nature of local law enforcement in this country and a police department's accountability and responsiveness to its jurisdictional clients isolates the department from the outside world.

The National Crime Information Center provides officers with access to other agencies indirectly, to obtain information on wanted persons and stolen property. However, the sharing of information on unsolved crimes and investigative leads is not a function of this extensive nationwide information system. Reciprocal relationships between homicide investigators are at best informal and usually within relatively limited geographical areas.

Linkage blindness exemplifies the major weakness of our structural defenses against crime and our ability to control it. Simply stated, the exchange of investigative information among police departments in this country is, at best, very poor. Linkage blindness is the nearly total lack of sharing or coordinating of investigative information and the lack of adequate networking by law enforcement agencies. This lack of sharing or networking is prevalent today with law enforcement officers and in their agencies. Thus linkages are rarely established among geographic areas of the country between similar crime patterns or modus operandi. Such a condition directly inhibits an early warning or detection system of the serial murderer preying on multiple victims. In those instances where serial murders are discovered or suspected, they are frequently being committed within a relatively small geographic area and therefore subject to obvious inferences. A law enforcement agency operates on information, yet agencies fail to seek it out, use or process it from the "outside," or share it with colleagues or their counterparts in other agencies.

Empirical analysis, albeit retrospective in nature, reveals numerous instances of linkage blindness in the investigations of serial murder across the United States. It should also be noted that this failure in communication and networking is not unique to this country, as evidenced by the Yorkshire Ripper investigation in England. Although it should be readily apparent to the informed reader that the concept of linkage blindness is applicable to all types of criminal mobility, examples will be limited to that of the serial murderer.

Norris (1989) misuses the term *linkage blindness* by defining it as professionals in disparate disciplines failing to relate causalities of behavior to one another's area of understanding and study. Norris also failed to understand the concept when it was first explained to him by the author in 1983 (see Darrach and Norris, 1984). True, the term does generally apply to faulty communication linkages among similar players in similar circumstances with similar responsibilities. But the term was coined and applied specifically to the law enforcement criminal investigation function. More important, the term was coined to denote a major investigative problem in the response to serial crime, not serial murder alone.

The fact that linkage blindness exists across the various components and role sectors of the criminal justice system and, more specifically, among the thousands of law enforcement agencies in the United States is not really debatable. The existence of linkage blindness has been documented in retrospective interpretations in an analysis of serial murder cases by Egger (1985). The problem has also become obvious to those journalists, researchers, and governmental officials who have examined numerous cases of serial murder. This is certainly true for the better-known nationally recognized cases, such as Bundy, Lucas, Gacy, or Ramirez and also for the lesser known or less publicized cases of Eyler, Gary, or Hatcher.

Police officers, particularly homicide investigators from Maine to Texas, are quick to agree (when it is explained) that linkage blindness exists. However, numerous police chiefs, sheriffs, and police commanders respond with a negative and unfortunately opposite opinion, arguing that agencies (more specifically, their agencies) communicate with one another on a daily basis, frequently across hundreds of miles of geography. Those law enforcement administrators not willing to admit this problem of communication and sharing only serve to exacerbate the problem

In discussing the mobility of serial killers and the difficulty of a multi–law enforcement agency investigation, Keyes (1986) describes Columbus, Ohio, homicide sergeant Bill Steckman's thinking about what he was facing in the investigation of the ".22 caliber murders:"

> Most serial murderers moved from city to city, stalking their victims across city, county or state lines, over weeks, months and even years. Because different law enforcement agencies were involved—county sheriff's deputies, city police and the FBI, each concerned primarily with their own cases—detectives often didn't notice the patterns. Conflicting investigative methods, interdepartmental jealousies, and prosecutors overreacting to the political pressures of a fearful and outraged public, often gave serial killers the advantage. Among the most difficult criminals to apprehend most often, when they were arrested, it was by accident. (p. 77)

It is thus difficult for the author to provide an optimistic or positive prognosis regarding the control or amelioration of serial murder in this country. It is equally disheartening when one realizes that the phenomenon of serial murder, that is, law enforcement's response to this phenomenon, is only symptomatic of the greater and all-encompassing problem of serial criminality. The traveling criminal who repeats his criminal acts in different law enforcement jurisdictions is indeed exploiting this systemic weakness, which frequently contributes to his or her continued immunity from detection or apprehension.

In a stranger-to-stranger murder lacking in physical evidence or witnesses, criminal investigators are left to deal with a very large set of suspects, with only a small probability of including the offender. A review of serial murders occurring over the last few years reveals that most serial murderers are caught by chance or coincidence, not by ratiocination or scientific investigation. Law enforcement agencies today are simply not adept at identifying or apprehending the murderer who kills strangers and moves from jurisdiction to jurisdiction and crosses state lines. Why, in this age of information and rapidly advancing computer technology, are multijurisdictional crimes of murder so difficult for law enforcement to solve? The answer is: linkage blindness.

The editors of *Forensic Science International* (1985) appear to be much too optimistic in their appraisal of U.S. law enforcement's response to the problem of linkage blindness. These editors state: "The development of close communication and systems of accumulation of nationwide data has brought very important results especially the respect of law enforcement organizations at various levels and in various locations for each other. These organizations have thus realized that their problem is shared by others" (p. 135).

The relatively recent development of VICAP by the FBI and the development of task forces in response to the Williams case in Atlanta, the Stano case in Florida, the Lucas–Toole case in Monroe, Louisiana, and the Green River case in Seattle are the only evidence the authors present to substantiate their optimistic assessment of law enforcement's response to the problem of linkage blindness. While these cases are of course noteworthy and VICAP's effort indeed laudable, they represent the efforts of a relatively few agencies, while VICAP is in effect the effort of only one federal agency.

Levin and Fox (1985) state that unless the serial murderer leaves a distinct or unique signature at the crime scene the police may not recognize the similarity of the killings. They also contend that if a pattern does exist, it may go undetected, due to the sheer volume of cases, particularly in large cities. For example, the Corll, Henley, and Brooks killings of 27 young boys from 1971 to 1973 in the Houston, Texas, area was completely unknown to the police until they received a telephone call from Henley in August 1973. In this case the police failed to thoroughly investigate missing persons reports or to correlate similarities in these reports (Levin and Fox, 1985, pp. 177–181).

Levin and Fox (1985) state: "Seeing a common element in several reports of missing or murdered persons in one large city is difficult enough. Seeing it across city or state lines magnifies the problem. Some killers are able to kill on the move so that they are already hundreds of miles away before police discover the crime" (p. 182). Goldstein (1977) refers to an acknowledgment by the New York City Police Department in September 1974 that it had failed to recognize the overall pattern in eight different murders and two assaults of women that occurred in the same hotel over a period of one and one-half years. This pattern was discovered when the killer confessed after being charged with another murder that occurred near the hotel (p. 67). This failure to identify patterns in different homicides may be the reason that the Houston, Texas, police department has recently initiated a number of internal changes in its homicide division in responses to a homicide clearance rate of only 64%. Two new shifts were created within the division that would overlap existing shifts to allow detectives more time to discuss cases and follow-ups with each other and possibly identify across-shift patterns.

Levin and Fox (1985) conclude that serial killers "may be hiding in the anonymity of large urban centers" (p. 186) or traveling across the country, and in either case the police will probably not detect their pattern of killing. This failure to detect a pattern is most certainly the result of a major law enforcement communication failure.

COMMITMENT TO A SERIAL MURDER INVESTIGATION

Most law enforcement administrators are very unwilling to make a public commitment to initiating a serial murder investigation. Since the public have been sold the concept that the police are responsible for the crime in their jurisdictions, chiefs and sheriffs are loath to admit that there is serial killer running loose throughout their jurisdictions, killing strangers at will. Given the tenuous employment risk of police chiefs in this country, it is no wonder that they strive to put their best appearance forward to the public. Serial killers make the police look bad. To commit to trying to catch one makes the hunters look inept, at the very least.

Commitment not only brings the police abilities, however misperceived by the public, into close scrutiny, it also means that one agency will have to work with at least one other, and frequently more than one. Police agencies don't work well together. They aren't trained to work together. Like all other vocations, the tasks at hand become habits—and habits that are hard to break.

When more than one agency is forced to work together when a criminal offender is committing his crimes in a number of jurisdictions, the first question to arise invariably is: "Who is in charge?" Unless this has been worked out specifically beforehand, determining who will lead the investigation takes a great deal of time to determine. Mutual-aid pacts are allowed in most states specified by state legislation; however, police agencies generally fail to take advantage of these laws until it is too late.

Commitment to a serial murder investigation means that an inordinate amount of investigatory personnel will have to be allocated to the effort. In addition to the reassignment of personnel, equipment will have to be dedicated to the investigation. Few agencies have the necessary contingency budget to allow for this without seeking additional funds from the policymakers of their respective governments. This can be time consuming and frequently a little embarrassing for the law enforcement administrator.

An additional consideration of committing to a serial murder investigation is that the mass media will undoubtedly cause a great deal of chaos for the investigatory personnel assigned to the case. In some cases the media become almost frenzied in their search for information. This was certainly the case in Gainesville, Florida, in late 1990 when five people were slain within 72 hours. For some observers this serial killing turned into a "media carnival" (Reynolds, 1992, p. 4). It has been reported that journalists used parabolic microphones to eavesdrop on members of the task force set up investigate these killings. Reynolds, a Reuters reporter, characterized his peers in Gainesville as having "brainstem behavior," and "[like] rats on methedrine, jabbering about semen and blood and missing nipples" (p. 4).

COORDINATION OF INVESTIGATIVE FUNCTIONS AND ACTIONS

The reallocation of personnel to the serial murder investigation also requires the reassignment of very skilled and experienced homicide investigators of supervisory- and command-level rank. This means that only less skilled investigators and less experienced supervisors and commanders are available to respond to ongoing cases and newly reported crimes.

It must be remembered that a serial murder investigation is a major, complicated effort that requires a tremendous amount of coordination. Commanders must know the status of assigned personnel and be able to monitor the activities of their personnel at all times. In other words, the left hand needs to know what the right hand is doing so that no mistakes are made and important pieces of information are acted upon and not lost in the confusion of multiple tasks and different assignments.

MANAGING LARGE AMOUNTS OF INVESTIGATIVE INFORMATION

In a serial murder investigation the amount of information and data that are generated is almost always unmanageable without the aid of the computer. The most novice student reviewing the literature of law enforcement and automated data processing will quickly realize that many police agencies operate from an almost illiterate grasp of the modern computer. In fact, most police departments simply use their computing machines as fast-retrieval file cabinets, not realizing the great potential of the computers of the 1990s.

To fully exploit the computer and the processing of information, the team of investigators must be able to cross-reference and retrieve aggregate data very rapidly. Indeed, a speedy electronic file drawer will almost certainly fail to provide timely and accurate information with the speed necessary for such an investigation. Command-level personnel who understand the necessity for such capability may not be available to the agencies involved. Outside consultants may be required, and this has not always worked very smoothly in these sensitive and stress-filled investigations.

Public Pressure and Mass-Media Pressure for Information

While adequately prepared to withstand a great deal of public pressure to capture the criminal and prevent crimes in the community, most law enforcement agencies are generally ill prepared to deal effectively with the mass media. The fact that serial murder investigations frequently involve more than one police jurisdiction only complicates the task of media relations. In some recent serial murder investigations, reporters have gone from one public information to another, seeking information about the investigation. Coordination with their counterparts in the other agencies involved is almost always neglected in training courses in police–media relations.

In addition to having to deal with public pressure, the result of intense mass media pressure is that the press come to be viewed as an adversarial and intolerant critic of the investigatory effort and all personnel assigned. A great deal of antagonism is therefore generated between investigators and journalists, resulting in poor and sometimes slanted reporting of the progress and effectiveness of the investigatory efforts.

The "Less-Dead": Low Priority Leads to Low Clearance Rate

When a victim of a homicide comes from a powerless and marginalized sector of our population, there is little pressure to solve the case and apprehend the killer. As homicide investigators are assigned additional homicides to investigate, the "less-dead" victims receive less and less priority. Without public or mass media pressure, such victims become less and less important. If, as the author has argued, the less-dead represent most of the serial killer's victims, law enforcement agencies are inadvertently placing a low priority on solving a homicide that has a fairly high probability of being part of a pattern of victims of a serial killer. Thus, by differentiating the value of homicide victims, the serial killer remains free to kill and kill again. In the final analysis, when this occurs, society's throwaways are indeed thrown away.

Law Enforcement's Lack of Knowledge of Other Agencies' Experiences with an Investigation: Documenting the Problem

Ted Bundy Case

Many of Theodore Bundy's murder victims were reported missing to the police by friends or relatives. In most cases, the victims' disappearances were treated as routine missing person reports by the police. In one instance in Utah, the police failed to file a missing report when a victim's mother reported her daughter's disappearance.

It was not until the fourth victim was reported missing, in May 1974, that the police established that there were some similarities among the disappearances of girls reported missing in Seattle, Olympia, and Ellensburg, Washington, and Corvallis, Oregon. It was not until early fall of that year that the missing girls' skeletal remains began to be discovered.

The task force in Seattle, Washington, established in March 1975 was a delayed response to the problem of missing and murdered girls. No victims missing specifically from Seattle's jurisdiction had been discovered until March of that year. However, the girls disappearing from Lake Sammamish in July 1974 and the discovery of their bodies in September of that year should have been sufficient, coupled with all the other disappearances, to have warranted joint investigative action much sooner (see Larsen, 1980; Rule, 1980; Winn and Merrill, 1980). The task force had a limited automated capability to cross-reference their information. Their access to computers did not occur until long after the investigation had begun. Even so, when Bundy was arrested in Salt Lake City, he was one of the task force's top 100 remaining suspects to be checked and entered into the computer.

Parents of the murdered girl in Utah County, Utah, asked the local sheriff's office to obtain assistance in their investigation from the Salt Lake City police. The sheriff's office refused, indicating that they didn't need any assistance. This agency had a reputation for not working well with other agencies in the state.

Following the Chi Omega sorority house murders in Tallahassee, Florida, officers from Washington and Colorado notified the Leon County Sheriff's Office to look for Ted Bundy as a suspect. This tip was apparently ignored by the sheriff's office. Also, the sheriff's office provided little cooperation to Colorado police who were interested in investigating Bundy's jail escape.

John Wayne Gacy Case

When John Wayne Gacy's crimes were discovered, he was in custody. Gacy had been separately connected to four of his victims who had been reported missing. However, the fact that Gacy was a common link to all the missing boys was not identified by the Chicago police. Due to the decentralized organizational arrangement of the Chicago police, computer files were not centralized so that any officer could have access to them. The Des Plaines police had connected Gacy to this thirty-third and last victim, who had been reported missing in Des Plaines, Illinois. Then, through their investigation, the Des Plaines police connected him to other missing boys, who turned out also to have been Gacy's victims. Nine of Gacy's victims were never identified by the police (see Linedecker, 1980; Sullivan and Maiken, 1983).

Four complaints had been lodged against Gacy in Chicago between 1971 and 1978 for homosexual assaultive behavior. One was still pending when he was arrested. However, since Gacy was never identified as a common link to the missing boys, this criminal information on Gacy was never linked to the boys' disappearances.

Hillside Strangler Case

It was not until Kenneth Bianchi acted on his own and killed in Washington that he became a suspect in the "Hillside Strangler" murders. He was arrested for a double homicide in Bellingham, Washington. The Bellingham police notified the Los Angeles County Sheriff's Office since Bianchi had a California driver's license and had recently moved to Washington (see Schwarz, 1981; Barnes, 1984). The first three victims in Los Angeles County had been found within three separate law enforcement jurisdictions. The Los Angeles Police Department, the Los Angeles County Sheriff's Office, and the Glendale Police Department were each investigating a murder.

When homicide investigators from the sheriff's office viewed the body of the third victim where she had been found in Glendale, they immediately saw similarities to the death of the second victim, who was found in their jurisdiction (F. Salerno, personal communication, August 1, 1985). From this point on, investigators from the Los Angeles Police Department began exchanging information with the other two jurisdictions. However, it was not until November 22, 1977, and the discovery of five additional victims, that these law enforcement jurisdictions met formally to share information on the killings and decided to form a joint task force to investigate the murders.

Bianchi had been contacted personally in connection with the "Hillside" murders on at least three separate occasions, twice by the Los Angeles officers and once by a Glendale police officer. These contacts were in response to tips called into the police. On a fourth and a fifth occasion, Bianchi's name was reported to the police, but no officer responded to this information. In all these cases, the information on Bianchi was either evaluated as unimportant, cleared with no additional follow-up necessary, or had become lost among the thousands of tips given to police during late 1977 and in 1978.

The task force formed in November 1977 grew to involve 130 officers assigned full time from three police agencies at the height of their investigation in early 1978. The size of the task force is reported to have created internal communication and coordination problems among its members, who were working around the clock to solve the murders. Of possibly more importance is the fact that the three police agencies were physically separated, working in different facilities, working their own clues and leads separately, and providing only summary information which was computerized without cross-referencing capability (F. Salerno, personal communication, August 30, 1985). Establishing linkages and common elements from all the data collected, transmitted, and stored in this manner became a difficult task.

Henry Lee Lucas Case

No patterns to Henry Lee Lucas's homicides were known to have been identified prior to his arrest and subsequent confessions, except for the homicides occurring between 1978 and 1980 along Interstate 35 from Austin, Texas, to the Texas–Oklahoma border north of Dallas, which Lucas is now strongly suspected of having committed. A law enforcement conference was held to discuss these murders and to share information among the various Texas jurisdictions involved.

The Lucas task force was formed after Lucas had been arrested and began confessing to the murders. Four major conferences in Texas, Louisiana, and California were held specifically to discuss Lucas and his killings. All of these efforts were, however, after the fact and too late for a number of victims (see Egger, 1985).

SUMMARY OF INVESTIGATIVE PROBLEMS

In the Bundy and Gacy cases the police responded to a number of reports on missing persons, most of them in their teens. Although responding to reports on missing young persons in a routine and perfunctory manner does not necessarily relate to linkage blindness, as defined, it does suggest the unwillingness of the police to make an effort to look for linkages among missing reports, when they are considered routine, assumed to be reports of runaways, not really considered a law enforcement problem by the police, and not seen as potentially life-threatening. A similar problem was apparent, although not well documented, in the Lucas case.

The Bundy and Lucas cases provide some examples of local and state agencies not sharing information or assisting one another. In the Bundy case there were numerous examples of sharing across local and state jurisdictions. However, there were at least two instances of a refusal to share information, seek assistance from another agency, or to cooperate with an investigation. The Lucas case represents the lack of sharing or coordination at a macro level, across numerous states as well as local jurisdictions. The difference here is that no patterns were identified to require interagency or interstate cooperation. However, the lack of such cooperation or a mechanism with which to communicate means that the patterns, identifiable in some cases on a large geographic scale, were not identified until after his arrest.

In the Gacy and Lucas cases, all coordinated responses to their killings were after the fact. No patterns to Lucas's criminal behavior were identified until after his arrest. The police in the Gacy case did finally begin to discern a pattern in his behavior, but only after 33 deaths.

In the "Hillside" and Bundy cases, police responded with a multijurisdictional task force operation. Both were delayed responses to a problem, with Seattle being the more delayed. Neither task force had adequate automated cross-referencing capability. In the "Hillside" case, the task force was also so decentralized that the problem of coordinating and sharing their information was undoubtedly magnified rather than reduced.

The subjectivity of hindsight is not necessarily a fair measure or a reliable measure of the effectiveness or efficiency of the numerous law enforcement agencies responding to these four serial murderers. Also, an after-the-fact assessment when all the facts are known, combined with recommendations beginning with phrases such as "They should have" or "If they had only," do not substantiate a cause-and-effect relationship and may facilitate very little change in the present intra- and inter-law enforcement communications. However, if the occurrences of linkage blindness found in the police response to these serial murderers are representative of the differing levels and degrees of this problem, workable solutions emerge and are the next logical step.

LINKAGE BLINDNESS: AN ANALYSIS

Interorganizational relations within the criminal justice system emerged as a major policy issue in the late 1960s and early 1970s. Recommendations of national commissions during this period attest to this concern (Johnson, 1977, pp. 5–6):

- In 1967, the President's Commission on Law Enforcement and the Administration of Justice recommended more cooperation between criminal justice agencies at the local level.

- In 1969, the National Commission on the Cause and Prevention of Violence called for local jurisdiction to establish criminal justice coordinating councils.
- In 1973, the National Advisory Commission on Criminal Justice Standards and Goals acclaimed those local areas that had adopted local criminal justice councils, then further recommended that all major metropolitan areas consider adopting this criminal justice linkage model.

Gray and Williams (1980) define coordination as the planned and self-conscious interdependence of two or more organizations. They note that coordination of functional and jurisdictional elements is an agreed-upon goal of the Omnibus Crime Control and Safe Streets Act of 1969 as amended (p. 138). However, neither the three commissions referred to above, nor the Safe Streets Act, refer specifically to coordination and communication between separate law enforcement agencies for the purpose of sharing information on unsolved crimes. The emphasis in these commission reports and legislation is on communication and coordination among components of the criminal justice system (police, prosecution, courts, and corrections), not on the interagency relations of law enforcement agencies.

Most references in the literature to the lack of communication, coordination, or networking among law enforcement agencies attribute this problem to the decentralized nature and local control of American policing. Vollmer concluded in 1936 that American peace officers employed by various units of government operated under a highly decentralized plan of organization with virtually no coordination among these governmental units (Vollmer, 1936, p. 236). Smith (1960) makes a similar observation:

> There is therefore no such thing in the United States as a police system, nor even a set of police systems within any reasonably accurate sense of the term. Our so-called systems are mere collections of police units having some similarity of authority, organization, or jurisdiction; but they lack any systematic relationship to each other. (pp. 20–21)

Leonard (1980) discussed governmental fragmentation and the police:

> The American system of government is based on a political philosophy of decentralized power and local control. As a result, governmental structures, including police agencies, have proliferated and often overlap one another. Semiautonomous governments (for example, towns, villages, cities, and the like) have established a wide variety of police agencies with differing formal structures and functions. (p. 11)

In discussing the organizational scale of U.S. law enforcement, Bayley (1977) stated:

The United States has the most decentralized police system in the world. Bruce Smith's famous figure is that there are 40,000 separate police forces in the United States. A more accurate figure may be 25,000. The United States does not really have a system, in the sense of development in accord with a considered plan; it has abutting and overlapping jurisdictions predicated on separate units of government. Like Topsy, the American police just grew. The strength of this tradition has been seen recently in the prevalence of the slogan "Support your local police." (p. 232)

Colton (1978) referred to the fragmented nature of law enforcement work:

Although there are federal police services (e.g., the Federal Bureau of Investigation, the Secret Service, etc.) the guiding principle in the United States is that police work is generally a local function and that recruiting, training, and levels of compensation are provided by local control. (p. 8)

In discussing why American police operate differently than their counterparts in England and France, Wilson (1978) stated:

The essential problem is that whereas other nations have either a national police force (as does France) or at least a single police force for each city (as does England), police responsibilities in the United States are divided among local, state, and federal authorities, each with a constitutionally distinct basis for existence. Federalism, in short, creates a system of different and even rival police organizations sharing powers over common problems. (p. 58)

In advocating a regional approach to policing, McCauley (1973) stated:

The demand for local autonomy and "home rule" has created rigid jurisdictional limitations. Traditionally, today's law enforcement officer has authority only within the confines of his territorial jurisdiction. Likewise, the responsibility for maintaining public peace and order is esoterically funneled, thus effecting a condition whereby law enforcement and the "national crime problem" are viewed as local problems. The implication, then, is that crime must be prevented and controlled primarily at the local levels of government. (p. 1)

Thibault et al. (1985) state that there is an abundance of police forces in this country due to the federal system of government and the wish of local communities to have control over their police. As a result, they find certain organizational realities in American policing today (p. 319):

1. Active competition between police organizations for calls, resources, and, at times, personnel.
2. De facto spheres of influence arranged by formal and informal agreements between agencies. For instance, while the state police have statewide jurisdiction, many will normally not answer calls in a village

that has a police department; the village police, in the same light, will not go outside municipal limits except in pursuit of an offender.

3. Informal relationships, usually based upon how well certain officers or agency heads get along, determine the distribution of intelligence information, assistance to other departments during emergencies, and the success or failure of interagency projects.

In addition to the decentralization, fragmentation, or balkanization of police agencies, references in the literature were also found that attributed the problem of linkage blindness to a jealousy or competitiveness among agencies, and in some cases, among individual officers. Alpert (1984) cited professional jealousy as a hindrance to interagency cooperation. He stated:

> Although investigations are an integral part of police work, the organization of detectives and other personnel can interfere with good police work. For example, if both a police department and the district (or state) attorney's office have investigators, professional jealousy and the desire to receive credit for an arrest may hinder cooperation. If more than one jurisdiction is involved, whether it be a city, a county, or a state and a federal one, professional jealousy may be harmful to effective and efficient law enforcement. (p. 45)

In determining critical problems facing smaller police agencies, McCauley (1973) said that "interdepartmental conflicts and jealousies inhibit coordination and cooperation" (p. 4). He also noted: "Cooperation between state and local police is not always genuine" (p. 229). McCauley (1973) believed that this ungenuine cooperation is a product of status manifestation due to the differential compensation, standards, equipment, and working conditions between state and local police agencies.

Smith (1960) argued that the competition among law enforcement agencies results from personalities and leadership style. He stated:

> The relationship between the varied types of police forces is difficult to explore in a systematic fashion. Partly it rests upon the personalities of the chief figures in the departments involved. As between forces in such specialized fields as narcotics suppression and liquor enforcement there is intense rivalry, based upon competition for informants and prestige. Numerous department heads imagine that interagency rivalry will develop a spirit among their own subordinates: rivalry thus becoming a device for leadership. (p. 23)

Strecher (1957) referred to both fragmentation and competitiveness among law enforcement agencies as contributing to coordination and communication problems. In his case study of the well-known Sam Shepard murder case of 1954 in the Cleveland, Ohio, metropolitan area, Strecher (1957) found that the administrative deficiencies in the investigation of Marilyn Shepard's murder occurred due to the jurisdictional overlapping and interagency rivalry of the law enforcement agencies involved. Strecher (1957) stated:

> The reaction of each of the assisting officials cognizant of the interagency rivalry and the distribution of legal power among rival officials, was to hasten into the investigative activity, assuming as large a role as possible without entirely supplanting any other organization. It is problematical, even if one competent official had assumed total responsibility for the inquiry, whether he could have elicited the cooperation of rival officials or their personnel. (p. 115)

Robert Daley (1983), a writer and former police commissioner of the New York City Police Department, commented on the jealousy, competitiveness, and territoriality of police officers in a recent work of fiction, which, for many, is fact disguised as fiction:

> Like politicians they fought over jurisdiction, over protocol. Like actors they fought for credit for a headline. Given the chance to make a major arrest, to break an important case, they were willing, figuratively speaking, to destroy each other. (pp. 125–126)

> Law enforcement personnel deal in secrets every day. Indeed their business relied on secrets almost exclusively. Which was not to say they were good at keeping them. Juicy tidbits were revealed to girl friends, to barmen and to the press almost as a matter of habit. Secrets were kept habitually—and with an almost religious fervor—only from each other.(p. 283)

Robert Keppel, who was involved with the Ted Bundy investigation in Seattle, Washington, and a consultant to the current Green River killings task force, found evidence of direct and intentional resistance to cooperation and coordination among police agencies. After trying to link serial killings in Seattle with murder in other locales, Keppel discovered some police agencies wanting no part of a serial murder investigation. One officer stated to Keppel, "I've had problems there in the big city. Stay away from us" (*Newsweek*, November 26, 1984, p. 106).

Forensic investigative services to many law enforcement jurisdictions are difficult, particularly in rural areas of this county. The lack of access to qualified forensic investigative support services by small rural police agencies causes them to rely on state or large police agencies for these services, which must be allocated to many geographic areas. Also, the medical examiner or coroner is frequently an elected official who is not a forensic pathologist. This problem of forensic support is further exacerbated by a lack of standardized procedures in many agencies for collection and processing of physical evidence.

Structural factors of the typical law enforcement agency's organizational arrangement also contribute to linkage blindness. The phenomenon of single-complaint policing rather than problem-based responses such as the problem-oriented approach (see Goldstein, 1977) result in police patrol units reacting to situations without identifying multiple situations of a similar nature as a problem or pattern to be resolved. The same is true for organization and resource allocation of the criminal investigation function. Here, the "case" basis of investigative assignment also precludes rapid identification of a developing crime pattern.

As indicated earlier, law enforcement's response, or lack thereof, to reports of missing persons fails to create the necessary information from which a readily identified pattern may emerge. Although this has recently been changing in agencies across the country, there are still many agencies unwilling to respond actively to reports of missing persons or to treat them as serious and potentially violent criminal acts.

Linkage blindness also occurs frequently due to the inability of policing organizations to deal with large amounts of information. Brooks et al. (1988) found that, historically, "the Achilles' heel of most prolonged serial murder investigations has not been that of the investigation function per se, but the viability of the law enforcement agencies involved to manage the massive amounts of information received and generated" (p. 2).

In most serial murder investigations, the vast amount of information and its rate of accumulation quickly exceeds human capabilities for effective management. While most governmental agencies in large metropolitan areas have installed computerized operations to increase the efficiency of their services, law enforcement agencies have, for the most part, been far behind the cutting edge of this development. Computer-assisted dispatching and automated records systems are commonplace today in many agencies; however, the development of computerized information systems to support investigation has lagged far behind. With the development of VICAP at the national level and HALT-like systems at the state level, the acceptance and utilization of these important tools, particularly for cross-jurisdictional information sharing, remains far from the normal operations of law enforcement agencies.

Further, law enforcement agencies are generally accustomed to operating as self-contained units specifically devoted to responding to service to the public within their respective jurisdictional boundaries. The organizational structure hierarchically designed for vertical downward and upward communication is sorely suited for communication and coordination with agencies outside their jurisdiction.

Linkage blindness is the real and ever-present cause of law enforcement's inability to respond to serial murder in a timely and effective manner. As indicated earlier, linkage blindness has been defined as the luck of sharing or coordination of investigative information and the lack of adequate networking among law enforcement agencies and law enforcement officers in this country. Numerous references to the communication problem have been directly or indirectly referred to by others. Further, this problem has been documented earlier in the text in the four well-known serial murder cases of Bundy, Gacy, the "Hillside Strangler," and Lucas.

In the day-to-day operations of law enforcement agencies in this country, little serious attention or resource allocation has been paid to interagency communication, cooperation, or coordination of the criminal investigation function. Today the chances of linkage blindness occurring within the law enforcement community are very good, due to the decentralized and fragmented nature of policing, resulting in thousands of law enforcement jurisdictions. Both the regionalization of policing services and the consolidation of police agencies have met with only limited success in this country. Jealousy, a sense of interagency competitiveness, and "turf" battles only add to the problem of linkage blindness, facilitating a systematic myopia. Limited forensic services with coroners ill-prepared to support criminal investigations is another contributor.

Structural factors such as single-complaint policing and "case"-based investigative assignments within hierarchically designed levels of control in most police agencies greatly inhibit interagency communication and increase the probability for linkage blindness to occur. Also, law enforcement's response to reports of missing persons, although currently changing, has clouded the lenses of many agencies in their view of these cases and evolving crime patterns. Fortunately, many such reports are beginning to be viewed with increased awareness of their potential criminality. Untimely and ineffective information management has also contributed to increased instances of linkage blindness. The inability to support criminal investigation with effective information management will greatly inhibit multijurisdictional investigations of serial murder.

By the late 1990s most police departments will have access to computer services. Access is only the first step, however. Standardized formats for the information and data processed by these services must be the next step. The next step must be training of police personnel. Otherwise, the benefits of this automation will be wiped out, due to the unwillingness of police personnel to take advantage of the computer, further exacerbating the problem of linkage blindness.

Serial killers are able to escape apprehension for long periods of times while they continue to kill. This has more to do with problems of law enforcement than with the special skills of these killers. Linkage blindness is the crux of the law enforcement problem. *Linkage blindness*, a term coined by the author in 1984, refers to a serious communication problem among law enforcement agencies in this country. Briefly stated, law enforcement agencies do not willingly and as a matter of accepted procedure readily share with one another information on unsolved murders. When it does occur, this sharing of information will greatly assist law enforcement investigators in identifying a pattern of homicides committed in different jurisdictions. Sadly, this sharing of information does not occur often enough. Many mobile serial killers have killed in numerous jurisdictions across the country, and this has protected them from being arrested. In effect, their mobility results in an immunity from quick and swift apprehension. It should also be noted that to be effective, this mobility does not have to occur across jurisdictions. Large urban police jurisdictions with numerous precincts or district stations have also had serial killers roaming their areas, killing, with what might be considered an immunity from detection or apprehension.

Linkage blindness results from the lack of sharing of information on unsolved murders among interested officers and among different jurisdictions: homicide investigative information that is not coordinated among multiple jurisdictions or areas of a single jurisdiction and the lack of adequate networking by law enforcement agencies and their officers. Linkage blindness is a systemic weakness of U.S. policing, due to the multitude of law enforcement agencies in every state and the different levels of policing (local, state, and national) that are present. The United States has the most decentralized policing system in the world, and since it appears to be the major hunting ground for serial killers, this decentralization, without a deliberate effort to share and communicate regarding unsolved cases, increases the probability that the serial killer can continue to kill with a great deal of immunity from detection.

As Robert Keppel, who was involved in the serial murder investigations of Ted Bundy and the Green River killer, has stated, for police departments to catch a serial killer, "they have to be more open to talk with other departments about what they have, because to identify the serial it may not be [all] within their jurisdiction . . . so just identifying the serial up front is one of the most important things" (Griffiths, 1993).

In most police responses to a serial murder, particularly those involving multiple jurisdictions, the author has found that the police were actively attempting to increase common linkages or networks among the law enforcement officers or agencies involved in the investigation (Egger, 1990a). Further, these investigations have focused on identifying, documenting, and verifying a serial murderer's trail of victims. In other words, these agencies have attempted to reduce the extent to which linkage blindness has allowed the serial killer to kill and kill again.

Information is necessary to establish that a single homicide event is part of a series of multiple homicide events. Second, information is necessary to establish modus operandi patterns. Information is also necessary to evaluate the physical evidence from the identified series. To obtain access to this kind of information, an investigator or his agency must expand and develop new sources of information beyond jurisdictional boundaries. The obvious sources for this information are other law enforcement agencies in other jurisdictions, which encompass the series of common homicide events.

Unfortunately, the lack of law enforcement efforts to expand sources of information to other jurisdictions has been characteristic in most of the incidents of serial murder in this country and to a great extent in other countries as well. Specifically, the U.S. law enforcement community very infrequently makes the necessary effort to seek sources of information outside their respective jurisdictional boundaries because of a blindness, forced or intentional, to the informational linkages necessary to respond effectively to the serial murder. Criminal investigators have not seen, have been prevented from seeing, or have made little attempt to see beyond their jurisdictional responsibilities in homicide investigations, which turned out to be of a serial nature.

The author has documented this problem of linkage blindness in a number of serial murder cases (Egger, 1985). In analyzing the four case studies presented earlier, this problem is evident in all the cases. In the Ted Bundy case, it was not until the fourth victim was reported missing in May 1974 that the police established that there were some similarities among the disappearances of girls reported missing in Seattle, Olympia, and Ellensburg, Washington, and Corvallis, Oregon. It was not until early fall that the missing girls' skeletons began to be discovered. It was not until a year later that a task force was established in Seattle, Washington. Further, following the Chi Omega sorority house murders in Tallahassee, Florida, law enforcement agencies provided little cooperation to Colorado and Washington police when they suggested that Bundy was a probable suspect in these killings.

When John Wayne Gacy's murders were discovered, he was in custody. Gacy had been separately connected to four of his victims who had been reported missing. Also, four complaints of sexual assault had been lodged against Gacy between 1971 and 1978. One of these complaints was still pending when he was arrested.

It was not until Kenneth Bianchi acted on his own in Washington that he became a suspect in the "Hillside Strangler" murders. The three police agencies involved (Los Angeles, Los Angeles County, and the city of Glendale) were physically separated during their investigations, working in different facilities, working their own leads, and providing only summary information to each other in the form of computer data, which was not cross-referenced.

No patterns to the murders committed by Henry Lee Lucas and Ottis Toole were known to have been identified as a serial pattern prior to the arrest of Lucas in 1983. No interagency or interstate cooperation had been initiated to investigate these murders until after his arrest.

It is not the intent of the author to focus on mistakes of law enforcement with such comments as "they should have," or "if they had only." It is nevertheless necessary when analyzing these case and many others to highlight a major problem, that of linkage blindness.

In the next chapter we discuss various police responses to serial murder. From this analysis we will see how linkage blindness plays a part in the various responses.

CHAPTER 12

≡⟩◇⟨≡

DIFFERENT POLICE STRATEGIES TO SERIAL MURDER

INTRODUCTION

Technically, the unsolved murder is never closed. Other murders occur and "old" cases receive reduced priorities. Resources are scarce and must be allocated on a cost-effective basis. Higher solvability factors, as well as the currency of the event, equate to higher priorities and the reallocation of investigative personnel to other cases. However, when the unsolved murder is part of an identified series, law enforcement agencies are under a great deal of pressure to continue the investigation regardless of the current probabilities of solving the crime or the cost-effectiveness of pursuing the case compared to other criminal cases. When the murder is identified and labeled as a serial murder, everything changes. As indicated in Chapter 11, the pressures from politicians, the media, and the general public create a different set of expectations, and agencies involved in the investigation of a serial murder seek a variety of solutions to catching the serial killer.

Unfortunately, regardless of the solutions selected, a serial murder case may remain unsolved. In the famous Green River investigation, after many years of trying to capture this elusive killer or killers, there have been no arrests. In the "Atlanta Child Murders" investigation, an arrest was made.

Wayne Williams was found guilty of two murders. However, few who have studied this case believe him to be responsible for all of the remaining 27 missing and murdered children.

Police have been successful in solving serial murder cases. However, this success has not always been the direct result of a specific law enforcement strategy aimed at the serial killer. At times this success may have little or nothing to do with a specific strategy. Bobbie Joe Long was not caught as a result of the formation of a task force in Hillsborough County, Florida. He was arrested when one of his intended victims got away to report her ordeal to the police. The subsequent investigation is a textbook example of good investigative techniques and interagency cooperation (noted later). However, the actions of the task force alone did not identify Long. Rather, it was their response to a reported assault that led to his arrest and conviction for nine murders, as well as convictions for kidnapping and rape in Pasco and Hillsborough counties, Florida.

Another example of success in a serial murder investigation having little to do with the police strategies being used to catch the killer is the case of the "Michigan Murders." The author was assigned to this investigation in 1969 while working for the Ann Arbor, Michigan, Police Department. This task force, which combined the resources of seven law enforcement agencies in Washtenaw County and the Michigan State Police, was indeed a frustrating exercise. Over a number of months the task force had not been successful in identifying a feasible suspect for the killings of seven young women in the area: that is, not until Michigan State Police Corporal David Leik returned to his home in Ypsilanti from a family vacation. While away, the Leiks had asked their nephew, John Norman Collins, to watch their house and care for their dog. Corporal Leik became suspicious of some red stains on washtubs in his basement after learning that his nephew had been questioned in the deaths of seven young women killed in the area since 1967. He scraped off samples of these stains and collected hair clippings from the basement area, where he had cut his children's hair before going on vacation. The stains revealed nothing connected to the murders. The hair clippings were, however, of great interest to the crime lab. By neutron activation analysis, crime lab technicians were able to match these clippings with the hair clippings taken from the body of the seventh female victim. Collins was arrested, and the hair clippings taken from his car also matched the clippings from the basement and the victim. Collins was convicted of this seventh murder. Most investigators on the case remain convinced that he was responsible for the deaths of at least four of the other six victims.

Luck, happenstance, being in the right place at the right time, routine police work, awareness of a serial murder investigation, or a fluke; they have played an important part in catching a number of serial killers. They probably always will. This doesn't mean we should assume that the police aren't doing much of a job at catching serial killers. With experience and the benefit and application of research, police do seem to be progressing in their efforts to catch serial killers. With the use of DNA fingerprinting, behavioral research, advanced crime link analysis, better utilization of the computer, and a greater awareness that sharing of information on unsolved cases should be a high priority, law enforcement agencies do appear to be moving forward in their effort to increase their effectiveness in serial murder investigations.

Notwithstanding these advances, police in this country (and in a number of other countries who have experienced serial murder) remain unsure of the correct response to a serial murder. A homicide investigation demands certain procedures and required skills. A multiple homicide that is serial in nature is quite another matter. When it involves more than one jurisdiction, it is indeed another matter. The police ask, "What strategy should we use?, How should we respond?" While law enforcement agencies are generally unwilling to admit to this frustration or lack of certainly on how to proceed, it will take only a quick review of the literature on serial murder to identify this problem. As indicated in Chapter 11, it is sometimes very difficult to get police to admit to the problem of linkage blindness. However, to get police to admit that they lack information and knowledge on the best way to proceed in a serial murder investigation is, as a colleague once stated, "Like pushing Jello up the side of a tree with a straw." Like any other profession, police don't like to acknowledge their uncertainty in responding to a difficult situation. Professionals are trained to respond to a variety of problems and situations. Unfortunately, this is not the case when police are confronted with a serial murder.

When police respond to what they believe is a serial murder, very traditional approaches are the rule. Frequently, an agency may begin the investigation as they would any other homicide investigation, only with more resources and determination to solve the murders. In some cases, police managers may consult other agencies that have had experience with a serial murder investigation. At other times, the agency may call on the expertise of the FBI Behavioral Science Unit in Quantico, Virginia. Very small agencies will sometimes call on the expertise of the state police. Request for assistance from other agencies frequently depends on the interagency relationships involved, the willingness of the agency administrator to seek outside assistance, and the agency's commitment to searching beyond their jurisdictional boundaries for a solution to a crime. Of course, the agency must first be willing to consider that homicides committed within their jurisdiction are linked to other homicides in other jurisdictions.

When homicides are identified as part of a serial sequence, either by confessions of an apprehended serial murderer or through the occurrence of a number of similar murders in a relatively small or contiguous geographical area, the police must respond. A review of the various ways in which law enforcement has responded to serial murder resulted in several categories: holding conferences with involved or potentially involved agencies, acting as a clearinghouse of information on the serial crimes, the formation of a task force for the coordination of multiple jurisdiction investigations, the uses of an outside investigative consultant team, or the use of psychological profiling. All of these responses are, of course, after the fact and reactive in nature. A less reactive response, although certainly not preventive in a pure sense, is the development of a centralized point of analysis from which to identify patterns of serial murders as they emerge and to communicate such patterns to the appropriate agencies for necessary and combined action. There are other responses to serial murder used less frequently than the aforementioned categories. These responses include the use of specially developed computer software programs, geoforensic pattern analysis, and paying an identified serial killer for criminal evidence necessary to locate all his murder victims. Each of these categories of law enforcement response to serial murder is described in this chapter.

Before we describe and analyze various responses by law enforcement to serial murder, we must, however, restate the major conclusion of Chapter 1 and, in effect, the premise of this book. A systematic search of the current literature and research on serial murder reveals that very little of scholarly substance and empirical knowledge is available on law enforcement's response to serial murder. Without such an empirically validated knowledge base, law enforcement's response to the serial murder is very frequently unsuccessful and, when successful, more a product of change than of a sophisticated and carefully planned approach. Jenkins' (1989) description of research on serial murder: "the very rudimentary state of our knowledge of serial murder, even when our access to the facts of particular cases is extensive" (p. 2) should be a warning to those who construe the following taxonomy as an indictment of law enforcement's investigative skills. In other words, those armed with the knowledge of this taxonomy and its apparent aggregate failures should temper their quickness to criticize.

Table 12–1 depicts the various strategies that police have used in responding to serial murder. These response strategies or a combination of these strategies were used by law enforcement agencies in serial murder investigations over the past 20 years in the United States, Canada, and England.

CONFERENCES

Law enforcement conferences are almost a tradition in police work. They are held on an annual basis by professional associations to socialize, share new

TABLE 12-1	LAW ENFORCEMENT RESPONSE STRATEGIES TO SERIAL MURDER			
Strategy	Examples	Networking Skills	Outside Assistance	Primary Expertise
Conference	National Conference on Serial Murder, Unidentified Bodies and Missing Persons, Oklahoma City, 1986 Green River Killer, 1986 Henry Lee Lucas, LA, 1983–84; WI and GA, 1984 Bobby J. Long, FL, 1984 Austin, TX, 1980	Cooperation and sharing of information Cross-case analysis	Interagency emphasis	Investigator skills Ability to identify possible similarities between cases
Information clearinghouse	Lucas Task Force, TX, 1983–85 Tennessee Bureau of Investigation, 1985	Collection and sharing of information	Interagency focus	Interagency relationships
Task force	Green River Atlanta Child Murders, 1980 San Diego, CA Hillside Strangler, 1977 Gainesville, FL, 1990 Zodiac, New York City, 1990	Coordination Organization of Information	Inter- and Intraagency concern	Same as above Willingness to to ignore "turf battles" and share information
Central coordination without forming a task force	Aileen Wuornos case, Marion Co., FL, 1990	Communication Coordination of information	Interagency	Same as above Willingness to trust agencies to share information and work together without a formal structure
Profiling	FBI Behavioral Science Unit State and local officers trained by FBI Psychologists Psychiatrists Geographic profiling Investigative psychology, University of Liverpool, UK	Cooperation Liaison Coordination	Yes	Investigative experience and exposure to a number of cases Psychology Psychiatry Empirical research and statistical analysis
Investigative consultants	Investigative team Atlanta, GA, 1980 Gainesville, FL, 1990	Cooperation Liaison Coordination	Yes	Special skills (investigation, criminology, research, analysis, and policing)
Forensic consultants	National, state, and local crime labs Medical examiner	Same as above	Yes	Forensic medicine Criminalistics DNA analysis Hypnosis

TABLE 12-1	CONTINUED			
Strategy	Examples	Networking Skills	Outside Assistance	Primary Expertise
Major incident room procedures	Police forces in the United Kingdom	Coordination	Intraagency focus Possibly	Investigative skills Training and use of standardized procedures in serious crime investigations
Solicitation from public	Clue tips or leads made to central telephone number (numerous cases) 2-hr TV special request; information on Green River Killer	Identifying and linking relevant information	Yes	Public relations Communication Electronic media
Computer analysis system	Holmes: UK, Toronto, and St. Petersburg, FL Dr. Watson case management system, Ontario, Canada Expert Systems Text management systems	If multiple jurisdictions involved	Possibly	Systems analysis Computer programs Software development
Centralized investigative network	Interpol VICAP (FBI) VICLAS (RCMP) HALT (NY State Police) HITS (WA) Other states	All of the above Collecting information from police agencies Communicating analysis results to appropriate agency	Interagency emphasis	Crime and pattern analysis Software and hardware support Communication Interagency relations
Psychics	Boston Strangler Michigan Murders J. W. Gacy Atlanta child murders Other cases where police don't acknowledge this assistance	Liaison Cooperation Coordination	Yes	Parapsychology Psychic phenomena
Offender rewards	R. Hansen (Anchorage, AK; confession and location of victims for out-of-state incarceration) Clifford Olsen [Vancouver, Canada; confession and location of victims for $110,000 (Canadian) to his family] Confession in return for no death penalty	If multiple jurisdictions involved	Yes	Willingness to "deal" with killer Interrogation
Rapid response team	FBI Rapid Start Team San Francisco: 15-yr investigation of 14 bombings aimed at educators St. Louis: kidnap murders of two girls Florida regional coordination teams	Development of mutual aid pact Liaison Cooperation Coordination	Yes	Crime and pattern analysis Communication with national data bases Interagency relations Investigative skills

techniques and technology, and generally be brought up to date on the particular world of policing germane to the specialization of the attendees or members. Conferences are convened to address specific problems facing multiple law enforcement jurisdictions, and only very recently have such conferences attempted to deal with serial murder. Conferences dealing with serial murder have been of two types, those dealing with numerous unsolved murders and those responding to the ramifications of the identification and confessions of a serial murderer.

One such conference dealing with numerous unsolved murders was held at the Texas Department of Public Safety Training Center in Austin, Texas, on October 28–30, 1980. The discovery of an unidentified homicide victim found along Interstate 35 near Waco, Texas, and numerous other unsolved homicides occurring along this highway in a three-year period was the catalyst for the conference. Conference coordinator Jim Boutwell, sheriff of Williamson County, Texas, stated: "We have a killer (or killers) still on the loose, traveling I-35. We know that the M.O. is not the same in all murders. Guns, knives, and strangulation have been utilized in killing these victims. Some may have been raped; some haven't" (J. Boutwell to F. Hacker, personal communication, August 29, 1980). Representatives from 32 cities, counties, and political jurisdictions in Texas attended this conference, and 19 new leads to unsolved area crimes resulted from the information shared among law enforcement officers Boutwell stated four years later: "If we'd only known about Henry [Henry Lee Lucas] back then!" (James Boutwell, personal communication, July 18, 1984). Other such conferences were held in response to the "Green River killings" in the Seattle, Washington, area (1983); the "Michigan murders" in the Ann Arbor–Ypsilanti, Michigan, area (1968); and the "Hillside Strangler" case in the Los Angeles, California, area (1979).

More recent examples of this type of conference were three conferences held in Canada. The Royal Canadian Mounted Police (RCMP) in Vancouver, British Columbia, sponsored the first conference in October 1991, entitled Project Eclipse. Experienced psychological profilers and crime analysts from New York, South Carolina, Seattle, the FBI, the Ontario Provincial Police, and the RCMP examined 25 unsolved homicides that had occurred in southwestern British Columbia. The primary purpose of this conference was to seek the opinion of the attendees regarding linkages between cases and to develop psychological profiles. In April 1992, the Ontario Provincial Police sponsored a second conference with the same format analyzing 11 unsolved homicides within the province of Ontario. Attendees at this second conference came from New York, the FBI, RCMP, Ontario, and Quebec. Building on the experience of these first two conferences, the RCMP sponsored a third conference entitled Project Kayo in Edmonton to analyze 14 unsolved homicides occurring in Alberta. Profilers, crime analysts, and homicide investigators from New Jersey, Iowa, the FBI, the

Ontario Provincial Police, the RCMP, and Montreal attended. They were provided with laptop computers. Thirteen investigative profiles of unknown offenders were developed. The RCMP plans to use the format and organization of Project Kayo as a model for future projects of this nature (MacKay, 1994).

An example of conferences convened in response to an identified, as well as confessing serial murder were the two conferences organized by the Monroe, Louisiana, Police Department in October 1983 and January 1984. In a direct response to the arrest and subsequent confessions of serial murderer Henry Lee Lucas in Texas, more than 150 investigators from 24 different states met during these two conferences and compared notes on unsolved murders in their area and were briefed by the Texas Rangers regarding Lucas's known travels and modus operandi. Similar conferences in 1984 in Wisconsin and Georgia focused primarily on Henry Lee Lucas and unsolved murders in those states (Gest, 1984; Lindsey, 1984).

Another example was the conference on December 10, 1984, organized by the Florida agencies following the arrest of Robert Joe Long, charged with eight counts of sexual battery, nine counts of kidnapping, one count of aggravated assault, seven counts of murder, and one count of first-degree murder in the Tampa, Florida, area. The Hillsborough County, Florida, Sheriff's Office, Tampa Police Department, and Florida Department of Law Enforcement officers from Florida, Georgia Bureau of Investigation, and the Regional Organized Crime Information Center in Nashville, Tennessee, attended. Information on Long and on a series of unsolved murders and rapes in Florida and Georgia was shared (Regional Organized Crime Information Center, 1985).

INFORMATION CLEARINGHOUSE

A response similar to the conference approach is the information clearinghouse. Again, such a response may occur due to the apprehension of a serial murderer or due to a number of unsolved murders involving multiple law enforcement jurisdictions. An example of the former, and on a national scale, was the Lucas Homicide Task Force in the state of Texas. The governor of Texas established this task force in November 1983. It was composed of Texas Rangers, the Texas Department of Public Safety, and the Williamson County sheriff's office. This task force operated until April 1985. This organization, while entitled a task force, performed the function of an information clearinghouse by communicating with law enforcement agencies requesting information on Lucas, coordinating interviews of Lucas conducted by law enforcement investigators from numerous states, compiling and distributing information on Lucas to requesting agencies, conducting preliminary interviews of Lucas for agencies that sent investigative information by mail, and providing security for Lucas. In addition, the Texas Rangers directly investi-gated 16 homicides committed in Texas in which Lucas was a suspect and assisted in numerous other investigations within the state. Between November 11, 1983 and April 12, 1985, approximately 600 different law enforcement agencies had interviewed Lucas. Total interviews of Lucas exceeded 1000 different people from 40 states and Canada. By the end of February 1985, a total of 210 homicide cases had been cleared by the task force, 189 of which were attributed directly to Lucas (B. Prince, personal communication, May 21, 1985). A more detailed description of this task force is documented in the Lucas case study in Chapter 7.

Another example of an information clearinghouse may be found in Tennessee. On April 24, 1985, the Tennessee Bureau of Investigation began serving as an information clearinghouse for law enforcement agencies from five different states (Pennsylvania, Kentucky, Tennessee, Mississippi, and Arkansas) and the Federal Bureau of Investigation in response to eight unsolved homicides of unidentified females occurring since October 1983. The clearinghouse provided information to all jurisdictions and was the cata-lyst for a network among them (*Tennessean*, April 25, 1984, p. 1). These homi-cides remain unsolved.

TASK FORCE

Gilbert (1983) contends that due to the increase in stranger criminal homi-cide, police administrators must seek nontraditional methods of case reduc-tion, such as aggressive patrol activity and interdepartmental task forces (pp. 162–63). However, the formation of a task force is one of the most tradi-tional methods of responding to a multijurisdiction criminal investigation.

In the early summer of 1969 a task force comprised of the Michigan State Police, Ann Arbor Police Department, Ypsilanti Police Department, Eastern Michigan University Police, and the Washtenaw County Sheriff's Office was established in Ann Arbor, Michigan, by the Washtenaw County Prosecutor's Office in response to six unsolved homicides of young females that had occurred in the county in the last two and one-half years. On July 28, 1969, a seventh young female homicide victim was found and on July 30, 1969, the governor of Michigan ordered the Michigan State Police to take charge of the investigations, "to concentrate and coordinate the efforts of all state and local agencies" (*Detroit News*, July 30, 1969, p. 1). John Norman Collins was arrested on August 1, 1969, for the murder of the seventh homi-cide victim and subsequently convicted. Homicide Captain Daniel C. Myre, Michigan State Police, who participated in this task force and later directed it after the governor's order, refers to a task force as a crime center in his book, *Death Investigation* (1974). Myre states:

The investigation of a major crime sometimes requires various police departments to unite and form a single investigative unit with a central headquarters.
Such major crime investigative centers are only as good as their organization
and information retrieval systems. To eliminate duplication of effort and insure
that evidence is handled properly by all investigators, a major crime center must
have a definite command structure and well-defined rules of procedure. (p. 153)

Levin and Fox (1985) state that the usual law enforcement response in
handling difficult investigations is to form a task force, which they argue,
"has never proven to be overly successful" (pp. 168–169). For Levin and Fox
(1985), the task force in the "Hillside Strangler" case was too large and
decentralized. They contend that had Bianchi not killed on his own in
Washington, the killings would never have been solved. "Until his arrest in
Washington, however, the Los Angeles task force had been stumped for a
year and had been labeled a total failure" (Levin and Fox, 1985, p. 169).

In July 1980, Chief Lee Brown announced the formation of a task force
to look into the problem of missing and murdered children in the Atlanta,
Georgia, area. The original task force consisted of five police officers
(Detlinger and Prugh, 1983, p. 68). This task force effort, which was to
grow a great deal larger, eventually resulted in the arrest and conviction of
Wayne Williams for murdering two of 28 homicide victims and suspected of
being responsible for the deaths of many of the other victims. Chet
Detlinger, formerly a police planner with the Kentucky Crime Commission
and a former assistant to Atlanta's chief of police, is extremely critical of the
Atlanta task force, particularly for their failure to place some homicide victims on a list of victims related to task force efforts and their analysis of the
geographic distribution of the homicides (Detlinger and Prugh, 1983).
Levin and Fox (1985) are also critical of the Atlanta task force for not being
formed earlier and for their failure to consider the geographic evidence in a
broader context.

Levin and Fox (1985) are also critical of the "Boston Strangler" task
force, which for them was poorly focused, with techniques as diverse as traditional forensics and the use of psychics. They state: "The capture of Albert
DeSalvo actually resulted from his arrest by the Cambridge Police for a
breaking and entering and an assault, rather than for one of the stranglings"
(p. 171).

Darrach and Norris (1984) contrast the Atlanta task force with the
Green River task force, set up to investigate the killings of over 30 young
women found in the general vicinity of the Green River in the Seattle,
Washington, area. They stated:

Everything that went wrong in the Atlanta investigation has been going right in
Seattle. The Green River Task Force, set up to investigate the killings, now
includes 30 talented detectives and is clearly one of the best organized, least

politicized and most effective units in the country. Protected by a strong sheriff, the group has shrewdly controlled the release of information to prevent hysteria and keep the killer guessing. (p. 64)

Unfortunately, however, the Green River task force was not successful in solving these homicides.

Past experience of multijurisdictional task forces reveals the crucial need for a well-managed and coordinated response. To meet this need, specific guidelines in the form of a manual, *Multi-Agency Investigative Team Manual* (MAIT) (Brooks, et al., 1988) was developed as a result of a National Institute of Justice grant of funds to Sam Houston State University in 1986. This manual resulted from the documentation and synthesis of a two-week conference of experienced serial murder investigators held in August 1986.

Although the MAIT manual was a disappointment for some because of its traditional approach to organization and management and its "cookbook" approach to the problem, there are indeed some particular points worth highlighting.

- The serial murderer often selects his victim from an urban area but disposes of the body in the privacy of a rural area, crossing jurisdictions in the process (p. 1).
- Law enforcement agencies are generally accustomed to operating as self-contained units and often do not have the organizational structure, personnel or inclination for coordinating with other agencies (p. 7).

Historically, the Achilles' heel of most prolonged serial murder investigations has not been that of the investigative function per se, but other factors:

- Management of the massive amounts of information received and effectively generated, and the ability to communicate internally or externally with other involved agencies are paramount (p. 23).
- With most serial murder investigations, the amount of information and the rate of accumulation far exceed human capabilities for management (p. 27).
- Case coordination, review, and analysis provide an opportunity to examine all investigative activities so that leads are not overlooked or links between them missed (p. 49).

A contemporary example of a task force formed to investigate a serial murder is the multistate task force formed to investigate the "I-70 Murders," involving police agencies in the states of Kansas, Indiana, Missouri, and Texas and the Federal Bureau of Investigation investigating possibly 10 homicides. These homicides have been tied to a single killer preying on retail clerks in stores located near interstate highways I-70 and I-35. These homicides occurred between April 8, 1992 and January 1994. Except for Texas, these killings were originally linked due to their close proximity to interstate highway systems and the fact that the victims were stalked before they were killed. This link was more firmly established when ballistics tests showed that the first six victims had all been shot with the same 22-caliber revolver. The links to Texas were confirmed due to the vocations of the victims and the fact that these killings were also near the interstate highway.

Law enforcement agencies from these states have been meeting periodically to share information. Recently it was determined that the St. Charles Police Department would set up a computerized data base to collect information related to the killings. Victims of these killings were all women except for one man with long hair and a ponytail (believed to have been mistaken for a woman by the killer) who worked in shoestores, bridal shops, a ceramics store, a video store, and a dance wear shop.

CENTRAL COORDINATION WITHOUT FORMING A TASK FORCE

In September 1990, law enforcement agencies in north-central Florida decided on a less than traditional approach to a serial murder investigation. Investigators from five county sheriffs' departments began to see similarities among a series of unsolved homicides that had occurred beginning in December of the preceding year. These investigators began to share the results of their investigations informally. Shortly after the discovery of a seventh homicide victim believed to be part of this series, two female suspects were identified and linked to these murders. On July 4 of that year these two suspects were seen leaving a car belonging to one of the victims after they had driven it off the road in the Ocala National Forest. Witnesses who saw these two women leaving the car and later hitchhiking away from the area assisted a police artist in developing a composite drawing of the two suspects.

In late November, the Marion County Sheriff's Office released information regarding these suspects and the composite drawing to a Reuters newspaper reporter and held a news conference the following day. For the first time reporters learned that investigators from five Florida counties were seeking two young women for questioning in a string of unsolved killings of men driving through the state on business. The bodies of five middle-aged men had been found in secluded areas of north-central Florida over the preceding seven months. The victims ranged in age from the forties to the mid-sixties and were traveling by car on business. Each victim had died from gunshot wounds from a small-caliber weapon.

This information was reported by a number of newspapers across the country, along with the composite drawing of the suspects. Within three weeks over 400 hundred people had called the Marion County Sheriff's

Office with leads to the case. Based on this information and fingerprints from a pawnshop where some of the victims' belongings had been pawned, the suspects were identified. By this time, the investigation, involving five county law enforcement agencies and the Florida Department of Law Enforcement, was being coordinated informally by the Marion County Sheriff's Office.

This informal coordination continued throughout the remainder of the investigation and included the arrest of one of the suspects. The investigation culminated with the interrogation of Aileen Carol Wuornos and her confession to seven homicides. Throughout this serial murder investigation, once agencies had agreed that the pattern of homicides indicated that the same killer or killers were involved, these six law enforcement agencies cooperated without a formal agreement or the development of a formal multiagency investigative task force or team. The Marion County Sheriff's Office took the initiative to serve as information coordinator to these agencies by collecting information on the various ongoing investigations and keeping each agency informed about progress and developments. In the final stages of the investigation the sheriff's office coordinated a multiagency surveillance of Wuornos, and her arrest.

PSYCHOLOGICAL PROFILING (INVESTIGATIVE PROFILING)

It is seldom that any man, unless he is very full-blooded, breaks out in this way through emotion, so I hazarded the opinion that the criminal was probably a robust and ruddy-faced man. Events proved that I had judged correctly.
—Sherlock Holmes, congratulating himself on the accuracy of his psychological profile in *A Study of Scarlet*

Psychological profiling is an attempt to provide investigators with more information on the serial murderer, who is yet to be identified. A more current and perhaps more descriptive term for this strategy is *investigative profiling*. The purpose of profiling is to develop a behavioral composite, combining sociological and psychological assessments of the offender. Profiling is generally based on the premise that an accurate analysis and interpretation of the crime scene and other locations related to the crime can indicate the type of person who committed the crime. Since certain personality types exhibit similar behavioral patterns (in other words, behavior that becomes routine), knowledge and an understanding of the patterns can lead investigators to potential suspects. Over the past 20 years three types of investigative profiling have emerged. The first type was developed primarily by the Federal Bureau of Investigation, an agency that consistently maintained a very visible role through the mass media as criminal profilers who assist local police in catching serial killers. While the bureau has changed the name of this service to investigative profiling, the media continues to use the term *psychological profiling*. Although the FBI conducts most of the profiles in serial murder cases in America, a number of psychologists, psychiatrists, and criminologists have also been involved in providing this service in serial murder cases. This type will be referred to as the *FBI model*.

The second type of investigative profiling to emerge was developed in England at the University of Surrey in Guildford. In 1985, David Canter, a psychologist at the university was approached by detective Vince McFadden, head of the Surrey Police Criminal Investigative Division and asked for his assistance in a major inquiry of two murders and at least 30 rapes under investigation by Scotland Yard, the British Transport Police, and the constabularies of Surrey and Hertfordshire. Canter agreed to help, and investigators from the London Metropolitan Police and Surrey Constabulary were assigned to assist him. Canter developed a profile of the unidentified murderer, who would be dubbed the "Railway Rapist" by the press. The profile was remarkably accurate and proved very useful in apprehension of the serial murderer and rapist, John Duffy. This second type will be referred to as the *Canter model*.

The third type of investigative profiling was developed by late Milton Newton, who referred to this strategy as *geoforensics*. A number of agencies investigating a serial murder have attempted to conduct geographical analysis for pattern identification. For the most part, these efforts have been nothing more than the extension of placing pins on a map to show geographic relationships typically used in traffic accident and enforcement analysis. Newton carried this analysis to a more sophisticated level through the use of geographic topical analysis.

Newton presented a preliminary analysis of his research entitled, "Geoforensic identification of localized serial crime," to the Southwest Division of the Association of American Geographers in Denton, Texas, in October 1985. Newton's latest and final research (unpublished) was entitled, "Geoforensic analysis of localized serial murder: The Hillside Stranglers Located," coauthored with Elizabeth Swoope, which the author received from Newton in January 1987. In this work, Newton developed a method through a post hoc analysis using a geographic method with points of fatal encounter and body dumps, resulting in a near geographic "hit" on Angelo Buono's home, where most of the murders had actually taken place.

Notwithstanding the author's loss of Milton Newton as a friend and colleague, the criminal investigation profession in the country, unknowingly, lost a valuable resource. Although it is true that Newton's analysis was conducted on a post hoc basis, his techniques could very easily be used as an integral part of an ongoing serial murder investigation. Had he lived, his further research would undoubtedly have provided this capability to an ongoing serial murder investigation. Newton's research has been recognized by the small but evolving forensic geographic community, and his research is being continued.

D. Kim Rossmo, an investigator with the Vancouver, Canada, Police Department has continued the study of geoforensics, which he now refers to as *geographic profiling*. Rossmo describes geographic profiling as the analysis of spatial behavioral patterns using a variety of techniques, including distance to crime research, demographical analysis, centrographic analysis, criminal geographic targeting, point pattern analysis, point spread analysis, crime site residual analysis, spatial-temporal ordering, and directional analysis (Rossmo, 1995). Each of the three types of investigative profiling are described in the following pages.

FBI Model

Hazelwood and Douglas (1980) define a psychological profile as:

> An educated attempt to provide investigative agencies with specific information as to the type of individual who committed a certain crime. . . . A profile is based on characteristic patterns or factors of uniqueness that distinguish certain individuals from the general population. (p. 5)

Reiser (1982) states:

> The arcane art of psychological profiling of suspects in bizarre and multiple murder cases is actually a variant of psycho-diagnostic assessment and psycho-biography. It involves an amalgam of case evidence, statistical probabilities based on similar cases, available suspect and victim psychodynamics, knowledge of unconscious processes, and interpretation of detectable symbolic communications. The factual materials and speculative possibilities are combined using an inferential-deductive process. (p. 53)

The actual origins of criminal profiling are obscure (Ault and Reese, 1980). However, it is known that during World War II, the Office of Strategic Services (OSS) employed psychiatrist William Langer to profile Adolf Hitler (Ault and Reese, 1980, p. 23). The material assembled by Langer included a psychological description of Hitler's personality, a diagnosis of his condition, and a predictive statement suggesting how Hitler would react to defeat (Pinnizzotto, 1984, p. 32). Furthermore, such cases as the "Boston Strangler" and the "Mad Bomber" of New York City in the 1960s were profiled in a similar manner by James A. Brussels (Geberth, 1983, p. 399).

The Federal Bureau of Investigation became involved in psychological profiling in 1970, when agent Howard Teten began developing profiles. Teten was teaching an applied criminology course at the FBI Academy and students from various police departments would bring their criminal cases to him (Porter, 1983). The FBI began formally developing psychological profiles shortly thereafter, for as Ressler et al. (1984) state: "The FBI agents at the Behavioral Science Unit have been profiling murderers for approximately twelve years" (p. 12). Roger L. Dupue, director of the FBI's Behavioral Science Unit states: "We believe that in most crime scenes, the killer leaves his signature there. If you're sensitized to what these things are, you can construct a profile of the killer"(Kessler, 1984, p. A-16).

Ressler et al. (1982) describe psychological profiling as "the process of identifying the gross psychological characteristics of an individual based upon an analysis of the crimes he or she committed and providing a general description of the person, utilizing those traits" (p. 3). Ressler et al. (1982) list five steps that normally occur in the process:

1. Comprehensive study of the nature of the criminal act and the types of persons who have committed the offense
2. Thorough inspection of the specific crime scene involved in the case
3. In-depth examination of the background and activities of the victim(s) and any known suspects
4. Formulation of the probable motivating factors of all parties involved
5. Development of a description of the perpetrator based on the overt characteristics associated with his or her probable psychological makeup (p. 3)

Swanson et al. (1984) state the purpose of the psychological profile: "The purpose of the psychological assessment of a crime scene is to produce a profile; that is, to identify and interpret certain items of evidence at the crime scene which would be indicative of the personality type of the individual or individuals committing the crime. The goal of the profiler is to provide enough information to investigators to enable them to limit or better direct their investigations" (pp. 700–701).

FBI agent Robert K. Ressler, a former member of the profiling team in the behavioral science unit, states:

> All people have personality traits that can be more or less identified. But an abnormal person becomes ritualized even more so and there's a pattern in his behavior. Often times, the behavior and the personality are reflected in the crime scene of that individual . . . by studying the crime scene from the psychological standpoint, rather than from the technical, evidence-gathering standpoint, you could recreate the personality of the individual who committed the crime. If the crime scene is abnormal, it would indicate their personality is abnormal. (*Law Enforcement News*, December 22, 1980, p. 7)

Geberth (1983) discusses the utility of psychological profiling:

Psychological profiling is usually productive in crimes where an unknown subject has demonstrated some form of psychopathology in his crime. For example,

- Sadistic torture in sexual assaults
- Evisceration
- Postmortem slashing and cutting
- Motiveless fire setting
- Lust and mutilation murders
- Ritualistic crimes
- Rapes

Practically speaking, in any crime where available evidence indicates a mental, emotional, or personality aberration by an unknown perpetrator, the psychological profile can be instrumental in providing the investigator with information that narrows down the leads. It is the behavior of the perpetrator as evidenced in the crime scene and not the offense per se that determines the degree of suitability of the case profiling. (pp. 400–401)

Roy Hazelwood, a former member of the FBI's profiling team states: "We don't get hung up on why the killer does the things he does. What we're interested in is that he does it, and that he does it in a way that leads us to him" (Porter, 1983, p. 6).

In 1982 the FBI Behavioral Science Unit received a grant from the National Institute of Justice, U.S. Department of Justice, to expand their profiling capabilities by building a file of taped interviews with convicted murderers (Porter, 1983; Ressler et al., 1984). As of September 18, 1984, thirty-six convicted sexual murderers representing solo, serial, and mass murderers had been interviewed (Ressler et al., 1984, p. 5).

The results or evaluations of psychological profiling reported in the literature have not been conclusive. Godwin (1978) is very critical of profiling. He characterizes it as dull, tedious, and of little use to the police. He states: "They play a blindman's bluff, groping in all directions in the hope of touching a sleeve. Occasionally they do, but not firmly enough to seize it, for the behaviorists producing them must necessarily deal in generalities and types. But policemen can't arrest a type. They require hard data: names, faces, fingerprints, locations, times, dates. None of which the psychiatrists can offer" (p. 276).

John Liebert, a Bellevue, Washington, psychiatrist and a consultant to Seattle's Green River Task Force, is distrustful of psychological profiles put together by police agencies and the FBI. He states: "I think the state of the art [profiling] leaves a lot to be desired" (McCarthy, 1984).

Liebert further urges that law enforcement involved in a serial murder investigation utilize the services of a psychiatric consultant. He warns against phenomenological generalizations about the murderer and states that "superficial behavioral scientific profiling that rigidly reduces serial murder to a few observable parameters can lead an investigation astray" (Liebert, 1985, p. 199).

Levin and Fox (1985) characterize psychological profiles as vague and general and thus basically useless in identifying a killer. They state:

> As with most things, however, the value and validity of a psychological profile depends mostly on the skills and experience of the profiler. Unlike a psychologist who might consult with police investigators on an occasional, ad hoc basis, a full-time team of FBI agents trained in behavioral sciences as well as law enforcement techniques prepares approximately three hundred criminal profiles a year. Because FBI profilers have extensive experience, they construct the most useful profiles. Unfortunately, this tool, no matter how expertly implemented, is inherently limited in its ability to help solve crimes. (p. 174)

> The FBI's own recent evaluation of its profiling efforts, in our minds, underscores the limitations of this approach. A survey of 192 users of these profiles indicated, first, that less than half the crimes for which the profiles had been solicited were eventually solved. Further, in only 17% of these 88 solved cases did the profile help directly to identify the subject. While a "success" rate of 17% of those 88 cases may appear low (and even lower if one includes the unsolved cases), the profiles are not expected, at least in most instances, to solve a case, but simply to provide an additional set of clues in cases found by local police to be unsolvable. Indeed in over three-fourths of the solved cases, the profile did at least help focus the investigation. (p. 176)

Holmes and DeBurger (1988) warn against a trend in law enforcement of contacting federal agencies to assist them in the development profiles. They argue that since federal agencies have little experience in murder cases, it would be far better for local agencies to train their homicide investigators in the recognition of psychological motives and other characteristics of the unknown killer that can be inferred from the crime scene rather than using a specialist.

Levin and Fox (1985) also indicate that the profile is intended to be a tool for use to focus on a range of suspects rather than pointing precisely to a particular suspect. Campbell (1976) sees intensive investigative work to locate a suspect and find corroborating evidence following the development of a psychological profile, due to its general and nonspecific descriptors. Reiser (1982), however, notes that the profile may provide a starting point or focus from which an investigation can proceed.

Robert Keppel, investigator for the Washington Attorney General's Office, is also critical of profiling: "For the most part, cases where you don't have a whole lot of information at the scene, profiling is nothing more than guess work. It's an art form number one, to begin with it's not real scientific, and there are some good profilers, and some very bad profilers, and the good ones are successful because they limit themselves to those cases where there is a lot of answers at the scene, and they're able to help the police in those matters" (Griffiths, 1993).

The FBI themselves urge caution in perceiving profiling as an automatic solution to a difficult case. Hazelwood et al. (1987) state: "Profiles have led directly to the solution of a case, but this is the exception rather than the rule, and to expect this will lead to failure in most cases. Rather, a profile will provide assistance to the investigator by focusing the investigation towards suspects possessing the characteristics described" (p. 147).

Psychological profiling is a relatively new tool in criminal investigation and has had some success in assisting in a serial murder investigation. Pinnizzotto (1984) stated that, "currently, the Behavioral Science Unit of the Federal Bureau of Investigation is developing a variety of research methods to statistically test for reliability and validity [of profiling]" (p. 37). However, as of 1996, there has been no evaluation forthcoming from the FBI.

In his discussion of psychological profiling, West (1987) states: "It can be seen that profiling owes more to experience and imagination than to scientific deduction. All the same, matches between the actual and predicted characteristics of an offender are sometimes very striking" (p. 183). Geberth (1983) notes that the psychological profile, "can be a valuable tool in identifying and pinpointing suspects; however, it must be noted that the profile has its limitations. It should be utilized in conjunction with the sound investigative techniques ordinarily employed at the scene of a homicide" (p. 399).

Most homicide investigators appear to be convinced of the potential value of the psychological profile. Geberth, an experienced homicide investigator of the New York City Police Department, argues that the serial murderer is a type of personality that can be profiled. Geberth (1983) states: "A description of the salient psychological and behavioral characteristics which identify personality and behavioral traits or patterns can be used to classify and distinguish such an individual from the general population" (p. 495).

The Behavioral Science Unit of the FBI had been working on an artificial intelligence software program to enhance the investigative tool's effectiveness. The status of this effort is currently not very certain. However, it should be noted that recently, private vendors have developed software programs for personal computers with an application for psychological profiling referred to as *computer-oriented profiling*.

Psychological profiling by FBI agents of the Bureau's Behavioral Science Unit has indeed received a great deal of criticism, as noted above. These profiles are not, however, without substantial support. Park Elliott Dietz, a noted forensic psychiatrist and a professor of law and behavioral science and psychiatry at the University of Virginia, argues that the FBI profiles have no peers. Dietz has stated, "I think I know as much about criminal behavior as any mental-health professional and I don't know as much as the bureau's profiles do" (Michaud, 1989, p. 42).

An example of part of a profile prepared by the FBI on the Green River killer is presented below.

⋙⋞◆⋟⋘

Psychological Profile of the Green River Killer

Their [the victims] ages and race showed a variance which indicated that the offender demonstrated no personal preference for race. It was determined through studies at the Behavioral Science Unit that even the best of the so-called street people can be tricked or fooled, and a frequent tactic repeatedly observed is where the offender impersonates a law enforcement official. During his contact with the victim, her safety will be the prime entree that he will use and he may even promise to take the victim home or to the police station. He may also admonish the victim for walking the streets in the evening hour and for soliciting sexual favors. The offender's biggest obstacle will be to gain control of the victims and while the victims will initially be willing to go with him for the solicited act of prostitution, at some point he will have to demonstrate power over the victim.

While in this particular case the victims are of different ages and races, including variances in modus operandi, the assumption is still made that all of the deaths are related and all are committed by the same individual. This is based on the location where the victims were initially confronted, that being the Pacific Highway South "stroll" area near the Seattle–Tacoma International Airport, and the location of the disposal of the bodies. Also due to the probable cause of death being strangulation asphyxia. All of the victims are categorized in this matter as high risk victims due to their involvement with drugs and prostitution, their life styles which makes them susceptive to be a victim of a violent crime. In other words, they are characterized as victim of opportunity, they are easy to approach on the street, and probably initiate the conversation with their prospective "John."

An analysis of the crime scene reflects a primary focal point being the disposal site for the offender. In the case of the Green River victims, namely [deleted], the offender dumped his victims in or near the Green River. Crime scene analysis further reflected the offender was comfortable at the crime scene where some of the victims were anchored down in the water with rocks. His efforts to secure victims to the bottom of the river by placing rocks on top of them demonstrates the fact that he spent a considerable period of time in or at this location. The other two bodies were dumped on the side of the Green River evidence, that the offender had to quickly dispose of his victims. The method of disposing of the victims indicates that offender does not, nor will not, demonstrate any remorse over the death of his victims and what the offender is telling the police is that the deaths of these victims are warranted and justified and he is even providing in his own mind a service to mankind.

The crime scene further reflects that the offender at this particular point in the investigation, is not seeking power or recognition or publicity as he is not displaying his victims after he kills them. He does not want his victims to be found and if they are eventually found, he has the mental faculties to understand that items of evidentiary value because of the bodies being place in the river, will not be found.

The offender is very familiar with the area where the victims are disposed, does not seek publicity, and demonstrates no remorse.

From the Medical Examiner reports and autopsy reports, it is learned the victims die from some sort of asphyxia. In some cases, the offender leaves the ligature around the victim's neck where in the other cases, none is evident. The primary element that surfaced with each victim is that the subject is not planning to kill his victim each night he sets out to the area where the victims solicit sexual favors. He does not bring a rape or murder kit with him, nor does he plan to put his victims through some sort of ritual sexual act of body positioning.

We learned that the offender commits post-mortem acts on two of the victims, that he placed pyramid rock in the vaginal canal, and by doing this act, the offender reveals further elements of his personality.

The offender is profiled basically as a psychopathic personality in that the offender is mobile, drives a vehicle quite a bit. The vehicle, according to the profile, will be conservative in make and model. Offenders of this type favor vans and four-door conservative automobiles. These vehicles would be a minimum of three years old, and will probably not be well maintained.

The offender, in all probability, has a prior criminal or psychological history, comes from a family background which includes marital discord between his mother and father, and in all probability was raised by a single parent. His mother attempted to fill the role of both parents by inflicting severe physical as well as mental pain on the victim. She consistently nagged her son, particularly when he rebelled against all authority figures. The subject had difficulty in school which caused him to probably drop-out during his junior or senior year and he had average or slightly average intelligence. The offender has dated and in all likelihood, if he has been married, he is separated or divorced at this time. He does not, nor has he ever been or had an aversion towards women. He had felt that he has been "burned" or "lied to and fooled by women one too many times." In his way of thinking, women are no good and cannot be trusted and he feels women will prostitute themselves for whatever reason and when he sees women openly prostituting themselves, this makes his blood boil.

He is drawn to the vicinity where there is open prostitution because of recent failures with other significant women in his life, and in all probability, he has been dumped by a woman for another man.

He seeks prostitutes because he is not the type of individual who can hustle women in a bar. He does not have any fancy line of speech as he is basically shy and has very strong personal feeling of inadequacy. Having sex with those victims may be the initial aim of the subject but when the conversation turns to "play for pay" this causes flashbacks in his memory to uncomfortable times he has had in the past with women. These memories, as stated previously, are not pleasant. The straight-forwardness of prostitutes is very threatening to him. They demonstrate too much power and control over him, because of his personal feelings toward women and the action of prostitutes that will make it mentally comfortable to him to kill them.

The offender will be in relatively good shape and will not be extremely thin or fat. He is somewhat of an outdoors man, and would be expected to have an occupation that required more strength than skill, a "laborer, maintenance, etc." He does not have an aversion to getting wet or soiled. His employment or hobbies will get him this way all the time.

When it comes to determining the race of the subject, the probability factor is decreasing inasmuch as some of the victims are white, some are black, women are mulatto. Generally, crimes to this type are intra-racial, black on black, white on white. Using the hypothesis that the first victim was white and is related to the other four victims, this would lead to the fact that the offender, in all probability, is white.

The age of the offender can be determined by the amount of control and confidence he exhibits in initially confronting his victims as mobility. These factors place him in an age category between his mid-twenties to early thirties. If the age grouping is correct, a previous criminal and psychological history for the offender can be found. Criminally cases of assault and rape would be his typical criminal background. Schizophrenia or manic depressive psychosis is typically found. It is felt, however, the offender is not insane as evidenced by his ability to conceal his victim, have little or any tangible evidence, and drive a vehicle. Someone that is insane does not rationally think of concealing his crimes nor is he capable of driving a vehicle safely.

It should be noted any suspects developed cannot be eliminated by age alone. There is no burn-out with these types of offenders and they can kill easily at 40 years of age just as at 20 years. These homicides reflect rage and anger on the part of the subject and he will not stop killing until he is caught or moves.

Under post offensive behavior, it was noted that the offender does not stay idle. He is a nocturnal individual and is a cruiser in his automobile. He feels comfortable during the evening hours, and when there is stress at work or at home, he cruises to the area where prostitutes are available. He, in all probability, has returned on several occasions to the disposal dump sites, both prior and subsequent to the victims being found and he has in all probability had additional encounters with prostitutes since these homicides. His primarily typical areas of conversation with the prostitutes would be the homicides.

He has followed the newspaper accounts of these homicides and clipped them out for posterity, and for further fantasy and further embellishment.

If items belonging to the victim are missing, he will take them as souvenirs and will in all probability give them to a girlfriend, wife, or his mother.

He has had difficulty sleeping and has been experiencing periods of anxiety. He fears being detected particularly if newspaper accounts report that investigators are conducting a thorough and exhaustive investigation.

—FBI, September 22, 1982

Canter Model

A primary difference between the profiling developed by David Canter and the FBI is that in Canter's case, he is continually building an empirical base from which to operate. The FBI model is based almost totally on intuition of the profiler and his or her experience in profiling previous crimes. Whereas with the FBI model little effort is spent on the victim of the crime, Canter's model considers victim information as crucial to development of the investigative profile. Canter relies on statistical analysis and the use of probabilities derived from his continually updated empirical base. He also bases his finding on accepted premises and theoretical concepts of the discipline of psychology, while FBI profilers rely almost solely on their own experience.

As a result of nine years of investigative profiling experience, Canter set up the first graduate degree in investigative psychology at the University of Surrey. He has recently moved to the University of Liverpool, where this degree will continue to be offered. All Canter's research focuses on the search for feasible psychological principles that can be used to generate profiles to assist in crime investigations. Canter's profiling research is broken down into five basic aspects of the criminal transaction between the offender and the victim. These aspects are interpersonal coherence, significance of time and place, criminal characteristics, criminal career, and forensic awareness.

Interpersonal coherence addresses whether variations in criminal activity relate to variations in the ways in which the offender deals with other people in noncriminal situations. Focusing on this aspect of the transaction highlights the selection of victims and the implied relationship of victim to offender. A coherence of behavior within subgroups provides a series of assumptions for the investigator to test.

The location and time of the criminal act may inform investigators regarding the way in which the offender conceptualizes temporal and spatial relationships. This may provide valuable information on the constraints of the offender's mobility.

Addressing the characteristics of the criminal allows researchers to determine whether the nature of the crime and the way it is committed can lead to classification of criminal characteristics. This may lead to common characteristics of a subgroup of offenders and provide some guidance for the direction of a criminal investigation.

Although the actual development of a person's criminal behavior may vary, the direction of this development determined from empirical data may provide a method for police to backtrack the probable career of the unidentified offender and to narrow the possibilities. In other words, solid and probative evidence may well be available in the offender's earlier crimes, which may have led to his contact with the police.

Forensic awareness, a term coined by Rupert Heritage during his research with Canter (see Canter, 1994), is any evidence that the offender has attempted to mask or hide physical evidence of the crime from the police. It implies that the offender probably has had earlier contact with the police and has learned some of the techniques and procedures of criminalistics. The presence of this awareness should lead investigators to suspect that the offender has a criminal record.

For Canter, research into the development of more accurate investigative profiles mean interpreting the "criminal's shadow" (see Canter, 1994). This shadow, or story of the criminal, which Canter refers to as the *inner narrative*, evolves from a series of cryptic signals given in the actions of the offender. These cryptic signals are (adapted from Canter, 1994, pp. 278–281):

- The personal world that the suspect inhabits
- The degree of care the offender takes in avoiding capture
- The degree of experience the offender shows in his crime
- The unusual aspects of the criminal act, which may reflect the type of person who may be recognized
- The habits of the offender, which may carry over into his daily life

In effect, Canter is saying that even though the serial murderer may be characterized as killing in a random manner, the killer will in fact act in a very coherent manner. For unless a person is totally out of control, random behavior does not occur.

Canter concludes his book *Criminal Shadows* by stating: "Although a shadow can be disguised, it can never be shaken off" (Canter, 1994, p. 285). This self challenge to his efforts in developing an applied investigative psychology with which to assist police in their investigation of crimes leads the author to believe that the efforts of David Canter and the students of his investigative psychology curriculum will indeed make a great deal of progress toward the integration of applied psychology into the criminal investigative procedures in the near future and substantially reduce the number of unsolved serial murder cases.

Geographic Profiling

Geographic profiling provides an analysis of spatial behavioral patterns of the offender and is based to some extent on the military intelligence interrogation technique called *map tracking* developed a number of years ago by U.S. Army Intelligence. It is also based on the criminal geography research of Brantingham and Brantingham (1978). Map tracking was used to debrief a captured combat soldier from his point of capture backward in time and space to his origination point or the point at which he has no more information of intelligence value. This crime geographic targeting analysis includes distance to crime research, demographical analysis, centrographic analysis, criminal geographic targeting, point pattern analysis, point spread analysis, crime site residual analysis, spatial-temporal ordering, and directional analysis (Rossmo, 1995). These analytical techniques are particularly useful in responding to serial rape and serial murder. By an examination of the spatial data connected to a series of crime sites, a criminal geographic targeting model generates a three-dimensional probability map that indicates those areas most likely to be associated with the offender, such as home, work site, social venue, or travel routes.

Geographic profiling analyzes spatial information associated with a series of crimes that have been linked and provides investigators with the most probable areas in which to locate the offender. This analysis requires a special software mapping program. Using the relevant variables of offender types, activity spaces, hunting styles, and target backcloths, geographic profiling infers the spatial characteristics of the offender behavior. At the very least, this profiling strategy can assist investigators in focusing their resources on specific geographic areas and narrow the alternative scenarios to explore.

The geographic profiling technique generally requires information regarding the crime, geography, victimology, and suspect information, when available. In addition, this technique can be integrated with the psychological profile, which should increase the specificity of profile information provided to the criminal investigators.

INVESTIGATIVE CONSULTANTS

In October 1980 the late chief of police of Stamford, Connecticut, Victor Cizanckas, contacted Commissioner Lee Brown, Department of Public Safety, Atlanta, Georgia, and offered his assistance regarding the investigation of the missing and murdered children in Atlanta. Specifically, Cizanckas offered to loan Atlanta one of his skilled investigators with experience in a similar case. Further discussions ensued between Cizanckas, Brown, and the Police Executive Research Forum, to which both men belonged. As a result of these discussions, the Forum agreed to underwrite a cooperative effort of providing a team of qualified investigators with experience to assist in dealing with the Atlanta child killings (Brooks, 1982). The Forum's ultimate goal in providing this investigative consultant team to Atlanta was "in the hope that it would serve as a model and prompt others to undertake similar efforts in the future" (Brooks, 1982, pp. v–vi).

A group of investigators was selected for the team by contacting homicide detectives in police departments from all regions of the country and asking them to name investigators in their area with expertise to deal with the Atlanta problem. Five investigators were selected from this pool. Pierce Brooks, retired police chief of Eugene, Oregon, and formerly a homicide investigator with the Los Angeles, California, Police Department, was selected as the team leader. Other members were detectives Alex Smith, Oakland, California; Gil Hill, Detroit, Michigan; George Mayer, Stamford, Connecticut; and Charles Nanton, New York City. On November 11, 1980, this team traveled to Atlanta and served as investigative consultants for two weeks. The police forum paid the $7000 cost for this team to travel and live in Atlanta.

The responsibility of this investigative consultant team was "to come to Atlanta as consultants to the task force investigators and share with them any insights they might have by virtue of their experience in working complex cases in their respective jurisdictions. To that end, they were expected to review the case files and interact with the investigators responsible for the investigation involving the missing and murdered children" (Brooks, 1982, p. iii). Commissioner Brown noted that the team's role "was akin to lawyers asking for consultation from other lawyers or doctors receiving consultation from other doctors—in short, asking for a second opinion" (Brooks, 1982, p. iii).

Brooks (1982) notes that the team could be considered the experimental product of established methods of interagency assistance; the formal mutual aid agreement and the informal one-on-one exchange of information between detectives. Whereas use of this team did not result directly in a successful resolution of the Atlanta homicides, Brooks states: "The November 1980, venture of the Investigative Consultant Team (ICT) in Atlanta is believed to be the first time police investigators, all from separate departments, were invited to participate as consultants in a major criminal investigation in a city other than their own" (p. 6).

While the utilization of psychiatrists, psychologists, forensic pathologists, and even psychics have been used by police as outside consultants in difficult criminal investigations, the participation of officers from other agencies not involved in the investigation was a bold and, for many, creative step by the Atlanta police. The use in a serial murder investigation of experienced homicide investigators from outside the involved jurisdictions brought fresh ideas and expertise to the case. This strategy, used in Atlanta, remains a unique experience. It has apparently not been replicated in other serial murder investigations.

FORENSIC CONSULTANTS

The term *forensics* means the application of scientific knowledge to answer legal questions. Since investigators are in effect attempting to answer legal questions so that the killer can be charged by the state with his crimes, it follows that forensic scientists will from time to time be asked to assist in serial murder investigation. Forensic scientists from a variety of disciplines have provided assistance to serial murder investigations. Scientists from national, state, and local crime laboratories provide a wide range of services in the analysis of physical evidence in order to make identifications and comparisons necessary to prove the elements of the crime in a court of law. These services include the actual identification of physical evidence at crime scenes, its preservation and collection, its examination (identification and comparison), and giving testimony in a criminal trial.

Experts on DNA, generally referred to as *genetic bloodprints*, are frequently used in serial murder investigations when semen is found at the crime scene or on the body of the victim. Hypnosis experts may be used to enhance the memories of crucial witnesses. The forensic pathologist is a frequent contributor in a serial murder investigation regarding specific information surrounding the actions of the killer and the victim, cause of death, time of death, manner of death, and other physiological evidence found from the autopsy of the victim. Aside from the normal forensic assistance in a serial murder investigation, forensic anthropologists have been used to reconstruct the head of an unidentified victim from the skull; forensic entomologists have been useful in determining time of death from the examination of maggot larvae on the victim's body, and forensic odontologists have assisted in the examination of teeth of the victims for identification purposes. This group of investigative response strategies are always used in some fashion in a murder investigation and frequently complement other response strategies described.

MAJOR INCIDENT ROOM PROCEDURES

Police services in the United Kingdom have by tradition used a somewhat standard procedure for organizing the investigation of a major crime. However, following the massive Yorkshire Ripper investigation, which culminated in 1981 in the conviction of Peter Sutcliffe, the need for a more uniform and systematic approach to a major inquiry was very evident. Based on this serial murder investigation and research on other major inquiries, the Metropolitan Police Academy in London introduced a standardized method of operating a major investigation incident room. Subsequent to the development of this standardized method and its implementation in the London Metropolitan Police, the Home Office required that this standardized method be implemented in police forces in the United Kingdom.

Much of this standardized method seeks to counter the problems identified in the Ripper case. During the Ripper investigation, several police forces possessed criminal information pertaining to the identity of suspects in the case. However, there was no systematic means for one of these agencies to cross-reference or retrieve information from the other. Thus the completion of investigative leads and the successful collation of criminal information was not well coordinated and "became a hit and miss proposition" (Hetzel, 1985, p. 15).

The primary purpose of the standardized incident room procedure is to improve the collation of criminal information and to enhance the flow of investigative documentation. In a criminal investigation in the United

Kingdom the major incident room is the nucleus of all investigative activity. This procedure is now standardized throughout all police forces in England, Scotland, Ireland, and Wales. Messages, reports, and calls, referred to as *actions*, are received at a central point, documented, assigned a control number, and forwarded to an action writer, who identifies leads to be documented and data to be recorded. Then the information is researched in a series of files and indexes, reviewed by administrative personnel, and then assigned for follow-up to investigative officers. This procedure assures that the investigation makes full use of all information on file before conducting interviews and taking further actions. While this standardized procedure appears complex compared to typical American police procedure, it does accomplish two very vital tasks: the efficient flow of investigative documentation and the efficient collation of criminal information in such a manner as to promote rapid retrieval (Hetzel, 1985).

SOLICITATION FROM THE PUBLIC

When and if an agency or group of agencies chooses to make public the fact that they are investigating a series of homicides believed to have been committed by the same killer or killers, it logically follows that leaders of the agencies involved would ask the public for assistance in providing information to the investigation. Often, when the police announce that they are searching for a serial killer they will set up a bank of telephones connected to a central number so that the public can call in information or leads to the police.

Making an investigation public is a strategic decision with a number of ramifications. A centralized telephone number made available to the public will require an additional allocation of investigative personnel to operate these telephones. Due to the large volume of information generated from these telephone banks, a number of potential suspects will be identified, requiring the necessary investigative follow-ups. In addition, a great deal of information will be received from the public requiring the necessity of computerizing these data so that it can be managed effectively.

For example, in the Green River murder investigation, still unsolved, 18,000 suspect names were collected, many from tips called in by the public to an advertised telephone hot-line number. In this well-known serial murder investigation, additional avenues were utilized to seek the public's help in identifying the killer. A two-hour TV special seeking assistance from the public was aired on December 7, 1988, entitled, "Manhunt Live: A Chance to End the Nightmare." A number of homicide investigators experienced in serial murder investigation were flown into Seattle by the local Crime Stoppers program. They were there to answer telephone calls from people viewing the program. During the program a toll-free telephone number constantly flashed on the bottom of viewers' TV screens. Prior to the broadcast a press release from the Green River Task Force stated: "The goal of this important special is straightforward and direct: to mobilize the country in an effort to track down the most prolific killer of all time, the Green River Killer. More vicious than Jack the Ripper, Ted Bundy, the Boston Strangler and Son of Sam combined, this killer has terrorized the West Coast for the last six years" (Smith and Guillen, 1991, p. 446).

As a result of this program, the telephone company in Washington reported that more than 100,000 people attempted to call the toll-free number. Fewer than 10,000 actually got through to the detectives operating the telephones for the broadcast. Notwithstanding this massive and unique effort to solicit information from a national television audience, it was to no avail. The Green River Killer has not yet been identified.

In Gainesville, Florida, in early September 1990, four young women and one 23-year-old man were found murdered—the work, apparently, of a single serial killer. Within the first 11 days of this serial murder investigation involving three police agencies, 3000 telephone calls were made to a central murder hot-line number.

There is currently no evaluation of this investigative response. Whether it has produced important information in a serial murder investigation has not been documented. However, given the difficulty of a serial murder investigation, police agencies are generally not willing to take the risk of not soliciting information from the public once the investigation goes public.

COMPUTERIZED ANALYSIS SYSTEM

Those who watch *Mystery* on PBS television, consider themselves anglophiles, or read British mysteries by P. D. James or Anne Perry will be familiar with the police sergeant who accompanies the inspector from Scotland Yard. This sergeant always has a "box" in which he maintains the records of the investigation. When the United Kingdom began to experience serial murder, the records of such an investigation necessarily outgrew this "box." Today, in the United Kingdom, the box has been replaced in all police jurisdictions with a small portable computer running a software program appropriately labeled with the acronym HOLMES for Home Office Large Major Inquiry System. This software is based on standardized criminal investigation procedures developed for major criminal incidents. The location of such an investigation is referred to as the major criminal investigation incident room (see Doney in Egger, 1990a for a more complete description).

The Major Crimes Files presently in operation in the Canadian Police Information Centre (CPIC) system is a national system that operates in a manner somewhat similar to VICAP and HOLMES. As opposed to VICAP, where the analysis is conducted at a central site, the Major Crimes File allows investigators to use the program for their own remotely located terminals (C. P. Clatney, personal communication, March 31, 1988). The utility of the system by a single investigator at a remote site is then similar to the function of HOLMES.

In addition to the computer software applications referred to earlier, there is other software being developed to assist law enforcement agencies in responding to serial murder. One such program, which operates on a personal computer, was recently implemented by the Peel Regional Police Force in Brampton, Ontario: the Dr. Watson Case Management System. This system, in some ways very similar to the HOLMES and HALT systems, was implemented in early 1988. Since that time the agency has utilized the system on several lengthy homicide investigations and has been given very positive evaluations (M. S. Trussler, personnel communication; January 27, 1989; see also *Government Computer News*, December 5, 1986, p. 78).

CENTRALIZED INVESTIGATIVE NETWORK

Interpol

Interpol is primarily a criminal information exchange service which provides it's members with studies and reports on individuals and groups involved in crime conducted on an international scale. "The purpose of Interpol is to facilitate, coordinate, and encourage international police cooperation as a means for embattling crime" (Interpol General Secretariat, 1978, p. 94).

Interpol is becoming an increasingly important tool for criminal investigation in the United States to satisfy investigative leads that go beyond our borders. To address the need for an international channel of communication for state and local law enforcement officials, each of the 50 states is setting up a point of contact within its own police system to serve as a focal point for all requests involving international matters. This effort was initiated and is being coordinated by the National Central Bureau of the U.S. Justice Department. Illinois was the first state to implement the program of state liaison, establishing this function within the Division of Criminal Investigation of the Illinois State Police.

Although Interpol was not designed specifically to respond to serial murder, the in-place system of this organization is uniquely qualified to provide assistance to investigators of a serial murder with potentially transnational characteristics. As each of the 50 states develops its liaison program, Interpol will become better known to the law enforcement community as a tool for international information and assistance.

Interpol has recently been instrumental in linking the location of 11 murders by a serial killer to Austria, Czechoslovakia, and the United States. As a result, on July 28, 1994, Jack Unterweger, an Austrian ex-convict, was found guilty of these murders in an Austrian court, where prosecution of crimes occurring in other countries is permissible.

FBI's Violent Criminal Apprehension Program

Control is currently law enforcement's only feasible strategy in responding to the phenomenon of serial murder. Control means to identify, locate, and apprehend. Identifying is to verify that similar patterns or modus operandi are present suggesting a serial murder. This usually requires information from various jurisdictional sources. Once this information is collated and the strong suggestion or probability of the serial events is identified, the collator, at a central point, can then distribute the information, from which a pattern has been determined, to the original sources. These sources, a group of discrete investigative agencies, can then share this information in order to coordinate investigative action. The collator is necessary to ensure that a high-value piece of information is not missed (Wilmer, 1970, p. 32). A central point of analysis precludes this from happening. An investigative network is then in a position through state-of-the-art investigative techniques to attempt to locate and apprehend the serial murderer.

Such a centralized investigative network or system is currently operational at the national and state level in the United States, and on a national level in Great Britain and to some extent in Canada. The U.S. network, referred to as the Violent Criminal Apprehension Program (VICAP), is located at the FBI National Academy in Quantico, Virginia, as a component of the National Center for the Analysis of Violent Crime (FBI, 1983). The Behavioral Science Unit at the academy is the central site for this system, and that unit performs the aforementioned functions of collator. This unit of agents also provides a psychological profile of the perpetrator of an unsolved violent crime when requested by a local agency.

VICAP is reported to have been the brainchild of Pierce Brooks, retired police chief of Eugene, Oregon, and a former homicide investigator with the Los Angeles, California, Police Department, and other police officials in the Pacific northwest. The VICAP concept was first operationalized during a multijurisdictional investigation of the killing of young children in Oakland County, Michigan, in 1976 and 1977 (Levin and Fox, 1985; see also McIntyre, 1988). This systematic approach coordinated the collection and distribution of case information to the team of investigators from different law enforcement jurisdictions in the county. On the basis of an LEAA grant, the Oakland County Task Force was to have served as a model in criminal investigation to other agencies facing a serial murder investigation. However, the task force's efforts have never been made available in document form to the law enforcement community.

Further developments concerning VICAP came in the form of a technical assistance task plan submitted to Integrated Criminal Apprehension Program (ICAP) program manager Robert O. Heck of the Law Enforcement Assistance Administration in September 1981. In this plan, written by Pierce Brooks, the following was stated:

> VI-CAP, a product of ICAP, is a process designed to integrate and analyze, on a nationwide basis, all aspects of the investigation of a series of similar pattern deaths by violence, regardless of the location or number of police agencies involved. The overall goal of the VI-CAP is the expeditious identification and apprehension of a criminal offender, or offenders, involved in multiple murders (also referred to as serial murders, sequential murders, or random and motiveless murders). (Brooks, 1981, p. 1)

Brooks (1981) also provided a statement of the problem that the proposed VI-CAP system would address:

> The lack of centralized automated computer information center and crime analysis system to collect, collate, analyze and disseminate information from and to all police agencies involved in the investigation of similar pattern multiple murders, regardless of date and location of occurrence, is the crux of the problem. Research of almost every multiple murder investigation indicates an absolute need for a centralized information center and crime analysis function as a nationwide all agency resource. . . . There is no question that on a number of occasions multiple killers could have been apprehended much sooner if the several agencies involved in the investigation could have pooled and correlated their information. Each agency alone had "bits and pieces" of suspect identity— together their information would have provided the murderers complete identity and early on apprehension. (p. 2)

Between November 1981 and May 1982, four VI-CAP planning sessions were held in Colorado, Texas, and Virginia. These sessions were funded from ICAP moneys and participants were investigators and crime analysts from law enforcement agencies involved in ICAP projects. As indicated in the notes of the first planning session, the definition, purpose, and goal of VI-CAP were as follows:

VI-CAP Defined

VI-CAP is a centralized computer information center and crime analysis system designed to collect, collate and analyze all aspects of the investigation of similar pattern multiple murders, on a nationwide basis regardless of location or number of police agencies involved;

VI-CAP Purpose

Through analysis and evaluation of data received, to identify the existence of similar characteristics (M.O., suspect description, physical evidence, etc.) that may exist in a series of deaths by criminal violence; and

VI-CAP Goal

The overall goal of VI-CAP is to provide police agencies reporting similar pattern homicides with the information necessary to initiate a coordinated multi-agency investigation to expedite the identification of the criminal offender, or offenders, responsible for the murders. (Brooks, 1981, p. 1)

Due to the demise of the Law Enforcement Assistance Administration, funds were suspended for any further VI-CAP planning efforts following the last planning session in May 1982. VI-CAP procedures, budgets, and forms had been developed as a result of these planning sessions. A third revised VI-CAP crime report form with instructions and summary sheets was the product of the final session (Briggs, 1982).

On July 1, 1983, Sam Houston State University received a planning grant award from the Office of Juvenile Justice and Delinquency Prevention (OJJDP) and the National Institute of Justice, U.S. Department of Justice, for a National Missing/Abducted Children and Serial Murder Tracking and Prevention Program (MACSMTP) (OJJDP, 1983). Activities of this planning grant included task force and workshop activities to plan, develop, and implement a National Center for the Analysis of Violent Crime, to include the VI-CAP system. A program workshop meeting in July 1983 included the following activities:

Preliminary development of a conceptual model of a National Center for the Analysis of Violent Crime (NCAVC), consisting of four major program components:

1. Training
2. Research and development
3. Profiling
4. The Violent Criminal Apprehension Program (VI-CAP)

The Behavioral Science Unit of the FBI Academy in Quantico, Virginia, was recommended as the site for the NCAVC: "Preliminary development of the procedures and reporting mechanisms for collecting information on serial murders and incidents of missing/abducted children. Included here was the first draft of an offense report for the collection of VI-CAP murder-incident information" (OJJDP memo, July 28, 1983). An MACSMTP workshop meeting in August 1983 included the following activities (OJJDP memo, September 15, 1983):

- A preliminary VI-CAP standardized form was developed for collecting murder-incident information. Selected members of the planning group were designated to perform content analysis on this form and to field test the document.
- The conceptual model of the National Center for the Analysis of Violent Crime to be located at the FBI Academy was discussed further and refined.
- Network linkages and collection, analysis, and dissemination processes of NCAVC were discussed.

The third workshop of the program, held in November 1983, included the revision of VI-CAP reporting forms (OJJDP memo, November 20, 1983). As a result of program efforts and activities referred to above, specific planning was initiated within the U.S. Department of Justice to fund the National Center for the Analysis of Violent Crime. On March 31, 1984, the FBI received approximately $3.3 million to support the organizational development of NCAVC for 24 months. Funding for this development was provided by the Office of Juvenile Justice and Delinquency Prevention, the National Institute of Justice, and the Office of Justice Assistance and Research Statistics. Under this funding arrangement, the project stipulated that it would:

- Create, develop, and test a criminal justice operations center for a national multijurisdictional investigative research information and assistance program addressing selective violent crimes. The center will be under the direction and control of the FBI training center at Quantico, Virginia.
- Include four major organizational components: research, training, investigative support, and information assistance.
- Provide a research and analysis center for the nation's law enforcement and criminal justice system that can coordinate, assist, and provide comparative investigative assistance between multijurisdictional criminal justice agencies having similar murder patterns showing violent sexual trauma, including mysterious disappearances of adults and children who may have been abducted, sexually exploited, molested, or raped. (OJJDP Interagency Agreement, December 19, 1983)

VICAP (the hyphen was deleted in 1984), a major component of the National Center for the Analysis of Violent Crime, is a centralized data information center and crime analysis system that collects, collates, and analyzes all aspects of the investigation of similar-pattern multiple murders on a nationwide basis, regardless of the location or number of police agencies involved. VICAP is described by Brooks et al. (1981) as a "nationwide clearinghouse . . . to provide all law enforcement agencies reporting similar pattern violent crimes with the information necessary to initiate a coordinated multi-agency investigation" (p. 41). VICAP attempts to identify any similar charac-teristics that may exist in a series of unsolved murders, and provide all police agencies reporting similar patterns with information necessary to initiate a coordinated multiagency investigation.

Cases that currently meet the criteria for VICAP are (Howlett, et al., 1986):

1. Solved or unsolved homicides or attempts, especially those that involve an abduction; are apparently random, motiveless, or sexually oriented; or are known or suspected to be part of a series

2. Missing persons, where the circumstances indicate a strong possibility of foul play and the victim is still missing

3. Unidentified dead bodies, where the manner of death is known or sus-pected to be homicide

Levin and Fox (1985) argue that the value of VICAP is predicated in part on the presumption that serial murderers roam the country. They state that "traveling serial killers like Bundy, Lucas and Wilder are in the minority to those like Williams, Gacy, Corll, Buono, and Berkowitz who 'stay at home' and at their jobs, killing on a part-time basis" (p. 183). However, this statement is based on a data set of 42 offenders involved in 33 acts of multiple murder, and only 10 of these were committed serially (Fox and Levin, 1983, p. 4).

The success of VICAP will not be known for some time. It is dependent on a number of factors, not the least of which is local law enforcement coop-eration in completing a very lengthy 16-page form and transmittal of this form on unsolved cases to the FBI. The concept appears to be moving in the right direction, however, since no data base from which to identify serial murders currently exists in this country. Depue notes that his VICAP system will be expanded to include the crimes of rape, child sexual abuse, and arson (Ressler, et al., 1988). Darrach and Norris (1984) state that for over 20 years there has been in the United States a national system for reporting and tracing stolen cars, but that no national computerized clearinghouse for reporting unsolved homicides currently exists. When VICAP develops the appropriate data base, the hope is that the identification of patterns will stimulate the necessary interagency communication and sharing of information, which is currently, with a few laudable exceptions, almost nonexistent.

NEW YORK STATE'S HOMICIDE ASSESSMENT AND LEAD TRACKING SYSTEM

By the mid-1980s a number of states initiated efforts to develop statewide analysis capabilities similar to the system evolving with VICAP. By 1986 there were 14 states involved in such an effort. The author was the project director of one such system for the state of New York, the first statewide system to become fully operational (in 1987). The Homicide Assessment and Lead Tracking System (HALT) was developed with state funds by the New York Division of Criminal Justice Services and turned over to the New York State Police in 1987 to be fully implemented. To date, HALT is far from realizing its full potential, due to the shortsightedness of the executive-level personnel of this agency, who have provided only one full-time investigator to the system. Nonetheless, HALT has become a model for other states to follow in terms of its design, computer software, functions, and established cooperative relationship with VICAP.

The development of HALT was a cooperative effort between the New York State Police and the Criminal Justice Institute, Division of Criminal Justice Services. From the onset of program development, plans were made for operational control of the program by the New York State Police. This was a major planning assumption in program development.

The HALT program was initiated in January 1986 and was designed to provide a systematic and timely criminal investigative tool to law enforcement agencies across the state. Through computer analysis of case incident information supplied by police agencies, HALT is able to determine when similar crime patterns exist in two or more jurisdictions. When patterns are identified, the appropriate local agencies are notified.

HALT was developed in cooperation with the Federal Bureau of Investigation national effort addressing serial homicide so as to be compatible with their program, VICAP. However, HALT was not simply a conduit from New York to VICAP. The system is "value added," to provide communication linkages within the state, investigative support services, and a source center to refer law enforcement agencies to specific services or to provide the appropriate applied research information.

HALT became fully operational by the New York State Police in 1987 and is considered to be a valuable resource in addressing the problem of serial violent crime in New York. The program goals of HALT were developed to be as follows (Egger, 1986a, p. 1–2):

1. To provide an informational and investigative resource for law enforcement agencies in the state by facilitating effective responses by local police agencies to serial homicides.
2. To promote and facilitate communication, coordination, and cooperation among law enforcement agencies in the state on unsolved serial homicides.
3. To be designed in a manner that will permit its extension to other serial crimes.

Examples of Other Computerized Analysis Systems

Another statewide computerized analysis system is the Homicide Investigation and Tracking System (HITS), in the state of Washington, which collects murder and sexual assault information and identifies similar characteristics across cases (see Keppel and Weis, 1993). In Canada the RCMP are currently in the process of implementing the Violent Crime Linkage Analysis System (VICLAS), which uses a modified version of the FBI's VICAP form to conduct computer analysis (RCMP, 1993). Although little information is currently available on the extent to which serial murder is an international phenomenon (except for research of Hickey, 1985, and Jenkins, 1992), Interpol, the international criminal police organization, provides a networking and communication system that can respond to the transnational character of serial crime. This is the organization best suited to provide a centralized investigative network for the world.

The extent to which conflict continues to exist between law enforcement agencies will contribute to the ongoing communication problem. Notwithstanding this conflict, a centralized investigative network can substantially contribute to the reduction of such conflict. Where there remains conflict between two organizations, there will be less of it when one outside person or group (such as VICAP or HALT) holds an acknowledged monopoly of relevant information. Thus, the ability of these agencies to access and retrieve information from a centralized investigative network may further reduce the conflict between involved agencies.

PSYCHICS

The extent to which the area of parapsychology or the utilization of a psychic has contributed to serial murder investigations has not been well documented. In fact, other than a survey by Sweat and Durm (1993), there are no empirical data on the police use of psychics in any type of investigation. Although the use of a psychic in a criminal investigation always receives a great deal of publicity in the press, psychic involvement in a serial murder investigation has generally received notice and attention only in the more publicized and infamous cases. Also, in many instances, regardless of the nature of the criminal investigation, police agencies have been reticent to admit to the use of psychics during or following the completion of an investigation given the risks of criticism from the public as well as other members of the law enforcement community. Psychics often become involved in highly publicized serial murder investigations. They either make predictions about the killer to the media or secretly provide advice to agencies or individual investigators.

During the early stages of searching for a missing teenage boy in December 1978, Des Plaines, Illinois, police began to strongly suspect that John Wayne Gacy was responsible for the boy's disappearance. A local psychic was utilized to uncover information about the missing youth. Information given to the police by this psychic was subsequently interpreted as very accurate in describing John Wayne Gacy, his method of killing his victims, and his disposal of their bodies. Gacy was arrested and convicted of killing 33 young men and boys in Cook County, Illinois. The young boy missing in Des Plaines had been one of Gacy's victims; however, the boy's body was still missing. (According to Gacy's confession to the police, the boy's body had been thrown off a bridge into the Des Plaines River, about 55 miles south of Chicago.)

Search for the missing boy's body continued until April of 1979 when his body was found floating in the Des Plaines River in Grundy County, Illinois. During the intensive search for the body, the local psychic and a well known psychic from the east assisted the Des Plaines Police.

The psychics used by the police did provide investigators with some "very pertinent information" (Kozenczak and Herickson, 1989, p. 24) regarding the location of the missing boy's body. Had weather conditions not been prohibitive, investigators argue that the boy's body might have been found earlier as a direct result of psychic assistance.

Peter Hurkos was well known to the law enforcement community in the early 1960s. This famous Dutch mystic had reportedly helped solve a number of murders in the United States and Europe. He also claimed to have helped Scotland Yard recover a famous painting that had been stolen.

In January 1964, at the urging of an anonymous citizen who offered to pay his fee, Hurkos was asked to assist the Massachusetts Attorney General's office in their investigation of a series of homicides occurring in and around Boston since 1962. The homicides were already being referred to as the "Boston Strangler" case.

After spending a week in Boston, Hurkos identified the killer as a 56-year-old shoe salesman with a history of mental illness. Hurkos assured the police that they need look no further. Boston police then coordinated an exhaustive investigation of this suspect, ruling him out as a suspect in the killings. Not long after this, Albert DeSalvo confessed to these killings (see Frank, 1967).

Over five years later in 1969, Hurkos, who by this time was working as a psychic detective in California theaters and nightclubs, was contacted by private citizens from Ann Arbor, Michigan, and asked to assist police in Washtenaw County in solving the "Coed Murders." At this time, these murders consisted of the deaths of six young females in the Ann Arbor–Ypsilanti area between 1967 and 1969.

Although there was a great deal of controversy as to whether the three major police agencies involved would cooperate with Hurkos, the Ann Arbor police finally agreed to provide some limited cooperation to the psychic. Hurkos agreed to come to Ann Arbor provided that his travel expenses were paid. With a great deal of fanfare and media publicity, Hurkos arrived in Michigan in late July 1969. For almost a week Hurkos was accompanied by two homicide detectives in his efforts to assist the investigation. Following the finding of a seventh homicide victim during this time, Hurkos left Ann Arbor claiming that the police were too hostile to his presence in the investigation (see Keyes, 1976).

In briefly discussing a psychic consultant brought in by the Atlanta Police Department to assist them in the Atlanta "Child Murders," Detlinger and Prugh (1983) states: "The Atlanta police did everything possible—including providing official police escort service—to facilitate her 'communion' with the killer(s) or the spirits driving the killer(s)" (p. 60). Detlinger is no less strident in his criticism of this psychic consultant and others who attempted to assist the Atlanta police in investigating a serial murder, which would officially list 30 victims. Media hype and self promotion was apparently a major problem in utilizing psychics during this investigation.

Notwithstanding the tendency of law enforcement and to a lesser extent, the public to be very negative regarding the use of psychics in a serial murder investigation, psychic consultants are often used in these investigations. The extent to which psychics are forced on the police or the amount of cooperation that police provide to these people is not well understood. In some cases, when all leads have been exhausted, turning to a psychic may be necessary, if only to show that the agency is willing to use any and all sources that might lead to resolution of the murders.

There has been no known or credible evaluation of psychic effectiveness in assisting a criminal investigation. A review of a number of serial murder investigations conducted over the last 20 years reveals the presence of psychics (invited and uninvited) in a large number of these cases. A number of investigators claim that psychics are very useful, but the majority appear to remain skeptical. However, the involvement of a psychic in a serial murder investigation may provide an unintentional benefit. Psychics approach the investigation from a very different perspective and this may, through the questions asked by the psychic, cause investigators themselves to begin to ask questions that have not been asked before. These answers may produce new information that provides further progress in the investigation.

OFFENDER REWARDS

On January 14, 1982, Clifford Robert Olson pleaded guilty in a Vancouver, British Columbia, courtroom to the rape and murder of 11 young boys and girls. Olson's pleas were entered in exchange for a promise by Canadian authorities to establish a $90,000 trust fund for Olson's wife and son. The story of this controversial plea received a great of deal of coverage in the Canadian press and was also reported extensively by the media in this country (*Criminal Justice Ethics*, Summer/Fall 1983, pp. 47–55). While the intense negative reaction from the public regarding this negotiated plea may preclude the probability of such an unusual event reoccurring, it is certainly worthy of note. One can only imagine the frustration of the criminal justice officials in Canada that caused such a negotiation to take place. It is not unrealistic to contemplate that such a negotiation in this country on such well-known cases as those of Ted Bundy and Henry Lee Lucas might have resulted in a resolution of the cases and an end to the "not-knowing" of their victims by relatives.

In other cases serial murderers have agreed to confess to their murders in return for prosecutors not seeking the death penalty against them or in return for incarceration at a specific location. Plea bargaining in serial murder criminal trials has not been well documented. However, the Robert Hansen case in Alaska does provide an example in which a serial murderer bargained with the legal system to assure his incarceration away from the state in which he was convicted. Robert Hansen pled guilty to the murders of 17 women and the rape of 30 additional women in Anchorage, Alaska, in early 1984. In return for this plea and confession, which enabled Alaska state troopers to locate and unearth his buried victims, Hansen was assured of incarceration at a federal prison outside Alaska, and state officials agreed to assist in the relocation of his family to another state (see Gilmour, 1991; DuClos, 1993).

SPECIALIZED RESPONSE TEAM

The FBI have recently developed a strategy to assist local law enforcement agencies in conducting major criminal investigations. Upon the request of a local or state law enforcement agency, an FBI Rapid Start Team is assembled to assist a local task force in their investigation. A team of FBI agents and computer specialists, numbering from 8 to 20, can be on the site of the investigation within four hours. This team provides laptop and desktop computers, telephone modems, customized software, a portable generator, and a tent for the team to use. The team assists the task force in transferring data into a specialized data base. The team members also recommend an organizational structure for the task force. The team is assigned to the task force on an indefinite basis; however, the overall goal of the team is to train the local departments involved and to provide appropriate software for the investigation. The team provides four basic services: help in organizing and delegating jobs within the task force, compiling and analyzing clues on the computer, establishing an electronic message system for the task force, providing links to national data bases, and establishing communication links to national or international police forces. Such teams have provided assistance in the Unabomber serial bombing case, involving 14 bombings across the country and in a serial kidnapping and murder case in the St. Louis area.

The Florida Department of Law Enforcement is planning a similar response at the state level. A series of six regional teams would be set up covering a specific geographic area of the state. These teams would consist of members from the Florida Department of Law Enforcement, police departments, sheriffs' offices, states attorneys, medical examiners, and persons with special training in polygraph and criminal profiling. The purposes of the regional coordination team would be to provide a vehicle for local law enforcement to obtain assistance on major violent crime cases, to ensure that work group resources are appropriately committed and that the most advanced technologies are applied in each situation. The special agent of the Florida Department of Law Enforcement in charge of each regional coordination team would have the primary duty of tracking the investigative case progress, ensuring that additional needs that surface during the course of the investigation are appropriately addressed and that additional agencies and/or expertise are involved in the case as needed.

ALL INVESTIGATIVE RESPONSE STRATEGIES SHARE A COMMON FOCUS

All of the law enforcement investigative responses encompassed within this taxonomy share a common focus: to reduce the extent to which linkage blindness occurs in a serial murder investigation (see Egger, 1984a). In the future, criteria for the success of a serial murder investigation will necessarily include the extent to which this shortsightedness or cross-jurisdictional myopia is reduced or excluded.

PART IV

—◆—

THE FUTURE

Part IV presents the reader with a futuristic perspective of serial murder. In Chapter 13 we discuss the future of the phenomenon by presenting an agenda for research of serial murder. Chapter 14 presents a brief discussion of the future of serial murder investigation by highlighting questions to be answered and recommendations made for training. Chapter 15 presents a detailed look at the Jeffrey Dahmer case and concludes with critical issues that must be addressed to reduce the incidence and prevalence of serial murder.

CHAPTER 13

━━▶◆◀━━

FUTURE OF THE PHENOMENON

INTRODUCTION

As the reader will have noticed by this point in the book, the preceding chapters have left more questions unanswered about serial murder than providing definitive answers and complete descriptions of this phenomenon. That is indeed appropriate since we still have a lot to learn about serial murder.

Rather than provide a summary of the earlier chapters highlighting what we know and what we don't know about serial murder, the intent of this brief chapter is to provide the structure and context for the necessary future study and research agenda on serial murder.

While all answers to the questions posed in this agenda may never be answered, it is the hope of the author that this agenda will stimulate sufficient research from the academic and law enforcement communities to provide answers or partial answers to many of them. If sufficient resources are allocated to this end, it is quite possible that in the near future the problem of linkage blindness can be applied to the much larger and more complicated phenomenon of serial crime.

What follows is an agenda for the research of serial murder. As the reader will note, a number of the questions posed in this agenda challenge the assertions and conclusions of this book. More research is needed to verify conclusions made by the author or prove them to be false and in need of revision. This agenda should serve graduate students seeking a thesis or dissertation topic, funding agencies developing priorities, law enforcement agencies developing criminal investigative strategies for the implementation of community policing or problem-oriented policing, and the rather intense and continuous curiosity of faculty members in criminology and criminal justice academic programs. It is hoped that no one who chooses to address a research question from this agenda will develop emotional calluses and that their research focus will continue to offend their sense of morality and value of life.

Ted Bundy stated to authors Michaud and Aynesworth (1983): "It has always been my theory that for every person arrested and charged with multiple homicide, there are probably a good five more out there" (p. 322). Hopefully, the research agenda that follows will test Bundy's theory as well as pique the interest of the research community to provide the necessary study and research that such a serious event as serial murder deserves. The agenda is presented in these categories, with questions about victimology, serial murderers, and policy.

Research Agenda for Serial Murder

VICTIMOLOGY

- Are prestigeless or powerless groups of people the most common victims of the serial murderer, or is their vulnerability a precipitating factor, creating "attractive" targets of opportunity for the serial murderer?
- Do the characteristics of powerlessness or lack of prestige of most serial murder victims contribute to the initial priority that law enforcement gives to singular acts of homicide prior to any identification of a serial pattern?
- Do serial murder victims' sexual preference or chosen vocation reduce the priority that law enforcement gives to their murder?
- How does the serial murderer select a victim, and how have selected victims escaped death?
- Can at-risk populations reduce the probability of their victimization from a serial murderer?

SERIAL MURDERERS

- What case study techniques or idiographic methodologies will better develop our understanding of the causes of serial murder?
- Is the definition of serial murder offered by the author or others noted in this work useful in facilitating a systematic framework from which to study the phenomenon?

- Is the apparent fact that most serial murderers are males a significant characteristic of the phenomenon?
- Why are a large number of serial murders committed by a team of killers? Do causation theories of solo serial killers also apply to these teams of killers?
- Will the development of a typology of serial murder facilitate a clearer understanding of serial murderers and thus increase meaningful research and study of serial murder?

POLICY

- How can the incidence and prevalence of serial murder be determined more accurately?
- Is the incidence of serial murder increasing in this country? If so, why?
- What clarifications or explanations of the phenomenon of serial murder are necessary to develop intervention, prevention, or deterrent strategies and policies?
- How can the significance or importance of serial murder be emphasized to warrant the necessary allocation of resources for its study?
- What are the preadolescent and adolescent characteristics of serial murderers that would distinguish them from their birth cohort? How can the identification of such characteristics be exploited to develop the necessary intervention techniques and strategies to prevent the development of these persons into serial murderers?
- What is the most effective methodology for estimating the number of serial murderers currently operating in a specific geographical area?
- Why does the United States appear to have so many serial murderers compared to the number in other countries?

It is the fervent hope of the author that this research agenda will stimulate the necessary research and study beyond that which has been provided in this book to establish a basis for the development of tactics and strategies that can readily be shared with the law enforcement community to reduce the prevalence and increase control of the incidence of serial murder—for the phenomenon of serial murder must indeed become less elusive.

CRIMINAL JUSTICE FAILURE: AN EXAMPLE

Larry G. Bell had a criminal history that should have alerted officials to his potential dangerousness. Unfortunately, the criminal court judges and probation officials in South Carolina seem to have made a number of faulty decisions in attempting to change Bell's behavior. Bell's juvenile record is reported to show involvement in a number of sexual offenses. When he was 26 he attempted to force a woman into his car at knife point. As an alternative to prison, the courts ordered him to undergo psychiatric treatment. He saw a psychiatrist only on two occasions. A few months later, using a handgun, he tried to force another woman into his car. A psychiatrist recommended to the court that Bell be given a long sentence and intensive psychiatric treatment. Instead, the judge sentenced Bell to only five years in prison. He was released on parole 21 months later and began to harass a woman and her 10-year-old daughter with over 70 obscene telephone calls. He was arrested for these calls, pled guilty, and was given probation with the stipulation that he see a psychiatrist. He saw a psychiatrist on only a few occasions and, as he had before, abandoned treatment. And as before, no one noticed that Bell had stopped seeing a psychiatrist.

Shortly thereafter, in 1985, Bell abducted a 17-year-old girl from her home and killed her. Two weeks later his victim was a 9-year-old girl. He was found guilty of both murders and is suspected of committing at least three other homicides in South Carolina. He is currently on death row in South Carolina. For many, the criminal justice system had failed and let Bell go free again and again, eventually to kill. One reporter stated: "Every time Bell got into trouble, he was ordered to get psychiatric treatment. Every time, he abandoned the treatment. And every time, the monitoring systems of the medical and criminal-justice systems failed" (Methvin, 1989, p. 138).

CHAPTER 14

—————◆◇◆—————

FUTURE INVESTIGATION OF SERIAL MURDER: RECOMMENDATIONS

- Is there a correlation between the demographic or geographic patterns of serial murder? For instance, there would appear to be a disproportionate number of serial murderers who have killed in the Pacific northwest (R. Keppel, personal communication, July 1985).
- Is a national centralized investigative network such as VICAP in the United States or HOLMES in the United Kingdom the most effective system for assisting local law enforcement agencies with unsolved and potentially serial homicides, or should other alternatives, such as regional distributive networks, be considered?
- How effective is VICAP or HOLMES in assisting local law enforcement agencies in responding to serial murder?
- What is the best method for developing a national data base on solved and unsolved serial murders?
- What investigative strategies or techniques are the most successful for law enforcement's response to an unsolved and potential serial murder?
- Can the technique of developing solvability factors be utilized in assessing the investigation of a serial murder?

- Is the collection of information on unsolved murders and communicating this information the most effective method of reducing the linkage blindness of law enforcement?
- What are the necessary components of a training program for criminal investigators to increase their effectiveness and efficiency in the investigation of serial murder?

These questions must be addressed to increase the effectiveness of law enforcement's response to serial murder.

Serial murderers defy deterrence. Nettler's (1982) lesson following his discussion of serial lust-murder makes the point, "Lock your doors" (p.138). More specific tactics are obviously necessary, but we don't know who the next victim will be. Until more research is conducted on serial murder, only the most general deterrence strategies can be suggested, which are of little use to the citizen.

Control is currently law enforcement's only feasible strategy in responding to the phenomenon of serial murder. Control means to identify, find, and apprehend. Identifying is to verify that similar patterns or modus operandi are present to suggest a serial murder. This requires information, and in most cases from different jurisdictional sources. Once it is collated and the strong suggestion or probability of serial events is present, the collator, a central point (functioning as a collector, processor, analyzer, and distributor of information), can then distribute the information, from which a pattern has been identified, to the original sources. These sources, a group of discrete investigative agencies, must then share this information to coordinate investigative action dictated by this distributed information. The collator is necessary to ensure that a high-value piece of information is not missed (Wilmer, 1970, p. 32). A central point of analysis precludes this. An investigative network is then in a position though state-of-the-art investigative techniques to attempt to locate and apprehend the serial murderer.

For those agencies or organizations developing training programs to increase effective serial murder investigations, the following topics are suggested:

- Review of appellate court decisions on serial murder cases to eliminate mistakes in the future
- Development of solvability factors (some clues may be more important than others) for a serial murder investigation
- Conduct psychological autopsies of serial murder victims to develop traits in identifying a serial killer
- Networking of information on unsolved murders

- Computer skills in analyzing large amounts of information in a serial murder investigation
- Basic skills in victimology of serial murder

CHAPTER 15

---⟿◈⟾---

JEFFREY DAHMER AND BEYOND

DAHMER'S HISTORY

June 18, 1978 — Stephen Mark Hicks, an 18-year-old white male of Coventry, Ohio, last seen hitchhiking to a rock concert. Dahmer meets him and brings him back to his home, where they have sex. When Hicks tries to leave, Dahmer strikes him in the head with a barbell, killing him. Dahmer smashes Hicks' body to bits with a sledgehammer, puts the remains in plastic bags, and buries them in the woods behind his house. It would be over nine years before Jeffrey Dahmer would kill again. However, this time he wouldn't stop with only one victim. He would kill and kill again.

In Milwaukee, Wisconsin, in December 1987, Steven W. Toumi, a 25-year-old white male was reported missing by his parents. He was already a victim of Jeffrey Dahmer. Dahmer picked up Toumi at Club 219 in Milwaukee and took him to a room at the Ambassador Hotel. The two got drunk and passed out. When Dahmer awoke, he claims Toumi was dead, with blood dripping from his mouth. Dahmer bought a large suitcase at a nearby mall and put the corpse inside. He took the suitcase by taxi to his grandmother's, where he had sex with the corpse in the basement. Dahmer then dismembered the corpse, placing the body parts in plastic bags, and throwing the bags in the trash. Toumi's remains were never found.

A Silent Psychopath

People who knew Jeffrey Dahmer in Milwaukee described him as a quiet, rather shy young man, who didn't have much to say. The silence of this psychopathic killer was, however, deafening to the souls of his victims, as he methodically assaulted and dismembered their corpses, placing their skulls on his death shrine in his apartment, and their entrails and body parts in his refrigerator and freezer.

Like other psychopaths who had become infamous serial killers in America, Jeffrey Dahmer appeared to be a very quiet person. But like his peers, he was filled with a rage or force that controlled him. This rage was driven by a particularly dangerous chemistry: an antisocial trait, so that he flouted the law with impunity; a "borderline" personality, which made him vulnerable to explosive rage when he felt he was being abandoned, and a bizarre sexual deviation, which culminated in necrophilia.

Dahmer appears to have been a sadist and necrophiliac. Sadists find their sexual pleasure in the sufferings of their victims; the sexual thrill stops when the victims die. But with necrophiliacs the thrill starts with the death. For Dahmer the pleasure was both for the suffering of his victims and for what he could do with them after their death.

After New Yorker Joel Rifkin recently confessed to murdering 17 prostitutes, a high school classmate said he was "quiet, shy, not the kind of guy who would do something like this." A friend of Juan Corona, who was convicted of killing 25 migrant farmworkers in California in 1971, stated: "Juan kept to himself and never said much, for the most part." An Army buddy of David Berkowitz, convicted of 6 "Son of Sam" murders in New York City in 1976 and 1977, described him as a man who "was quiet and reserved and kept pretty much to himself." "That's the way he was here, nice—a quiet, shy fellow," said Berkowitz's former boss. Westley Allan Dodd, executed this year for the kidnapping, rape, and murder of three small boys in Oregon, was described by a neighbor as "a quiet young man who seemed so harmless."

Quiet and deadly! Like a viper, waiting and ready to strike. When Jeffrey Dahmer struck and picked up a young man in one of the Milwaukee gay bars he frequented, on the near south side of the city, the result was almost always death. Few would escape after entering number 213 of the Oxford Apartment Complex.

Neighbors said Dahmer always brought his guests in through the back door of the complex. All his guests would eventually leave through this door:

their torsos floating in a chemical bath in a large blue barrel, their arms and legs in plastic bags, some of their skulls in cardboard boxes labeled "Skull Parts," and some of their frozen heads in Dahmer's refrigerator. They would be carried out by police officers, hazardous waste removal specialists, and staff from the county medical examiner's office. As Dahmer's guests left apartment 213, their remains passed by a bright yellow tape that read **"POLICE LINE. DO NOT CROSS."** For these victims, the warning came much too late.

As Dahmer's refrigerator was removed on a dolly, down the back steps of the Oxford Apartments, Doug Jackson, a short black man stood by watching from the neatly kept lawn of the complex. "My head could've been in that refrigerator," he said in a low, cracking voice. A few days earlier Dahmer had invited Jackson to his apartment for a beer. His girlfriend had talked him out of going. He was very thankful.

Milwaukee's Horror

For months after the grisly discovery in apartment 213, many people in the city would double-check the locks on their doors and windows before going to bed for the night. Some would keep a constant log of phone numbers and addresses of where their kids were supposed to be. Many would pay more attention to "things that go bump in the night." And if they had them, many would load their guns and put them within easy reach.

Milwaukee police received numerous calls to check out suspicious strangers, day and night. A mind-numbing fear and paranoia seemed to envelope the city. Milwaukee had become a city of victims. Victims of fear, horror, and disbelief of what had gone on behind the door of number 213.

The breweries, beer halls, German restaurants, and various ethnic neighborhoods were no longer linked to this midwestern city in eastern Wisconsin on the shores of Lake Michigan. When people heard "Milwaukee," they immediately thought of Jeffrey Dahmer. Of course for some, who had been mesmerized by Anthony Hopkins' portrayal of Dr. Hannibal Lecter in the movie *Silence of the Lambs*, Milwaukee would become the "City of the Lambs," whose silence had been shattered by the screaming of innocent, slaughtered lambs.

Killing Close to Home: A Megastat Serial Killer

Jeffrey Dahmer is what experts call a *megastat, local,* or *place-specific* serial killer. This type of serial killer stays within the general area of a city or county in search of his victims. Most of Dahmer's victims were lured from the immediate area of his home, where he killed them. However, Dahmer doesn't totally fit into this category since he did lure two of his victims from Chicago, Illinois, 50 miles south of Milwaukee.

Dahmer's victims were lured into his lair, where he could control the situation and the assault of his prey. He didn't stalk them on the streets and then quickly slay them for the police to find. Dahmer was much smarter and he needed time with his dead victims. Time was important to Dahmer; time to have sex with the corpses, time to dismember and fillet the bodies at his leisure, and time to select a trophy before disposing of the victim's remains.

A Curious Evil: Self-Taught Anatomy

Jeffrey's morbid curiosity about death, bodies, bones, and flesh began at an early age. He started with a collection of insects preserved in jars full of chemicals. Then he began to collect dead animals run over on the roads near his home. Once while fishing with some other boys, he chopped up the fish he had caught into little pieces so he could see their insides. A group of boys walking in the woods behind the Dahmer home found the head of a dog impaled on a stick. They were so shocked at the sight that they took photographs, but they didn't tell the police until years later after Dahmer was arrested in his apartment in Milwaukee. Neighbors of the Dahmers also found frogs and cats impaled or staked to trees. A boy who grew up across the street from the Dahmer home said that young Jeffrey kept chipmunk and squirrel skeletons in a backyard shed and maintained a pet cemetery nearby with small crosses to mark each grave.

A neighborhood dog would disappear once in a while but no one suspected that Jeffrey was killing them for his autopsies. In 1975 when Jeffrey was 15, a neighbor boy walking in the woods behind the Dahmer home came upon a mutilated dog carcass. The head was mounted on a stick next to a wooden cross. The body, skinned and gutted, was nailed to a nearby tree. Dahmer's father had given him a chemistry set. According to Jeffrey's stepmother: "He liked to use acid to scrape the meat off dead animals." No one, including his parents, seemed to think this behavior warranted much attention or concern.

Most psychiatrists agree that cruelty to animals is one common childhood characteristic of the sadistic criminal. Many serial killer experts agree that many of these killers started out by torturing and killing animals as kids. Jeffrey's behavior should have been a warning. Had this warning been heeded, a number of lives might have been saved. In 1978 he began experimenting with human beings.

Killing for Company and Sex

As in the case of Dennis Nilsen, Britain's notorious and gruesome serial killer, Dahmer wanted company. Whether his urge to kill was driven by a longing for simple companionship or sex, Dahmer killed for it. He wanted to be with them. He wanted to keep them with him. As his obsession grew, he began saving body parts. He wanted to remember their appearance and took pictures of the corpses. They belonged to him.

Addicted to the Slaughter

Soon the offer of money for posing in the nude or for sex, the killing, sex with the corpse, dismemberment and examination of the bodies, trophy selection, and disposal became habit-forming for Dahmer. He was performing a ritual each time he convinced his prey to come with him to their slaughter. His reverse sculpturing of their bodies became the driving force of his existence, the search for his next work of art. It was an addiction to bodies.

Easy Prey: The Powerless and Vulnerable

Most serial killers select easy prey. The victims are those with little prestige or power in society. If they are missed, authorities spend little time looking for them. Often, victims are not missed for weeks or months. Some are never missed. No one cares. They are almost always strangers to their killer and are generally easy to dominate, lure, or manipulate.

Victims of serial killers are selected because of their vulnerability. This doesn't mean the serial killer is a coward. It means that he is smart! It reduces the time and effort of the selection, the lure, or the "con." It provided Dahmer more time for the control and the kill.

Dahmer was gay and he selected his own kind. He knew them. He understood their sexual frustration and their problems of meeting sexual partners. He knew how the rest of society felt about them. He knew that their parents had not sat down with them when they started dating men and warned them about certain kinds of men to watch for. Persuading them to go with him was seldom a problem. He knew what they wanted. Only he wanted something more. Unfortunately for his victims, their death was required to fulfill his wants.

A victim's lifestyle is frequently the critical factor in their falling prey to a serial killer. Prostitutes and gays very often become victims of serial killers. Dahmer chose gays. Boys and men from age 14 to 31 became his victims. Most of them were African-American.

A Drunk, a Loner, and a Weirdo

It would appear that Jeffrey Dahmer remained unattached during his childhood and never really bonded with anyone. Further, there is no evidence that Dahmer ever developed an intimate deep relationship. He seemed to trust no one.

In grade school the other kids noticed that Dahmer never had any sympathy for others. When other kids got hurt on the school playground, he would laugh or watch the scene without compassion.

By high school he was considered so weird that no one wanted to associate with him. He played on the tennis team but was not a popular student. He was very shy toward girls, but aggressive toward authority figures.

A neighbor remembers Dahmer's ritual as he walked to the school bus stop: four steps forward, two steps back, four steps forward, one step back, day after day, week after week. Little kids thought it was funny and watched him. He seemed to be seeking attention everywhere he went. He would reportedly fake epileptic fits in the classroom and at the nearby mall. He would frequently draw outlines of nonexistent bodies on the floors at school.

One of his former classmates, now a sociology professor, considered him a friend for a short period of time. However, "at 16 years of age, he was lost," she said. "He seemed to cry out for help, but nobody paid attention to him at all. . . . He would come in with a cup of scotch—not coffee with something in it, scotch whiskey. If a 16-year-old drinking in an 8 A.M. class isn't calling out for help, I don't know what is."

He spent most of his first semester drinking at Ohio State University in Columbus, Ohio. He never made it through the second semester. A classmate remembers the last time she saw him. "He was passed out on a street in Columbus," she said.

After his failure with college, Dahmer joined the Army and served in a medical unit in Germany. His roommate said, "Jeff would drink his gin. He had an eight-track stereo with headphones, and he'd sit there and get plastered. He'd be on a two- or three-day drink. He wouldn't even leave his room to go eat." Dahmer was discharged from the Army in 1981 because of his drinking.

Returning home from the Army, Dahmer was arrested in a hotel lobby where he was drinking vodka and threatening people. On his way to jail, he kept insisting that the police stop the car and beat him up. In 1982 he moved in with his grandmother in West Allis, a Milwaukee suburb. He began hanging out in gay bars and would sometimes bring men home through a private entrance to his grandmother's basement.

Trauma of His Parents' Divorce

Jeffrey's parents were headed for divorce when he killed his first human victim. It became a very bitter battle as Lionel and Joyce Dahmer fought over custody of Jeffrey's younger brother David, who was then 12. Jeffrey was already 18 and not an issue in the custody battle. His father was the first to sue for divorce, charging his mother with "gross neglect of duty and extreme cruelty." Dahmer's mother countersued, charging his father with the same charges. In the court documents of the divorce, Jeffrey's father had accused his mother of having an "extreme mental illness."

During the time that Jeffrey's parents were arguing over custody of his brother, they divided the house, each living on one side. His father set up a warning system with a string of keys to alert him if his wife was trying to enter his half. Both parents pressured Jeffrey to side with them in the divorce. He later told Milwaukee police that his parents were "constantly at each other's throats" before they divorced.

After his father had moved out of the house to a motel and his mother had left for Wisconsin with his brother, Jeffrey lured his first victim to his abandoned home and killed him. Dahmer may have been abandoned by his parents, but now he was someone very different. He now had a self-image. He was a killer.

Joyce Dahmer won custody of David. In August 1978, Lionel stopped by the house for a court-ordered visitation with David. He found Jeffrey home alone. The house was a shambles and there was no food in the refrigerator. Joyce Dahmer had moved with David to Wisconsin, instructing Jeffrey not to tell his father where they had gone. His mother had left Jeffrey with no money.

Beating the System

Since June 1978 Jeffrey Dahmer had beaten the system. When stopped by Bath, Ohio, police with a dismembered body in garbage bags on the back seat of his car, Dahmer told police he was taking them to the dump. The police let him drive on. In April 1988, a man reported that he had been drugged and robbed by Dahmer. Milwaukee police spoke to Dahmer but lacked evidence to pursue the charges. In March 1989 a friend of Anthony Sears reported him missing. The friend took police to the street corner, where he left Sears with another man. The other man was Jeffrey Dahmer and his grandmother's house was nearby. Police turned up nothing.

When Dahmer was released from the Milwaukee County jail, where he had been sentenced under work release for second-degree sexual assault and enticing a child for immoral purposes, he was on probation. Probation procedures required that his probation officer meet with him twice a month and make regular home visits. Dahmer's probation officer, who was supervising 121 clients at the time, requested that she be excused from making home visits with Dahmer. She argued that she had a heavy caseload and that Dahmer lived in a bad neighborhood. Her supervisors agreed to waive the home visit requirement with Dahmer. Jeffrey Dahmer was then free to pursue his INFERNO in apartment 213. And when one of Dahmer's victims escaped, the police helped him return the victim to the apartment and his death.

Milwaukee Police Thought It Was Just a Lover's Quarrel

Police Officer: *Intoxicated Asian naked male. (Laughter) Was returned to his sober boyfriend. (More laughter)*

Dispatcher: *10-4 64 and 65.*

Police Officer: *10-4. It will be a minute. My partner is going to get deloused at the station. (Laughter)*

—*Milwaukee Police Communications transcript, 2:00 A.M., May 27, 1991*

The "intoxicated Asian naked male" would become Jeffrey's Dahmer's twelfth victim, and his youngest. After his arrest Dahmer told the police that he had drugged the 14-year-old boy and the boy feel asleep. Dahmer left the boy in his apartment and went out to buy some beer. When Dahmer returned he saw the naked boy in the street talking to police officers. Neighbors described a young Laotian boy as naked and bleeding from his buttocks, staggering in the street. Dahmer told the officers he would take care of his friend and that he was drunk. The officers then escorted Dahmer and the naked boy back to his apartment. The officers had considered it a routine domestic dispute between homosexuals. It only became routine for Dahmer, who strangled the young boy as he had his other victims, after the police left.

On July 26, four days after Dahmer's arrest, Milwaukee Police Chief Philip Arreola suspended with pay the officers involved in this previous incident, pending an investigation. On September 6, Arreola announced that he had fired two of the officers involved in the incident, who had been members of the department for six and seven years. Arreola noted that the officers had failed to protect a child, to interview witnesses at the scene, and to consider impassioned pleas of a witness who later called the police. The Milwaukee County District Attorney's Office had already advised the Milwaukee Police Department that no criminal charges would be filed against the police officers involved. The two officers were reinstated to their jobs in 1995.

Escape From Apartment 213: The Arrest

It was the night of the arrest. . . . I heard a knock on the door and the police were there with the last victim. They asked me where the key was to the handcuffs. My mind was in a haze. I sort of pointed to the bedroom and that's where they found the pictures and they yelled "Cuff him" and I was handcuffed. And it was the realization that there was no point in trying to hide my actions anymore, the best route was to help the police identify all the victims and just make a complete confession.

—Television Program *Inside Edition:*
excerpts of Jeffrey Dahmer interview, February 8, 1993.

Just before midnight, Monday evening, July 22, 1991, two Milwaukee police officers sitting in their squad car were approached by a short African-American man with handcuffs dangling from his left wrist. The man, 31-year-old Tracy Edwards, told the officers about a "weird dude" who had handcuffed him in a nearby apartment. The officers were reluctant to respond but eventually agreed to go with Edwards to the apartment to investigate.

Once inside the Oxford Apartment Complex, the officers noticed a heavy rancid odor in the air. Jeffrey Dahmer opened the door for the three men. Dahmer was asked for the key to the handcuffs and he told the officers the key was in the bedroom. One of the officers walked into the bedroom and looked into an open dresser drawer. The officer was horrified! There were Polaroid pictures of dismembered bodies, skulls, and a skeleton hanging from a showerhead.

Jeffrey Dahmer was arrested immediately. As the officers began to look over the apartment, one of them opened the refrigerator door. The officer found a human severed head staring out at him. And the search of apartment 213 had only just begun.

For the remainder of his life, Jeffrey Dahmer's home was to be a prison cell at the Columbia Correctional Facility in Portage, Wisconsin. Columbia's five guard towers rise above Wisconsin farmland as tall as the silos of nearby dairy farms. It is the newest and most secure of the state's maximum-security prisons. "He's very glad that he's in there," his mother, Joyce Flint, 57, told reporters. "He still has those thoughts," she said.

Jeffrey Dahmer's "thoughts" or fantasies drove him into a decade-long orgy of murder, necrophilia, and cannibalism. Dahmer's orgy of death left at least 17 people dead and scores of surviving relatives and loved ones crying for the execution of this serial killer. Fortunately for Dahmer, the state of Wisconsin doesn't allow the death penalty. However, he would not live long. On November, 28, 1994, he was killed by another inmate.

The Trial: Was He Insane?

Jeffrey Dahmer choose to plead guilty but insane and changed the nature of his criminal trial. It was no longer a question of guilt, but a question of responsibility. It was not for the court to determine the strange or perverted behavior of Dahmer, or for that matter, his bizarre motivations. The question was whether Jeffrey Dahmer understood what he was doing and whether he knew the difference between right and wrong. Further, Wisconsin criminal statutes required that the court determine whether he could have stopped himself. The burden was no longer on the state to prove him guilty. It was now the burden of the defense to demonstrate his insanity.

Trial Judge Gram had warned the jurors that they were going to hear testimony unlike anything they had heard before. That was exactly what they heard. During the first two days of testimony the jury heard the reading of Dahmer's confession, in which Dahmer related how he skinned victims, boiled and cleaned their skulls, and even ate the biceps of one man after seasoning it with salt, pepper, and A-1 sauce.

Dahmer's defense attorneys would have to prove that he was suffering from some form of mental illness at the time of his crimes and that he lacked capacity to understand the wrongfulness of his action or to conform his conduct to the law. The trial became a battle of psychiatrists. Those hired for the defense would testify to Dahmer's mental illness and those hired by the prosecution would testify to his sanity.

Dahmer's intense sexual craving was described as a "cancer of the mind" by Fred Berlin of Johns Hopkins University, testifying for the defense. Berlin viewed Dahmer as "out of control. . . . The power of what was driving him basically took over." Berlin stated further: "I don't think the normal man could even force himself to walk around thinking about having sexual contact with dead bodies."

Park Dietz, testifying for the prosecution, stated that Dahmer suffers from a variety of sexual disorders, but none would have made him unable to know right from wrong or unable to stop himself from killing. Dietz described Dahmer's sexual urges as "less than many teenagers experience in back seats with their girlfriends" (Dahmer wore condoms when having sex with his dead victims).

George Palermo, court-appointed psychiatrist, said Dahmer was "sick" but "not psychotic" and was "legally sane at the time of the offenses."

Frederick Fosdal, testifying for the prosecution, said Dahmer suffered from necrophilia "before, during and after" killing 17 young males, but the disorder didn't prevent him from stopping. Fosdal stated, "He was able to refrain and had some control as to when he followed through on his sexual desires." Fosdal stated that Dahmer appreciated the wrongfulness of his acts, was prepared and did have the capacity to conform to the law, and could have controlled his behavior at the time of the acts.

Four of the testifying psychiatrists referred to Dahmer as a necrophiliac. Two of them classified him as having an antisocial personality disorder. One described Dahmer's behavior as clinically rare, unusual, and bizarre and for which there was no current diagnostic category.

The jury heard from a total of 28 witnesses before attorneys provided their summation of the case. "He couldn't stop killing because of a sickness he discovered, not chose," Dahmer's defense attorney, Gerald Boyle told the jurors. "He had to do what he did because he couldn't stop. This isn't a matter of choice," Boyle said.

Prosecutor E. Michael McCann described Dahmer as a sane, cowardly killer who sacrificed others for his own sexual pleasure and was now "seeking to escape responsibility. Please, please don't let this murderous killer fool you with this special defense," McCann told jurors. After 12 days of testimony, jurors deliberated a little more than five hours to find Jeffrey Dahmer sane on all 15 counts of murder.

His Father Writes a Book

Jeffrey Dahmer's mother, Joyce Flint, who took her maiden name after divorcing Lionel Dahmer, recently told reporters that she is worried that her ex-husband's soon-to-be published book, *A Father's Tale* (Dahmer, 1994), will blame her for the gruesome deeds of her son. Dahmer's mother made her first public statement since her son's arrest. "We're still blaming mothers," she said.

Advance publicity for Lionel Dahmer's book stated that it will examine "the origins of madness and role of kinship in the legacy of evil." In a TV interview Dahmer's father suggested it was possible that drugs his wife took while pregnant could have helped shape the person Jeffrey became. His mother admitted that she was treated for depression in 1978 and was taking prescribed drugs for the problem the year Jeffrey graduated from high school. It was also the year he first killed.

Alone With His Thoughts

It is difficult to understand what made Jeffrey Dahmer commit such horrendous acts against his fellow human beings. The crimes he committed were just not normal. What normal man would systematically murder and mutilate 17 victims? Our morbid fascination with him and his terrible acts may be a way of attempting to define him as separate and different from the rest of society. We seem to need the comfort or peace of mind in knowing that this serial killer is an aberration, that he is simply not one of us. To consider him normal would mean anyone could be capable of these savage acts of terror and death.

Jeffrey Dahmer was sentenced to 15 consecutive life sentences plus an additional 10 years for habitual criminality on each of the 15 counts. The judge structured Dahmer's sentences in such a way that he will never again see freedom. He will have the rest of his life to contemplate his murders, away from society, behind bars. Few disagree with the Judge's wisdom in sentencing Dahmer. Certainly not Jeffrey's mother, who recently told reporters, "He still has those thoughts." Dahmer may relive his deeds in his own macabre fantasy world but he won't add any more trophies to his gruesome collection.

THE VICTIMS: THE FORGOTTEN ONES

- *January 16, 1988.* Dahmer met James Doxtator, a 14-year-old Native American boy outside Club 219 and offered him some money to pose nude. Dahmer took the boy to his grandmother's, where they had sex. Dahmer then gave him a drink with sleeping pills in it, and when the boy fell asleep, Dahmer strangled him. Dahmer dismembered the body with a knife and a sledgehammer, placed the remains in plastic bags which he put in the trash.

- *March 24, 1988.* Richard Guerrero, a 25-year-old, Mexican-American, met Dahmer near Club 219 and agreed to go home with him. After they had sex in his grandmother's basement, Dahmer again drugged his victim with sleeping pills and strangled him. Dahmer had sex with the corpse, dismembered it, and threw the remains away. For Jeffrey Dahmer, it was becoming a way of life.

- *September 26, 1988.* The day after Dahmer moved from his grandmother's to an apartment at 808 North 24th Street in Milwaukee, Dahmer offered a 13-year-old Laotian boy money to come to his apartment, where he attempted to seduce the boy and laced his drink with sleeping pills. The boy left and when he passed out at home his parents took him to the hospital, where the police were notified. Dahmer was arrested the next day for sexual assault. Dahmer pled guilty to the charge and was sentenced to five years' probation and to one year at a correctional center in a work release program.

- *March 25, 1989.* Dahmer met Anthony Sears, a 24-year-old African-American at the La Cage Aux Folles bar and offered him money to be photographed. The two drove to Dahmer's grandmother's, where they had sex, after which Dahmer drugged Sears and strangled him. Dahmer disposed of his victim as before, however, he kept the head. He boiled the head so that only the skull remained. Dahmer painted his trophy with gray paint.

- *June 1990.* Raymond L. Smith, a 28-year-old African-American, met Dahmer at Club 219 and agreed to go to his apartment to be photographed. Dahmer drugged him, strangled him to death, and had sex with his corpse. Dahmer dismembered and disposed of the remains as he had before. He kept Smith's skull as another trophy.

- *Late June 1990.* Dahmer offered money for sex and to pose for pictures to Edward W. Smith, a 28-year old African-American whom he met in the Phoenix Bar. They returned to apartment 213, where they had sex, after which Dahmer drugged and strangled Smith. Dahmer disposed of Smith's dismembered body in trash bags. His only trophy was pictures of the dead man.

- *September 24, 1990.* Ernest Miller, a 24-year-old African-American, was lured by Dahmer from in front of an adult book store. After taking a number of pictures of Miller, Dahmer drugged him, and when he passed out, cut his throat with a hunting knife. Dahmer placed the corpse in his bathtub, removed the flesh from the body, and photographed the skeleton. This time his trophy was the entire skeleton. Dahmer put some of the flesh from the corpse in his freezer. He claims he ate the flesh.

- *Late September 1990.* The girlfriend of David Thomas reported him missing on September 24, 1990. This 22-year-old African-American died at the hands of Jeffrey Dahmer. His only trophy this time was photographs, taken by Dahmer as he dismembered Thomas's corpse.

- *February 1991.* Curtis Straughter, an 18-year-old African American, met his death after Dahmer lured him from a bus stop to his nearby apartment. Sex, followed by strangulation, more sex, and then dismemberment—it was becoming a ritual for Dahmer. Dahmer photographed the corpse and kept the skull.

- *April 7, 1991.* Errol Lindsey's mother last saw her son when he left home to have a key made. This 19-year-old African-American made a fatal mistake. He accepted Jeffrey Dahmer's offer of money to go to apartment 213. All that remains of Lindsey is his skull and some horrific photos of his corpse.

- *May 24, 1991.* The next victim Dahmer would lure to his death was deaf-mute Tony A. Hughes. They met in front of club 219. Dahmer communicated with this 31-year-old African-American in writing and convinced him to go to apartment 213. Another skull trophy had been added to Dahmer's collection.

- *May 27, 1991.* Like Dahmer's other victims, 14-year-old Konerak Sinthasomphone was lured with money, and once in Dahmer's apartment, was drugged with sleeping pills. However, in this case Dahmer left to get some beer before killing this young Laotian boy. Sinthasomphone awoke and Milwaukee police found him staggering in the street near Dahmer's apartment. Dahmer told police that the boy was drunk and had done this before. He stated that he would "take care of his friend." The police escorted Dahmer and the boy back into apartment 213, where the remains of Tony Hughes lay decomposing in the back bedroom. After the police left, Dahmer strangled the boy, photographed the corpse, and after having sex with it, dismembered the remains and kept the skull.

- *June 30, 1991.* Dahmer traveled to Chicago for his next victim. He met Matt Turner, a 20-year-old African-American at a bus station, after they had both attended the Gay Pride Parade in Chicago. Turner agreed to pose nude for money and they both returned on the bus to Dahmer's apartment in Milwaukee. Turner passed out from the drink laced with sleeping pills and his horrific fate was sealed. After dismembering the corpse, Dahmer placed Turner's head in the freezer and his torso in a 57-gallon barrel.

- *July 5, 1991.* Returning to Chicago, Dahmer lured his next victim from Carol's Speakeasy, promising money in return for posing in the nude. Jeremiah Weinberger, a 23-year-old Puerto Rican man, stayed in apartment 213 with Dahmer for two days before deciding to leave. The deadly ritual was triggered again and another head was added to Dahmer's freezer and a second torso to the 57-gallon barrel.

- *July 15, 1991.* Jeffrey Dahmer found his sixteenth victim just around the corner from his Milwaukee apartment building. Oliver Lacy's remains would be found in Dahmer's apartment. Seven days later police would find this 23-year-old African-American's head in the refrigerator and his disemboweled body in the freezer. His heart was also in the freezer.

- *July 19, 1991.* Joseph Bradehoft, a 25-year-old white man, fell prey to Dahmer's lure of money for posing in the nude while they were riding a Milwaukee bus. In apartment 213, Bradehoft's head was added to Dahmer's gruesome refrigerator collection and his torso was stuffed into the 57-gallon barrel, which was getting full. Bradehoft would be Jeffrey Dahmer's seventeenth and last homicide victim.

FROM JEFFREY DAHMER'S 179-PAGE CONFESSION

My consuming lust was to experience their bodies. I viewed them as objects, as strangers. If I knew them, I could not have done it. It's hard for me to believe that a human being could have done what I've done, but I know I did it. It would be me who has to stand before God and admit my wrongdoing.

I realize what I have done is my fault, but I have to question if there is an evil force in the world and if I am influenced by it. If I am honest with myself, I would have to admit that if I was set up in another apartment and had the opportunity, I probably would not be able to stop.

A power higher than myself had been fed up with my deeds and decided it was time for me to be stopped.

Jeffrey Dahmer was killed in prison by another inmate on November 28, 1994.

BEYOND THE DAHMERS OF THE 1990s

What kind of serial killers will hunt our world in the next century? Given the selectivity of our mass media, our newspapers and TV news programs will find them somehow more horrific than Jeffrey Dahmer. Possibly they will be mass-serial killers, using letter bombs, poison in our water supply, or poison gas in the subways of our urban centers.

For our society and the criminal justice system to respond and catch these serial killers in the next century, we must pay special attention to a number of critical issues.

1. Research into the phenomenon of serial murder must focus on the motivation of these killers and critically analyze how our society spawns these horrific and deadly craftsmen.

2. An extensive and detailed data base on serial killers must be developed to facilitate the generation of correlations used to build an accurate profile of these killers.

3. The "less dead" victims of serial killers must be given more effective protection from the serial killers. This can only be realized by implementing numbers 1 and 2 above.

4. The mass media must be held accountable for the generation of myths and falsehoods regarding serial murder so that the public becomes accurately informed about the serial murder phenomenon.

5. More case studies of serial killers should be conducted by criminologists using a standardized protocol similar to the cases presented in Chapters 6 to 9, so that cross-case analysis can be presented for a significant number of cases.

6. The seven major problems confronting a serial murder investigation (as detailed in Chapter 11):
   (1)   Linkage blindness
   (2)   Public commitment
   (3)   Coordination of investigations
   (4)   Management of information
   (5)   Public pressure and adversarial news media
   (6)   Unrecognized victim information
   (7)   Lack of exposure to the various strategies available in serial murder investigations

FINAL COMMENTS

It is the fervent hope of the author that this book will stimulate the research and study necessary to make this book obsolete in the near future. Notwithstanding this idealism, it is his more realistic hope that a number of law enforcement officials will read the book and understand the imperative of sharing information on unsolved murders with their counterparts on our rapidly shrinking globe.

The phenomenon of serial murder must become less elusive and better understood. *Serial killers remain among us.* They must be found and apprehended! Without the necessary research and study of these killers, they will remain free to kill and kill again. And they will remain, *the killers among us.*

REFERENCES

ABRAHAMSEN, D. (1985). *Confessions of Son of Sam.* New York: Columbia University Press.

———. The murdering mind. New York: Harper and Row.

APA. (1994) *Electronic DSM-IV,* HDT Software. Jackson, WY: Teton Data Systems.

———. (1987). *Diagnostic and statistical manual for mental disorders,* 3rd ed., revised. Washington, DC: American Psychiatric Association.

———. (1980). *Diagnostic and statistical manual for mental disorders,* 2nd ed. Washington, DC: American Psychiatric Association.

———. (1968). *Diagnostic and statistical manual of mental disorders,* Washington, DC: American Psychiatric Association.

———. (1952). *Diagnostic and statistical manual of mental disorders,* Washington, DC: American Psychiatric Association.

APSCHE, J. A. (1993). *Probing the mind of a serial killer.* Morrisville, PA: International Information Associates.

AULT, R. L., AND REESE, J. T. (1980), A psychological assessment of crime profiling. *FBI Law Enforcement Bulletin,* March, pp. 1–4.

BANAY, R. S. (1956). Psychology of a mass murderer. *Journal of Forensic Science,* vol. 1, no. 1, pp. 1–7.

BARNES, M. (producer and director) (1984). "The mind of a murderer" (videotape). Washington, DC: Public Broadcasting Service.

BAYLEY, D. H. (1977). The limits of police reform. David H. Bayley, (ed.), *Police and society*, Beverly Hills, CA: Sage, pp. 219–36.

BERGER, J. (1984). Mass killers baffle authorities. *New York Times*, September 8, p. 1.

BIONDI, R., AND HECOX, W. (1988). *All his father's sins: Inside the Gerald Gallego sex-slave murders*. Rocklin, CA: Prima Publishing and Communications.

BJERE, A. (1981). *The psychology of murder: A study in criminal psychology* (reprint of 1927 ed.) New York: De Capo Press.

BLACKBURN, D. J. (1990). *Human harvest: The Sacramento murder story*. Los Angeles: Knightsbridge.

BRANTINGHAM, P. J., AND BRANTINGHAM, P. L. (1978). A theoretical model of crime site selection. In M. Krohn and R. Akers (Eds.), *Theoretical Perspectives*. Thousand Oaks, CA: Sage, pp. 105–118.

BRIGGS, T. (1982). VI-CAP memo. Colorado Springs Police Department, March 4, pp. 1–10.

BRITTAIN, R. P. (1970). The sadistic murderer. *Medical Science and the Law*, vol. 10, pp. 198–207.

BROOKS, P. R. (1982). *The investigative consultant team: A new approach for law enforcement cooperation*. Washington, DC: Police Executive Research Forum.

———. (1981). VI-CAP. Unpublished report.

BROOKS, P. R., DEVINE, M. J., GREEN, T. J., HART, B. L. AND MOORE, M. D. (1988). *Multi-agency investigation team manual*. Washington, DC: U.S. Department of Justice.

BROWN, N., AND EDWARDS, R. (1992). Genene Jones: Deliver us from evil. Unpublished case study, University of Illinois at Springfield, Springfield, ILL.

CALL, M. (1985). *Hand of death: The Henry Lee Lucas Story*. Lafayette, LA: Prescott Press.

CAMPBELL, C. (1976). Portrait of a mass killer. *Psychology Today*, May, pp. 110–119.

CANTER, D. (1994). *Criminal shadows: Inside the mind of a serial killer*. London: Harper Collins.

CENTER FOR DISEASE CENTRAL. (1982). *Homicide-United States: Morbidity and mortality report, 31* (44), pp. 594, 599–602.

CHAMBLISS, W. (1972). *Box man: A professional thief's journey*. New York: Harper & Row.

CHENEY, M. (1976). *The co-ed killer*. New York: Walker.

CLARK, S., AND MORLEY, M. (1993). *Murder in mind: Mindhunting the serial killers*. London: Boxtree.

CLECKLEY, H. (1964). *The mask of sanity*, 4th ed., St. Louis; MO: C.V. Mosby.

COLTON, K. W. (1978). *Police computer technology*. Lexington, MA: Lexington Books.

CONRADE, P. (1992). *The red ripper*. New York: Dell

CONNOR, S. (1994). Crimes of violence: Birth of a solution. *The Independent*, March 6, p. 19.

COSTON, J. (1992). *To kill and kill again*. New York: Penguin Books.

CRESSEY, P. G. (1932). *The taxi-dance hall*. Chicago: IL: University of Chicago Press.

CULLEN, R. (1993). *The killer department: Detective Viktor Burakov's eight-year hunt for the most savage serial killer in Russian history*. New York: Pantheon Books.

DAHMER, L. (1994). *A father's story*. New York: William Morrow.

DALEY, R. (1983). *The dangerous edge*. New York: Dell.

DARRACH, B., AND NORRIS, J. (1984). An american tragedy. *Life*, August, pp. 58–74.

DAVIES, N. (1981). Inside the mind. *The Guardian*, May 23, p. 6.

DE RIVER, J. P. (1958) *Crime and the sexual psychopath*. Springfield, IL: Charles C. Thomas.

DETLINGER, C., AND PRUGH, J. (1983). *List*. Atlanta, GA: Philmay Enterprises.

DIETZ, M. L. (1983). *Killing for profit*. Chicago: Nelson-Hull.

DIETZ, P. E. (1986). Mass, serial and sensational homicides. *Bulletin of the New York Academy of Medicine*, vol. 62, no. 5, pp. 477–491.

DOBSON, J. (1992). Special report: Ted Bundy's last words. *Policy Counsel*, Spring, pp. 31–38.

DOMINICK, J. R. (1978). Crime and law enforcement in the mass media. In Charles Winick (Ed.), *Deviance and mass media*. Thousand Oaks, CA: Sage, pp. 105–128.

DUCLOS, B. (1993). *Fair game*. New York: St. Martin's Press.

EGGER, S. (1990a). *Serial murder: An elusive phenomenon*. Westport, CT: Praeger.

———. (1986a). *Homicide Assessment and Lead Tracking System (HALT) briefing document*. Albany, NY: New York Division of Criminal Justice Services.

———. (1985b). Serial murder and the law enforcement response. Unpublished dissertation, College of Criminal Justice, Sam Houston State University, Huntsville, TX.

———. (1984a). A working definition of serial murder and the reduction of linkage blindness. *Journal of Police Science and Administration*, vol. 12 , no. 3, pp. 348–357.

EGGINTON, J. (1989). *From cradle to grave: The short lives and strange death of Marybeth Tinning's nine children*. New York: William Morrow.

ELKIND, P. (1990). *The death shift: Nurse Genene Jones and the Texas baby murders*. New York: Onyx.

ELLIS, A., AND GULLO, J. (1971). *Murder and assassination*. New York: Lyle Stuart Inc.

FAIR, K. (1994). Kenneth McDuff: Death row. *Police*, July, pp. 56–58.

FBI (1983). *Violent criminal apprehension program:* Conceptual model. Unpublished working document, July, pp. 1–4.

FOX, J. A. AND LEVIN, J. (1983). Killing in numbers: An exploratory study of multiple-victim murder. Unpublished manuscript.

FRANK, G. (1967). *The Boston strangler*. New York: New American Library.

FRANKLIN, C. (1965). *The world's worst murderers*. New York: Taplingce Publishing Co.

GACY, J. W. (1991). *A question of doubt: The John Wayne Gacy story*. Craig Bowley Consultants.

GEBERTH, V. J. (1983). *Practical homicide investigation*. New York: Elsevier.

GEST, T. (1984). On the trail of America's "serial killers." *U.S. News & World Report*, April 30, p. 53.

GIANNANGELO, S. (1996). *The psychopathology of serial murder: A theory of violence.* Westport, CT: Praeger.

GIBBONS, D. C. (1965). *Changing the lawbreaker.* Upper Saddle River, NJ: Prentice Hall.

GILBERT, J. (1983). A study of the increased rate of unsolved criminal homicide in San Diego, California and its relationship to police investigative effectiveness. *American Journal of Police*, vol. 2, pp. 149–166.

GILMOUR, W. (1991). *Butcher, baker: A true account of a serial murderer.* New York: Onyx.

GODWIN, J. (1978). *Murder USA: The ways we kill each other.* New York: Ballantine Books.

GOLDSTEIN, H. (1977). *Policing a free society.* Cambridge, MA: Ballinger.

GRAY, V., AND WILLIAMS, G. (1980). *The organizational politics of criminal justice.* Lexington, MA: Lexington Books.

GRAYSMITH, R. (1976). *Zodiac.* New York: Berkley Books, St. Martin's Press.

GRIFFITHS, R. (producer and director). (1993). "Murder by number" (videotape). Atlanta, GA: CNN.

GUTTMACHER, M. (1960). *The mind of the murderer.* New York: Grove Press.

HARE, R. D. (1993). *Without conscience.* New York: Pocket Books.

HARE, R. D., FORTH, A. E., AND STRACHAN, K. E. (1992). Psychopathy and crime across the life span. In R. D. Peters, R. J. McMahon, and V. L. Quinsey (Eds.), *Aggression and violence throughout the life span.* Thousand Oaks, CA: Sage, pp. 285–300

HARRINGTON, J., AND BURGER, R. (1993). *Eye of evil.* New York: St. Martin's Press.

HARRIS, T. (1988). *The silence of the lambs.* New York: St. Martin's Press.

HAZELWOOD, R. R., AND DOUGLAS, J. E. (1980). The lust murderer. *FBI Law Enforcement Bulletin*, April, pp. 1–5.

HAZELWOOD, R. R. , RESSLER, R. K., DEPUE, R. L., AND DOUGLAS, J. E. (1987). Criminal personality profiling: An overview. In R. R. Hazelwood and A.W. Burgess (Eds.). *Practical aspects of rape investigation: A multidisciplinary approach.* New York: Elsevier, pp. 137–149.

HETZEL, R. L. (1985). The organization of a major incident room. *The Detective: Journal of Army Criminal Investigation*, vol. 12, no. 1, pp. 15–17.

HICKEY, E. W. (1991). *Serial murderers and their victims.* Pacific Grove, CA: Brooks/Cole.

———. (1985). Serial murderers: Profiles in psychopathology. Paper presented at annual meeting of Academy of Criminal Justice Sciences, Las Vegas, NV.

HILBERRY, C. (1987). *Luke Karamazov.* Detroit, MI: Wayne State University Press.

HOLMES, R. M., AND DEBURGER, J. (1988). *Serial murder.* Thousand Oaks, CA: Sage.

———. (1985). *Profiles in terror: The serial murderers.* Paper presented at annual meeting of Academy of Clinical Justice Sciences, Las Vegas, NV, March 18.

HOWLETT, J. B., HANFLAND, K. A., AND RESSLER, R. K. (1986). The violent criminal apprehension program VICAP: A progress report. *FBI Law Enforcement Bulletin*, December pp. 15–16.

INTERPOL GENERAL SECRETARIAT (1978). The I.C.P.O.—Interpol. *International Review of Criminal Policy*, vol. 34, pp. 93–96.

ISSACSON, W. (1982). A web of fiber and fact. *Time*, March 28, p. 18.

JENKINS, P. (1989). Serial murder in the United States 1900–1940: A historical perspective. *Journal of Criminal Justice*, vol. 17, pp. 377–392.

JESSE, F. T. (1924). *Murder and it's motive*. New York: Alfred A. Knopf.

JOHNSON, K. W. (1977). *Police interagency relations: Some research findings*. Thousand Oaks, CA: Sage.

JOUVE, N. W. (1986). *"The street cleaner": The Yorkshire ripper case on trial*. London: Marion Boyars.

KARMEN, A. (1983). Deviants as victims. In D. E. MacNamara, and A. Karmen, (Eds.), *Deviants: Victims or victimizers?* Thousand Oaks, CA: Sage, pp. 237–254.

KARPMAN, B. (1954). *The sexual offender and his offenses*. New York: Julian Press.

KATZ, J. (1982). A theory of qualitative methodogy: The social system of analytic fieldwork. In R. M. Emerson, (Ed.), *Contemporary field research*. Boston: Little, Brown, pp. 127–148.

KENDALL, E. (1981). *The phantom prince: My life with Ted Bundy*. Seattle, WA: Madrona Publishers.

KEPPEL, R., AND WEIS, J. (1993). *Improving the investigation of violent crime: The homicide investigation and tracking system*. Washington DC: National Institute of Justice, August.

KESSLER, R. (1984). Crime profiles. *Washington Post*, February 20, pp. 1, 16.

KEYES, D. (1986). *Unveiling Claudia: A true story of serial murder*. New York: Bantam Books.

KEYES, E. (1976). *The Michigan murders*. New York: Pocket Books.

KIDDER, T. (1974). *The road to Yuba City*. Garden City, NY: Doubleday.

KING, H., AND CHAMBLISS, W. J. (1984). *Harry King: A professional thiefs journey*. New York: John Wiley & Sons.

KIOCKARS, C. B. (1974). *The professional fence*. New York: The Free Press.

KOZENCZAK, J., AND HERICKSON, K. (1992). *A passing acquaintance*. New York: Carlton Press.

————. (1989). The use of psychics in a serial murder investigation. Unpublished manuscript.

KRAUS, R. T. (1995). An enigmatic personality: Case report of a serial killer. *Journal of Orthomolecular Medicine*, vol. 10, no. 1.

KRIVICH, M., AND OLGERT, O. (1993). *Comrade Chikatilo: The psychopathology of Russia's notorious serial killer*. Fort Lee, NJ: Barricade Books:

LANE, B., AND GREGG, W. (1992). *The encyclopedia of serial killers*. London: Headline House.

LARSON, B. (1984). *The story of mass murderer Henry Lee Lucas*. Bolder, CO: Bob Larson.

LEONARD, V. A. (1980). *Fundamentals of law enforcement*. St. Paul. MN: West Publishing Co.

LEVIN, J., AND FOX, J. A. (1985). *Mass Murder*. New York: Plenum Press.

LEYTON, E. (1986). *Hunting humans: The rise of the modern multiple murderer*. Toronto, Onario, Canada: McClelland & Stewart.

LIEBERT, J. A. (1985). Contributions of psychiatric consultation in the investigation of serial murder. *International Journal of Offender Therapy and Comparative Criminology*, vol. 29, December, pp. 187–199.

LINDSEY, R. (1984). Officials cite a rise in killers who roam U.S. for victims. *New York Times*, January 21, pp. 1, 7.

LINEDECKER, C. L. (1991). *Night stalker*. New York: St. Martin's Press.

———. (1980). *The man who killed boys*. New York: St. Martin's Press.

———. (1990). *Serial thrill killers*. New York: Knights bridge.

LINEDECKER, C. L., AND BURT, W. A. (1990). *Nurses who kill*. New York: Pinacle.

LOURIE, R. (1993). *Hunting the devil: The pursuit, capture and confession of the most savage killer in history*. New York: HarperCollins.

LUNDE, D. T. (1976) *Murder and madness*. Stanford, CA: Stanford Alumni Association.

MACNAMARA, M. (1990). Letters from San Quentin: Playing for time. *Vanity Fair*, November, pp. 80, 86, 88, 90, 92.

MACPHERSON, M. (1980). The roots of evil. *Vanity Fair*, May, pp. 140–49, 188–98.

MAGHAN, J., AND SAGARIN, E. (1983).Homosexuals as victimizers and victims. In D. E. J. McNamara and A. Karmen. (Eds.), *Deviants: Victims or victimizers?* Thousand Oaks, CA: Sage, pp. 147–162.

MARKMAN, R., AND DOMINICK, B. (1989). *Alone with the devil: Famous cases of a courtroom psychiatrist*. New York: Doubleday.

MARSH, H. L. (1989) Newspaper crime coverage in the U.S.: 1983-1988. *Criminal Justice Abstracts*. September, pp. 506–14.

MCCAULEY, R. P. (1973). *A place for the implementation of a state-wide regional police system*. Unpublished doctoral dissertation. South Houston State University, Huntsville, TX.

MASTERS, B. (1985). *Killing for company: The case of Dennis Nilsen*. London: Jonathan Cape.

———. (1991). Dahmer's inferno. *Vanity Fair*, May pp. 183–189, 264–269.

MCCARTHY, K. (1984). Serial killers: Their deadly bent may be set in cradle. *Los Angeles Times*, June 28, p. 1.

MCINTYRE, T. (1988). *Wolf in sheep's clothing: The search for a child killer*. Detroit, MI: Wayne State University Press.

MEGARGEE, E. I. (1982). Psychological determinants and correlates of criminal violence. In M. E. Wolfgang and N. A. Weiner (Eds.), *Criminal violence*. Thousand Oaks, CA: Sage, pp. 14–23.

MELOY, J. R. (1988). *The psychopathic mind: Origins, dynamics, and treatment.* Northvale, NJ: Jason Aronson.

————. (1989) Serial murder: A four-book review. *Journal of Psychiatry and Law*, pp. 85–108.

MEREDITH, N. (1984). The murder epidemic. *Science 84*, December, pp. 43–48.

METHRIN, E. H. (1989). Beauty and the Beast. *Reader's Digest*, February, pp. 132–38.

MICHAUD, S. G., AND AYNESWORTH, H. (1983). *The only living witness.* New York: Linden Press, a subsidiary of Simon & Schuster.

MILLIKAN, R. (1994). Backpacker murders. *The independent*, December 13, p. 15

MOORE, K., AND REED, D. (1988). *Deadly medicine.* New York: St. Martin's Press.

MORRIS, T., AND BLOOM-COOPER, L. (1964). *A calendar of murder.* London: Michael Joseph.

MYRE, D. C. (1974). *Death investigation.* Washington, DC: International Association of Chiefs of Police.

NELSON, T. (1984). Serial killings on increase, study shows. *Houston Post*, March 23, p. 11.

NETTLER, G. (1982). *Killing one another*, Vol. 2, *Criminal careers.* Cincinnati, OH: Anderson.

NEWTON, M. (1990). *Hunting humans: An encyclopedia of serial murder.* Port Townsend, WA: Loompanics Unlimited.

————. (1988). *Mass murder: An annotated bibliography.* New York: Garland.

NORRIS, J. (1989). *Serial killers.* New York: Anchor Books.

NORTON, C. (1994). *Disturbed ground: The true story of a diabolical female serial killer.* New York: William Morrow.

OJJDP. (1983). *National missing/abducted children and serial murder tracking and prevention program.* Washington, DC: U.S. Department of Justice.

O'BRIEN, D. (1985). *Two of a kind: The hillside stranglers.* New York: NAL Books.

OLSEN, J. (1993). *The misbegotten son: A serial killer and his victims—The true story of Arthur J. Shawcross.* New York: Delacorte Press.

PETTIT, M. (1990). *A need to kill.* New York: Ivy Books.

PINNIZZOTTO, A. J. (1984). Forensic psychology: Criminal personality profiling. *Journal of Police Science and Administration*, vol. 12 no. 1, pp. 32–37.

PORTER, B. (1983). Mind hunters. *Psychology Today*, April, pp. 1–8.

PRON AND DUNCUSON. (1994). Six sex slayings may be linked. *The Toronto Star*, May 1, p. 5.

RAE, G. W. (1967). *Confessions of the Boston strangler.* New York: Pyramid.

RCMP (1993). *VICLAS: Violent Crime Linakage Analysis System* [Crime Analysis Report Form 3364 eng. (93-07)]. Royal Canadian Mounted Police, July.

REIDEL, M. (1992). *Stranger violence: A theoretical inquiry.* New York: Marland Publishing.

REIDEL, M. (1987). Stranger violence: Perspectives, issues and problems. *The Journal of Criminal Law and Criminology*, 78(2), pp. 223–58.

REGIONAL ORGANIZED CRIME INFORMATION CENTER (1985). *ROCIC Bulletin,* January, p. 13.

———. (1984). *ROCIC Bulletin,* February.

REINHARDT, J. M. (1962). *The psychology of a strange killer.* Springfield, IL: Charles C. Thomas.

REISER, M. (1982). Crime-specific psychological consultation. *The Police Chief,* March, pp. 53–56.

RESSLER, R. K. (1992). *Whoever fights monsters.* New York: St. Martin's Press.

RESSLER, R. K., BURGESS, A. W., AND DOUGLAS, J. E. (1988). *Sexual homicide.* Lexington, MA. Lexington Books.

RESSLER ET AL. (1984). *Serial murder: A new phenomenon of homicide.* Paper presented at the annual meeting of International Association of Forensic Sciences, Oxford, England, September, 17.

RESSLER, R. K., BURGESS, A. W., HARTMAN, C. R., DOUGLAS, J. E., AND MCCORMACK, A. (1986). Murderers who rape and mutilate. *Journal of Interpersonal Violence,* vol. 1, no. 3, pp. 273–287.

RESSLER, R. K., ET AL (1982). *Criminal profiling research on homicide.* Unpublished research report.

REVITCH, E., AND SCHLESINGER, L. B. (1981). *Psychopathology of homicide.* Springfield, IL: Charles C. Thomas.

REVITCH, E., AND SCHLESINGER, L. B. (1978). Murder, evaluation, classification, and prediction. In I. L. Kutask, S. B. Kutash, L. B. Schlesinger and Associates (Eds.). *Violence: Perspectives on murder and aggression.* pp. 138–164, San Fransisco: Jassey. Bass Publishers.

REYNOLDS, M. (1992). *Dead ends.* New York: Warner Books.

ROSE, H. M. (1979). *Lethal aspects of urban violence.* Lexington, MA: D. C. Heath and Co.

ROSSMO, D. K. (1995). Geographical profiling: Target patterns of serial murderers. Unpublished dissertation, Simon Frasier University, Vancouver, British Columbia, Canada.

RULE, A. (1980). *The stranger beside me.* New York: New American Library.

SAGARIN, E., AND MAGHAN, J. (1983). Homosexuals as victimizers and victims. In I. MacNamara and A. Karmen, (Eds.), *Deviants: Victims or victimizers?* Thousand Oaks, CA: Sage, pp. 147–162.

SARE, J. (1986). Other slaying linked to Lancaster suspect. *Dallas Morning News,* pp. 21, 43.

SAM HOUSTON STATE UNIVERSITY CRIMINAL JUSTICE CENTER (1983). National missing/abducted children and serial murder tracking and prevention program. (Grant application to Office of Juvenile Justice and Delinquency Prevention, U.S. Department of Justice). The Center, Huntsville, TX.

SCHWARZ, T. (1981). *The hillside strangler: A murderer's mind.* New York: Doubleday.

SCOTT, H. (1992). The female serial killer: A well kept secret of the "gentler sex." Unpublished thesis, University of Guelph, Guelph, Ontario: Canada.

SEWELL, J. D. (1991). Trauma stress of multiple murder investigations. *Journal of Traumatic Stress,* vol. 6, no. 1, pp. 103–118.

————. (1985). An application of Megargee's algebra of aggression to the case of Theodore Bundy. *Journal of Police and Criminal Psychology,* vol. 1, pp. 14–24.

SHAW, C. (1930). *The jack-roller.* Chicago: The University of Chicago Press.

SMITH, B. (1960). *Police systems in the United States,* rev. 2nd ed.: B. Smith, Jr. New York: Harper & Row.

SMITH, H. (1987). Serial killers. *Criminal Justice International,* 3(1), p. 1, 4.

SMITH, C., AND GUILLEN, T. (1991). *The search for the Green River killer.* New York: Onyx.

SONNENSCHEIN, A. (1985). Serial killers. *Penthouse,* February, pp. 32, 34–35, 44, 128, 132–134.

STAFF. (1985). Serial murder in America. *Forensic Science International,* vol. 3, pp. 130–37.

STARR, M., ET AL. (1984). The random killers. *Newsweek,* November 26, pp. 100–106.

STORR, A. (1972). *Human destructiveness.* New York: Basic Books.

STRECHER, V. G. (1957). An administrative analysis of a multiple-agency criminal investigation within the suburban district of a large metropolitan area. Unpublished master's thesis, Michigan State University, East Lansing, MI.

SULLIVAN, T. AND MAIKEN, P. (1983). *Killer clown.* New York: Grosset & Dunlap.

SUTHERLAND, E. (1937). *The professional thief.* Chicago, IL: University of Chicago Press.

SWANSON, C. R., CHAMELIN, N. C., AND TERRIETO, L. (1984). *Criminal investigation.* New York: Random House.

SWEAT, J. A., AND DURM, M. W. (1993). Psychics: Do police departments really use them? *Skeptical Inquirer,* pp. 148–165.

TANAY, E. (undated). The murderers. Unpublished report.

THILBAULT, E. A., LYNCH, L. M., AND MCBRIDE, R. B. (1985). *Proactive Police Management,* Englewood Cliffs, NJ: Prentice-Hall, Inc.

THOMPSON, T. (1979). *Serpentine.* New York: Dell.

U.S. DEPARTMENT OF JUSTICE. (1982) *Crime Report, 1981,* Washington, DC., U.S. Government Printing Office.

————. *(1995) Crime Report, 1994,* Washington, DC., U.S. Government Printing Office.

VOLLMER, A. (1936). *The police and modern society.* Berkely, California: Regents of University of California.

WERTHAM, F. (1966). *A Sign For Cain.* New York: Paperback Library.

WEST, D. J. (1987). *Sexual crimes and confrontations: A study of victims and offenders.* Brookfield, Vermont: Gower.

WILKINSON, A. (1994). Conversation with a killer. *The New Yorker,* April 18, pp. 58–76.

WILLIE, W. S. (1975). *Citizens who commit murder: A psychiatric study.* St. Louis, MO: Warren H. Green

WILMER, M. A. P. (1970). *Crime and information theory.* Edinburgh: University Press.

WILSON, C., AND PUTNAM, P. (1961). *The encyclopedia of murder.* New York: Putnam.

WILSON, J. Q. (1978). *The investigators.* New York: Basic Books, Inc.

WILSON, C., AND SEAMAN, D. (1990). *The serial killers.* N.Y.: Carol Publishing Group.

———. (1983). *The encyclopedia of modern murder, 1962-1982.* New York: Putnam.

WILSON, P. R. (1988). *Murder of the innocents: Child-killers and their victims.* Rigby, Australia: Adelaide.

WINN, S. & MERRILL, D. (1980). *Ted Bundy: The killer next door.* New York: Bantam.

WOOD, W. P. (1994). *The bone garden: The Sacramento boardinghouse murders.* New York: Pocket Books.

YALLOP, D. (1982). *Deliver us from evil.* New York: Coward, McCann.

YIN, R. K. (1984). *Case study research. Design and methods.* Beverly Hills, California: Sage.

ZAHN, M. A. (1981). Homicide in America: A research review. In I. L. Barak- Glantz, & R, Huff, (Eds.) *The mad, the bad and the different: Essays in honor of Simon Dinitz.* pp. 43–55, Lexington, Mass: Lexington Books.

ZAHN, M. A. (1980). Homicide in the twentieth century. In J. A. Meicude & C. Farepel, (Eds.) *History and crime: Implications for criminal justice policy.* Beverly Hill, CA: Sage.

APPENDIX A

CASE STUDY SOURCE MATERIAL

Theodore Robert Bundy

Books

KENDALL, E. (1981). *The phantom prince: My life with Ted Bundy*. Seattle, WA: Madrona Publishers.

LARSEN, R. W. (1980). *Bundy: The deliberate stranger*. Upper Saddle River, NJ: Prentice Hall.

MICHAUD, S. G., AND AYNESWORTH, H. (1983). *The only living witness*. New York: Linden Press, a subsidiary of Simon & Schuster.

RULE, A. (1980). *The stranger beside me*. New York: W. W. Norton.

WINN, S., AND MERRILL, D. (1980). *Ted Bundy: The killer next door*. New York: Bantam.

Magazine Articles

MACPHERSON, M. (1989). The roots of evil. *Vanity Fair*, May, pp. 140–49, 188–98.

STAFF. (1979). Bundy: Guilty. *Time*, August 6, p. 22.

STAFF. (1979). Camera in the courtroom. *Time*, July 23, p. 22

STAFF. (1979). *The case of the Chi Omega killer. Time*, pp. 12, 13.

Newspaper Articles

Jacksonville Journal, June 19, 1984.

Lake City Reporter (Florida): May 10, 13, 1985.

Orlando Sentinel, February 10, 1980.

Sentinel Star (Orlando, Florida): June 30, July 15, August 1, 1979; March 16, May 20, 1982; May 10, 1985.

Other Sources

Interviews with Robert D. Keppel, Investigator, Attorney General's Office, State of Washington, various dates 1983–1985.

King County Department of Public Safety (1974). Summary of events July 14 and September 7, Seattle, WA: King County Department of Public Safety. (Case 74 - 123376)

Letter from R. D. Keppel to R. H. Robertson, September 26, 1983, regarding Bundy travels, known victims, and list of ninety similar victims.

John Wayne Gacy

Books

GACY, J. W. (C. I. MCCLELLAND, ED.) (1991). *A question of doubt: The John Wayne Gacy story.*

KOZENCZAK, J., AND HENRICKSON, K. (1992). *A passing acquaintance.* New York: Carlton Press.

LINEDECKER, C. L. (1980). *The man who killed boys.* New York: St. Martin's Press.

SULLIVAN, T., AND MAIKEN, P. T. (1983). *Killer clown: The John Wayne Gacy murders.* New York: St. Martin's Press.

Magazine Articles

DARRACH, B., AND NORRIS, J. (1984). An American Tragedy. *Life,* August, pp. 58–74.

STAFF (1979). Double life of a clown. *Newsweek,* January, pp. 93, 24.

STAFF (1984). Dahmer, *Newsweek,* November 26, p. 106.

WILKINSON, A. (1994). Conversation with a killer. *The New Yorker,* April 18, pp. 58–76.

Other Source

Sociological Evaluation of John Wayne Gacy by F. Osanka for W. J. Kunkle, Jr., March 6, 1980.

Newspaper Articles

New York Times December, 23, 24, 25, 28, 29, 30, 31, 1978. January 1, 2, 3, 8, 9, 10, 11, 12; March 1, 3, 11, 17; April 8, 10, 24, 1979. January 28, 29; February 2, 7, 16, 17, 22, 23, 24; March 8, 9, 11, 12, 13, 14, 16, 27, April 1; May 4, 1980. September 8, 1984.

Washington Post: March 3, 1980.

"Hillside Strangler"

Books

SCHWARZ, T. (1981). *The hillside strangler: A murderer's mind.* New York: Doubleday.

Newspaper Articles

Bellingham Herald (Washington): January 1, 1980.

Glendale News Press (California): February 22, 1979.

Herald Examiner (Los Angeles): March 8, 1978; January 7; March 30; April 29; November 14, 15, 16; October 2, 16; November 2, 20, 21, 23, 25, 1983. January 8, 11; March 19, 31, 1984.

Houston Chronicle: February 5, 1984.

Los Angeles Daily News: August 18; November 16, 19; December 2, 1982. January 7; March 20, 28; April 27, 29; May 4; June 22; August 3, 8; Sept. 3, 29; November 1, 4, 7, 9, 11, 14, 15, 17, 18, 19, 20, 23, 25, 1983. Jan. 5, 11, 14, March 19, 1984. January 14, 1985.

Los Angeles Times: November 22; December 15, 1977. August 22, 1978. January 1; March 5, 20, 27; May 6, 8, 12, 13; June 13, 17; September 11; October 3, 4, 6, 22, 25; November 14; December 4, 6, 1980. January 6; February 6; March 15; July 7, 8, 11, 13, 22, 23, 27, 29, 30, 31; August 6, 7, 9, 10, 11, 13, 14, 21, 28, 29; October 5, 23, 1981. February 8, 11, 27; March 2, 3, 4, 8, 9, 10, 11, 12, 15, 17, 19, 24, 25; April 6, 9, 14, 27, 29; May 31; June 5, 24; July 1, 8; October 4, 13, 26; November 1, 8, 10, 1982. January 7; February 24; September 2; October 21; November 1, 2, 4, 6, 8, 9, 10, 11, 12, 15, 16, 17, 19, 30, 1983. January 5; March 9, 19; August 19, 1984.

New York Times: February 24, 1979.

San Francisco Chronicle: May 7, 1994.

Other Sources

Barnes, M. (producer and director). (1984). "The mind of a murderer" (videotape). Washington, DC: Public Broadcasting Service.

Interviews with Frank Salerno, Sergeant, Los Angeles Sheriff's Office (various dates 1983–1985).

Henry Lee Lucas

Books

CALL, M. (1985). *Hand of death: The Henry Lee Lucas story.* Lafayette, LA: Prescott Press.

LARSON, B. (1984). *The story of mass-murderer Henry Lee Lucas.* Bolder, CO: Bob Larson.

Newspaper Articles

The Atlanta Constitution: April 10, 1985

The Atlanta Journal: December 21, 1984; April 22, 1985.

Austin American Statesman: June 29; July 3; November 23; December 8, 1983. March 9, 12; April 4, 18, 24; May 11; July 26, 1984. April 21, 1985.

Avalanche Journal (Lubbock, TX): June 3, 4, 5, 6, 28; September 2; October 31, 1984.

The Baltimore Sun: February 20, 1984.

Beaumonth Enterprise: July 1, 29, 1984.

Dallas Morning News: June 30; July 7; August 3, 11, 25; December 8, 1983. June 8; August 1, 2, 9; October 28, 1984.

Dallas Times Herald: August 11, 1982. June 24, 26; August 13, 25, 26; November 26, 1983. April 5, 7, 11, 14, 23, 27; May 11, 17; October 6, 27; September 7, 1984 April 14, 15, 16, 17, 18, 19, 20, 23, 24, 1985.

El Paso Herald Post: October 26, 27, 1984.

Fort Worth Star Telegraph: January 16, 29, 1984.

Herald Dispatch (Huntington, WV): December 11, 17, 28; April 7, 13, 23; May 12; June 2, 17, 23; August 1; September 7; October 6, 1984. January 14; April 15, 16, 18, 22, 23, 24, 25, 30; May 4; June 24, 1985.

Houston Chronicle: April 7, 1984.

Houston Post: June 30; August 11, 28; September 8, 9, 22, 23 30; October 1, 4, 5, 8, 22, 23, 25; April 5; July 1; August 18, 1984. April 15, 16, 18, 19, 20, 1985.

Law Enforcement News: September 24, 1984.

New York Times: April 18, 24, 29, 1985.

Rocky Mountain News: (Denver, CO): September 13, 1984.

Tampa Tribune: June 9, 1985.

The Toledo Blade: January 17, 19, 20, 1960.

Other Sources

Cuba, N. (1985). The life and deaths of Henry Lee Lucas. *Third Coast*, vol, 4, no. 12, July, pp. 44–59.

Henry Lee Lucas Homicide Task Force Investigative Reports

  Index of Confirmed Homicides

  Court Action Involving Henry Lee Lucas

  Index to Supplements of Synopsis

  Synopsis of Confirmed Homicides

  Daily Log Activities of Lucas and Toole

Interviews with Henry Lee Lucas by Steven A. Egger

  June 5, 1984

  June 22, 1984

  June 24, 1984

  July 7, 1984

  July 18, 1984

  August 2, 1984

  August 14, 1984

September 25, 1984

October 25, 1984

November 30, 1984

February 2, 1985

February 8, 1985

March 22, 1985

Egger, S. A. (1985). Case study of serial murder: Henry Lee Lucas. Presented at Academy of Criminal Justice Sciences 1985 annual meeting, Las Vegas, NV, March.

Psychiatric Reports

Transfer to Ionia State Hospital, Michigan, July 14, 1961.

Ionia State Hospital Diagnosis, August 10, 1061.

Ionia State Hospital Record, January 28, 1965.

Psychological Evaluation, Center for Forensic Psychiatry, Ypsilanti, Michigan, November 17, 1971.

Regional Organized Crime Information Center (1984). *ROCIC Bulletin*, February.

Regional Organized Crime Information Center (1985). *Travel movements of Henry Lee Lucas and Ottis Elwood Toole, 1952–1985*. Nashville, TN: ROCIC

APPENDIX B

SOURCES FOR JEFFREY DAHMER CASE STUDY (CHAPTER 15)

Books and Reports

DAVIS, J. (1991) . *Milwaukee murders: Nightmare in Apt. 213*. New York: St. Martin's Press.

DIETZ, P. (1992). Statement in reaction to Dahmer verdict. Press release, February 15.

DVORCHAK, R. J., AND HOLEWA, L. (1991). *Milwaukee massacre*. New York: Dell.

FISHER, H. (1992). *Jeffrey Dahmer: An unauthorized biography of a serial killer*. Champaign, IL: Boneyard Press.

JAEGER, R. W., AND BALOUSEK, M. W. (1991). *Massacre In Milwaukee*. Madison, WI: Waubesa Press.

MAYOR'S CITIZEN COMMISSION ON POLICE-COMMUNITY RELATIONS (1991). A Report to Mayor John O. Norquist and the Board of Fire and Police Commissioners, October 15.

NORRIS, J. (1992). *Jeffrey Dahmer*. New York: Shadow Long Press.

SCHWARTZ, A. E. (1992). *The man who could not kill enough: The secret murders of Milwaukee's Jeffrey Dahmer*. Secaucus, NJ: Carol Publishing Group.

Newspaper Articles

January 26, 1992: Defense gears for battle over Dahmer's sanity. *Springfield (IL) State Journal Register*, p. 3.

January 28, 1992: Two serial killers' day in court. *USA Today*, p. 3A.

January 29, 1992: Victims' kin bring anger for Dahmer. *Chicago Tribune*.

January 28, 1992: A horror warning for Dahmer trial. *Chicago Sun-Times*. p. 14.

January 31, 1992: Lawyer: Dahmer driven to sex with the dead. *Springfield (IL) State Journal Register*.

February 1, 1992: Witness: Dahmer said he'd "eat my heart." *Springfield (IL) State Journal Register*, p. 3.

February 3, 1992: He wanted "excitement, gratification." *USA Today*, p. 3A.

February 4,1992: Psychiatrist says Dahmer fought his necrophilia. *Chicago Sun-Times*, p. 5.

February 5, 1992: Expert tells of Dahmer's twisted acts. *Boston Herald-American*, p. 1.

February 6, 1992: Expert says killer lived for morbid sex fantasies. *Boston Herald-American*, p. 3.

February 9, 1992: Expert: Dahmer sought control. *Boston Herald-American*, p. 4.

February 9, 1992: Necrophilia drove Dahmer. *Decatur (IL) Herald & Review*, p. A4.

February 13, 1992: Psychiatrist: Dahmer gave up idea of freeze-drying victim. *Springfield (IL) State Journal Register*.

February 15,1992: Jury debates Dahmer's sanity after hearing final arguments. *Springfield (IL) State Journal Register*, p. 3.

February 16, 1992: Juror: Dahmer is a con artist. *Springfield (IL) State Journal Register*, p. 1.

February 16, 1992: Killer-cannibal Dahmer declared sane by jury . *Boston Herald-American*, p. 2.

February 18, 1992 Dahmer is given life in prison. *Boston Globe*, p. 3.

February 18, 1992: Dahmer shocks even expert on deviant psyches. *Los Angeles Times*, p. B4.

October 12, 1992: Officers in Dahmer's case try to regain jobs. *The New York Times*, p. 7.

October 17, 1992: Police in Dahmer case admit making error. *The New York Times*, p. 14.

November 29, 1992: Officers dismissed in Dahmer case lose bid to get their job back. *The New York Times*, p. 35.

Articles in Journals and Magazines

CAPLAN, L. (1992). Not so nutty. *New Republic,* March 2, p. 18–20.

CHIN, P. (1991). The door of evil. *People Weekly*, August 12, pp. 32–37.

CHIN, P., AND TAMARKIN, C. (1991). The door of evil. *People*, August 12, p. 34.

DAVIDS, D. (1992). The serial murderer as superstar. *McCalls*, February, p. 150.

DEBENEDICTIS, D. J. (1992). Sane serial killer. *ABA Journal*, April, p. 78, 22.

DIETZ, P. (1992). Court testimony. *Court TV*, February 12.

GELMAN, D. (1991). The secrets of Apt. 213. *Newsweek*, August 5, pp. 40–42.

KAPLAN, D. A. (1992). Secrets of a serial killer. *Newsweek*, February 3, pp. 45–51.

Kaufman, I. (1982, August). The insanity plea on trial. *New York Times Magazine*, p. 18.

Mackenzie, H. (1991). Infamous in Milwaukee. *MacLean's*, September 23, p. 28.

Masters, B. (1991). Dahmer's inferno. *Vanity Fair*, November, pp. 183–189, 264–269.

Mathews, T. (1992). Secrets of a serial killer. *Newsweek*, February 3, pp. 46–49.

———. (1992). He wanted to listen to my heart. *Newsweek*, February 10, p. 31.

Miller A. (1991). Serial murder aftershocks. *Newsweek*, August 12, pp. 28–29.

Prudhome, A. (1991). The little flat of horrors. *Time*, August 5, p. 26.

———. (1991). Did they all have to die? *Time*, August 12, p. 28.

Salholz, E. (1992). Insanity: A defense of last resort. *Newsweek*, February 3, p. 49.

Schneider, K S. (1992). Day of reckoning. *People Weekly*, March 2, pp. 38–39.

Staff (1991). Black men tragic victims of white Milwaukee man's gruesome murder spree. *Jet*, August 12, pp. 16–17.

Staff (1991). Jeffrey Dahmer. *People Weekly*, January 6, p. 70.

Staff (1992). I carried it too far, that's for sure. *Psychology Today*, May/June, pp. 28–31.

Staff (1992). Jeffrey Dahmer. *People Weekly*, December 30, p. 25.

Staff (1992). The jury finds Dahmer sane. *Jet*, March 2, p. 15.

Staff (1992). Post-mortem on the Dahmer trial coverage. *Editor & Publisher*, February 29, pp. 125, 129.

Staff (1992). Secrets of a killer. *Newsweek*, February 3, pp. 44–47.

Staff (1992). Secrets of a serial killer. *Newsweek*, February 3, p. 49.

Staff (1992). The Socrates option. *Reason*, May 24, p. 47.

Staff (1992). So guilty they're innocent. *National Review*, March 2, pp. 17–18.

Tayman, J. C. (1991). The door of evil. *People*, August 12, pp. 32–35.

Treen, J., Toufexis, A., and Tamarkin, C. (1992). Probing the mind of a 1-70 killer. *People Weekly*, August 20, pp. 37, 75–78.

Toufexis, A. (1992). Do mad acts a madman make? *Time*, February 3, p. 17.

INDEX

A

25-Caliber Killer 47
Abrahamsen 24, 40, 91
Allison, Ralph 134, 136
Allitt, Beverly 70
Alpert 192
Angel of Death 40, 41
Angelo, Richard 41
Anthropological explanations 35–36
Anti-social personality disorder 7, 26, 27, 28
Apsche 23
Atkins, Benjamin 41
Atlanta Child murders (*see* Williams, Wayne)
Ault and Reese, 213
Australia, serial killers in, 68
Aynesworth, 9

B

Backpack Murders, 68
Baker, David, 69
Banay, 25
Barfield, Velma, 53, 55
Barnes, 132, 187
Bayley, 190
Behavioral characteristics, 20, 21, 22, 23, 58
Bell, Larry, 246–47
Berdella, Robert, 42
Berger, 25, 63, 78, 98
Berkowitz, David, 24, 40, 44, 62, 233, 252
Berlin, 260
Bianchi, Kenneth, 3, 10, 11, 13, 26, 40, 62, 128–43, 167–74, 187, 188, 189, 195, 197, 205, 208, 212
Biological explanations, 15, 33–35
Biondi and Hecox, 42

Bittaker, Lawrence, 10, 41, 42
Bjere, 29, 91
Black, Robert, 70–71,
Blackburn, 55
Black-widow killer, 21, 52
Bonin, William, 42
Boone, Carole (see Bundy, Theodore), 148
Boston Strangler (see DeSalvo, Albert)
Brady, Ian, 10
Brantingham and Brantingham, 222
Brittain, 24
Brooks (see Corll), 182
Brooks, Pierce, 4, 6, 63, 194, 209, 223, 224,
      229, 230, 231, 232
Brown and Edwards, 54
Brudos, Jerome, 41
Brussels, James, 213
Bundy, Carol, 10, 41
Bundy, Theodore, 8, 10, 13, 23, 25, 30, 31,
      39, 44, 56, 75, 84, 143–66, 167–74,
      178, 181, 188, 189, 195, 196, 233,
      238, 245
Buono, Angelo, 8, 10, 11, 40, 128, 129,
      132, 135, 136, 137, 138, 139, 140,
      141, 142, 167–74, 189, 195, 205, 208,
      212, 233
Burn, 69
Burt, 41

C

Call, 123
Canada, serial killers in, 72
Canter, David, 27, 28, 31, 86, 212, 220–22
Case studies, 13, 19, 23, 29, 91–166
Centers for Disease Control (CDC), 59
Central Indiana Multiagency Investigative
      Team, 81
Centralized investigative network, 204
Cheney, 43
Chikatilo, Andrei, 6, 66–67,
Childhood trauma, 8, 13, 28–29, 33
Chi-Omega sorority (see Bundy,
      Theodore), 154, 160, 165
Christie, John Reginald, 66
Clark and Morley, 42

Clark, Douglas, 41, 42
Cleckley, 25, 155
CNN Special Reports, 64
Collins, John, 200, 205, 207, 236
Colton, 191
Computerized analysis systems, 204,
      227–28
Conferences, 203, 206
Confessions, 17, 53
Connor, 33
Conradi, 67
Copeland, Roy and Faye, 43
Corll, Dean, 30, 182, 233
Cornwall, Patricia, 89
Corona, Juan, 40, 44, 252
Coston, 43
Cowell, Theodore (see Bundy, Ted), 146
Cultural explanations, 7, 16, 20, 21
Cummins, Gordon, 66
Curriden, 40

D

Dahmer, Jeffrey, 14, 19, 39, 44, 82, 93, 178,
      251–64
Dahmer, Lionel, 256–57, 260
Daley, Robert, 193
Darrach and Norris, 5, 61, 110, 180, 208,
      233
Davies, 69
Depue, Robert, 63, 214
DeRiver, 6, 24, 58
DeSalvo, Albert, 30, 40, 213, 236
Detlinger and Prugh, 208, 237
Diagnostic and Statistical Manual
      of Mental Disorders (DSM), 7,
      26–28, 121
Dietz, Park, 65, 78, 87, 217, 260
Disorganized offender, 58, 89
Dobson, 164
Dodd, Westley Allan, 40, 44, 252
Dominick, 61
Doney, 227
Dr. Watson Case Management System,
      228
Duffy, John, 212

E

Egger, Steven, 7, 12, 20, 30, 31, 52, 57, 61, 64, 69, 77, 81, 82, 181, 188, 196, 197, 227, 234, 239
Egginton, 55
Eidetic memory, 127
Elkind, 54
Ellis and Gullo, 8, 29
Eyler, Larry, 181

F

Faerstein, Saul, 135
Fair, 43
Falling, Christine, 42, 54
Federal Bureau of Investigation (FBI), 5, 6, 14, 44, 46, 53, 59, 60, 61, 64, 65, 85, 88, 89, 153, 182, 201, 205, 209, 211, 212, 213, 214, 216, 217, 218, 220, 229, 232, 233, 238
Female serial killer, 21, 52, 53
Fish, Albert, 57
Flint, Joyce, 256, 257–60
Fontana, Nicholas (see Bianchi, Kenneth), 138
Ford, David, 81, 82
Forensic awareness, 221
Forensic consultants, 203, 224–25
Fort, 26
Fosdal, 259
Frank, 40
Franklin, 66
Freeway Killer, (see Bonin, William), 42

G

Gacy, John Wayne, 8, 9, 13, 25, 30, 40, 44, 56, 57, 75, 82, 95–114, 167, 167–74, 181, 187, 188, 189, 197, 233, 236
Gallego, Charlene, 42
Gallego, Gerald, 42
Gary, 181
Gauron, Eugene, 101
Geberth, 213, 214, 217
Gein, Ed, 57
Geoforensics, 212

Geographic profiling, 213, 222–23
Geographical location, 5, 56, 57, 83
Geographical types, 56, 57
Geographically stable, 57
Geographically transient, 57
Gest, 78
Giannangelo, 28
Gibbons, 92
Gilbert, 59
Godwin, 26, 40, 59, 215
Goldstein, 183, 194
Gray and Williams, 19, 80
Graysmith, 51
Green River Killer, 14, 49–50, 57, 62, 75, 182, 196, 199, 205, 208, 209, 215, 218, 226, 227
Griffiths, Richard, 6, 33, 34, 40, 41, 42, 64, 87, 196, 217
Gullen, 67
Guttmacher, 24, 58

H

Hansen, Robert, 56, 238
Hare, 25, 27
Harrington and Burger, 43
Harris, Thomas, 86, 89
Hartman, Arthur, 105
Harvey, Donald, 40, 178
Hatcher, 181
Hazelwood and Douglas, 4, 8, 29, 58, 213
Hazelwood, Roy, 32, 215, 217
Heck, Robert, 62
Heidnik, Gary, 23
Henley, Elmer, 82, 109, 182
Heritage, Rupert, 221
Hetzel, 225, 226
Hickey, Eric, 8, 10, 20, 21–22, 23, 27, 52, 53, 57, 64, 66, 84, 235
High-risk lifestyles, 83
Hilberry, 26
Hillside Strangler (see Bianchi, Kenneth and Buono, Angelo)
Hindley, Myra, 10, 21
Holmes and DeBurger, 6, 20, 21, 23, 57, 65, 216

HOLMES computer program, 228, 248
Holmes, Sherlock, 211
Homicide assessment and lead tracking
   system (HALT), 194, 228, 233–34,
   235
Homicide Investigation and Tracking
   System (HITS), 235
Howlett, 233
Huberty, James Oliver, 5
Hurkos, Peter, 236
Hypernesia, 127

I

I-70 robbery murders, 48, 209
Inadequate socialization, 28
India, serial killers in, 67
Informational clearing house, 203, 206–7
Internet, 45
INTERPOL, 228–29
Investigation of serial murder, 12–13
Investigative Consultants, 203, 223–24
Issacson, 39

J

Jack the Ripper, 66
Jenkins, Phillip, 10, 202, 235
Jesse, 58
Jones, Genene, 54
Joubert, John, 42
Jouve, 69

K

Kacyznski, Ted, 45, 239
Karamozov, 26
Karmen, 77, 78, 83
Karpman, 58
Katz, 92
Kearney, Patrick, 40
Kemper, Edmund, 12, 26, 30, 43, 56, 57
Kendall, 160
Keppel, Robert, 56, 78, 83, 143, 149, 160,
   161, 193, 196, 216, 248
Keys, 181
Kidder, 40

Kiger, 64
Killer Clown (see Gacy, John Wayne)
King and Chambliss, 124
Kiss, Bela, 66
Kozenczak and Herickson, 113, 236
Kraft, Randy, 42
Kraus, Richard, 34, 35
Krivieh, 67
Krytopyrrolos, 35
Kurten, Peter, 66

L

Lake, Leonard (see also Ng, Charles), 43
Landru, Desire, 66
Lane and Gregg, 19, 40, 67
Larsen, 143, 144, 147, 148, 149, 152, 153,
   162, 165, 166, 186
Larson, 123
Leonard, 190
Less-dead, 74–84, 185, 265
Levin and Fox, 7, 24, 26, 30, 56, 61, 62, 77,
   83, 132, 134, 140, 182, 183, 208, 216,
   229, 233
Leyton, Elliott, 7, 36, 43, 65, 66, 90
Liebert, 26, 215, 216
Lindsey, David, 56, 62, 78, 83, 89
Linedecker, 19, 42, 65, 187
Linkage blindness, 12–13, 179, 180, 181,
   188, 189–98, 201, 239, 265
Long, Bobby Joe, 200, 206
Long, David, 43
Lorenz, Konrad, 15,
Lourie, 67
Lucas, Henry Lee, 8, 9, 10–11, 13, 39,44,
   56, 62, 115–27, 167–74, 179, 181,
   182, 188, 189, 195, 197, 205, 206,
   233, 238
Lunde, 7, 29, 78, 91, 133
Lust murder, 4, 24, 89

M

MacNamara, 41, 42
MacPherson, 164
Magazines, 5

Maghan and Sagarin, 77, 83
Major incident room, 204, 225–26
Markman, Dominick, and Bosco, 41
Marsh, 87
Mass media, 3–4, 13, 20, 25, 37, 85–90,
    179, 184, 226, 265
Mass Murder, 5, 14
Masters, 65, 69
McCann, F. Michael, 260
McCarthy, 30, 78, 215
McCauley, 191, 192
McDuff, Kenneth, 42
McIntyre, 229
Megamobile, 57, 92
Megaree, 31, 58
Megastat, 57, 92, 253
Meloy, 21, 27
Meredith, 59
Methvin, 247
Michaud, 218
Michaud and Aynesworth, 144, 145, 147,
    148, 149, 164, 166, 245
Michigan Murders (see Collins, John)
Midland Ripper, 71
Milat, Ivan, 68
Miller, 43
Miller, James, 84
Milliken, 68
Moor Murders, 10
Moore and Reid, 54
Morris and Bloom-Cooper, 59
Morrison, Helen, 25, 30, 78, 105, 111
Movies, 4, 85, 86,
Mudgett, Herman, 3, 57
Multi-Agency Investigative Team Manual
    (MAIT), 209
Myre, 207
Myths of serial murder, 13–14

N

Nance, Wayne, 43
National Center for Analysis of Violent
    Crime (NCAVC), 63, 64, 229, 231, 232
Native Americans, 51
Nelson, 62

Nepal, serial killers in, 67
Nettler, 58, 249
Newspapers, 3, 4, 13, 18, 20, 64
Newton, Michael, 55
Newton, Milton, 212, 213
Ng, Charles (see also Lake, Leonard), 43
Nilsen, Dennis, 24, 30, 68, 69, 254
Norris, J, 6, 36–37, 65, 180
Norris, Roy, 10, 24, 41, 42
Norton, 55

O

O'Brien, Darcy, 141
Oakland County child killer, 51
Offender rewards, 204, 237–38
Office of Juvenile Justice and Delinquency
    Prevention, 62
Olsen, Jack, 19, 35
Olson, Clifford, 237
Organized offender, 58, 89
Orne, Martin, 134
Osanka, Frank, 105

P

Palermo, George, 260
Pennsylvania Train Sniper, 47
Petiot, Marcel, 66
Pincus, Jonathon, 33
Pinnizzotto, 213, 217
Poland, serial killers in, 73
Porter, 215
Power and control, 7, 30, 32
Profiling, 16, 37, 86, 88, 89, 203, 205, 211–23
Pron and Duncanson, 72
Psychics, 204, 235–37
Psychological explanations, 15, 16
Psychopath, 7, 25, 26, 27
Puente, Dorothea, 53, 55

R

Rae, 40
Railway Rapist (see Duffy, John), 212
Raine, Adrian, 33
Ramirez, Richard, 8, 13, 15, 39, 75, 181

Rape, 7, 22, 31, 32, 40, 41
Rapid Response Team, 204
Regional Organized Crime Information
     Center, 124
Reinhardt, 8, 29
Reiser, 213, 216
Ressler, Robert, 23, 24, 30, 56, 62, 63, 214,
     215, 233
Restak, Richard, 33, 34
Revitch and Schlesinger, 6, 24, 58
Reynolds, Mike, 41, 184
Riedel, 59, 65
Rifkin, Joel, 44, 82, 178, 252
Rolling, Danny, 14, 75
Rose, 25
Rossmo, D. Kim, 213, 222
Rule, Ann, 146, 147, 150, 163, 165, 166, 186
Russia, serial killers in, 66

S

Sare, 43
Sartre, Jean-Paul, 38
Schwarz, 130, 131, 132, 133, 141, 187
Scott, H, 54, 55
Serial killer syndrome, 7
Serial Murder definition, 5, 245
Serial murder victims, 6, 12, 77–78
Serial murder, research agenda, 245
Serial murder, term, 4, 5
Serial murder, the future of, 244–46
Sewell, 31
Sex as a motive, 6, 23, 24, 30
Shawcross, Arthur, 8, 14, 19, 34–35, 39,
     46, 177
Shepard, Sam, 192
Silence of the Lambs, 4, 13, 43, 74, 86, 89,
     253
Simons, Norman, 67
Smith, 65, 190, 192
Smith and Guillen, 50, 227
Sobhraj, Charles, 67
Sociological explanations, 15, 16, 25
Sociopath, 7, 25, 26, 27, 28
Solicitation from the public, 204, 226–27
Solo killers, 9, 22

Son of Sam (see Berkowitz, David)
Sonnenschein, 56
South Africa, serial killers in, 67
Specialized Response Team, 238–39
Speck, Richard, 5
Spree killers, 19
Stano, 182
Starr, 5, 29, 63
Station Strangler (see Simons, Norman), 67
Storr, 28, 30
Stranger-to-stranger crime, 11, 38, 60, 80
Strecher, 192
Sullivan and Maiken, 96, 97, 100, 101,
     102, 103, 105, 106, 109, 110, 111,
     112, 113, 187
Sunset Strip Slayer (see Clark, Douglas)
Sutcliffe, Peter, 68, 225
Swanson, 214
Sweden, serial killers in, 73
Swoope, Elizabeth, 212

T

Tanay, 25, 155
Task force, 200, 203, 207–10, 229
Team killer, 10, 22
Television, 4, 13, 89
Teten, Howard, 213
Texas Rangers, 120, 122, 125, 206
Thailand, serial killers in, 67
Thibault, 191
Thompson, 67
Throw-aways, 79–80
Tinning, Marybeth, 53, 54
Toole, Ottis (see also Lucas, Henry Lee),
     10, 119, 123, 182, 197
True-crime books, 18, 19, 20
Turkey, serial killers in, 67

U

Unabomber (see Kacyznski, Ted), 45
Uniform Crime Report (UCR), 18, 63, 65
United Kingdom, serial killers in, 68–71,
     71–72
United States, serial killers in, 59–66

Unterweger, Jack, 229

V

Violent Crime Linkage Analysis System
    (VICLAS), 235
Violent Criminal Apprehension Program
    (VICAP), 5, 88, 182, 194, 227,
    229–33, 234, 235, 248
Vollmer, 190

W

Walker, Steven (*see* Bianchi, Kenneth), 135
Watkins, John, 134
Wertham, Fredric, 38, 91
West, 30, 31, 217
West, Frederick and Rosemary, 69, 70
Wilder, Christopher, 233
Wilkinson, 113
Wille, 29
Williams, Wayne, 8, 39, 56, 57, 199, 200,
    233

Wilson, 191
Wilson and Putman, 35
Wilson and Seaman, 3,7, 84
Wingo, Cecil, 57, 82
Winn and Merrill, 144, 149, 151, 152, 154,
    155, 161, 162, 163, 164, 186
Wood, James, 32–33
Wood, W.P, 55
Wray, Bob, 54
Wuornos, Aileen, 9, 52, 211

Y

Yallop, 69
Yin, 92
Yorkshire Ripper (*see* Sutcliffe, Peter), 180

Z

Zahn, 63
Zimring, 59
Zodiac Killer, 51

Author Index

A

Abrahamsen, 24, 40, 91
Alpert, 192
Apsche, 23
Ault and Reese, 213
Aynesworth, 9

B

Baker, David, 69
Banay, 25
Barnes, 132, 187
Bayley, 190
Berger, 25, 63, 78, 98
Berlin, 260
Biondi and Hecox, 42
Bjere, 29, 91
Blackburn, 55
Brantingham and Brantingham, 222

Brittain, 24
Brooks, Pierce, 4, 6, 63, 194, 209, 223, 224, 229, 230, 231, 232
Brown and Edwards, 54
Burn, 69
Burt, 41

C

Call, 123
Canter, David, 27, 28, 31, 86, 212, 220–22
Cheney, 43
Clark and Morley, 42
Cleckley, 25, 155
Colton, 191
Connor, 33
Conradi, 67
Cornwall, Patricia, 89
Coston, 43
Curriden, 40

D

Dahmer, Lionel, 256–57, 260
Daley, Robert, 193
Darrach and Norris, 5, 61, 110, 180, 208, 233
Davies, 69
Depue, Robert, 63, 214
DeRiver, 6, 24, 58
DeSalvo, Albert, 30, 40, 213, 236
Detlinger and Prugh, 208, 237
Diagnostic and Statistical Manual of Mental Disorders (DSM), 7, 26–28, 121
Dietz, Park, 65, 78, 87, 217, 260
Dobson, 164
Dominick, 61
Doney, 227

E

Egger, Steven, 7, 12, 20, 30, 31, 52, 57, 61, 64, 69, 77, 81, 82, 181, 188, 196, 197, 227, 234, 239
Egginton, 55
Elkind, 54
Ellis and Gullo, 8, 29

F

Faerstein, Saul, 135
Fair, 43
Ford, David, 81, 82
Fort, 26
Fosdal, 259
Frank, 40
Franklin, 66

G

Gauron, Eugene, 101
Geberth, 213, 214, 217
Gest, 78
Giannangelo, 28
Gibbons, 92
Gilbert, 59
Godwin, 26, 40, 59, 215

Goldstein, 183, 194
Gray and Williams, 1980
Graysmith, 51
Gullen, 67
Guttmacher, 24, 58

H

Hare, 25, 27
Harrington and Burger, 43
Harris, Thomas, 86, 89
Hartman, Arthur, 105
Hazelwood and Douglas, 4, 8, 29, 58, 213
Hazelwood, Roy, 32, 215, 217
Hetzel, 225, 226
Hickey, Eric, 8, 10, 20, 21–22, 23, 27, 52, 53, 57, 64, 66, 84, 235
Hilberry, 26
Holmes and DeBurger, 6, 20, 21, 23, 57, 65, 216
Howlett, 233

I

Issacson, 39

J

Jenkins, Phillip, 10, 202, 235
Jesse, 58
Jouve, 69

K

Karamazov, 26
Karmen, 77, 78, 83
Karpman, 58
Katz, 92
Kendall, 160
Keppel, Robert, 56, 78, 83, 143, 149, 160, 161, 193, 196, 216, 248
Keys, 181
Kidder, 40
Kiger, 64
King and Chambliss, 124
Kraus, Richard, 34, 35
Krivieh, 67

L

Lane and Gregg, 19, 40, 67
Larsen, 143, 144, 147, 148, 149, 152, 153, 162, 165, 166, 186
Larson, 123
Leonard, 190
Less-dead, 74–84, 185, 265
Levin and Fox, 7, 24, 26, 30, 56, 61, 62, 77, 83, 132, 134, 140, 182, 183, 208, 216, 229, 233
Leyton, Elliott, 7, 36, 43, 65, 66, 90
Liebert, 26, 215, 216
Lindsey, David, 56, 62, 78, 83, 89
Linedecker, 19, 42, 65, 187
Lourie, 67
Lunde, 7, 29, 78, 91, 133

M

MacNamara, 41, 42
MacPherson, 164
Maghan and Sagarin, 77, 83
Markman and Dominick, and Bosco, 41
Marsh, 87
Masters, 65, 69
McCann, F. Michael, 260
McCarthy, 30, 78, 215
McCauley, 191, 192
McIntyre, 229
Megaree, 31, 58
Meloy, 21, 27
Meredith, 59
Methvin, 247
Michaud, 218
Michaud and Aynesworth, 144, 145, 147, 148, 149, 164, 166, 245
Miller, 43
Miller, James, 84
Milliken, 68
Moore and Reid, 54
Morris and Bloom-Cooper, 59
Myre, 207

N

Nelson, 62

Nettler, 58, 249
Newton, Michael, 55
Newton, Milton, 212, 213
Norris, J, 6, 36–37, 65, 180
Norton, 55

O

O'Brien, Darcy, 141
Olsen, Jack, 19, 35
Orne, Martin, 134

P

Pincus, Jonothon, 33
Pinnizzotto, 213, 217
Porter, 215
Pron and Duncanson, 72

R

Rae, 40
Raine, Adrian, 33
Reinhardt, 8, 29
Reiser, 213, 216
Ressler, Robert, 23, 24, 30, 56, 62, 63, 214, 215, 233
Restak, Richard, 33, 34
Revitch and Schlesinger, 6, 24, 58
Reynolds, Mike, 41, 184
Riedel, 59, 65
Rose, 25
Rossmo, D. Kim, 213, 222
Rule, Ann, 146, 147, 150, 163, 165, 166, 186

S

Sare, 43
Sartre, Jean-Paul, 38
Schwarz, 130, 131, 132, 133, 141, 187
Scott, H, 54, 55
Sewell, 31
Smith, 65, 190, 192
Smith and Guillen, 50, 227
Sonnenschein, 56
Starr, 5, 29, 63
Storr, 28, 30

Strecher, 192
Sullivan and Maiken, 96, 97, 100, 101,
        102, 103, 105, 106, 109, 110, 111,
        112, 113, 187
Swanson, 214

T

Tanay, 25, 155
Thibault, 191
Thompson, 67

V

Vollmer, 190

W

Watkins, John, 134
Wertham, Fredric, 38, 91

West, 30, 31, 217
Wilkinson, 113
Wille, 29
Wilson, 191
Wilson and Putman, 35
Wilson and Seaman, 3,7, 84
Winn and Merrill, 144, 149, 151, 152, 154,
        155, 161, 162, 163, 164, 186
Wood, W.P., 55

Y

Yallop, 69
Yin, 92

Z

Zahn, 63
Zimring, 59